Off The Beaten Track
POLAND

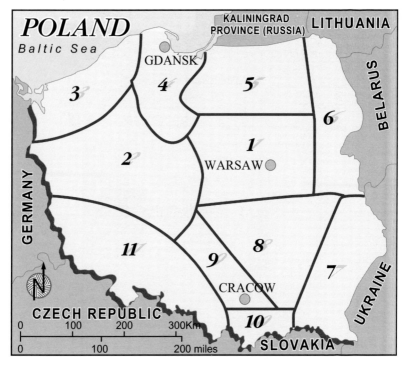

POLAND
Baltic Sea

KALININGRAD
PROVINCE (RUSSIA)

LITHUANIA

GERMANY

BELARUS

UKRAINE

CZECH REPUBLIC

SLOVAKIA

GDANSK

WARSAW

CRACOW

N

3
4
5
6
1
2
8
9
11
7
10

0   100   200   300Km

0   100   200 miles

Off The Beaten Track
POLAND

Gordon McLachlan

MOORLAND PUBLISHING

The Globe Pequot press

Published by:
Moorland Publishing Co Ltd,
Moor Farm Road West, Ashbourne,
Derbyshire, DE6 1HD England

ISBN 0 86190 553 9 (UK)

The Globe Pequot Press,
6 Business Park Road,
PO Box 833, Old Saybrook,
Connecticut 06475-0833

ISBN 1-56440-718-7 (USA)

© Moorland Publishing Co Ltd 1995

Colour illustrations by:
Gordon McLachlan

Origination by:
ga Graphics, Lincolnshire

Printed by:
Wing King Tong Co Ltd, Hong Kong

MPC Production Team:
Editorial: Tonya Monk
Editorial Assistant: Christine Haines
Design: Ashley Emery
Cartography: Mark Titterton

British Library Cataloguing in Publication Data:
A catalogue record for this book is available from the British Library.

Library of Congress Cataloging-in-Publication Data
McLachlan, Gordon W.
    Off the beaten track. Poland/Gordon McLachlan
        p. cm.
    ISBN 1-56440-718-7
    1. Poland -- Guidebooks.   I. Title.
DK4037. M39   1995
914.3804'56--dc20   95-12755
                                                         CIP

Contents

About the Author

Gordon McLachlan was born in Edinburgh in 1956 and graduated MA with Honours in Politics and Modern History from the University of Edinburgh in 1978. Following several years working in the sales side of publishing, he turned to full time writing in 1987. His special interests include music, art and architecture, reading, photography and gastronomy.

Note on Maps

The maps for each chapter, while comprehensive, are not designed to be used as route maps, but to locate the main towns, villages and places of interest.

Opening Times

Museums and other places to visit are listed at the end of each chapter, but these are liable to change.

Polish Addresses

Rynek — the main (market) square. Virtually all Polish towns have one, though occasionally it is given a different name

plac (abbreviation pl.) — square
ulica (abbreviation pl.) — street
aleja (abbreviation pl.) — avenue

Introduction

To the English-speaking world, Poland is so unfamiliar as a tourist destination that the country as a whole readily fits the phrase 'off the beaten track'. Exactly why this should be so is rather strange, as this is not, either geographically or historically, a country with a low profile. It lies at the very heart of the European continent, as properly understood. By any standards, it is a significant nation, with a population of 40 million and a land area greater than Italy's and not much less than that of reunified Germany. Its history dates back over a thousand years, and for more than a century of this, following the formal union with neighbouring Lithuania in 1569, it was the largest and arguably the most powerful empire in Europe. The violation of its territorial integrity by Hitler was the direct cause of World War II, while throughout the 1980s it was seldom out of the international spotlight as it played the vanguard role in the overthrow of Soviet-imposed Communism throughout Eastern Europe.

In the past few years, Poland has made a remarkably successful transition to a market economy while remaining a very safe place to visit, one whose hospitality is legendary and where almost everything is remarkably inexpensive for Westerners. All of this notwithstanding, foreign tourism is largely confined to three famous cities — Warsaw, Cracow and Gdańsk — and to two scenic areas — the Tatra and Pieniny mountains — lying on either side of the one internationally renowned resort, Zakopane.

Yet these are only a few of the highlights of an endlessly rewarding country that is full of paradoxes. Not the least of Poland's fascinations is that its present make-up, ethnically homogenous and the most fervently Roman Catholic country in the world, stands firmly at odds with its own history. Modern Poland is a direct result of outside interference: firstly by the Nazis, who indulged in a murderous programme of ethnic 'cleansing' and then by the Soviets, who instituted massive forced transfers of populations and were also responsible for shifting it bodily across the map of Europe, allocating it territories which had spent centuries under German rule as compensation for those they themselves had annexed in the east.

A wealth of surviving historic monuments bear witness to a very different past. Poland was in many ways the first-ever multi-racial and multi-cultural society; from the Middle Ages onwards, it was a melting-pot of different peoples, traditions and religions. German settlers regularly took the lead in the commercial development of Polish towns. Italian architects and craftsmen built and decorated a high percentage of the greatest churches and palaces. There were substantial communities of Lithuanians, Ukrainians, Belarussians, Armenians and Tatars. Those persecuted in other countries found the country a ready refuge: thus for about half a millennium Poland was home to the largest Jewish community in the world.

There are also plenty of visual reminders of the other major theme of Poland's history, the regular subjugation it has suffered in its heroic struggle to preserve its own identity and independence against the predatory designs of the Germans and Russians. These range from the awesome medieval castles of the Teutonic Knights, via the administration buildings of the Partitioning powers which combined to wipe Poland off the map from 1795 until 1918, to the Nazi concentration camps of World War II where most of Polish Jewry was exterminated, and the monuments of Socialist Realism sponsored by the Soviets in the post-war period.

Another paradox is that, while much of Poland is unrelievedly flat and featureless — and moreover has a reputation as an environmental disaster area because of the pollution which was the inevitable consequence of the Communist infatuation with outmoded heavy industry — it also contains some of the strangest and most beautiful landscapes in Europe. The Tatras and Pieniny are just two out of a score of regions of outstanding natural interest which are now under careful observation and protection as national parks. Others include Europe's only surviving primeval forest, its last intact wetland, and its largest group of moving sand dunes. For the sake of completeness, this book covers the whole of Poland, including the few destinations already on the established tourist circuit, but the emphasis is firmly on those which are less familiar. It features many places which are omitted or glossed over in other English-language guidebooks: this is, for example, the first to give details on all the national parks.

The chapters are based on the historic regions of Poland, which retain their distinctive identities even although most have not functioned as political or even administrative units for a very long time. All can be explored in a week or less, though many have the potential for a much longer visit. Some are suitable for visiting from a single base, whereas others can only be covered by means of a touring route. Within the national parks, it is usually (though not always) necessary to walk to see the best of the scenery, and details of the best trails are given. Otherwise, even the smallest and remotest villages are serviced by a public transport network that is extensive, regular and very cheap, if seldom speedy. Bringing a car offers obvious advantages, with the proviso that the organised theft of Western vehicles, particularly by mafia groups from the former Soviet Union, is the one major problem of tourist security.

1 • Mazovia

Mazovia or **Mazowsze** lies in the very heart of Poland, and it is this centrality which has been the key factor in the pre-eminent role it has held in the life of the nation over the past four centuries. Although watered by the mighty Vistula, and by other major rivers such as the Narew, Bug, Wieprz and Pilica, it is predominantly a land of infertile sandy soils which, under different historical circumstances, might well have languished as a rural backwater. Indeed, Mazovia had no permanent settlements until the eleventh century, though soon afterwards it became a constituent part of the Polish state, with its first capital, Płock, gaining the status of a royal residence before the century was over. However, when King Bolesław the Wrymouthed divided his territory among his sons in 1138, Mazovia was reduced to being one of several competing Polish principalities. Even after centralized government was re-established in the fourteenth century under King Kazimierz the Great, it continued to function as a quasi-autonomous vassal state of the crown until the last of its dukes died without issue in 1526.

The turning-point in Mazovia's fortunes came later the same century with the impending extinction of the Jagellonians, the royal house which had ruled Poland and Lithuania in personal union since 1386. Anxious to provide a secure future for both his realms in the face of an increasing threat from Russia, the last of the line, King Zygmunt August, negotiated the fusion of the two nations into the Polish-Lithuanian Commonwealth, which was founded in 1569. Stretching continuously from the Baltic to the Black Sea, it was, at the time, the largest country in Europe. Lying near its south-western extremity, the Polish royal capital of Cracow was in an unsuitable position for governing this vast empire. The Sejm, the national parliament, immediately decided to transfer its seat to a location midway between Cracow and the Lithuanian capital Vilnius, and its choice fell on Warsaw, which had risen from obscurity to become the main residence of the Mazovian dukes in the early fifteenth century. Four years later, Warsaw's position was consolidated with the birth of the so-called Republic of Nobles, whereby the nobility — which comprised around 10 per cent of the total population — convened in an open field outside the city to elect a new king. Its status as undisputed capital was sealed in 1596 when King Zygmunt Waza moved the royal court from Cracow.

This supremacy has been maintained without challenge ever since,

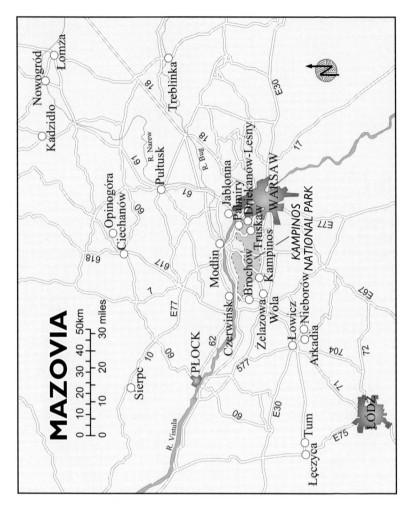

though the city's fortunes have been mixed, to say the least. In the eighteenth century it was one of the most cultured and refined of European capitals, but this golden era came to an abrupt end with the Partitions which wiped Poland off the map and Warsaw, like the nation as a whole, sank into decline. It began to recover in the second half of the nineteenth century, to flourish once again after 1918 as capital of the resurrected Polish state. However, World War II brought a virtual Armageddon: following the failure of the 1944 Uprising, the Nazis engaged in systematic and ruthless revenge, reducing around 65 per cent of the city to rubble and boasting that it had been erased altogether from the map. In an act of supreme national faith, the city was painstakingly reconstructed after the war, confounding the sceptics who believed it was so badly damaged that it could not continue to function as the capital.

Warsaw lags far behind Cracow and Gdańsk in terms of conventional beauty. Yet, despite all the vicissitudes of its past, it has a wealth of sightseeing attractions. Moreover, it is an excellent touring base, offering easy and convenient access to all places of interest in Mazovia. The province's attractions are mostly low-key — but it has a fair number of historic towns and stately homes as well as extensive tracts of forest which still preserve some primeval characteristics.

Warsaw

With a population of well over a million and a half, **Warsaw** (**Warszawa** in Polish) is by far the largest city in Poland, and is the hub of most aspects of national life — even if is does not dominate the rest of the country to quite the same extent as do other European capitals such as London and Paris. Like many of its counterparts, it is almost wholly untypical of the country as a whole, its dynamism being strikingly at odds with the strongly traditional culture and economy to be found throughout so much of Poland. Since the fall of Communism, the city has become quite heavily western-ized, and is now amply endowed with luxury hotels, restaurants offering all kinds of ethnic cuisines, an ever-growing number of bars and pubs of a type previously unknown in Poland, and shops stocked with all the internation-ally renowned brands of consumer products.

Warsaw occupies a large geographical area, and its attractions are well spread out. The compact Old and New Towns form the historic core, and are where foreign visitors tend to spend most of their time, often overlooking the extensive Baroque quarter immediately to the west. Plenty more sights can be found on and near the Royal Way, which stretches southwards from the Old Town to the two great palace complexes at Łazienki and Wilanów, the only suburbs which lie on any tourist trail, though by no means the only ones which warrant a visit. The itineraries below are designed to cover the city as quickly and efficiently as possible, and include a host of rewarding sights which most tourists manage to miss.

The Old Town

Warsaw's **Old Town** (Stare Miasto) has gained a place on UNESCO's highly prestigious World Heritage List. This is, however, not on account of its size (which is very modest), nor because of the architectural worth of the buildings (few of which are in the class of their counterparts in Cracow, the only other Polish city so honoured). Instead, the listing is intended as a tribute to the work of the Polish restorers who skilfully transformed the heap of rubble left by the Nazis into an accurate re-creation of the pre-war appearance of the quarter — minus a few unwanted accretions. Almost equally remarkable has been the way the Old Town has recovered its soul: it has none of the over-sanitized, museum-piece appearance of so many rebuilt historic town centres in Germany. Instead, it provides a fitting

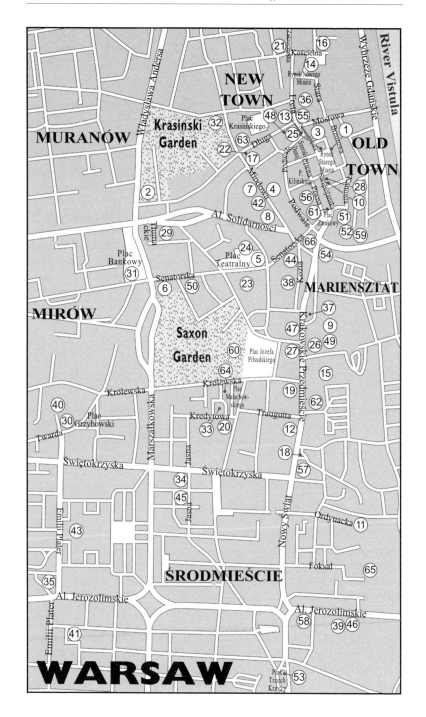

KEY

1 Adam Mickiewicz Literary Museum
2 Archaeological Museum
3 Barbican
4 Basilian Monastery
5 Blank Palace
6 Blue Palace
7 Borchów Palace
8 Capuchin Church
9 Carmelite Church
10 Cathedral
11 Chopin Museum
12 Church of the Holy Cross
13 Church of the Holy Ghost
14 Church of the Holy Sacrament
15 Church of the Nuns of the Visitation
16 Church of the Visitation
17 Collegium Nobilum
18 Copernicus Monument
19 Czapsk Palace
20 Ethnographic Museum
21 Franciscan Church
22 Garrison Church
23 Grand Theatre
24 Heroes of Warsaw Monument
25 Historical Museum of Warsaw
26 Hotel Bristol
27 Hotel Europejski
28 Jesuit Church
29 Jewish Historical Institute
30 Jewish Theatre
31 John Paul II Collection of European Paintings
32 Krasiński Palace
33 Lutheran Church
34 Main Post Office
35 Main Railway Station
36 Maria Skłodowska-Curie Museum
37 Mickiewicz Monument
38 Museum of Caricatures
39 National Museum
40 Nożyk Synagogue
41 Operetta
42 Pac-Radziwiłł Palace
43 Palace of Culture
44 Palace of the Primates of Poland
45 Philharmonic Hall
46 Polish Army Museum
47 Potocki-Czartoryski Palace
48 Raczyński Palace
49 Radziwiłł Palace
50 Reformed Franciscan Church
51 Royal Castle
52 Royal Library
53 St Alexander's Church
54 St Anne's Church
55 St Hyacinth's Church
56 St Martin's Church
57 Staszic Palace
58 Stock Exchange
59 Tin-Roofed Palace
60 Tomb of the Unknown Soldier
61 Tourist Office
62 Tykskiewicz Palace
63 Warsaw Uprising Mounument
64 Zachęta Gallery
65 Zamoyski Palace
66 Zygmunt August Monument

showpiece focal point for the modern city, one frequented as much by locals as by tourists, and enlivened, particularly in summer, by the presence of artists, hawkers and street performers.

Entry to the Old Town is via plac Zamkowy, a large and spacious square in the middle of which stands a 72ft (22m) high Corinthian column bearing a bronze **statue of King Zygmunt Waza** (or Vasa), the monarch who sealed Warsaw's position as the national capital. Erected in 1633, a year after his death, by order of his son, King Władysław Waza, it was the most grandiose monument to a political ruler erected anywhere in Europe since the time of the Roman Empire. The statue, by the Italian sculptor Clemente Molli, serves as a glorification not only of Zygmunt, but also of the Polish crown, the Waza dynasty and the Counter-Reformation he championed so resolutely — a stance which lost him the throne of Sweden, his staunchly Protestant native land.

The **Royal Castle** on the east side of the square is by far the most important and imposing building in the Old Town. Its kernel is the Gothic fortress of the Mazovian dukes, which was progressively expanded in the seventeenth and eighteenth centuries in accordance with its unique dual role as the principal royal residence and the national parliament. It acquired its final appearance during the reign of the last Polish king, Stanisław August Poniatowski, who gathered together a talented artistic team from Italy, Germany, France and Poland — the architects Jacopo Fontana, Domenico Merlini and Jan Kamsetzer, the painters Marcello Bacciarelli, Bernardo Bellotto and Jan Bogumił Plersch, and the sculptor and stuccoist André Le Brun. Having been almost totally destroyed by the Nazis, the site of the Royal Castle served as a promenade until long after the rest of the Old Town had been rebuilt. In 1971, work finally began on its reconstruction, and by 1984 it had risen like a phoenix from its own ashes. The movable works of art which had been spirited away to safety at the outbreak of the war returned to adorn painstakingly accurate reproductions of the chambers they formerly occupied.

A visit to the Royal Castle falls into several constituent parts, and a separate admission ticket is required for each. Except on Sundays, the first floor of the east wing, containing the main chambers of state built during the reign of Stanisław August, can only be seen on guided tours. The private apartments of the king begin with the so-called Canaletto Room, containing twenty-three meticulously painted views of Warsaw by Bellotto, who appropriated the surname of his famous uncle, the great view-painter of Venice. One depicts Stanisław August's election by the nobility; the others are full of architectural detail and thus proved to be an invaluable reference for the post-1945 restoration of the city. Adjoining is the Small Chapel, designed by Merlini in the emergent neo-Classical style, rather than the late Baroque used for the secular apartments. It contains the regalia of Stanisław August — sword, sceptre and chain of the Order of the White Eagle — as well as an urn with the ashes of Tadeusz Kościuszko, a general in the American Wars of Independence who returned to his native Poland to lead the heroic but unsuccessful fight against the Partitions which wiped the country off the map.

Beyond the Audience Chamber, with symbolic paintings by Bacciarelli extolling the king's reign, and the rooms of the Royal Bedchamber, are the state reception halls, collectively known as the Great Apartment. These include the National Hall, whose walls are lined with paintings by Bacciarelli depicting famous Poles and key events in the nation's history; the Marble Room, with portraits by the same artist of Poland's kings from Bolesław the Brave to Stanisław August; the Throne Room, with its closet dedicated to other European monarchs of the day; and the Great Assembly Hall, which also served as the ballroom.

Other apartments can be visited independently. On the ground floor of the east wing is a suite of Gothic and Renaissance rooms, centred on the Deputies' Chamber, where the Sejm originally convened. Parliamentary functions were subsequently transferred to the western wing of the first floor, at the northern end of which is the splendid Senators' Chamber, where the first parliamentary constitution in Europe, and the second in the world, was passed on 3 May 1791 — just 4 years before the demise of the Polish state. To the west are the Crown Prince's Rooms, which are hung with canvases by the nineteenth-century history painter Jan Matejko, the country's best-known native-born artist. In addition to a cycle chronicling Polish civilization, there are several canvases in his most grandly heroic vein, such as *Rejtan*, which illustrates the protest of the eponymous parliamentarian against the First Partition.

Several permanent exhibitions are mounted in the Castle's Gothic cellars, and in the more modest interiors of the second floor. Displayed in the former are the everyday objects discovered during archaeological excavations of the Old Town, and silverware donated to the National Defence Fund prior to the outbreak of World War II. The latter has a numismatic cabinet and a treasury displaying the insignia of all the Polish knightly orders. On the same floor are a room containing furnishings brought from Eaton Place in London, the long-time headquarters of the Polish government in exile; the study of inter-war President, Ignacy Mościcki; and the apartment which served as novelist Stefan Żeromski's home for the last 4 years of his life.

Temporary exhibitions are staged in the Lubomirski Palace, colloquially known as the Tin-Roofed Palace, which is entered through a courtyard on the south side of the Royal. To its north is Merlini's Royal Library, the only part of the whole Castle complex which was not destroyed by the Nazis. An elegant columned hall adorned with stucco medallions illustrating the arts and sciences, it too is used for temporary exhibitions, but in due course will become the home of a permanent display on the Polish Enlightenment.

On ul. Świętojanska, immediately north of plac Zamkowy, is the **cathedral**, which was formerly the collegiate church of St John the Baptist. As the seat of the present Primate of Poland it is the mother church of the nation, though this role will probably revert in the future to its traditional home, Gniezno in Great Poland. In the post-war rebuilding, the cathedral was returned to its original Gothic appearance. Most of its furnishings were destroyed; those which survived include the Renaissance tomb of the last two Mazovian dukes and the monument to Stanisław Małachowski, the Speaker of the Sejm, by the great Danish neo-Classical sculptor Bertel Thorwaldsen. The crypt houses the plain tombs of a number of famous Poles, including the Nobel Prize-winning novelist Henryk Sienkiewicz and the redoubtable post-war Primate and unofficial leader of the opposition to Communist rule, Cardinal Stefan Wyszyński. They were joined in 1992 by the remains of Ignacy Jan Paderewski, the virtuoso pianist-composer and post-World War I premier, which were brought back from the United States in recognition of Poland's newly-won national freedom.

Alongside the cathedral is the **Jesuit church**, a plain early Baroque building whose tower rises high above the rest of the Old Town's roofline. Inside is a much venerate painted of Our Lady of Grace. The only other church in the quarter is **St Martin's**, a block to the west on ul. Piwna. Originally Gothic, but almost totally rebuilt in the Baroque era, it was formerly part of an Augustinian monastery, though nowadays it belongs to a convent of Franciscan nuns.

At the heart of the Old Town is the inevitable market square, the **Rynek Starego Miasta**. Until 1817, it resembled most of its Polish counterparts in having a Town Hall in the middle, but this was demolished in order to create more space for traders. The four sides of the square, each of which is named after a civic dignitary of the time of King Stanisław August, are lined with tall mansions. These were built for wealthy merchants but were later sub-divided into tenement flats after the Old Town lost its lustre following the establishment of more capacious inner suburbs. With only two exceptions (numbers 34 and 35), the houses had to be reconstructed following destruction in World War II. Most are predominantly Baroque in appearance, though a few preserve Gothic and Renaissance features, notably St Anne's House (number 31), which takes its name from the devotional statue of St Anne with the Virgin and Child.

The mansions along the north side of the square contain the **Historical Museum of Warsaw**. Entry is via the Negro House (number 36), named after a carving which symbolizes the trading interests of the Italian-born merchant who commissioned it. Spread over some sixty rooms, the museum features a host of artefacts connected with the city, ranging from lapidary fragments, arms and armour, furniture, goldware and silverware to reconstructed interiors and documentary material on the destruction of World War II. At house number 20 on the east side of the square is the **Adam Mickiewicz Literary Museum**, which focuses on the output of the national bard after whom it is named, an epic poet of the Romantic era in the Byron mould.

A block to the west of the Rynek is the **Szeroki Dunaj** (literally, 'Broad Tributary'), a smaller market square once used for selling meat and fish. The house at number 5 was the home of Jan Kiliński, the shoemaker who led the Warsaw citizenry in Kościuszko's national insurrection of 1794. He is

The main square of Warsaw's Old Town (Chapter 1)

The Tin-Roofed Palace, an extension to Warsaw's Royal Castle (Chapter 1)

A song and dance troupe rehearsing in the Theatre on the Island in Łazienki Park, Warsaw (Chapter 1)

The main front of Wilanów Palace in Warsaw (Chapter 1)

commemorated by a monument which stands close to the town walls at the junction of ul. Podwale and ul. Piekarsa, a block further south.

The walls themselves have been rebuilt to about half their former length, and stretch from plac Zamkowy all the way round the western and northern boundaries of the Old Town. Guarding the latter end is the **Barbican**, a small fort by a sixteenth-century military architect, Giovanni Battista da Venezia, which is now used as a commercial art gallery. A little to its east is a statue, formerly part of the Rynek's fountain, of the symbol of Warsaw, the mermaid Syrena. According to legend, she lived in the Vistula and was responsible for luring a brother and sister named Wars and Sawa to found a town on this spot.

The New Town

Immediately beyond the Barbican is the **New Town** (Nowe Miasto), which is actually only slightly younger than its counterpart. Although historically a self-contained town in its own right, it lacked its own defensive system and had a far less prosperous populace. At the head of ul. Freta, the southern part of its central axis, are two large Baroque monasteries. To the left is the **church of the Holy Ghost**, which belongs to the Paulite order and is the starting-point of the Warsaw leg of the great annual pilgrimage to Częstochowa described in Chapter 9. Inside is an altarpiece of *The Crucifixion* by the great Silesian painter Michael Willmann. Across the road is the Dominican **church of St Hyacinth** (or Jacek), built in the first half of the seventeenth century to plans by Giovanni Battista Trevano, who also worked on the Royal Castle. Off its north aisle is the chapel of the Kotowski family by Tylman van Gameren, a Dutch-born architect from the latter part of the same century, whose severe Palladian-derived style made a decisive imprint on the face of the city.

Further up the same street is the **birthplace of Maria Skłodowska-Curie**, the great scientist known outside Poland as Marie Curie, the name she used in her adopted home of France. The house is now a memorial museum, focusing on her early life in Warsaw as well as on her scientific achievements, notably the discovery and isolation of radium, which brought the unprecedented award of Nobel Prizes for both physics and chemistry.

A short distance beyond is the New Town's own market square, the **Rynek Nowego Miasta**, which also formerly had a Town Hall in the middle. On its eastern side is one of Warsaw's most distinguished buildings, the **church of the Holy Sacrament**, designed by Tylman van Gameren to a Greek-cross plan, with a large central dome resting on an octagonal drum. It was commissioned by Queen Maria Kazimierza as a votive offering for the victory of her husband, King Jan Sobieski, over the Turks at the Battle of Vienna in 1683, an event which ended the longstanding Ottoman threat to Western Europe and brought Poland to the peak of her international power and influence — albeit at a cost which precipitated her long slide into disintegration and eventual oblivion. The church was gutted in the war, and the only notable adornment left is the neo-Classical monument to Maria de

Bouillon, granddaughter of the foundress and the last of the Sobieski dynasty.

Overlooking the Vistula to the north is the New Town parish church, which is dedicated to the **Visitation of the Virgin Mary**. As a result of the post-war restoration, it has reverted to its original Gothic shape. A block to the west, on ul. Zacroczymska, the northern continuation of ul. Freta, is the **Franciscan church**, the only one of the New Town's monasteries to have preserved much in the way of old furnishings, The most important of these is the Crucifix in the north transept, which was carved by Andreas Schlüter, who later became the leading sculptor and architect at the Prussian royal court in Berlin. Across the road is **Sapieha Palace**, a splendid Baroque residence by the Dresden architect Johann Sigismund Deibel, nowadays a school for the deaf.

The Baroque Quarter

Immediately west of the Old and New Towns lies another historic quarter, one which came to the fore in the seventeenth and eighteenth centuries as the setting for the grand palaces built as the Warsaw residences of the great aristocratic families who dominated the life of the Polish-Lithuanian Commonwealth. Because the interiors of many of the historic monuments in this quarter cannot be visited, it lies well off the beaten tourist track, but is nonetheless among the most rewarding parts of the city.

In the Middle Ages, Ul. Długa, which leads west from the **church of the Holy Ghost**, was one of the two main roads leading out of the city. Immediately to the rear of the church is the **Raczyński Palace**, which was remodelled in neo-Classical style by the royal architect Jan Kamsetzer for the family whose name it bears. It now houses the Historic Records Office. Near the road junction a little further along the street is a fine seventeenth-century church in the Roman Baroque style. It was built for a **Piarist monastery**, was converted for Orthodox worship when Warsaw came under Russian rule during the Partitions, and has served as the church of the local military garrison since 1918.

Opposite is the open space of plac Krasińskich, in which stands the **Monument to the Warsaw Uprising**, a belated tribute to those who died in the most tragic episode in the city's history. It was unveiled on 1 August 1989, the forty-fifth anniversary of the launch of the ill-fated revolt against the Nazis. On the east side of the square is the late seventeenth-century **Krasiński Palace**, arguably the most magnificent of all the city's aristocratic residences. The architect was Tylman van Gameren, while the sculptures are by Andreas Schlüter. On the façade and garden fronts are tympana of Roman triumphal scenes, references to the Valerius family, from whom the Krasińskis claimed to be descended. Nowadays, the special collections of the National Library are housed in the palace. To the rear is the Krasiński Garden, likewise designed by Tylman, but altered in the middle of the following century, when it was thrown open to the general public.

From the garrison church, the diagonal ul. Miodowa, one of Warsaw's most impressive thoroughfares, links ul. Długa with the other original main road out of the city, ul. Senatorska. Past the **Collegium Nobilium**, the former Piarist boarding school, is the **Basilian monastery of the Assumption**, designed by Domenico Merlini for the Uniate or Greek Catholic Church, which follows Orthodox traditions but accepts the authority of the pope. The chapel, a domed octagon, is a little-visited architectural gem containing three altarpieces, including one of *The Assumption*, by Franciszek Smuglewicz, an eighteenth-century Polish painter who trained in Rome.

Opposite is the **Borchów Palace**, the current residence of the Archbishop of Warsaw. Alongside is the enormous **Pac-Radziwiłł Palace**, currently occupied by the Ministry of Health. It was built by Tylman van Gameren for the powerful Radziwiłł clan, and extended in the 1820s by Henrico Marconi, a prolific Italian-born architect who practised a wide variety of styles. Next in line is the **Capuchin church**, founded by Jan Sobieski in thanks for his victory over the Turks. Off the south aisle is the Royal chapel, which was founded by King August III to shelter the heart of his notorious father King August II, nicknamed Augustus the Strong on account both of his physical strength and legendary sexual prowess, which is said to have included the siring of a child for each day of the year. An urn containing Sobieski's heart was subsequently placed in the chapel as well.

At the head of ul. Seantorska is the former **Palace of the Primates of Poland**, designed by Tylman van Gameren and now housing Warsaw's main registry office. Diagonally opposite is the horseshoe-shaped **Blank Palace**, a French-style château built by Szymon Bogumił Zug, a German-born architect who introduced the full-blown neo-Classical style in Poland. On the open square immediately to its west is a statue of the goddess Nike, a monument to the heroes of the city. This faces the **Grand Theatre**, a huge pile erected between 1825 and 1833 by Antonio Corazzi, the leading Warsaw practitioner of late neo-Classicism. Its main auditorium, Poland's leading venue for opera and ballet, is capable of seating over 2,000 people. A small Theatre Museum, detailing Poland's theatrical history, is also housed inside.

Further west is the **monastery of Reformed Franciscans**, a well-preserved Baroque complex. Beyond, marking the end of ul. Senatorska, is the **Blue Palace**, formerly the residence of the Zamoyski family, and the setting for one of Chopin's first concerts, given when he was just 6 years old. It stands at the edge of the **Saxon Garden** (Ogród Saski), a large park which was, until its destruction in the war, the backdrop for the palace built for King August II, who was also Elector of Saxony. The park's present appearance is largely due to a landscaping carried out in the early nineteenth century by an English gardener, James Savage. At its far eastern end, facing plac Piłsudskiego, is the Tomb of the Unknown Soldier.

Immediately north of the Blue Palace is plac Bankowy, a large square designed by Antonio Corazzi to serve as a self-contained financial district. At the south-west corner is a building which accommodated both the Stock Exchange and the Bank of Poland. It now contains the **John Paul II Collection of European Paintings**, established in 1987 by English-based émigrés, the Carroll-Borczyński family. Assembled in only a few years, mainly at auction, the collection has attracted a great deal of controversy, with many of its attributions challenged as being too optimistic. Nonetheless, it has an impressive roster of old masters, with Tintoretto, Pontormo, Guido Reni, Domenichino, Rubens, Van Dyck, Rembrandt, Terburgghen, Velàzquez, Murillo, Ribera and Goya being among those represented. There are also a few examples of Impressionism plus one of the better representations of British art to be seen on the continent. An oddity is that the paintings are not hung chronologically or by national schools, but by subject matter.

On the minute ul. Tłomackie, on the north side of plac Bankowy, is the **Jewish Historical Institute**. In addition to its research facilities, this contains a museum with displays of Judaic liturgical objects and photographs illustrating Jewish life in the city. Prior to World War II, Jews made up about a third of Warsaw's population — the highest figure anywhere in Europe. Their main place of worship, the Great Synagogue, stood on the site now occupied by the blue-coloured skyscraper.

Across the busy al. Solidarności, at the western end of ul. Długa and at the corner of the Krasiński Garden, is King Władysław Waza's Arsenal. Several times remodelled, it is now home to the **Archaeological Museum**, with displays on the history of Poland from prehistoric times until the disintegration of the state on the death of King Bolesław the Wrymouthed. There is a special section on the Iron Age village of Biskupin in Great Poland, and another on the mysterious Baltic tribes, the Prussians and Jatzvingians, who for centuries inhabited the areas which are now Poland's coastal regions.

The Royal Way

The first section of the **Royal Way** (Trakt Królewski), which links the Royal Castle with the residences at Łazienki 4km south, is along the broad Krakowskie Przedmieście, another street lined with a host of predominantly Baroque churches and palaces. Its name, which literally means 'Cracow Suburb' is explained by the fact that, when it was first built up, it marked the beginning of the road linking the new royal capital of Warsaw with its immediate predecessor.

At the top end, just off plac Zamkowy, is **St Anne's church**, which was founded in the fifteenth century by Anna, Duchess of Mazovia, for the Bernardine order. It is best viewed from across al. Solidarności to the north, from where the surviving Gothic outline of the east end is still apparent. However, the church otherwise has a predominantly Baroque appearance, including a full complement of decoration and furnishings — trompe l'oeil frescos, altars, pulpit and organ. The façade, modelled on that of San Giorgio Maggiore in Venice, was built by Poland's finest Romantic architect, Christian Piotr Aigner, who also designed the detached belfry in a free re-interpretation of the Italian Renaissance idiom. In summer, the latter can be ascended for a marvellous view over the city.

Further down the street is a **statue to Adam Mickiewicz**, which was financed by public subscription and unveiled in 1898, the centenary of the poet's birth. Although 12,000 people were present, the ceremony was conducted in silence because of Russian-imposed restrictions on public meetings. From there, it is worth making a detour to the tiny ul. Kozia a block to the west, to see the **Museum of Caricatures**, whose highly entertaining exhibitions usually include plenty of subjects which are readily intelligible even to those who do not speak Polish.

South of the Mickiewicz statue is the former **Carmelite church;** it was not destroyed in the war and still preserves its eighteenth-century furnishings intact. Alongside is the **Radziwiłł Palace**, which was remodelled by Aigner to serve as the residence of the Governor of the Congress Kingdom of Poland. In 1951, it was the setting for the meetings leading to the formation of the Warsaw Pact, the Eastern bloc military alliance; in 1989, it hosted the Round Table Negotiations which resulted in the transfer of power from the Communists to a democratically-elected government. The equestrian statue in the courtyard, modelled on that of the Roman Emperor Marcus Aurelius, is of Józef Poniatowski, nephew of King Stanisław August and commander-in-chief of Napoleon's Polish forces. He died the death of a Romantic hero at the Battle of Leipzig in 1813, having seen all hopes of the revival of Polish independence end with the French defeat. The statue is a copy of the original by Bertel Thorwaldsen, which was destroyed by the Nazis.

On the opposite side of the street is the **Potocki-Czartoryski Palace**, now the headquarters of the Ministry of Culture and Art. Beyond it is Warsaw's oldest grand hotel, the Europejski, designed by Henrico Marconi in the 1850s. In due course, it came to be overshadowed by the yet more luxurious Bristol Hotel which faces it, built by his son Władysław at the turn of the century in the Viennese Secessionist style. After a long period of closure, it was restored by Trusthouse Forte, and has once again taken its place among the most exclusive hotels in Europe.

Beyond the little park is the **church of the Nuns of the Visitation**, where Chopin used to play the organ for children's services. At the high altar is a mid-seventeenth-century silver tabernacle donated by Queen Luisa Maria; the eighteenth-century pulpit is in the shape of a boat, a popular format in Poland at that time. The buildings to the south belong to the University of Warsaw, which was founded in 1816, shut down by the Czarist authorities in 1831, to be re-opened by them as a Russian-language institution in 1869, with Polish outlawed until 1915. Closest to the church is the former **Tykskiewicz Palace**, now containing pat of the University Library. Designed by Jan Kamsetzer, it is one of the few Warsaw palaces to have a street front rather than a courtyard.

Across the street is the **Czapsk Palace**, which was built by Tylman van Gameren but subsequently remodelled. Chopin lived for a time in the wing on the left side of the courtyard. On the opposite side of ul. Traugutta is the **church of the Holy Cross**, one of whose nave pillars bears a plaque to the great composer, together with an urn containing his heart. Several leading

Polish literary figures — Julius Słowacki, Józef Kraszewski, Bolesław Prus and Władysław Reymont — are also commemorated by plaques, as is Władysław Sikorski, the wartime leader of the Polish government-in-exile.

A few worthwhile sights just off the Royal Way can be seen by taking a short detour down ul. Traugutta. Just beyond the end of the street is the domed **Holy Trinity church**, built in the 1770s by Szymon Bogumił Zug for his fellow Lutherans, utilising the central plan design so appropriate for Protestant worship. Just to the north is the **Zachęta Gallery**, a grandiose turn-of-the-century building which is Warsaw's main venue for temporary artistic exhibitions. On the other side of the Lutheran church is the **Ethnographic Museum**, which has displays of artefacts from Africa, South America and Oceania on its ground floor, with items from Poland, including a colourful array of folk dresses from all over the country, upstairs.

Back on the Royal Way, the end of Krakowskie Przedmieście comes with the **Staszic Palace**, a neo-Classical design by Antonio Corazzi which is now home to the Academy of Science. In front is a statue of the Renaissance astronomer Nicolaus Copernicus by Bertel Thorwaldsen. Thereafter, the street narrows perceptibly, with its name changed to Nowy Świat (literally, 'New World'). Instead of palaces and churches, there are tenements, shops and eateries, among them Warsaw's oldest and best-known café, Blikle (number 35).

Just east of Nowy Świat, reached via ul. Ordynacka, is the **Ostrogski Palace**, an aristocratic residence designed by Tylman van Gameren which is now the headquarters of the Chopin Society, which incorporates a museum of memorabilia pertaining to the composer. In addition to letters and manuscripts, the displays include a piano at which he composed some of his greatest works. Just to the south, at the end of ul. Foksal, is the **Zamoyski Palace**, part of which now serves as a commercial art gallery.

Further south, Nowy Świat is bisected by al. Jerozolimskie, a busy boulevard which is one of the main axes of Warsaw's commercial quarter, a district spreading over a large area to the west. At the corner of the two is a large concrete structure which was built as the headquarters of the ruling Communist Party but is now, in a neat twist of fate, the **Stock Exchange**.

Alongside is the **National Museum**, which, despite its forbidding exterior, is one of the most rewarding destinations in the city. The archaeology department on the ground floor contains a spectacular group of murals and architectural fragments, dating from the eighth to the thirteenth centuries, from the cathedral of Faras in Nubia (the present-day Sudan), which was excavated by Polish archaeologists in the 1960s. On the same level is a magnificent collection of medieval sacred art from all over present-day Poland, with a particular emphasis on former German territories such as Royal Prussia and Silesia. Much of the first floor is taken up by Polish painting. This begins with a number of examples of a distinctive national art form, the coffin portrait, and continues with the immigrant artists of the following century, such as Bacciarelli, Bellotto and the Frenchman Jean-Pierre Norblin. There are a number of historical blockbusters by Matejko, notably *The Battle of Grunwald*, along with plenty of examples of all the other leading Polish painters of the past two centuries: names to look out for include Piotr Michałowski, Wojciech Gerson, Józef Brandt, Józef Chełmoński, Stanisław Wyspiański, Olga Boznańska, Jacek Malczewski and Witold Wojtkiewicz. The left wing of the first floor and nearly all the second floor are devoted to foreign paintings, with Botticelli, Tintoretto, Cranach, Baldung, Terbrugghen, Watteau and Ingres being just some of the artists represented. Displays of decorative art are found on all three floors, while the east wing of the building contains the Polish Army Museum.

Back on the Royal Way, Nowy Świat terminates at the plac Trzech Krzyży, in the middle of which stands **St Alexander's church**, built by Christian Piotr Aigner on the model of the Pantheon in Rome. To the south, the street takes the name of ul. Ujazdowski, and changes character once more, becoming a leafy suburban boulevard lined with grand nineteenth- and early twentieth-century palaces which are now occupied by ministries and foreign embassies. The Sejm, a 1920s building which is the home of the current parliament, is located a block to the east, on ul. Wiejska.

Łazienki

The palace and park complex at **Łazienki**, just to the south of the city centre, is undoubtedly among the most attractive spots in Warsaw. By origin, it belonged to the Ujadzów estate, and was a marshy woodland used by aristocratic hunting parties, but it was completely transformed after King Stanisław August acquired it in 1766, commissioning the same artistic team who worked on the Royal Castle to turn it into a fitting summer residence.

The main part of the park lies south of ul. Agrykola, with a smaller section north of the same road. Within the latter is **Ujadzów Castle**, which was built in the 1620s by order of King Zygmunt Waza, probably to designs by Giovanni Battista Trevano. It has a strongly Italianate appearance, with four corner towers and a loggia on the side overlooking the River Vistula. Housed inside is the Centre of Modern Art, which presents temporary exhibitions by contemporary artists from Poland and abroad. At the southern end of this section of the park is a **monument to King Jan Sobieski**, depicting his in his favourite guise as the scourge of the Turkish infidel.

From the monument, there is a fine view across the pond to the main Łazienki palace, generally known as the **Palace on the Water**. The name Lazienki, which literally means 'bath house' is a reference to the original building on the site, which was designed in the 1680s by Tylman van Gameren for Stanisław Lubomirski, the Grand Marshal of Poland. King Stanisław August's court architects, Domenico Merlini and Jan Kamsetzer, skilfully incorporated this bath house into the framework of the new palace, adding a second storey, two contrasting fronts — one playful, one severe — overlooking the garden and the water, and two side pavilions linked by colonnades to the main block. Inside, the original Bathroom, with bas-reliefs of aquatic scenes from Ovid's *Metamorphosis* survives in a modified form, as does the central Rotunda, with its statues of the Roman emperors and Polish kings most admired by Stanisław August. The larger ground-floor chambers, such as the Ballroom and the Hall of Solomon, belong to the royal additions. Upstairs, the intimate private apartments of the king are hung with Dutch and Flemish cabinet paintings; also on view is a large canvas by Bellotto showing the appearance of the bath house prior to its reconstruction.

To the north-east is the **Old Guardhouse**, designed by Kamsetzer in a style echoing that of the palace's north front. Temporary exhibitions of modern art are often held inside. On its eastern side is the Great Outbuilding, a large U-shaped pile by Merlini which initially contained the royal kitchens and servant quarters. It is now home to the **Paderewski Museum**, which contains memorabilia of the musician-turned-statesman, including his piano, plus his personal collection of Oriental art.

Immediately opposite is the **Myślewicki Palace**, which Merlini designed to an unusual quarter-circle groundplan. It served for a time as Józef Poniatowski's private residence, and in recent years has often been used to accommodate visiting foreign dignitaries, which means that public access is sometimes suspended. The interiors, which have never been altered or destroyed, are intimate in scale. Among the most notable are the Dining Room, with murals by Jan Bogumił Plersch of Italian views, and the Bathroom, with a ceiling by the same artist of Flora and Zephyr.

A little to the south is the **Theatre on the Island**, an equally idiosyncratic creation, this time by Kamsetzer, which is still regularly used for its original purpose of hosting all kinds of open-air spectacles. Its most curious feature is that the stage, which is based on the ruined Temple of Jupiter at Baalbeck in the Lebanon, is separated from the amphitheatre, which is modelled on that in Herculaneum near Naples, by a narrow canal — an arrangement unique in Europe.

A short distance west of the palace is the **Trou Madame**, a pavilion by Merlini designed for the game after which it is named. Later remodelled to serve as the New Guard House, it has been given back its original name for its latest incarnation as a café. Beyond is the **White House**, which Merlini built to serve as a residence for Stanisław August while the main palace was under construction. He chose a revolutionary cube-shaped design with four identical elevations, whose sobriety contrasts sharply with the frothy decoration of the interiors. The most notable of these are the Dining Room, whose walls are covered with painted grotesques by Plersch, and the octagonal Study, with its trompe l'oeil depiction of a rose bower, again by Plersch.

Further west are two more buildings by Merlini. First of these is the **Water Tower**, a free copy of the tomb of Cecilia Metella in Rome. On the rise above, fronted by a formal garden with antique statues, is the **Old Orangery**. Inside, the Winter Garden serves both as a café and a sculpture gallery. The east wing contains the former Court Theatre, one of the few in Europe to have retained its eighteenth-century appearance. To ensure the best possible acoustics, it was built entirely of wood, but painted inside by Plersch to resemble marble. The artist created another illusion by painting a second tier of boxes, peopled with courtiers of the day, above the real ones below; he was also responsible for the ceiling fresco of Apollo and his chariot.

To the south, close to the al. Ujadzowskie entrance to the park, is an Art Nouveau **monument to Chopin**, the setting for open-air piano recitals on summer Sundays. Further south are two small garden buildings, the **Temple of Diana** and the **Egyptian Temple**, built by Jakub Kubicki in the 1820s. A short walk to the west of the latter is the **New Orangery**, which dates from four decades later and nowadays contains one of Warsaw's top restaurants.

Towards the south-west corner of the park, but outside its actual boundaries and not accessible to the public, is the **Belvedere Palace**, the official residence of the Polish President. In its present form, it dates back to the 1820s, when the previous palace on the site was remodelled in neo-Classical style by Kubicki for Grand Duke Constantin, the commander-in-chief of the Polish section of the Tsarist army.

Wilanów

Wilanów Palace, 4 miles (6km) south of Łazienki, is often described as 'The Polish Versailles', though this is applicable more to its location on the outer fringe of the city than to its size, which is on a relatively human scale when judged by the usual standards of royal residences. The estate was acquired in 1677 by King Jan Sobieski, who proceeded with the construction of a typical Polish manor house on the site. As his prestige soared, both at home and abroad, as a result of his successful campaigns against the Turks, so did this simple house become ever grander, gradually evolving, under the direction of the his architect Agostino Locci, into a splendid palace in the Roman Baroque style. Being the private property of Sobieski, it lost its royal function on his death, and in 1720 was acquired by Stanisław Lubomirski's daughter Elżbieta Seniawska, who added the two wings, so creating a French cour d'honneur. After a brief return to royal status under Augustus the Strong, it passed through the hands of several of Poland's most celebrated aristocratic dynasties before coming into state ownership in 1945.

Entry to the courtyard is via a Baroque gateway with statues of Pax and Mars, symbolizing the peace brought by Sobieski's military victories. The main block of the palace is festooned with an unashamedly hagiographic programme of sculptures, mostly by Stefan Szwanger. Above the entrance, the sun's rays beam down on the Sobieski armorial bearings held aloft by putti. On the attic, bas-reliefs illustrate the king's triumphs in war. Fronting his private apartments to the north are allegorical figures symbolizing his virtues, while those in the corresponding position to the south celebrate those of his queen, Maria Kazimierza. The garden front has even more elaborate decoration, including frescos of scenes from Homer's *Odyssey* and Virgil's **Aeneid**, portrait medallions of the royal couple, emblems of Poland and Lithuania, and a sundial based on the principles of the great Gdańsk astronomer Johannes Hevelius.

Inside, the apartments, although crammed with furnishings, are mostly quite homely in feel. The most impressive are the private apartments of the

Sobieskis, particularly the bedrooms and antechambers, which have a set of ceiling frescos of the Four Seasons. In the south wing is the only large reception room in the palace, a two-storey Dining Hall built for Augustus the Strong by the Dresden architect Johann Sigismund Deibel. The rooms of the north wing are decorated in the early nineteenth-century Empire style favoured by the then owners, the Potockis. Among the works of art is Jacques Louis David's equestrian portrait of Stanisław Kostka Potocki, one of the supreme masterpieces of neo-Classical painting. Several hundred more portraits, albeit of a much lower artistic standard, are housed in the upstairs galleries, which present a survey of Polish portraiture from the sixteenth to the nineteenth century, including many made for coffin lids.

The **Palace Park** falls into three readily identifiable sections. Immediately to the rear of the palace is a formal Baroque garden on two levels, featuring flowerbeds, clipped hedges and Rococo sculptures above, and arbors and a grotto below. To the side of the upper level is the Orangery, which now contains the **Museum of Decorative Arts**, featuring valuable objects from all over Europe and the Orient, including notable displays of Limoges enamels and Dresden china. South of the palace is a park laid out by Szymon Bogumił Zug in a mixed English and Chinese idiom, later adorned with monuments to various members of the Potocki family. Another English park occupies the corresponding position to the north. Among its garden buildings are a neo-Gothic pumphouse, a Chinese bower and a mock Roman bridge.

Just to the south of the gateway to the palace courtyard is the former coach house and riding school, which now contains the **Poster Museum**. This features both permanent and temporary displays of an art form taken very seriously in Poland; when it opened in 1968, it was the first of its kind in the world. In the park fronting the gateway is the neo-Gothic mausoleum of Stanisław Kostka Potocki and his wife Aleksandra by Henrico Marconi. The same architect remodelled the nearby **church of St Anne** in grand neo-Baroque, and lined the wall of its close with a picturesque series of shrines of the Stations of the Cross.

Other City Districts

This section offers a brief coverage of some of Warsaw's other districts, of which only one sees many foreign visitors — proof of how easy it is to get well off the beaten track in this city. While there are few attractions to compare with the set-pieces already described, anyone prepared to be adventurous will be rewarded with a few surprises.

Śródmieście, Warsaw's modern commercial centre, occupies a large area to the west of the Royal Way, Despite some recent intrusion, it is essentially a creation of the Communist years, displaying all the most characteristic features of Stalinist planning, with soulless high-rise offices, shops and blocks of flats grouped around intimidatingly wide boulevards. It is completely devoid of tourist sights, though a certain fascination is attached to the building which not only provides its focal point, but is also easily the most prominent landmark in Warsaw, visible from miles around.

Known as the Palace of Culture, this was a 'gift' from Stalin to the Polish people, and was raised between 1952 and 1955. It exemplifies Soviet wedding cake architecture at its most bloated — it is 833ft (254m) long and 754ft (230m) high — and is detested by most Varsovians, who resent the way it has become the most familiar symbol of their city. Although there has been talk of demolishing it, the chances are that it will be preserved, if only because it can be put to such a wide variety of uses: in addition to hosting trade fairs and exhibitions, it houses research institutes, offices, shops, theatres, cinemas, museums, libraries and a casino. A fine panorama of the city can be enjoyed from the viewing platform on the thirtieth floor: the local joke goes that this is the best viewpoint in the city as it is the only one from which the Palace of Culture cannot be seen.

North of the commercial centre are the districts of **Mirów** and **Muranów**. Until the Nazi Holocaust, these were the home of the bulk of Warsaw's Jewish population, which numbered over 300,000. From his American exile, the Yiddish writer Isaac Bashevis Singer described the life of this vanished community in a series of memoirs, novels and short stories which reached a wide international audience and won him the Nobel Prize for Literature. Unfortunately, Singer's beloved ul. Krochmalna is now unrecognizable from its pre-war self, and the same is true of virtually every street in both districts. However, on plac Grybowski in Mirów there is an active Jewish theatre, while down the alley to the rear is the Nożyk Synagogue, the only surviving Jewish temple in Warsaw. It was built in the early years of the century in neo-Romanesque style, and is open to the general public on Thursday mornings.

In Muranów, the Monument to the Heroes of the Ghetto in a little park on the western side of ul. Zamenhofa commemorates the heroic but doomed uprising mounted against the Nazis by the inhabitants of the closed ghetto in 1943. On ul. Strawki, four blocks further north, another monument stands on the site of the Umschlagplatz, the starting-point for the transports to Treblinka and other death camps.

The main Jewish cemetery is on ul. Okopowa in the western part of Muranów. Among the luminaries buried there are Ludwik Zamenhof, the inventor of Esperanto, and Solomon An-ski, whose play *The Dybbuk*, the undisputed masterpiece of Yiddish theatre, is still regularly performed around the world. This is actually one of a group of adjacent cemeteries, each devoted to a different religious or ethnic group. Much the largest is the Roman Catholic Powązki cemetery. At its eastern edge is the church of St Charles Borromeo, which was endowed by Primate Michał Poniatowski, brother of King Stanisław August, and built by Domenico Merlini, both of whom are buried in its catacombs. To the north, across ul. Tatarska, is a Tatar cemetery, while further south are separate cemeteries for Caucasians, Lutherans and Reformed Protestants.

The large district stretching north of both Muranów and the New Town is known as **Żoliborz**. It grew very rapidly during the inter-war years in line with Warsaw's revived importance as the capital of an independent country, and was endowed with a number of housing developments of the garden city type, which can still be seen on all sides of the central plac Wilson. Also from this period is the church of St Stanisław Kostka on ul. Hozjuska, a short distance west of the square, though it was not completed until after the war. This church is now one of Poland's leading shrines, as in the graveyard alongside is the tomb of the parish priest, Father Jerzy Popiełuszko, a pro-Solidarity activist who was murdered by the secret police in 1984, so becoming the great martyr of the popular resistance to Communist rule.

Further south, overlooking the Vistula, is the colossal Citadel, which was built by the Russians following the failed insurrection of 1830-1. Whole streets were razed to make way for it, but these have since been re-instated within the well-preserved outer walls of the fortress. The former prison, located towards the north-eastern end, is now open as a branch of the Historical Museum, with displays commemorating the victims of this earlier struggle against Russian tyranny.

The suburb of **Praga** on the right bank of the Vistula was founded as a separate town in the fifteenth century and functioned as such until 1791, when it was incorporated into Warsaw. It developed as a predominantly working-class district, and was spared destruction in World War II, when the Red Army cynically waited on its outer fringes while the Home Army mounted its ill-fated uprising against the Nazis, only moving across the river to liberate the city after most of it had been devastated.

From either the Praga waterfront, or from Most Śląsko Dąbrowski, the bridge which links it with the city centre, there is a fine view of the Old Town. Bordering the river is an extensive stretch of greenery made up of the Park Praski and the Zoological Gardens. Just beyond the eastern edge of these is the Loretto chapel, the oldest of several Polish reproductions of the Casa Santa at Loretto in southern Italy, which according to legend was transported there from Nazareth by angels. It was built in the 1640s by Constantino Tencallo, the designer of the Zygnunt Waza Column, and formed part of a now demolished Bernardine monastery.

Praga's skyline is dominated by St Michael and St Florian on plac Weteranów to the south, a bold twin-towered neo-Gothic church from the end of the nineteenth century. Further east is the Orthodox church of St Mary Magdalene, built in a traditional Byzantine-inspired style in the 1860s at a time when many Russians lived in the quarter. It is now the seat of the Metropolitan of the Polish Orthodox Church. Behind it is the Brotherhood of Arms Monument, one of the few surviving examples in Poland of the once ubiquitous memorials proclaiming an overtly Communist message.

On ul. Targowa to the south is the Różycki Bazaar, Warsaw's most colourful open-air market, albeit one that has lost much of its former lustre since the onset of capitalism. A couple of blocks to the north is the Warsaw Distillery, housed in mock medieval premises from the turn of the century. Another notable industrial landmark is the celebrated Wedel chocolate factory on ul. Zamoyskiego, the southern continuation of ul. Targowa.

Further down the same street are the Grochów tollbooths, a pair of columned pavilions by Jakub Kubicki. In the park to the south is the Tenth Anniversary Stadium, which is not only the biggest sports venue in the city, but also the setting for the main open-air market.

South of the main business district is the inner suburb of **Mokotów**, which is liberally endowed with parks and gardens. The Mokotów Palace on ul. Puławska dates back to the eighteenth century, but was given a neo-Gothic remodelling by Henrico Marconi. Its grounds were landscaped by Szymon Bogumił Zug, who was also responsible for adding a couple of eccentric little garden buildings — a tower with dovecot and a Moorish pavilion which was later changed into a Flemish gloriette. Further south is the Królikarnia Palace, a re-interpretation by Merlini of one of the seminal buildings of the Italian Renaissance, Palladio's Villa Rotunda near Vicenza. Built as the residence of the director of the court theatre, it is now a museum devoted to the work of Xavery Dunikowski, one of the most inventive and accomplished Polish sculptors of the century.

Also in the southern part of the city, approximately midway between Łazienki and Wilanów, is **Czerniaki**, which was formerly a village belonging to the Ujadzów estate. In the 1680s, Tylman van Gameren built a Bernardine monastery there at the behest of Stanisław Lubomirski, who wished it to serve as his family mausoleum. The complex, which stands in isolation on the eastern side of ul. Czerniakowska, a major arterial road into the city, survives intact and little altered. Its church, dedicated to St Anthony of Padua and St Boniface, has a domed nave in the shape of a Greek cross and an octagonal presbytery. The life and cult of St Anthony, whose relics are kept in the crypt, are depicted on the frescos which cover most of the walls, while a double-sided altarpiece with sculptures by Andreas Schlüter closes off the area reserved for the monks.

Excursions from Warsaw

The most enticing excursions from Warsaw all lie south of the River Vistula and have good communications links with the city. Even without a car, it is possible to visit two or three of the destinations described below in the course of a day trip. Those to the north of the river are more spread out, though every place included here is the feasible object of a day excursion; some or all can easily be combined to make a longer circular tour, while many are possible stop-offs on journeys to or from a neighbouring province.

South of the Vistula

Warsaw is the only major European city fortunate enough to have a large area of protected landscape — namely the **Kampinos National Park** (Kampinoski Park Narodowy) — right on its doorstep. Even although its closeness to the capital is its most remarkable feature, it deserves to be considered as one of Poland's premier attractions in its own right, being a predominantly natural wilderness area inhabited by over 4,000 different animal species. Beginning not far from the city boundaries, it stretches westwards for some 25 miles (40km), and at times measures 12 miles (20km) from north to south, with its total area ranking as the second largest of all the country's national parks. Small wonder, therefore, that it has often been the haven of resistance fighters throughout Poland's turbulent history, most notably during the 1863 uprising against the Russians, and during World War II.

The park's alternative name of the Puszcza Kampinoska signifies that it retains some of the characteristics of the primeval forests which once covered much of Europe. Particularly notable in this regard is the existence of dramatically different types of scenery in close proximity to one another. Among the chief components of the landscape is one of the largest complexes of sand dunes to be found anywhere in inland Europe. These dunes reach heights of up to 92ft (28m) and are generally covered with pine forests. Although they only occupy a small proportion of the total area, alder swamps are another ubiquitous feature of the park. On clammy summer days, when ridden with mosquitoes, they can seem uncannily like the tropics — yet it may be no more than a stone's throw to a flower-strewn meadow or a wood of oaks, lindens or poplars.

The symbol of the park is the elk, which, together with the beaver and the lynx, has been re-introduced in recent years to this former natural habitat. All of these animals, however, tend to keep well away from humans, and visitors are more likely to spot red or roe deer, wild boar, badgers or foxes. Thanks to lying on the migratory routes south, the park has a rich birdlife. Several birds of prey, including eagles, buzzards, goshawks, ospreys and ravens, nest there, as do cranes, herons and both white and black storks. The park's flora is exceptionally diverse: among the most characteristic are wild cherries, lily-of-the-valley, mezereons and pasque-flowers.

There are some 186 miles (300km) of marked trails in the park. The predominance of sandy soils makes for unusually comfortable and easy conditions underfoot, but some sections of the paths can become impassable after extended periods of heavy rainfall. Inevitably, the easternmost part of the park gets the most visitors, particularly at weekends, when droves of Varsovians take advantage of a swift and easy break from city life.

Dziekanów-Leśny, a village just beyond the boundaries of Warsaw, is the starting-place for the two trails which traverse the entire length of the park — the green route to Żelazowa Wola and the red route to Brochów. These are both over 30 miles (50km) in length, rather too long under normal circumstances to be accomplished in a single day, though there are camping facilities (but not any other type of accommodation) en route.

For a shorter walk, the best jumping-off point is probably **Truskaw**, a farming settlement which lies well within the park, the dead-end terminus of a road from Warsaw which is plied by fairly regular urban buses. A good cross-section of the park's scenery can be seen in a just a few hours by walking between Truskaw and Dziekanów-Leśny: this involves taking either the black or the blue trail to the cemetery at **Palmiry** (3 miles/5km south of the eponymous village), which has the graves of hundreds of partisans shot by the Nazis, then switching to the red trail.

For the less visited western half of the park, the obvious base is **Kampinos**, some 28 miles (45km) from Warsaw by road, site of the only tourist lodge in the immediate vicinity of the forest. The village is itself of note for its fine wooden parish church, a late eighteenth-century building whose twin towers are crowned by highly idiosyncratic spires shaped like obelisks.

Under normal circumstances, **Żelazowa Wola**, which lies 6 miles (10km) west of Kampinos by road, or 14 miles (22km) away via the last stretch of the green trail, would be a village sunk in total obscurity. Instead, it has gained international renown as the birthplace of Frédéric Chopin, the composer par excellence for the piano, whose creative output has reached an audience unmatched by any other Pole in the artistic sphere. Chopin was born in 1810 in a typical Mazovian *dwór* or manor house on the estate of the Skarbek family, to whom his French-born father served as a tutor. The family moved to Warsaw a year later, though the village held a special place in the composer's affections, and he returned there at regular intervals until 1830, when he left his subjugated native land for good, settling among the already well-established Polish émigré community in Paris. Just before the outbreak of World War II, Chopin's birthplace was made into a memorial museum, with a landscaped park created around it. No original furnishings survive, but it has been decked out in the style of the period. The best time to visit is on a summer Sunday, as piano recitals are given then, usually at 11am and 3pm.

Chopin was baptized at the late Gothic church of St Roch in **Brochów**, 4 miles (7km) to the north-west, where his parents had married in 1806. This has an interest well beyond its associations with the composer, as it is arguably the best surviving example in Poland of a fortified village church. The walled enclosure, the three barbican-like towers with their gun loops, the steeply pitched roof and the tall narrow windows are all evidence of the building's defensive function. However, the interior was remodelled in late Renaissance style in the 1660s and has a bright and airy feel.

Łowicz, which is 20 miles (32km) south-west of Żelazowa Wola, was for many centuries the preferred main residence of the Archbishops of Gniezno, who were traditionally also the Primates of Poland. It is also the hub of a region with a long-established reputation for handicrafts. These religious and folklore traditions are combined to spectacular effect in the big church festivals, most notably Corpus Christi, which takes place in late May or early June, the exact date varying each year in accordance with that designated for Easter.

This colourful yet deeply spiritual event, one of the most potent demonstrations of the central role of Roman Catholicism in Polish life, begins with an open-air mass on the main square, the Rynek Kościuszki, followed around 12noon by a solemn procession, lasting for about 90 minutes, round its perimeter and into the collegiate church on the west side. For this, the local women wear traditional handmade folk costumes — headscarfs, blouses, waistcoats and full-length skirts — adorned with a kaleidoscopic variety of patterned and floral motifs. They process in parish groups, each participant holding a ribbon attached to an embroidered banner held aloft by a standard bearer. Walking in neat files behind the adults, decked out in long white robes or dresses, are children preparing to receive their first Communion. The rear of the procession is formed by nuns, monks and priests, with the sacred host displayed on a triumphal car at the tail. After a short service, the groups disperse and parade back informally to their individual parish churches.

When there is not a religious festival taking place, Łowicz can seem a very monochromal town, but it does have several monuments of note. The collegiate church itself is, in its present form, essentially a mid-seventeenth building by the brothers Tommaso and Andrea Poncino, poised between late Renaissance and early Baroque in style. It is far less of note for its architecture than for its rich and varied furnishings, among which are the funerary monuments of several Polish Primates, These include two Renaissance masterpieces: the tomb of Archbishop Przerębski by the Milanese Hieronimo Canavesi, and its counterpart to Archbishop Uchański by the only major Polish sculptor of the period, Jan Michałowicz.

On the east side of the Rynek Kościuszki is the town's most distinguished building, the Missionary college by Tylman van Gameren. Now the Regional Museum, it houses sections on the history of the town and on local folklore, with wide-ranging displays of costumes, painted Easter eggs, paper cut-outs and woodcarvings. Sacred treasury items are on view in the chapel, one of Tylman's finest creations, which is frescoed with scenes narrating the life of St Charles Borromeo by Michelangelo Palloni, court painter to King Jan Sobieski. In the garden to the rear is a small *skansen*, consisting of several large and comical folk sculptures plus two cottages furnished in traditional country style.

The Town Hall on the north side of the square is a typical example of the grand neo-Classical public buildings erected during the short-lived period of the Congress Kingdom of Poland; also from this era is the Post Office on nearby ul. 3 Maja. Of the town's many Baroque churches, the most interesting is the late eighteenth-century Piarist church off the south-west corner of the square, which has a resplendent convex-concave façade. At the far north-western end of the town centre, overlooking the River Bruza, is the castle of the archbishops. It was sacked by the Swedes in the seventeenth century, and little now remains beyond the foundations, set atop a mound commanding a pleasant view over the surrounding countryside.

Arkadia, some 3 miles (5km) south-east of Łowicz, is one of the finest of a number of English-style country estates specially created at the end of the eighteenth century for leading members of the Polish aristocracy, in this case by Szymon Bogumił Zug for Princess Helena Radziwiłł. Unlike its models, it was not based around a stately home, but instead consists only of a landscaped park with a number of whimsical garden pavilions. Many of

Woods and meadows in the Kampinos National Park (Chapter 1)

Participants in the Corpus Christi parade in Łowicz (Chapter 1)

The palace in Gołuchów (Chapter 2)

Windmills in the Ethnographic Park by Lake Lednica (Chapter 2)

these are Classical in inspiration, and include a Temple of Diana, an aqueduct and an amphitheatre deliberately built as a ruin, as well as many original statues and lapidary fragments from Roman times. However, in true Romantic fashion, inspiration comes from other sources, as is witnessed by the neo-Gothic chapel and the Swiss-style chalet at the park entrance.

The Radziwiłłs also owned the palace at **Nieborów**, a further 2 miles (4km) to the south-east, which was built in the 1690s by Tylman van Gameren for Cardinal Michał Radziejowski. Now a museum, the ground floor is used to display the family's valuable collection of Classical sculpture, the star piece being the Nieborów Niobe, a first-century Roman copy of a Greek original from the fourth century BC. Upstairs, the rooms are furnished in period style, and display many notable artefacts, such as a pair of Renaissance globes from Venice, as well as tiled stoves made in the local porcelain factory which operated, as the only one in Poland, between 1881 and 1906. Other products from this are on display in the former granary, located a couple of minutes' walk east of the entrance to the grounds. Immediately to the rear of the palace is a formal Baroque garden in the French manner, while beyond is a much more extensive English park laid out by Zug for the Radziwiłłs.

North of the Vistula

Jablonna, just 12 miles (20km) north of central Warsaw, is a small satellite town on whose fringes is a fine late Baroque palace designed by Domenico Merlini and extended by Szymon Bogumił Zug. It was built for Primate Michał Poniatowski, brother of the last Polish king, later passing to his nephew, the military hero Józef Poniatowski, and then to the Potocki dynasty. Since the war, the palace has been used as a conference venue by the Polish Academy of Sciences, though on completion of a restoration programme there are plans to make it into a regular tourist attraction. In the meantime, there is public access to the park, which has a Chinese-style pagoda, a neo-Classical Orangery and a triumphal arch commemorating the military victories of Józef Poniatowski.

Modlin, a further 12 miles (20km) downstream at the confluence of the Vistula with the Narew, has a huge hilltop fortress built in the first decade of the nineteenth century by order of Napoleon, and subsequently extended on several occasions by the Russians, growing into a garrison capable of accommodating over 25,000 soldiers. It remained of strategic importance right up until World War II, when it was reduced to its present ruinous state.

Another 19 miles (30km) west, facing the far end of the Kampinos National Park, is **Czerwińsk**, an old world village of wooden houses that was once a town of some significance. On the cliff high above the river is the abbey, founded in the twelfth century by an evangelizing congregation of Canons Regular from France. Following damage in World War II, the twin-towered church was stripped of many of its later accretions and returned to something approaching its original Romanesque shape. It has a beautifully carved entrance porch, and a number of frescos of various epochs, the oldest of which date back to the thirteenth century. The detached belfry, a Gothic structure from the end of the fifteenth century, can be ascended in summer for a view over the village and the river. It is also possible to visit the monastic buildings, which are currently inhabited by a small community of Salesian Fathers. Within are a number of fine Gothic interiors, notably the former refectory, which houses a small museum on their missionary activities.

Płock, 28 miles (45km) west, was a place of major importance long before Warsaw. It served as the main seat of the Mazovian dukes for half a millennium, and for several decades in the late eleventh and early twelfth centuries was a favourite royal residence and thus effectively the national capital. However, its long period of decline began when it was supplanted by Warsaw in the fifteenth century. Only after World War II did it belatedly develop into a city, thanks to being accorded the dubious honour of becoming the hub of Poland's oil and petrochemical industries.

The city's key historic buildings are located on another of the Vistula's escarpments, high above the river. Of these, the cathedral is the oldest, dating back to the twelfth century. As so often in Poland, it was remodelled repeatedly, losing much of its original Romanesque shape in the process. Although a restoration at the beginning of the twentieth century returned it to a partially medieval appearance, it still retains many later accretions, including the neo-Classical façade by Merlini. The bronze entrance doors are modern copies of the originals, which were cast in Magdeburg in Germany in the mid-twelfth century, and transferred a couple of hundred years later to St Sophia's church in the Russian city of Novgorod, where they remain to this day. Under one of the Gothic towers is a chapel containing the mortal remains of Władysław Herman and his son Bolesław the Wrymouthed, the two Polish kings who resided in Płock. The vivacious and rather unecclesiastical murals in the main body of the building are in the Secessionist style, and were added soon after the completion of the restoration programme.

Alongside the cathedral are the fourteenth-century Nobleman's Tower and the fifteenth-century Clock Tower, the latter of which serves as its belfry. These both belonged to the castle of the Mazovian Dukes, most of which was destroyed by the Swedes in the seventeenth century. However, a residential wing has been restored to serve as the Mazovian Museum, which is principally of note for containing the finest collection of Secessionist and Art Nouveau artefacts to be seen anywhere in Poland. Across the road is the Diocesan Museum, which has displays of sacred art, including folk woodcarvings. There are many eighteenth- and nineteenth-century houses in the centre, including a fine group on the Rynek. Also on this square are the neo-Classical Town Hall and the parish church; the latter is Gothic by origin, but was completely transformed in the Baroque era, when it was re-aligned to face to the square.

Sierpc, 20 miles (32km) north of Płock, is the home of the Mazovian Village Museum (Museum Wsi Mazowieckiej), which is located 2 miles

(3km) west of the town centre, near the village of Bojanowo. This *skansen* displays a dozen farmsteads from the northern part of Mazovia, as well as an inn and a number of wayside shrines. There is also a Regional Museum in the Town Hall on Sierpc's Rynek, featuring exhibits on local history and folklore.

Ciechanów, 53 miles (85km) north-east of Płock, and a similar distance north-west of Warsaw, was a stronghold and secondary residence of the Mazovian dukes. At the eastern edge of town is their castle, which is dominated by two round towers of glazed bricks. A fine specimen of fifteenth-century military architecture, it owes much to the earlier fortresses of the Teutonic Knights in its rigorous symmetry, yet has a definite character of its own. It was partially remodelled in the sixteenth century as a Renaissance palace for Bona Sforza, the widow of King Zygmunt the Old, but was allowed to fall into disrepair soon after her death and has remained semi-ruinous ever since. Just off the town centre Rynek is the Gothic church of St Joseph, while the neo-Gothic Town Hall on nearby ul. Sienkiewicza houses the District Museum, with displays of folk art and crafts.

Some 5 miles (8km) to the north-east of Ciechanów is the village of **Opinogóra**, with a palace and English-style park commissioned by Wicenty Krasiński, a one-time general in Napoleon's army who — in total contrast to Józef Poniatowski — managed to overcome the bitter disappointment of the failure to re-establish Polish independence, choosing to accept a senior administrative post in the Russian-ruled Congress Kingdom. In 1843, he gifted the palace and estate to his son Zygmunt, one of Poland's greatest-ever poets, as a wedding present. The palace is a true piece of Romantic fantasy, dominated by a four-storey octagonal tower asymmetrically placed at the south-east corner. Fittingly, it is now designated as the Museum of Romanticism, and furnished accordingly. Wicenty Krasiński was also responsible for the more sober neo-Classical parish church in the village, which doubled as the family mausoleum.

Yet another place with a Napoleonic connection is **Pułtusk**, 24 miles (38km) south-west of Ciechanów and 37 miles (60km) north of Warsaw, scene of a hard-won French victory over the Russians in 1806. The Old Town, which is situated on an island between branches of the River Narew, is centred on the 1,312ft (400m) long Rynek, one of the largest squares in Europe. In the middle of this is a Baroque Town Hall which still preserves the tower of its Gothic predecessor. The latter now contains the Regional Museum, which includes archaeological excavations as well as examples of the distinctive folk art of the Kurpie region described below. To the north of the Rynek is the collegiate church. Although this preserves its original Gothic exterior, it received a highly distinctive internal transformation by the Italian Renaissance architect Giovanni Battista da Venezia, who gave it a roomy, tunnel-like appearance and highly distinctive network vaults.

South of the square is the former Castle of the Bishops of Płock, whose main residence this was. In its present form, it dates back to a Renaissance rebuilding carried out in the 1520s. Napoleon lodged there in 1806, and again 6 years later following his retreat from Moscow. Nowadays, it has been refurbished to serve as the *Dom Polonii*, a luxury hotel and conference centre specially geared towards members of the Polish diaspora. Between the castle and the square is the former court chapel, the Renaissance church of St Mary Magdalene.

The Kurpie region to the north-east of Pułtusk is centred on a marshy forest, the Puszcza Kurpiowska, and is a place where traditional rural lifestyles are still the norm. It is best-known for its handicrafts, in particular weaving and decorative paper cut-outs, but also has its own dialect and distinctive musical tradition. In the village of **Kadzidło** 48 miles (77km) from Pułtusk, there is a co-operative crafts workshop, as well as a small museum, the Izba Kurpiowska, in a cottage decorated in the local style. The inhabitants don colourful costumes for the main religious festivals, most notably Corpus Christi.

At the opposite end of the region, about 31 miles (50km) from Kadzidło by the roundabout main road, is **Nowogród**, home of an Ethnographic Park which is the second-oldest open-air museum in Poland. Splendidly situated high above the River Narew, it has a fine collection of eighteenth- and nineteenth-century houses from throughout the Kurpie region, as well as many old beehives of all shapes and sizes.

Upstream from Nowogród, 10 miles (16km) to the south-east by road, is **Łomża**, one of Mazovia's oldest towns, situated hard by the historic boundary with Podlasie, which forms the subject of Chapter 6. It was badly damaged in World War II, and in the post-war construction the cathedral was stripped of many of its Baroque accretions, and returned to its original late Gothic form. Built as a parish church in the sixteenth century, it boasts beautiful stellar and cellular vaulting and several impressive Renaissance funerary monuments. Immediately to the north is the Rynek, now unfortunately lined with modern buildings, with the exception of the neo-Classical Town Hall and one old mansion. A couple of blocks beyond is the Capuchin monastery, a late eighteenth-century Baroque complex which survived the war intact.

Treblinka, 40 miles (65km) due south of Łomża, and about 62 miles (100km) north-east of Warsaw, was the site of one of the most notorious Nazi concentration camps, which functioned from 1941 until liquidated 2 years later, by which time up to 800,000 people may have perished — a total surpassed only at Auschwitz-Birkenau. The camp's setting was chosen as a matter of cynical calculation: it was a secluded rural location well away from prying eyes, yet only 3 miles (5km) south of the town of Małinka, which lay on the main railway line from Warsaw to Russia via Białystok. Moreover, it was almost directly on the border partitioning Poland between Germany and the Soviet Union which had been agreed as a secret provision of the Molotov-Ribbentrop Pact of 1939, suggesting that the Nazis intended to make it appear that the Soviets had founded the camp.

As at Auschwitz, there were actually two camps, a couple of kilometres apart: Treblinka I was created to exploit slave labour, while Treblinka II, set up a year later, was for systematic mass murder. The Nazis excised virtually all traces of both in a vain attempt to cover up their crimes. However, memorials to the victims were set up on the site of both camps in 1964. That at Treblinka II is surrounded by a stylized cemetery, with several thousand rough granite blocks serving as symbolic tombstones.

Łódź

Łódź, Poland's second largest city, lies 32 miles (52km) south-west of Łowicz, right in the very centre of the country. It sees very few tourists, and is a place even patriotic Poles are inclined to view as a major national embarrassment. The reason for this is that it still presents an almost unaltered industrialised cityscape, of a type which has vanished completely from Western Europe. Yet the time-capsule feel of the smoking castellated factories and the grand villas of the captains of industry has a potent attraction of its own, making the city well worth a visit. Long nicknamed 'The Polish Manchester', it has plenty of similarities with its English counterpart — albeit as it was a few decades ago.

Two further curiosities are that all the notable buildings belong to a relatively short historical period, and that prior to World War II, the life of the city was dominated by people who were not ethnic Poles. Indeed, although Łódź is documented as early as the twelfth century, it remained a small village until 1820, when an edict of the Russian-ruled Congress Kingdom of Poland designated it as a new industrial centre and encouraged foreigners to come and settle. It quickly underwent a mushroom growth under an economic elite dominated by German entrepreneurs, most of whom were Protestant, and Jews from all over Europe. Łódź therefore became renowned as a melting-pot of four great peoples and religions, but this was reduced to three after the Russians relinquished political power in 1918, and had disintegrated completely by the end of World War II, when nearly all the Jews were massacred and the Germans expelled.

Most of Łódź's sights are located on or around ul. Piotrkowska, a 2¹/₂ mile (4km) long avenue which bisects the city from north to south. Just beyond its northern end is the original Rynek, which soon lost its market function as the city expanded rapidly southwards. One block south and another west, at the junction of ul. Zachodnia and ul. Ogrodowa, is one of the best-preserved complexes from the Industrial Revolution to be seen anywhere in Europe. On the corner itself is the neo-Baroque Poznański Palace, formerly the main residence of a leading Jewish manufacturing family. Alongside is their still-functioning factory, behind whose mock-Gothic brickwork façade are weaving and spinning mills plus a number of warehouses. Across the street are the tenement flats of the workforce.

The Poznański Palace, which mimmicks the appearance of a stately home, is now the City Historical Museum. Downstairs are temporary exhibitions of modern art and photography, while up the grandiose staircase are the showpiece chambers, the dining room and the ballroom, along with others of more modest size which are now devoted to displays on different aspects of the city's history. Archive photographs show the appearance of prewar Łódź, including the now-demolished synagogues, while there is an extensive collection of memorabilia of the pianist Artur Rubinstein, one of the most fêted pianists of the century, whose recordings of the music of Chopin remain the interpretative touchstone for Poland's greatest composer.

A block to the south then one to the east is the circular plac Wolności. Its monuments include the neo-Classical Town Hall, a statue of Tadeusz Kościuszko, and the domed church of the Holy Ghost, which is built to a Greek-cross plan. There is also the Archaeology and Ethnography Museum, featuring a wide-ranging collection of local artefacts, costumes and archaeological finds.

A couple of blocks further south, then off to the right on ul. Więckowskiego, is the Modern Art Gallery or Galeria Sztuki, installed in a neo-Renaissance palace, complete with stained glass windows, which formerly belonged to the Poznański dynasty. Founded in 1925, when it was one of the world's first museums devoted to the avant-garde, it is the finest modern art collection in the country. Major artists represented include Marc Chagall, Pablo Picasso, Paul Klee, Max Ernst and Ferdinand Léger. There is also an excellent selection of work by twentieth-century Polish artists, such as Łódź's own Władysław Strzemiński, who practised a highly individual form of abstraction; his sculptress wife Katarzyna Kobro; and the Jewish painter Jankiel Adler, who spent his final years in England.

One block to the south, and six to the east, facing the main railway station, Łódź Fabryczna, is the Orthodox church, a rare reminder of the era of Russian rule. A short distance to the south-west, at the back of the Grand Hotel, is ul. Moniuszki, an uninterrupted row of plush neo-Renaissance family houses. More fine mansions can be seen three blocks further south, on the west side of ul. Piotrkowska. Another three blocks on, this time on the opposite side of the street, is the large Olympia factory, followed by several more villas of the old industrial tycoons, often set in spacious grounds and showing a mixture of architectural styles.

Across from them are two of the city's most important churches. The neo-Gothic cathedral, dedicated to St Stanisław Kosta, has a plain yellowbrick exterior, though the spacious interior, with its luminous stained glass windows, is much more impressive. A little further on is the Lutheran church of St Matthew, which is still used by the few remaining descendants of the old German oligarchy. Frequent recitals are given on its Romantic-style organ, the finest instrument of its kind in Poland.

Towards the southern end of ul. Piotrkowska is the huge White Factory, the oldest mechanically operated mill in the city. Part of it is now occupied by the Textile Museum, which features a large number of historic looms, documentary material on the history of the industry in Łódź, and an exhibition of contemporary examples of the art of weaving.

On ul. Przędzalniana in the eastern part of the city is the Herbst Palace or Księży Młyn, the residence of one of the leading German manufacturing families. Outwardly, it imitates the great Renaissance villas built by Palladio in northern Italy. Both the grand reception rooms downstairs and the intimate family ones above display a wide range of influences in their decor, ranging from ancient Rome via the Orient to Art Nouveau. The ballroom, added as an afterthought, is a pastiche of the English Tudor style.

On ul. Tylna a short distance to the west is the Grohmann Villa, which is also due to be opened as a museum in due course. Further north, spanning both sides of the busy al. Piłsudskiego, is the vast plac Zwycięstwa, whose southern side is almost entirely occupied by the castellated Scheibler Palace, the former home of the most powerful of the German textile families. Part of it now houses the Cinematography Museum, which celebrates Łódź's status as the leading Polish training ground for film makers, among whom Andrzej Wajda and Roman Polański have gained world renown.

It is not inappropriate that cemeteries provide the most poignant reminders of the cultural diversity of Łódź's past. The main Christian necropolis, which lies about ½ mile (1km) west of the Poznański factory along ul. Ogrodowa, is divided into three interconnected plots. By far the largest is the Catholic cemetery, whose monuments, with rare exceptions, are fairly simple. Even less ostentatious is its Orthodox counterpart, containing the graves of civil servants, soldiers and policemen from the Tsarist period. In contrast, the Protestant cemetery is full of appropriately grandiose memorials to the manufacturing dynasties. Towering over all the other graves is the Scheibler family mausoleum, which is built in the form of a miniature Gothic cathedral, complete with a characteristically Germanic openwork spire. The Jewish cemetery, the largest in Europe with some 180,000 tombstones, including many of great beauty, is situated in the north of the city on ul. Bracka.

Łódź is located within a territory which was, in the Middle Ages, a separate county between Mazovia and Great Poland named after its principal town, **Łęczyca**. This lies 29 miles (46km) north-west of Łódź and 32 miles (52km) west of Łowicz, and is nowadays a modest-sized regional centre. The one monument of note is the surviving part of the medieval castle, whose tower contains a museum with displays on archaeology, local history and ethnography.

Following its sacking at the hands of the Teutonic Knights in the fourteenth century, Łęczyca was relocated to its present position from its original site 1 mile (2km) to the south-east, which is now a separate village called **Tum**. The twelfth-century collegiate church, now set among open fields, is probably the best-known Romanesque building in Poland, though it was the subject of a rather drastic restoration after being damaged in World War II. Crafted of hard pink and grey granite, the church has apses at both ends, each of which is flanked by twin towers — square to the west, cylindrical to the east — which served a defensive function. The battered north portal still preserves some of its carvings, but the interior was altered in the Gothic period, receiving pointed arcades made partly from bricks.

Further Information
— Mazovia —

Places to Visit

Ciechanów
Castle of the Mazovian Dukes
Open: Tuesday to Sunday 10am to 4pm.

Regional Museum
ul. Sienkiewicza
Open: Tuesday to Sunday 10am to 4pm.

Kadzidło
Izba Kurpiowska
Open: Wednesday to Saturday 10am
to 5pm, Sunday 10am to 3pm.

Łęczyca
Castle (Regional Museum)
Open: Tuesday to Friday 10am to 4pm,
Saturday and Sunday 9am to 2pm.

Łódź
Archaeology and Ethnography Museum
plac Wolności 14
Open: Tuesday and Friday 11am to
6pm, Wednesday and Thursday 10am
to 5pm, Saturday 9am to 3pm, Sunday
10am to 3pm.

Cinematographic Museum
pl. Zwycięstwa 1
Open: Wednesday to Friday 10am to
2pm, Saturday and Sunday 11am to 5pm.

Herbst Palace
ul. Przędzalniana 72
Open: Tuesday 10am to 5pm,
Wednesday and Friday 12noon to
5pm, Thursday noon to 7pm, Saturday
and Sunday 11am to 4pm.

Modern Art Gallery
ul. Więckowskiego 36
Open: Tuesday 10am to 5pm,
Wednesday and Friday 11am to 5pm,
Thursday 12noon to 7pm, Saturday
and Sunday 10am to 4pm.

*Poznański Palace (City Historical
Museum)*
ul. Ogrodowa 15
Open: Tuesday and Thursday to
Saturday 10am to 2pm, Wednesday
10am to 6pm.

Textile Museum
ul. Piotrkowska 280
Open: Tuesday and Saturday 10am to
5pm, Wednesday and Friday 9am to
5pm, Thursday 10am to 5pm, Sunday
10am to 3pm.

Łowicz
Regional Museum
Rynek Kościuszki
Open: Tuesday to Sunday 10am to 4pm.

Nieborów
Palace
Open: Tuesday to Sunday 10am to
3.30pm.

Nowogród
Ethnographic Park
Open: April to October Tuesday to
Friday 9am to 4pm, Saturday and
Sunday 10am to 5pm.

Opinogóra
Palace
Open: Tuesday to Sunday 10am to
3.30pm.

Płock
Diocesan Museum
Wzgórze Tumskie
Open: Wednesday to Saturday 10am
to 3pm, Sunday 11am to 2pm.

Mazovian Museum
ul. Tumska 2
Open: Tuesday, Thursday and
Saturday 9am to 3pm, Friday 10am to
5pm, Sunday 10am to 3pm.

Pułtusk
Regional Museum
Rynek
Open: Tuesday to Saturday 10am to
4pm, Sunday 10am to 2pm.

Sierpc
Mazovian Village Museum
Open: May to September Tuesday to
Sunday 10am to 5pm, October to
April Tuesday to Sunday 9am to 3pm.

Regional Museum
Rynek
Open: Tuesday to Sunday 10am to 4pm.

Warsaw
Adam Mickiewicz Literary Museum
Rynek Starego Miasta 20
Open: Monday, Tuesday and Friday
10am to 3pm, Wednesday and
Thursday 11am to 6pm, Sunday 11am
to 5pm.

Archaeological Museum
ul. Długa 52
Open: Monday to Friday 9am to 4pm,
Sunday 10am to 4pm.

Chopin Museum
ul. Okólnik 1
Open: Monday to Wednesday, Friday
and Saturday 10am to 2pm, Thursday
12noon to 6pm.

Citadel (Independence Museum)
ul. Skazańców 25
Open: Tuesday to Friday 10am to
5pm, Saturday and Sunday 10am to
4pm.

Ethnographic Museum
ul. Kredytowa 1
Open: Tuesday, Thursday and Friday
9am to 4pm, Wednesday 11am to
6pm, Saturday and Sunday 10am to
5pm.

Historical Museum of Warsaw
Rynek Starego Miasta 28
Open: Tuesday and Thursday 12noon
to 7pm, Wednesday and Friday 10am
to 3.30pm, Saturday and Sunday
10.30am to 4.30pm.

Jewish Historical Institute
ul. Tłomackie 3-5
Open: Monday to Friday 9am to 3pm.

*John Paul II Collection of European
   Paintings*
plac Bankowy 1
Open: Tuesday to Sunday 9.30am to
4.30pm.

*Łazienki Palaces (Myślewicki Palace,
Old Orangery, Palace on the Water)*
Park Łazienkowski
Open: Tuesday to Sunday 9.30am to
3.30pm.

Maria Skłodowska-Curie Museum
ul. Freta 16
Open: Tuesday to Saturday 10am to
4pm, Sunday 10am to 2pm.

Museum of Caricatures
ul. Kozia 11
Open: Tuesday to Friday 11am to
5pm, Saturday and Sunday 12noon to
5pm.

National Museum
al. Jerozolimskie 3
Open: Tuesday and Sunday 10am to
5pm, Wednesday, Friday and Saturday
10am to 4pm, Thursday 12noon to 6pm.

Paderewski Museum
Park Łazienkowski
Open: Tuesday to Sunday 10am to 5pm.

*Palace of Culture Observation
   Platform*
plac Defilad
Open: Monday to Saturday 9am to
5pm, Sunday 10am to 5pm.

Polish Army Museum
al. Jerozolimskie 3
Open: Wednesday to Sunday 10am to
4pm.

Royal Castle
plac Zamkowy 4
Exhibitions: Open: Tuesday to Sunday
10am to 4pm.
State aparments: Open: 16 April to 30
September Tuesday to Sunday 10am
to 6pm, 1 October to 15 April
Tuesday to Sunday 10am to 4pm.

Theatre Museum
plac Teatralny
Open: Tuesday, Thursday and Friday
11am to 2pm.

*Ujadzów Castle and Centre of Modern
    Art*
al. Ujadzowskiè 6
Open: Tuesday to Sunday 11am to
5pm, Friday 11am to 9pm.

*Wilanów Orangery and Museum of
Decorative Arts*
Park Wilanowski
Open: Monday and Wednesday to
Saturday 10am to 3.30pm.

Wilanów Palace
Park Wilanowski
Open: Wednesday to Monday 9.30am
to 2.30pm.

Wilanów Poster Museum
ul. Wiertnicza 1
Open: Tuesday to Sunday 10am to
3.30pm.

Zachęta Gallery
plac Małachowskiego 3
Open: Tuesday to Sunday 10am to 6pm.

Żelazowa Wola
Chopin Museum
Open: May to September Tuesday to
Friday and Sunday 10am to 5.30pm,
Saturday 10am to 2pm, October to
April Tuesday to Friday and Sunday
10am to 4pm, Saturday 10am to 2pm.

Tourist Offices

Łódź
ul. Traugutta 18
☎ 337-169

Warsaw
plac Zamkowy 1-3
☎ 27-00-00

2 • Great Poland and Kujawy

S cenically, **Great Poland** or **Wielkopolska** is one of the least remarkable parts of the country, being a flat plain interrupted by low-lying
hills, forests and lakes formed in geologically recent times by retreating
glaciers. Its human story is an altogether different matter, however, as it has
been inhabited since the Stone Age by numerous tribes, some nomadic,
others settlers. The exact period when it was settled by Slavs remains
uncertain, but it may have been as late as the eighth century. Within the area
approximately equivalent to that of modern Poland there may have been
fifty or so Slav tribes but, although they shared a similar language and
culture, they initially retained separate identities.

It was the Polonians (literally, the people of the open fields), living
around the banks of the River Warta between what subsequently became the
cities of Poznań and Gniezno, who took the lead in forging these peoples into
a coherent nation. From the early ninth century, they were ruled by the Piast
dynasty, whose early story is shrouded in legend but which emerges into
something more definite with the beginnings of recorded history in the
second half of the tenth century.

In AD965, Duke Mieszko I underwent public baptism, thus placing
himself under the protection of the papacy and thereby thwarting the
eastward expansion of the Holy Roman Empire of Germany, which had
expanded deep into what had previously been Slav territory. By 990,
Mieszko had succeeded in uniting his tribal area, henceforth known as Great
Poland, with that of the Vistulanians (called Little Poland, though it was no
smaller in size) and Silesians. Mieszko's policies were continued by his
warrior son Bolesław the Brave, who gained formal recognition as a king,
and expanded Poland's boundaries to incorporate the other related tribes.

Great Poland's pre-eminence lasted for no more than a century, as the
nation's centre of gravity shifted eastwards and southwards. Nonetheless, it
has always been one of the most authentically Polish parts of Poland,
relatively little touched by the myriad outside influences that have left such
a profound mark on most of the nation.

The obvious base for exploring Great Poland is Poznań, its chief city,
which lies midway along the major international routes between Berlin and
Warsaw. Many of the province's most interesting places can easily be
reached from there on day trips, though it is best to allocate a longer period
for exploring the main tourist trail, the Piast Route, which covers all the other

43

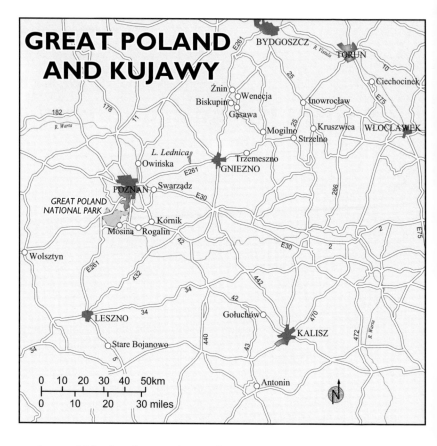

GREAT POLAND AND KUJAWY

places which played a prominent role in the nation's early life. The latter stage of this passes into **Kujawy** or **Kuyawia**, which, despite its tiny size, was a separate constituent part of the early Polish state.

Poznań

Poznań, founded as a fortified settlement on an island in the River Warta, was one of the two main centres of the early Polish state, and the seat of its first bishop. Although the commercial life of the city subsequently moved to the west bank of the river, what became known as Ostrów Tumski ('Cathedral Island'), has remained the episocpal quarter. Nowadays it functions solely as a holy isle, and is a world away in spirit, though not in distance, from the bustle of the centre, one of Poland's most dynamic cities, the setting for big international trade fairs.

Ostrów Tumski's streets, lined by the handsome eighteenth-century houses of the canons, stand very much in the shadow of the cathedral itself. Following damage in World War II, this was returned to its original Gothic brickwork appearance, though some of the Baroque and neo-Classical accretions, such as the steeples and the apse chapels, were retained. Inside, the crypt has been excavated, uncovering remains of the earlier cathedrals on the site, plus parts of the sarcophagi of Mieszko I and Bolesław the Brave. Their current resting place is the Golden Chapel in the ambulatory, a sumptuous co-operative venture of the 1830s between neo-Byzantine mosaic artists from Venice and a painter and a sculptor from the heroic neo-Classical tradition of Berlin. The cathedral has many other outstanding funerary monuments, including two Renaissance masterpieces: that to Bishop Benedykt Izdbieński just to the left of the entrance to the Golden Chapel was carved by Jan Michałowicz, the one major native Polish artist of the period, while the Górka family tomb in the Holy Sacrament chapel at the northern end of the nave is the work of one of the many itinerant Italian craftsmen, Hieronimo Canavesi.

At the western end of Ostrów Tumski is the late Gothic Psalteria, characterised by its elaborate stepped gable. It was built in the early sixteenth century to serve as the residence of members of the cathedral choir. Immediately behind is an earlier brick structure, St Mary's, a lofty chapel of unusual grace and purity of design. This was given a controversial but effective interior decoration of stained glass and murals after the war. Across the street is the Lubrański Academy, the oldest high school in Poland, founded in 1516. Nowadays, it houses the Archdiocesan Museum, which offers a typical array of paintings, sculptures, textiles and treasury items from the Middle Ages to the present day, displayed in a homely, old-fashioned manner.

The right-bank suburb of Śródka, just over the bridge from Ostrów Tumski, is the second oldest part of the city. Though there is nothing special to see, it preserves something of the atmosphere of an old market quarter (its name, meaning Wednesday, signifies the day on which these were originally held). Just beyond is another distinct settlement, known as Komandoria after the commanders of the Knights of Saint John of Jerusalem, who founded it towards the end of the twelfth century. St John's, the late Romanesque church of this community, survives — albeit with Gothic and Baroque additions — and now stands in splendid isolation to the side of one of the busiest traffic intersections in the city. Beyond is the artifical Lake Malta (Jezioro Maltańskie), a popular watersports centre.

Poznań's other sights are all located on the west bank of the Warta, where the original chessboard pattern of the streets is still very apparent. For seven centuries the grandiose old market place, the Stary Rynek, has been the hub of the city's life. In form and layout it is archetypally Polish, with the important public buildings sited in the middle, ensuring that prime space is not wasted.

Here, the Town Hall stands predominant. Originally a two-storeyed Gothic brick structure, it was radically rebuilt in Renaissance style in the 1550s by Giovanni Battista Quadro of Lugano. Its façade, apparently based on an engraving of the Crypta Balbi, a celebrated but vanished building of ancient Rome, features castellated turrets and three tiers of loggias. Every midday, the effigies of two rams emerge on to the platform of the clock, and butt their heads twelve times. The source for this is a legend which maintains that these creatures locked horns on the steps of the Town Hall, whereupon a crowd quickly formed to view their combat. As a result, attention was drawn to a fire which had just begun, and the city was saved from one of the conflagrations to which it was prone. In grateful thanks, the rams were immortalised on the local coat-of-arms, as well as by this timepiece.

The Town Hall's interior is now designated as the Museum of the History of Poznań. Surviving from the Gothic period are the vaulted cellars, which house the earliest objects in the display, notably items excavated on Ostrów Tumski, and the medieval pillory. However, the showpiece is the Renaissance Great Hall on the first floor, formerly the scene of council meetings. Its resplendent coffered vault is adorned with polychrome bas-reliefs of scenes from the lives of Samson, King David, Venus and Hercules along with astrological personifications. Around the walls are marble busts of Roman emperors, symbolizing the weighty historical tradition of municipal leadership.

Outside the Town Hall stands a fine but blackened Rococo fountain, showing the abduction of Prosperine by Pluto. Alongside, in its traditional location, is a copy of the aforementioned pillory. Further to the south is a colourful block known as the Houses of the Keepers. These were the homes of the market traders, many of whom sold their wares in the arcaded passageway. The present structures, though very heavily restored, date back to the sixteenth century and are thus the oldest in the square.

At the back of the Town Hall is a reproduction of Giovanni Battista Quadro's Weigh House, the original of which was pulled down in the nineteenth century. Round the corner from there is the sternly neo-Classical Guardhouse, built for the 'defence and decoration' of the city in the 1780s — just before the whole Polish state crumbled. It now contains the Great Poland Historical Museum. Between there and the Houses of the Keepers are two ugly Communist legacies which mar the harmony of the square. One of these houses the Great Poland Museum of Arms, a display of the history of weapons in the province from the Middle Ages onwards, with special emphasis on the struggle against the Germans. The other, the Gallery of Modern Art, hosts temporary exhibitions only.

Many a medieval or Renaissance interior lurks behind the Baroque façades of the gabled houses lining the outer sides of the Stary Rynek. Although not regular tourist sights, these can often be visited, as most of the buildings are shops, restaurants, cafés or public offices. Particularly fine are those on the eastern side: look out for the apothecary at no.41, and for the Gothic gables on numbers 42, 50 and 51. Housed in number 45 is the Museum of Musical Instruments, the only collection of its kind in Poland. Its exhibits range from folk instruments from all over the world, including some peculiar to Poland, through memorabilia of Chopin to an impressive assemblage of violins.

The western side of the square is almost equally imposing, especially the massive green and white Działyński Palace at number 78, one of the leading headquarters of the nineteenth-century struggles to keep Polish culture alive during the period of enforced Germanisation. Architecturally, it shows the Baroque style melting into neo-Classicism, notably in the attic, which has friezes of a Roman sacrificial procession and a triumphal parade. The houses at the extreme ends of this side were the homes of prominent Poznań personalities. Number 71 belonged to Jan Chróściejewski, twice the mayor of the city around the turn of the seventeenth century and the author of the first book on children's diseases. Giovanni Battista Quadro lived in no.84, whose present façade has murals narrating his life. Inside is the Henryk Sienkiewicz Literary Museum, dedicated to the life and work of the Nobel Prize-winning epic novelist, best-known for *Quo Vadis*, a great favourite with Hollywood film makers.

Just to the west of the Stary Rynek stands a hill with remnants of the inner circle of the medieval walls. This particular section guarded the castle above. Progressively modified down the centuries, it was almost completely destroyed in 1945 but has been partially restored to house the Museum of Decorative Arts, featuring objets d'art from medieval times to the present day. The Gothic cellars are used for changing displays of posters, an art form taken very seriously in Poland.

Below the hill is the Baroque Franciscan church, whose integrated decoration, including the ornate stalls and grandiose high altar, was executed by the Franciscan brothers (in both senses of the word) Adam and Antonin Swach, the former being a painter, the latter a sculptor and stuccoist. On the interior of the west wall are examples of a uniquely Polish art: portraits of nobles painted on sheet metal, which were placed on the deceased's coffin for the funeral procession.

From there it is only a short walk round the corner to the vast elongated space of plac Wolności, whose name (meaning Liberty Square), commemorates the successful Great Poland Uprising of 1918, which ensured that the Poznań area formed part of the resurrected Polish state. The Bazar Hotel was a favourite meeting place of Polish patriots throughout the Partition period, and was where Ignace Jan Paderewski, the pianist-turned-politician, lodged while leading the rebellion against the German garrison. Diagonally opposite stands another key institution in the fight to keep Polish culture alive, the Raczyński Library. Architecturally, it is one of the most distinguished buildings in the city, erected in the 1820s in the grand neo-Classical style of the Louvre.

Directly facing this is the National Museum, one of the few important displays of old master paintings in Poland. The Italian Renaissance section features examples of Bellini, Bassano and Bronzino, along with *The Game of Chess* (featuring a series of portraits of the artist's family) by Sofonisba Anguissiola, the most accomplished female painter of the period. A small but choice Spanish section has masterpieces by Zurbarán and Ribera, including the former's *Madonna of the Rosary*, which incorporates portraits of the silent Carthusian monks who commissioned it. Polish painters are strongly represented, highlights being the roomful of works by the versatile Jacek Malczewski, the historical scenes by Jan Matejko, the landscapes of Wojciech Gerson, the nocturnes of Aleksander Gierymski and the subdued portraits of Olga Boznańska. Also hung in this section is the huge *Election of Stanisław August* by the Italian Bernardo Bellotto, a fascinating documentary record of the way a Polish king was chosen.

Just off the south-east corner of the Stary Rynek is the Górków Palace, still preserving its intricate Renaissance portico and sober inner courtyard. It now houses the Archaeology Museum, which traces the history of Great Poland from the time of the nomadic reindeer hunters who lived there between 15000 and 8000BC all the way to the early feudal society of the seventh century AD. A block further south is the complex of former Jesuit buildings, one of the finest Baroque ensembles in Poland. This includes what is now generally known as the parish church, completed to designs by the Italian architect Pompeo Ferrari just 40 years before the expulsion of the order in 1773. Its interior, with its grandiose coloured columns, gilded Corinthian capitals, monumental sculptures, large painted altarpieces and rich stucco work, is based on the best Roman churches of the period. Across the road is the Jesuit school, now a ballet academy, with a lovely miniature patio. To the east of the church is the Jesuit college, currently the seat of the city council. The Jesuits have returned to Poznań, but were unable to reclaim their buildings. Instead, they now occupy the oldest left-bank building, the Dominican church to the north-east of the Stary Rynek. Despite a Baroque recasing, this still preserves original Romanesque and Gothic features, as well as a star-vaulted Rosary chapel.

Poznań's other attractions are scattered on all sides of the centre. West of the business thoroughfares which branch out from plac Wolności is the Theatr Polski, erected in the 1870s as part of the struggle to preserve Polish culture during the Partition period. The uphill nature of this task is reflected in the inscription on the façade: 'the nation by itself'. Overlooking the busy junction a little further along is the city's most distinguished post-war building, the Dom Tomarowy department store, a ten-storey cylinder constructed round a hollow core with three spiral staircases.

In the streets beyond are a number of bombastic Historicist buildings erected around the turn of the twentieth century by the German authorities, who had by then been in control for a hundred years. Among them is the colossal Kaiser's House, which was built to accommodate the German emperor during his visits to this corner of his realm, but is nowadays a Palace of Culture with a distinctly populist slant. In the nearby park is a monument consisting of two huge crosses bound together. This commemorates the birth of the Solidarity trade union and at the same time honours the victims of the local food riots of 1956, the first major act of resistance to Communism. Remarkably, it was erected on the twenty-fifth anniversary of the latter event, at a time when the Communists had placed the country under martial law.

The wooden saltworks in Ciechocinek (Chapter 2)

The parish church of St John in Włocławek (Chapter 2)

Fisherfolk working on the beach at Międzyzdroje (Chapter 3)

The Mill Gate in Słupsk (Chapter 3)

Facing each other across the brow of the hill which rises north of the city centre are two fine churches. To the right is the Gothic St Adalbert, whose stumpy little seventeenth-century detached belfry is the only piece of wooden architecture left in the city. Opposite, the handsome early Baroque façade of the Carmelite monastery makes a highly effective contrast. Further uphill is the most exclusive cemetery in Poznań, reserved for people deemed to have made a valuable contribution to the life of Great Poland; there is also a grandiose monument to the defenders of the city during the German invasion of 1939. Higher up is the vast former Citadel, a nineteenth-century Prussian fortress levelled after the war to make a public park. It has a cemetery for the 6,000 Russians and Poles who lost their lives in the month-long siege which led to its capture, while in a special area to the east are the graves of British and Commonwealth soldiers. Another plot is dedicated to French prisoners who died in the Franco-Prussian war of 1870-1.

Almost due east of the Stary Rynek is the church of the Holy Cross, a late Baroque period piece. It illustrates the architecture and furnishings favoured by the city's once strong Lutheran community, though the altar inserted following its takeover by the Catholics strikes a jarring note. Round the corner is the former lodge of the freemasons, a building of identical vintage now housing the Ethnographical Museum. Further south is the very different Baroque church of the Bernardine monastery, which has been gleamingly restored by the monks who repossessed it following its wartime use as a workshop for the local opera house. At the southern extremity of the old town is Corpus Christi, a soaring fifteenth-century Gothic church, formerly belonging to a Carmelite monastery.

Excursions from Poznań

It is easy to escape from the big city feel of Poznań, as the outskirts soon give way to peaceful agricultural villages set in a lake-strewn landscape. Within a 15$^1/_2$ mile (25km) radius of the city is some of the finest scenery in Great Poland, along with two of the country's best-known castles.

Kórnik is 22km south-east of Poznań on the eastern bank of Lakes Skrzynki and Kónickie, the first two in a long north-south chain of six. At the extreme southern edge of the village is the castle of the Górka family. A fragment of the fifteenth-century original survives, together with the medieval layout with surrounding moat. The rest was rebuilt in the nineteenth century to plans by Karl Friedrich Schinkel, one of the greatest architects of the period, and the creator of many of the main public buildings in Berlin. However, his designs were considerably modified, and credit for the final shape of the castle is due to the owner, Tytus Działyński, whose aim was as much to show off his collection of arms and armour, books and objets d'art as to provide a suitably luxurious home for himself.

In contrast to the exterior, with its mock defensive towers and battlements, the interior is on an intimate scale, and creates the impression of trespassing into a private residence of a century or more ago. The one really theatrical gesture is the Moorish Hall, which imitates the spectacular Arab palace of the the Alhambra in Granada — albeit in whitewash rather than the stucco and ceramic splendour of its model. Originally in the formal French style, the park, Arboretum, was transformed and greatly extended at the time of the castle's reconstruction in the seemingly arbitrary manner of a *jardin anglais*. There are over 2,000 species of trees and shrubs, many of them specially brought from all corners of the world.

Rogalin, 7 miles (11km) west, has the palace of another eminent Poznań family, the Raczyńskis. In contrast to Kórnik, it is a grand country residence without medieval antecedents, built in a style which shows the late Baroque melting into neo-Classicism. There are also a couple of subsidiary attractions: an art gallery containing the bulk of the nineteenth-century holdings of Poznań's National Museum; and the coach house, with an array of historic carriages, including the last horse-drawn cab to be used in in the city. Just outside the gates is the mausoleum of the Raczyński family, a slightly reduced copy of one of the best-preserved monuments of Classical antiquity, the Maison Carrée in Nîmes in southern France, built in pink sandstone.

At the back of the palace is an enclosed garden in the formal French geometric manner. Beyond is an English-style park, laid out on the site of a primeval forest. This is chiefly remarkable for its oak trees, three of the most ancient of which have been fenced off for protection. Among the most celebrated natural wonders of Poland, they are popularly known as Lech, Czech and Rus after the three mythical brothers who founded the Polish, Czech and Russian nations; with all due modesty, the largest of the three is designated as Rus. It has been calculated that they are at least 1,000 years old, and thus of a similar vintage to the Polish nation itself.

The only area of protected landscape in the province, the **Great Poland National Park** (Wielkopolski Park Narodowy), occupies an area of some 38sq miles (100sq km) to the south of Poznań. In many ways it is typical of the region as a whole, having been formed in geologically recent times. These glacial and post-glacial formations consist of both ground and terminal moraine, plus gentle ridges known as drumlin; there are also eleven lakes, some quite large. Almost exactly half the park is taken up by forest. The trees are predominantly pine and birch, modern replacements for the original hardwoods; sadly, their youth has not saved them from the effects of pollution from the city. Although the scenery in the park is hardly dramatic, it undoubtedly has its own character, and is unspoiled by any kind of development.

There are several possible access points, among them the straggling little town of Mosina, 5 miles (8km) from Rogalin. Just to the west is Osowa Góra station, the terminus of a branch line from Poznań; above this is a rise where cars can be parked, and from where a rare panoramic view of the park can be enjoyed. From this point, the blue trail leads round the small heart-shaped Lake Kociołek, which is beautifully shaded by trees, then continues through the forest to the southern end of Lake Góreckie. It then climbs uphill, again through thick woods, before passing through open countryside to Lake Łódźkie, from where it leads along the northern shore of Lake Witobelskie to its terminus at the village of Stęszew.

The alternative red trail also passes Lake Kociołek, then travels circuitously uphill, skirting the small Lake Skrzynka just before crossing the blue trail. It arrives at the bend in the sausage-shaped Lake Góreckie, from where there is a view across to an islet with a ruined castle — a former fortress of the Działyński family, and a meeting point for the Polish insurgents of 1863. The path then leads about halfway round the perimeter of the lake as far as Jeziory, where there is another car park.

Broadly similar in character to the Wielkopolska National Park, and about half as large again in area, is the **Puszcza Zielonka** to the north-east of Poznań. Much of this area is under the management of the Agricultural Acadamy, though there are also nature reservations, such as Dziewicza Góra, just north of Czerwonak, which is about 7 miles (12km) from Poznań. The next village up the line, **Owińska**, boasts a handsome neo-Classical palace, but is chiefly of interest for the domed Baroque church of a dissolved Cistercian convent, designed by Pompeo Ferrari. Its lavishly ornate interior has frescoes by Adam Swach illustrating the story of the True Cross and the history of the order, while the square outside is dominated by one of the huge ancient oaks so characteristic of the region.

Even closer to Poznań, practically joined on to its eastern suburbs, is the furniture-producing town of **Swarzędz**. This is home to Poland's most unusual skansen, one devoted entirely to beehives. Over 200 examples are on view, ranging from plain medieval examples made out of hollowed wood to elaborate modern folk art creations, including accurate models of Poznań's cathedral and town hall.

South of Poznań

Leszno, some 56 miles (90km) south of Poznań, was founded in the late fourteenth century by one of Poland's most remarkable dynasties, the Leszczyński family, and remained a family fiefdom for four centuries. The town was a bastion of the Polish Reformation and in the seventeenth century became the refuge of the Bohemian Brethren, a group of exiled Czech Protestants. An academy established by them developed into one of Europe's most prestigious centres of learning, and the picture textbook developed by the school's director, the great educationalist Jan Comenius, remains a staple tool of classrooms to this day. In 1704, Stanisław Leszczyński, the last of the male line, was elected Polish king in a defiant attempt to halt the nation's slide towards outside domination; his deposition 6 years later marked the effective end of the country's independence.

Though there is little about modern Leszno to suggest its illustrious past, its Rynek is one of Poland's prettiest main squares, lined with a series of colourful Baroque buildings erected in the aftermath of the Swedish wars which had caused the devastation of the town and the departure of the Bohemian Brethren. Prominently sited in the middle of the square, its belfry serving as the main local landmark, is the red, yellow and white town hall by the Italian Pompeo Ferrari, the favourite architect of the Leszczyńskis.

Just south of the Rynek, the exterior of the church of St Nicholas strikes a more sombre note. Its interior, on the other hand, boasts an extravagant set of Rococo furnishings, notably the huge funerary monuments of the Leszczyńskis. A fascinating contrast with its richness is provided by the clean, sober lines of the Lutheran Holy Cross church, a couple of minutes' walk to the south-west. On the same square is the Regional Museum, a miscellaneous local collection featuring a room devoted to Comenius. A few streets east of there, off ul. Bolesława Chrobrego, is the church of St John, where the Bohemian Brethren held their services.

Stare Bojanowo, 11 miles (18km) south of Leszno, is the starting-point for one of Poland's still-surviving narrow gauge railways, whose numbers have unfortunately declined since the fall of Communism. Modern, immaculately maintained little diesels ply the 9 miles (15km) long line to **Wielichowa**, passing through a series of sparsely populated farming communities en route.

An even bigger attraction for railway buffs is the lakeside town of **Wolsztyn**, 31 miles (50km) north-west of Leszno. Its station has a huge siding in which steam engines can be seen shunting throughout the day; some of the local passenger trains are pulled by steam locomotives, but double-decker commuter diesels are more commonly used. In the centre of town are some fine buildings, notably a neo-Classical palace and a Baroque church with an impressive frescoed vault. On the main street, ul. 5 Stycznia, is the Marcin Rożek Museum, occupying the home of this artist, one of the best Poland ever produced, who was murdered in Auschwitz. A roomful of oils show his talents as a painter, but it is his sculptures which stand out, notably the Classically-inspired portrait busts in the garden (mostly re-creations of originals destroyed by the Nazis), and the large reliefs on musical themes placed on the rear of the house. There is also a small *skansen* (open-air museum) of traditional farm buildings from the region, located on the outskirts of town on the shore of Lake Wolsztyn.

Kalisz, which lies at the extreme south-east corner of Great Poland, about 81 miles (130km) from both Poznań and Leszno, is generally held to be the oldest city in the country. It was mentioned under the name of Calissia by Pliny in the first century and by Ptolemy in the second century as a trading settlement on the Amber Route between the Baltic and Adriatic. Though apparently inhabited without interruption ever since, it has never been a place of more than moderate importance. While mainly of interest as a jumping-off point for visiting two of the country's finest palaces, its reasonably well-preserved Old Town is worth a look.

The Rynek is dominated by a large Baroque town hall, whose tower can be ascended for a fine view. A couple of blocks north-west of the square is the brick Gothic church of St Nicholas, which has been subject to a fair amount of neo-Gothic tinkering, though not entirely to its disadvantage: the silhouette given to the tower is undeniably picturesque. Inside is a copy of Rubens' altarpiece of *The Descent from the Cross*, the original of which was brought directly from the master's workshop in Antwerp, but which was destroyed by fire (or perhaps stolen) a couple of decades ago. Off the south-eastern corner of the Rynek is a smaller square, dominated by the Franciscan church, an older and simpler example of Gothic brickwork, but with ample Baroque interior decorations, including a pulpit in the shape of a boat.

From there, it is just a short walk to ul. Kolegialna, which defines the eastern perimeter of the old town. This is dominated by the long three-storeyed façade of the Jesuit college, a neo-Classical composition incorporating an older Renaissance portal. The one part of it which can be visited is the church, which is in the plain early Baroque idiom pioneered at this order's mother house, Il Gesù in Rome. Immediately beyond the college, standing beside the surviving fragment of the city's ramparts, is the single-towered Collegiate church, a rather more adventurous example of Baroque incorporating parts of its Gothic predecessor. The interior bristles with works of art, the most notable being a Silesian polyptych of around 1500. On ul. Tadeusza Kościuszki on the opposite side of the River Prosna from the Old Town is the Regional Museum, which contains material from the many archaeological excavations carried out in the area, along with a varied display of textiles.

The village of **Gołuchów**, some 12 miles (20km) from Kalisz on the Poznan road, is virtually an appendage to its palace, which was originally a small defensive castle erected for Rafał Leszczyński of the famous Leszno family in 1560. Early the following century, his son Wacław completely transformed this into a palatial residence worthy of someone who had risen to be Royal Chancellor. It subsequently fell into ruin, but was purchased in 1853 by Tytus Działyński, the owner of Kórnik, as a present for his son Jan, who married Izabella, daughter of the formidable Adam Czartoryski. While her husband languished in exile for his part in the 1863 uprising, Izabella devoted her life to recreating the glory of the castle, eventually opening it as one of Poland's first museums.

Rather than revert to the Italianate form of the original, she followed contemporary taste and opted for a distinctively French accent, with steeply pitched slate roofs, prominent chimneys, towers and a graceful arcaded courtyard, all modelled on the château of the Loire. The intimate apartments are crammed with paintings and furnishings. Highlight of the display is a distinguished collection of (mostly Greek) antique vases; only a small section of this is now on view here, with the rest kept in the National Museum in Warsaw. The park, like that of Kórnik, is cultivated for serious scientific purposes, and a small herd of bison is kept in an enclosed part of the forest beyond. Also in the grounds are a Museum of Forestry and the neo-Gothic funerary chapel of Izabella Działyńska.

In the little holiday resort of **Antonin**, 22 miles (35km) from Kalisz on the main road to Wrocław, is another remarkable palace, now a hotel. This was built in the 1820s as a hunting lodge for Prince Antoni Radziwiłł, a member of another leading Polish dynasty. He was then regent of the Grand Duchy of Posen, the puppet state set up by the Prussians on the territory of Great Poland. This connection enabled Radziwiłł to secure the services of Karl Friedrich Schinkel, who responded with one of his most audacious designs. Constructed in wood, it is centred on an extraordinary three-storey octagonal hall surrounded by two levels of galleries with a cylindrical chimneypiece in the middle. Chopin was twice a house guest, a fact commemorated in a memorabilia room, and in frequent concerts. Alongside the palace is the mausoleum of the Radziwiłłs, which was also probably the work of Schinkel. The former hunting ground is now a fine forest park.

The Great Poland Piast Route

The Piast Route is the name given to a tourist trail between Poznań and Inowrocław in the adjoining province of Kujawy. As the name implies, it offers constant reminders of the dynasty which forged the Polish nation and ruled it until 1370, though the range of sightseeing attractions is considerably wider than this suggests, particularly if a detour is made to see the astonishing Iron Age village of Biskupin.

The first stop, about 23 miles (40km) east of Poznań, is **Lake Lednica**, a long, narrow finger lake so typical of the peaceful post-glacial landscape of the region, but one with its own remarkable history. At the southern end of the lake, close to the village of Dziekanowice, is the Great Poland Ethnographic Park. This reassembles around fifty traditional rural buildings from the last 250 years or so from all over the province. These range from three windmills still in full working order, through a Baroque cemetery chapel with all its furnishings, to several farmsteads.

About 1 mile (2km) north of the main road is the disparate tourist complex known as the Museum of the First Piasts at Lednica. There are a few more examples of rural architecture, including the oldest surviving windmill in Poland, a small museum of archaeological finds, and stylized over-life-sized statues of Polish warriors of a millennium ago. More importantly, this is the departure point for Ostrów Lednicki, the largest of the three islands in the lake, which is reached in a couple of minutes by the chained ferry.

Once among the most important royal seats in Poland, this began life in the ninth century as a fortified town covering about a third of the island and linked to the mainland by a causeway. In the following century, a massive palace was constructed, along with a church. Unfortunately, the excavated remains can only hint at its former grandeur, but the presence of stairways prove it must have been at least two storeys high. Bolesław the Brave was born there, and it may also have been where his coronation by Emperor Otto III took place, rather than, as in normally assumed, in Gniezno. The buildings were destroyed in 1038 by the Czech Prince Brzetysław, but the church was rebuilt soon afterwards, only to fall gradually into disuse, along with the town itself, which subsequently became a cemetery.

A further 11 miles (18km) east is **Gniezno**, which, despite several competing claims, is normally credited with having been the first capital of Poland. Lech, the legendary sixth-century founding father of the Poles, supposedly came across the nest (*gniazdo* in Polish) of a white eagle there;

he founded a town on the spot, and made the bird the emblem of his people, a role it has maintained to the present day.

Whatever the substance of this story, at the turn of the millennium Gniezno was the scene of one of the crucial events in the country's history. In AD997 St Adalbert, the former Bishop of Prague, set out from there on a mission to convert the Prussians, a fierce Baltic tribe who lived on Poland's eastern borders, but was quickly sent to a martyr's death. Bolesław the Brave was forced to pay the saint's weight in gold in order to recover the body. At the instigation of the pope, the Holy Roman Emperor Otto III made a pilgrimage to Gniezno, where he crowned Bolesław with his own crown, thus confirming Poland's right to be regarded as a fully-fledged kingdom.

The cathedral is the normal seat of the Primate of Poland, though it temporarily lost this status in 1992. Strongly reminiscent of its Poznań counterpart, it was built in the fourteenth century in the severest style of Gothic brickwork, but was enlivened in the Baroque period by a ring of stone chapels and by the addition of steeples to the twin towers. Memorials to St Adalbert dominate the interior. His red marble tomb at the entrance to the sanctuary was carved around 1480 by Hans Brandt of Gdańsk; a later craftsman from the same city, Peter van Rennen, made the silver shrine above the high altar.

Even more precious is the magnificent pair of bronze doors in the south aisle. These were cast around 1170, and depict the saint's life in eighteen scenes, forming a remarkable documetary record in which even the physiognomy of the Prussians is accurately depicted. On the west wall are two outstanding fifteenth-century funerary monuments; the marble slab of Zbigniew Oleśnicki by the great Cracow-based German sculptor Veit Stoss; and the brass memorial to Jakub ze Sienna alongside, the product of a Flemish workshop.

The cathedral archive off the northern aisle houses a valuable collection of manuscripts, including a ninth-century gospel book with annotations by Irish missionaries which has prompted suggestions that it was the Irish who converted the Poles to Christianity. Other treasures are kept in the Archdiocesan Museum, which occupies one of the cluster of houses on the north side of the cathedral. The most valuable piece is an agate chalice said to have belonged to St Adalbert himself.

Just west of the cathedral is Lake Jelonek, greatly contracted from its former size, but still providing a peaceful spot with a wonderful view of the town. Overlooking its far bank is a large modern building containing the Museum of the Origins of the Polish State. This contains archaeological finds from various sites in Great Poland, along with changing art exhibitions. There is also a video show on the early history of Poland, with screenings in English on request.

The town centre of Gniezno is surprisingly small-scale, though it has three more Gothic churches. Just off the southern side of the Rynek is the Holy Trinity, which was partly rebuilt in the Baroque style following a fire, and beside which stand the only surviving remains of the city walls. Off the opposite side of the Rynek towers the Franciscan church, while further to the north is St John's. The latter, a foundation of the Knights Templars, preserves fourteenth-century frescos in its chancel, and has vigorously carved bosses and corbels depicting virtues and vices.

The Iron Age village of **Biskupin**, some 19 miles (30km) north of Gniezno, is one of the most evocative archaeological sites in Europe. Though the area had long been a fruitful source for excavations, its full significance only became apparent in 1933, when the local schoolmaster noticed what were obviously stakes fashioned by hand standing up in the reeds at the edge of Lake Biskupin. He also learned from a landowner that artefacts, poles and boards had been found during peat cutting. Experts were able to pronounce that the site had been a fortified village of the Lusatian culture, founded around 550BC and destroyed in tribal warfare some 150 years later.

The excavations fall starkly into two parts, with one section consisting of the usual uncovered foundations of various buildings, while the other presents full-scale conjectural re-creations of the Iron Age buildings, best appreciated from the steamer which plies the lake. The palisade is particularly ingenious: it originally consisted of 35,000 stakes grouped in rows up to nine deep and driven into the bed of the lake at an angle of 45 degrees. It acted both as a breakwater and as the first line of the fortifications. Immediately behind was a circular wall of oak logs guarded by a tall watchtower. Inside the defences were a ring road plus eleven symmetrical streets, again made of logs and filled in with earth, sand and clay; the houses were grouped in terraces ranged from east to west to catch the sun. An entire extended family would have lived in each house, so the population of the settlement probably numbered over 1,000.

In the museum are all manner of items dug up on site — tools, household utensils, weapons, jewellery, ornaments and objects for worship. Archaeologists have been able to draw a picture of a society which was advanced for its time: hunting had been relegated to a minor role in favour of arable farming and livestock breeding. The trade patterns were surprisingly extensive — the iron seems to have come from Transylvania, while there is a fascinating group of exhibits imported from even further afield, the most exotic being the Egyptian beads. Beyond the museum buildings is an enclosure in which several tarpans are kept. These miniature working horses have evolved very little since the time of the settlement.

Biskupin lies on the line of a narrow gauge steam railway which runs throughout the tourist season. It begins at **Gąsawa**, a village with an eighteenth-century wooden church 1 mile (2km) south. The next stop after Biskupin is **Wenecja**, whose open-air Museum of Narrow Gauge Railways has a collection of engines and rolling stock from all over Europe. On the other side of the tracks are the remains of the fourteenth-century castle of Mikołaj Nałęcz, a notorious figure known by the nickname of the 'Bloody Devil of Wenecja'. The northern terminus of the 7 miles (12km) long route is **Żnin**, a small town set between two lakes, part of a long north—south chain. In the centre of the Rynek stands the tower of the otherwise demolished fifteenth-century Town Hall, whose interior has been fitted out as the local museum.

Returning to the Piast Route, the next stop beyond Gniezno is the little lakeside town of **Trzemeszno**, 10 miles (16km) away. According to tradition, it was founded by Saint Adalbert. His original church was succeeded a couple of centuries later by a Romanesque structure, parts of which are incorporated in the Baroque basilica which completely dominates the town. From the outside, it appears rather austere, but the interior, from the tiled pavement to the frescoed dome, is lavishly decorated. In the main square is a monument to the local hero, the shoemaker Jan Kiliński, who played a leading role in the 1794 insurrection against the Partitioning powers.

A further 10 miles (16km) north-east is **Mogilno**, again set on the bank of a lake. Overlooking the water are a couple of churches, the Gothic St James and the Romanesque St John the Evangelist. The latter preserves its original crypt and apse, complete with carved frieze, though the main body of the building was heavily transformed in both the Gothic and Baroque epochs.

Far more appealling is **Strzelno**, another 11 miles (17km) east. Enclosed in a precinct a short distance from the Rynek are two outstanding Romanesque buildings, though these are not the earliest evidence of this site as a place of worship, as the large stone block in front of them is thought to have been used for pagan rites. The former Premonstratensian monastery of the Holy Trinity illustrates the very Polish habit of grafting features in the architectural fashion of the day on top of an existing structure: brick Gothic gables and a monumental Baroque façade sprout from a dignified late twelfth-century Romanesque shell. After the war, some of the interior encrustations were removed, to reveal, in well-nigh perfect condition, four original nave pillars. Two of these, adorned with figurative carvings set in a foliage surround, are crafted with a delicacy found in few other European sculptures of the period; a third is reminiscent of Arab art in its abstract geometrical shapes. Another column of almost equal quality forms the sole support of the beautiful vault of the chapel of St Barbara to the right of the chancel. Beside the monastery church stands the slightly older red sandstone rotunda of St Procopius, which has preserved the purity of its original form intact.

Kujawy

For its last two stops, the Piast Route leaves Great Poland and enters Kujawy, a separate old province which itself played a leading role in the molding of the Polish state. Indeed **Kruszwica**, 10 miles (16km) north-east of Strzelno, is enshrined in folklore as the cradle of the Piast dynasty. According to the legend, the descendants of Lech were supplanted by the evil Popiel, who massacred all his male kinsmen except his own sons, and established himself in a castle at Kruszwica, where he subjected his people to a reign of terror. One day, Saints John and Paul arrived in the guise of poor travellers, but the king refused them hospitality, forcing them to lodge with a peasant named Piast. They baptised him and his family and promised that he would be first in a long line of monarchs, whereupon they vanished into thin air. Shortly afterwards, the Poles rose up against their own ruler, who took refuge in his castle tower, where he was eventually devoured by rats. The righteous Piast was then chosen as his successor.

South of the town centre, at the head of the pencil slim Lake Gopło, the largest of western Poland's lakes, is a shady tree-lined peninsula dominated by a brick octagon known as the Mouse Tower. This was supposedly where Popiel met his death, but it was actually part of a castle built in the fourteenth century by the last of the Piast kings, Kazimierz the Great. During the summer season, it is possible to ascend to the top for a sweeping view down the length of Lake Gopło.

On the eastern shore of the small lake to the north is the twelfth-century Collegiate church. A plain granite basilica in Romanesque style, it has been stripped of most of its later accretions, except for the brick Gothic tower. Supposedly occupying the miraculous site of Piast's cottage, it served as the cathedral of the Kujawy diocese for the first half-century of its life, but was then supplanted by Włocławek.

The end of the Piast Route comes 9 miles (15km) north of Kruszwica at **Inowrocław**. Here the main monument is the Church of the Assumption, a contemporary of the basilicas in Strzelno and Kruszwica, albeit one remodelled early in the twentieth century. It occupies a pleasantly landscaped position in a park, a few minutes' walk east of the big roundabout north of the commercial centre. In the heart of the old town is St Nicholas, a Gothic parish church with Renaissance and Baroque additions. Around the time this was being built in the fifteenth century, underground salt springs were discovered in the area, but it was not until the 1870s that Inowrocław became a popular spa, with thermal establishments built to the west of the old town. The prosperity this brought is reflected in the grand turn-of-the-century buildings erected along the town's main axis, ul. Królowej Jadwigi, which are now re-emerging from decades of neglect in their full colourful pomp. Unfortunately, although the baths are still in use, the modern town has harnessed the waters as the basis of a chemical industry which has led to heavy pollution and the construction of rings of concrete suburbs.

The largest city in Kujawy is **Bydgoszcz**, strategically located on the River Brda, just before its confluence with the Vistula, a little over 20 miles (40km) north of Inowrocław. It was of little significance until the eighteenth century when, as the Prussian town of Bromberg, it became the hub of an important canal system linking the Vistula to the Oder.

The medieval centre is very small in relation to the sprawling industrial mass of the modern city. As ever, the focal point is the Rynek, on which stands a typical Communist monument to the victims of the Nazis, who murdered around a quarter of the local population. There are also a few Baroque and neo-Classical mansions, notably number 24, which contains the municipal library. These are rather overshadowed by the vast bulk of the

Jesuit college, which closes the west side of the square, with another fine frontage along ul. Jeznicka. Begun at the end of the seventeenth century, this was for long the town's leading educational establishment, but it is now used for the municipal offices.

In a secluded corner just to the north is the redbrick fifteenth-century parish church. This has recently been raised to the status of a cathedral, though its dimensions and appearance are more modest than those of many a village church. Nonetheless, its exterior is graced by a fine Gothic gable, while inside, among the usual Baroque ornamentation, is the sixteenth-century high altar of *The Madonna with the Rose*. The church overlooks what is fancifully styled the 'Bydgoszcz Venice', the banks on either side of the island formed by two arms of the Brda. On the peninsula at the edge of this island are an old granary and mill, the latter being a branch of the Historical Museum.

The south side of the main waterfront is dominated by two much larger half-timbered granaries of the eighteenth century. One of these contains the main part of the Historical Museum, with displays on the history of the town, including archive material on the Nazi atrocities. From the quay outside, boats regularly depart in summer for excursions along the Brda.

On the opposite bank is the former convent church of the Poor Clares, a curious amalgam of late Gothic and Renaissance, with later alterations. Its conventual buildings now contain the District Museum, which is mostly given over to the work of the eclectic local artist Leon Wyczółkowski. This marks the start of al. 1 Maja, the main commercial axis of the modern part of town, along which are a number of colourful turn-of-the-century build-ings, including Pod Orłem, which has always ranked as the best hotel in town.

Five blocks east of there is a historical curiosity — the basilica of St Vincent de Paul, a vast circular brick church modelled on the Pantheon in Rome, and capable of accommodating 12,000 worshippers. Its construction was a direct result of the city's change in ownership after World War I from Protestant Prussia to Catholic Poland, which necessitated a much larger space for the main feast days than the small existing churches were able to provide.

Ciechocinek, a spa town with its own microclimate, is set slightly back from the Vistula, some 37 miles (60km) south-east of Bydgoszcz. The Park Zdrojowy is a restful spot with floral gardens, tree-lined avenues and the usual spa buildings — pump room, concert hall and bandstand. Far more intriguing, however, is the Park Tężniówy on the opposite side of the railway tracks from the town. Here, in three separate sections stretching for over 1 mile (1^1/$_2$km), is the mass of wooden poles and twigs which make up the saltworks, begun in 1824 but not completed until several decades later. A truly amazing sight, it still functions as originally intended. The technology behind it is simple: water from the town's saline springs is pumped to the top of the structure, from where it trickles back down through the twigs. This not only concentrates the salt, it also creates a wondrously healthy atmosphere in the covered space below. Formerly, patients would walk through the saltworks, breathing in deeply as they went, but, for conservation reasons, this is no longer permitted.

Włocławek, Kujawy's historic capital, lies on the River Vistula, about 19 miles (30km) upstream of Ciechocinek, and 31 miles (50km) south-east of Inowrocław. Primarily an industrial city, it is best known for its production of one of Poland's favourite tourist souvenirs — glazed earthenware hand-painted with brown floral motifs. However, it has been the seat of a bishop since the mid-twelfth century, and remains an important episcopal centre; the formidable Stefan Wyszyński, scourge of successive Communist governments, spent most of his early priesthood there.

The cathedral, directly overlooking the river, dates back to the fourteenth century, but was ruthlessly remodelled in neo-Gothic style, notably by the addition of a pair of fantastical spires, and by the painted decorative scheme of the interior. However, there remain some beautiful old chapels, such as that dedicated to St Joseph on the north side, which contains the Hungarian marble tomb of Bishop Piotr Moszyński by Veit Stoss. This adopts the highly original but subsequently much imitated format of a full-length relief portrait of the deceased on the sloping lid of the sarcophagus. In the same chapel is a fine funerary monument, to Monsiegneur Karnowski by another, this time anonymous, sculptor from Nuremberg. Also of note is the late Renaissance mausoleum of the Tarnowski family, a showy protrusion on the opposite side of the cathedral, its coloured marble exterior adorned with sundials, its interior richly furnished with statues and busts.

Just to the west is the Rynek, which has lost its function as the commercial heart of the city and now has a certain dilapidated charm. Its historic houses range in date from the seventeenth to the nineteenth centuries; a fine Baroque example on the east side now contains the District Museum, with displays on the archaeology, history, art and folklore of Kujawy. On the north side of the square is the parish church of St John, originally Gothic but heavily remodelled in the Baroque period. A modern cantilever bridge traverses the Vistula, which is here dotted by a number of sandbanks. From the northern side is an excellent view over the city and the river.

Further Information
— Great Poland and Kujawy —

Places to Visit

Biskupin
Archaeological Park
Open: mid-April to September daily 8am to 6pm, October (subject to good weather) daily 8am to 5pm.

Bydgoszcz
District Museum
ul. 1 Maja
Open: Tuesday and Wednesday 10am to 6pm, Thursday to Saturday 10am to 4pm, Sunday 10am to 2pm.

Historical Museum
ul. Spichlerna
Open: Tuesday and Wednesday 10am to 6pm, Thursday to Saturday 10am to 4pm, Sunday 10am to 2pm.

Gniezno
Archdiocesan Museum
ul. Kolegiaty 2
Open: Tuesday to Saturday 10am to 4pm.

Museum of the Origins of the Polish State
ul. Kostrzewskiego 1
Open: Tuesday to Sunday 10am to 5pm.

Gołuchów
Palace
Open: Wednesday to Saturday 10am to 4pm, Sunday 11am to 5pm.

Museum of Forestry
Open: Tuesday to Sunday 10am to 3pm.

Kalisz
Regional Museum
ul. Kościuszki 12
Open: Tuesday, Thursday, Saturday and Sunday 10am to 2.30pm, Wednesday and Friday 12noon to 5.30pm.

Kórnik
Palace
Open: March to November Tuesday to Friday and Sunday 9am to 3pm, Saturday 9am to 2pm.

Kruszwica
Mouse Tower
Open: May to September daily 9am to 4.30pm.

Lake Lednica
Great Poland Ethnographic Park
Open: April to October Tuesday to Sunday 9am to 5pm, November to March Tuesday to Sunday 9am to 3pm.

Museum of the First Piasts and Ostrów Lednicki
Open: April to October Tuesday to Sunday 9am to 5pm, November to April (museum only) Tuesday to Sunday 9am to 3pm.

Leszno
Regional Museum
Plac Metziga 17
Open: Tuesday and Thursday 2pm to 7pm, Wednesday and Friday 9am to 2pm, Saturday and Sunday 10am to 2pm.

Poznań
Archaeological Museum
ul. Wodna 27
Open: Tuesday to Friday 10am to 4pm, Saturday 10am to 6pm, Sunday 10am to 3pm.

Archdiocesan Museum
ul. Lubrańskiego 1
Open: Monday to Friday 9am to 3pm, Saturday and Sunday 1 to 3pm.

Ethnographical Museum
ul. Grobla 15
Open: Tuesday, Wednesday, Friday
and Saturday 10am to 4pm, Sunday
10am to 3pm.

Great Poland Historical Museum
Stary Rynek 3
Open: Tuesday 12noon to 6pm,
Wednesday and Friday 10am to 4pm,
Saturday and Sunday 10am to 3pm.

Great Poland Museum of Arms
Stary Rynek 9
Open: Tuesday 12noon to 6pm,
Wednesday and Friday 10am to 4pm,
Saturday and Sunday 10am to 3pm.

Henryk Sienkiewicz Literary Museum
Stary Rynek 84
Open: Monday to Friday 10am to 5pm.

Museum of Decorative Arts
Góra Przemysława
Open: Tuesday and Sunday 10am to
5pm, Wednesday, Friday and Saturday 10am to 4pm.

Museum of Musical Instruments
Stary Rynek 45
Open: Tuesday 11am to 5pm,
Wednesday and Friday 10am to 4pm,
Saturday 10am to 5pm, Sunday 10am
to 3pm.

National Museum
Plac Wolności
Open: Tuesday 12noon to 6pm,
Wednesday, Friday and Saturday
10am to 4pm, Sunday 10am to 3pm.

*Town Hall (Museum of the History of
    Poznań)*
Stary Rynek 1
Open: Monday, Tuesday and Friday
10am to 4pm, Wednesday 12noon to
6pm, Sunday 10am to 3pm.

Rogalin
Palace
Open: Wednesday to Sunday 10am to
4pm (stays open until 6pm on
Saturday from May to September).

Swarzędz
Skansen
Open: Monday to Friday 8am to 3pm.

Wenecja
Museum of Narrow-Gauge Railways
Open: daily 9am to 4pm.

Włocławek
District Museum
ul. Szpichlerna 2
Open: Tuesday 10am to 6pm, Wednesday, Friday and Saturday 10am to 3pm,
Thursday 10am to 12noon and 3pm to
6pm, Sunday 10am to 2pm.

Wolsztyn
Marcin Rożek Museum
ul. 5 Styczna
Open: Tuesday to Friday 9am to 4pm,
Saturday and Sunday 10am to 2pm.

Żnin
Town Hall (Local Museum)
Plac Wolności
Open: Tuesday to Friday 9am to 4pm,
Saturday 9am to 3pm, Sunday 10am
to 3pm.

Tourist Office
Poznań
Stary Rynek 59
☎ 52-61-56

3 • Pomerania

The much-disputed maritime territory of **Pomerania** (known as **Pomorze** in Polish) has come under the suzerainty of several countries throughout its history and is nowadays, appropriately enough, divided between Poland and Germany. Like Great Poland, Pomerania was settled during the Dark Ages by Slav tribes, and formed part of the nation established by Mieszko I and Bolesław the Brave. However, it drifted in and out of central control and had a period of occupation by the Danes before eventually establishing itself as a quasi-independent duchy. Although ruled by a Slav dynasty, the Gryfits, Germans were encouraged to settle, playing a prominent role in the development of the towns, several of which became members of the Hanseatic League, the powerful German-dominated trading alliance.

As Poland expanded its borders to the east, Pomerania became increasingly marginal, and in 1521 the Holy Roman Emperor of Germany, rather than the Polish king, gained formal acceptance as its overlord. Eleven years later, the Gryfits divided into two lines, and their territory was partitioned along a line west of the Odra delta. The smaller western duchy, known as Lower or Hither Pomerania, has never subsequently been part of Poland. The larger one to the east, called Farther Pomerania, had very similar boundaries to the area understood as Pomerania in present-day Poland, which forms the subject of this chapter.

However, the identification of this territory with Poland is a relatively recent phenomenon. During the Thirty Years War of 1618-48, the Swedes conquered not only Hither Pomerania, but also part of the coastline of Farther Pomerania, including the capital Szczecin, or Stettin, as it was then called. This remained part of the Swedish Empire until 1720, when it fell once more into the German orbit, being subsumed into the emergent Kingdom of Prussia, which re-united the partitioned duchy as a single administrative unit. This situation lasted until 1945 when all except a small sliver of Farther Pomerania was allocated to Poland as part of the compensation package for the formal annexation of the Eastern Territories by the Soviet Union.

Given this background, it is not surprising that Pomerania is one of the least obviously Polish parts of Poland. Those historic monuments which survived the intense fighting of World War II, in which whole towns were

63

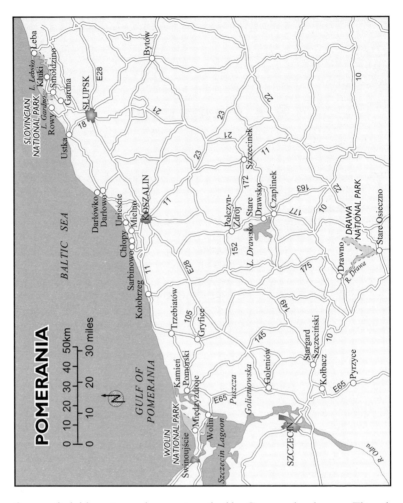

frequently laid waste, evoke a past marked by German dominance. Though the province's main attractions are well spaced out and can thus only be properly explored via a continuous touring route, rather than from a central base, there is much worth travelling far to see.

Especially impressive is the wonderful stretch of almost uninterrupted sandy coast, lapped by the virtually tideless Baltic Sea. Not only is this wonderful for beachcombing during the brief but often extremely hot summers, there are two sections, both now national parks, which are among the most spectacular and unusual natural features in the country. Inland is another of Poland's beautiful lake districts, one which is off the beaten tourist track even for the Poles themselves.

The Slovincian Open-Air Museum in Kluki (Chapter 3)

View over Lake Łebsko from the top of Łacka, the highest of the moving sand dunes in the Slovincian National Park (Chapter 3)

Old houses in Czaplinek, in the Pomeranian Lake District (Chapter 3)

The pier at Sopot, with a Hel-bound steamer (Chapter 4)

Szczecin

The huge port of **Szczecin** is by far the largest city in Pomerania as well as its historic capital. It lies on the banks of the River Odra, not far from the southern shore of the vast Szczecin Lagoon (Zalew Szczeciński), which stretches all the way up to the Baltic. Despite a distinguished history and a fine natural setting, it has often been given a bad press — not least from normally patriotic Poles uncomfortable about a place with such a predominantly German past. Indeed, the allocation to Poland of what had long been Berlin's main outlet to the sea was the most humiliating of all the territorial losses suffered by Germany in 1945. Some have even dubbed this decision as 'Stalin's joke', maintaining that it was ploy by the Soviet dictator to set up a long running bone of contention between Poland and Germany.

In the event, German claims on Szczecin are now a distant memory, and the city has evolved a distinctive Polish character. This has gone hand in hand with a shift in its centre from the medieval Old Town, which was heavily bombed during the war, to the New Town further uphill, which had survived in far better shape and is characterised by the grandiose nineteenth-century architecture favoured by the Prussian authorities.

Typical of these is the bulky neo-Gothic New Town Hall, now the seat of the maritime authorities, which towers above the harbour area. In the square below is a fountain in the form of an anchor, symbolising Szczecin's indebtedness to the sea; unfortunately, the allegorical female figure which formerly stood aloft was a casualty of the war. Across the street, steps lead up to the former Savings Bank, a typical example of Jugendstil, the German form of Art Nouveau.

At the very heart of modern Szczecin is a large and busy square, plac Zwycięstwa, in front of which stands the Harbour Gate, a stately Baroque archway built by the Prussians in 1725 to mark their purchase of the city. This is exuberantly adorned with relief carvings, including a depiction of the god of the Odra leaning on the jug from which the waters of the river flow. Ahead stretches al. Niepodległości, the city's main axis, on whose western side stand two more Prussian-era public buildings — the Post Office, still fulfilling its original function, and the administration building of the Pomeranian district, which has been taken over by the displaced Savings Bank.

Downhill from the Harbour Gate is the former parish church of St James, which was raised to the dignity of a cathedral in 1982, the same year as the restoration work to repair the grievous damage it has suffered in the war was finally completed. The oldest parts of the church date back to the fourteenth century, and are by Hinrich Brunsberg, the most accomplished of the specialist brickwork architects of the Baltic lands; the hall design he used here is notable for its consummate simplicity. In the middle of the following century, the single massive tower was constructed; this is now only half of its pre-war height of 394ft (120m), having been rebuilt minus the tapering spire which for long dominated the city's skyline. Its $5^1/_2$ ton bell now stands outside, as does a memorial to Carl Loewe, one of the great popular ballad composers and singers of the nineteenth century, who was for several decades the church's organist and the municipal music director. To the rear of the church are its dependencies, including a pretty little Gothic rectory.

On the square on the north-west side of the cathedral is the Baroque Pod Globusem Palace, originally built for the ruler of the Prussian province of Pomerania, and now used as the medical academy. Across from it stands a covered fountain adorned with satyrs and an eagle, which began life in the eighteenth century as an outlet of the municipal waterworks. Hidden among the trees a few paces away is another piece of Baroque frippery, a statue of the goddess Flora.

Szczecin's oldest surviving building is the Franciscan monastery of St John near the waterfront, part of which dates back to the thirteenth century. It provides a vivid illustration of the fact that medieval builders could and did get their calculations wrong, being marked by geometric inconsistencies: the chancel is in the shape of an irregular decagon, yet has a seven-part vault, while the nave, which was added later, adjoins at an oblique angle, its off-centre vaulting a vain attempt to align the bays with the aisle windows.

Further east is the Rynek, which was flattened in the war and replaced by concrete blocks of flats. The only reminder of its former appearance and status is the attractively gabled Old Town Hall in the middle of the square. This is a reconstruction of the fourteenth-century original, probably designed by Hinrich Brunsberg, with a single Baroque gable retained as a reminder of the successive modifications it had undergone prior to its wartime destruction. A museum of the history of Szczecin has been installed inside.

Just uphill is the only burgher's mansion left in the city, the mid-sixteenth-century Loitz House. Of a strikingly angular design, this Renaissance tower house was the home of a prominent local banking and trading dynasty. Nearby are two rare medieval survivors, a barn and the municipal weigh-house. Of the once formidable fifteenth-century fortification system, almost nothing remains save the graceful Maiden's Tower, now stranded in a park to the north of the Rynek in the lee of a huge spaghetti junction.

Above this, commanding the river from its hillside perch, is the Castle of the Pomeranian Dukes. The kernel of this dates back to the mid-fourteenth century, but its present appearance is due to a Renaissance enlargement carried out a couple of centuries later. There is a handsome central courtyard, often used for open-air theatrical performances in summer. Unfortunately, the original interiors were destroyed in the war, though various chambers have been restored to house temporary exhibitions. The chapel has been given a new lease of life as a concert hall, while the crypt contains the tin sarcophagi of the Gryfit dynasty. From the top of the tower is a really marvellous bird's-eye view over the city centre and the port.

Immediately to the west of the castle is ul. Farna, where the residence of the commandant formerly stood. This was the birthplace in 1729 of Sophie von Anhalt-Zerbst, a princess of a minor German aristocratic line who, having deposed her own husband, became Empress Catherine the Great of Russia. Her desire for territorial expansion led her to play a leading role in the three Partitions which wiped Poland off the map, making it all the more ironic that her native city is now Polish.

A couple of blocks further west is ul. Staromłyńska, at the corner of which rises an elegant Baroque palace, formerly the Pomeranian parliament, now home of a section of the National Museum. On the ground floor is an impressive display of medieval Pomeranian sculpture, the highlights being some beautifully carved columns from the nearby monastery of Kołbacz, a monumental wooden Crucifix from Kamień Pomorski, and a carved and painted polyptych from Stargard Szczeciński. Upstairs is a dazzling collection of Renaissance jewellery, providing telling evidence of the splendour of the Pomeranian court during this epoch. Paintings and sculpture from the nineteenth century onwards are on display in the annexe across the street.

Over the broad open space of plac Żołnierza Polskiego is the Baroque Gate of Prussian Homage (also known as the Royal Gate), whose carved arches, with reliefs of military trophies, echo those of the Harbour Gate. The interior is now used for changing exhibitions of the work of contemporary painters and photographers. Facing it to the east is the pretty Gothic church of Saints Peter and Paul. This was given a painted wooden ceiling in the seventeenth century, and also has a number of memorial tablets of the same date, all with tell-tale German inscriptions.

To the north is Wały Chrobrego, a showpiece boulevard lined with self-confidently grandiose public buildings from the beginning of the twentieth century. One of these houses a branch of the National Museum, this time devoted mainly to maritime history, notably the seafaring culture of the early Pomeranian Slavs; there is also an unexpected section on African ethnology. Immediately below is the ferry terminal, the departure point for boat trips round the port and harbour, and for the hydrofoil across the vast Szczecin Lagoon to Świnoujście. It is also worth crossing the Odra to Łasztownia, a free port constructed at the end of the nineteenth century, and still preserving many buildings from that period.

Despite the heavily built-up character of its centre, Szczecin has plenty of stretches of greenery, which are ideal for a quick break from the urban bustle, particularly on summer evenings. Just to the north of the centre is the Park Kasprowicza, which is best known for the huge triple eagle monument. Erected in commemoration of the fortieth anniversary of the outbreak of World War II, it symbolizes the three generations of Poles who lost their lives. Across the narrow Lake Rusałka is the Dendrological Garden, which contains over 200 species of trees and shrubs, including a host of exotic varieties. At the northern extremity of the city is the Park Głębokie, centred on the sausage-shaped lake of the same name. A small part of this is developed, but the rest is preserved in rustic tranquillity.

Szczecin's most distinctive park is that in the eastern suburb of Zdroje, where there are a number of hiking trails, a couple of restaurants, and the Emerald Lake (Jezioro Szmaragdowe). The last, whose name is justified by its deep green waters, was created in the 1920s by flooding a former quarry, and is a popular bathing spot.

Further east is Dąbie, for centuries a separate town, and one formerly prosperous enough to have been a member of the Hanseatic League in its own right. It lies at the mouth of the River Regalica, part of the Odra's delta, at the head of the Dąbie Lagoon, a miniature version of the Szczecin Lagoon immediately to the north. The attractive waterfront is a popular sailing area, while the town centre boasts the Gothic church of St Mary, an archetypal example of Baltic brickwork, and the Renaissance Princes' Palace.

Excursions from Szczecin

Szczecin is not the most obvious base for excursions, but there are a few places of note in the surrounding area. Closest to the city, about 7 miles (12km) to the south down a side road, is **Kołbacz**, the first monastery to be established in Pomerania. It was founded in 1175 by Cistercian monks from Denmark, who built the church in the severe Transitional style — using both Romanesque and Gothic elements — characteristic of the order. Initially, the monastery flourished, and in the fourteenth century a new Gothic chancel was raised. However, it later fell into terminal decline, leading to the demolition of part of the church and most of the monastic buildings, though enough remains to hint at its former greatness.

A further 12 miles (20km) south is **Pyrzyce**. Prior to World War II, this was considered one of the prettiest small towns not only in Pomerania, but anywhere in Germany. Alas, most of it was destroyed, and the transfer in ownership to Communist Poland meant that the old centre was replaced by characterless concrete blocks. Nonetheless, sections of the medieval walls remain, including the Szczecin Gate, the Bańska Gate, the Owl Tower and five bastions. The fourteenth- and fifteenth-century parish church of St Maurice, left as a ruin in the war, was belatedly rebuilt in the 1960s.

Rather more substantial reminders of the Middle Ages can be seen at **Stargard Szczeciński**, 12 miles (20km) north-east of Pyrzyce and 15^1/$_2$ miles (25km) south-east of Szczecin, which it replaced as Pomeranian capital for the duration of the Swedish occupation. Situated on the River Ina, a tributary of the Odra, Stargard owed its early development to its position on the old trade routes to and from the Baltic. Although it suffered severe damage in World War II, most of the principal monuments of the medieval old town survived. Thanks to the outstanding quality of the setpieces, this deserves to be considered as the most impressive historic townscape in Pomerania, despite the presence of a lot of ugly post-war concrete.

Considerable portions of the fifteenth-century town walls, which are made of brick and some 13ft (4m) thick, still survive, including five towers and four gateways. The shady Park Chrobrego has been laid out as a promenade along the western side, the longest surviving stretch. Another uninterrupted section can be seen round to the north, at the back of the Gothic church of St John, whose 295ft (90m) tower is now the highest in Pomerania, given the reduced height at which St James' in Szczecin was rebuilt. The most impressive part of the fortification system is the Mill Gate, which takes the form of a covered bridge over the Ina. It was built high enough for boats to pass underneath, and has a pair of battlemented octagonal towers topped with sharply-pointed steeples.

The Rynek, which occupies an unusually off-centre location towards the south-eastern end of the Old Town, has a number of impressive reconstructed burghers' houses. At the corner stands the Town Hall, a plain Gothic structure dramatically altered by the addition of a florid Renaissance gable adorned with polychromed terracotta tracery. Next to it is the Guard House, whose open arcades and loggia suggest the Mediterranean rather than the Baltic. Together with the Weigh House next door, it houses the local museum.

Fine as all these buildings are, they are outclassed by the magnificent church of of St Mary to the rear. One of the most original and decorative examples of the characteristic Gothic brickwork style of the Baltic lands, it was begun around 1400, probably by Hinrich Brunsberg. The two towers, with their glazed green and white ceramics, can be seen from all over the town: the southern one is topped with a fancy gable, whereas its higher northern counterpart features chimney-like turrets and a great central octagon, itself crowned in the Baroque era with a two-storey copper lantern. In contrast to this monumentality, the east end and the protruding octagonal chapel dedicated to the Virgin are adorned with brickwork of the utmost delicacy, proving conclusively that this is far from being the intransigent building material it is often assumed to be. After this, the stately interior seems very low-key, though it does have some highly ornate vaults, which were only added in the seventeenth century.

North of Szczecin is the **Puszca Goleniowska**, a vast forested area, most of it wilderness, which stretches almost all the way up to the island of Wolin. It makes for a particularly scenic approach to the Baltic coast, particularly if travelling by train, as the line cuts right through the heart of the forest.

Within the Puszca, about 25 miles (40km) from Szczecin, is **Goleniów**, a former Hanseatic trading town which is important junction on the transport routes to and from Świnoujście, Kołobrzeg and Kamień Pomorski. Its main church, St Catherine, is a typical example of Baltic Gothic, but was remodelled in the nineteenth century, when the tower was added. The surviving towers and gateways of the town walls make up a nicely varied group, with the most impressive being the Wolin Gate, the largest to be found anywhere in Pomerania. There is also a noteworthy half-timbered eighteenth-century granary on the banks of the River Ina.

Wolin

Poland's only significant island is **Wolin**, the easterly of two heavily indented islands between the Szczecin Lagoon and the inshore part of the Baltic known as the Gulf of Pomerania. The gap dividing Wolin from the mainland is so narrow that it is often described as a peninsula; indeed, at the island's eastern and southern extremities there are roads built directly over the short stretches of the River Dziwna which separate them.

Wolin, which is 22 miles (35km) long and between 5 miles (8km) and

12 miles (20km) across, offers a wonderfully contrasted landscape of sand dunes, lakes, forest, meadows, moors and both ground and terminal moraines. Its most memorable feature is undoubtedly its dramatic coastline, which has attracted crowds of holidaymakers since last century. This is likely to be heavily developed in the future, but in the meantime it remains relatively unspoilt, with a sizeable portion under guaranteed protection as a national park.

Both the road and the railway from Szczecin enter the island at the town of **Wolin**, which occupies the site of one of the oldest Slav settlements in the country. According to Nordic chronicles, a tribe known as the Wolinians established themselves at this spot in the eighth century. Excavations have uncovered plenty of artefacts from the settlement, and these are now displayed in the Archaeology Museum on the main street. Otherwise, Wolin is a rundown provincial town, not at all typical of the island as a whole. There are some nineteenth-century mansions on the Rynek, with a ruined Gothic church nearby.

At the far western end of Wolin is **Świnoujście**, a bustling fishing port, naval base and frontier post. It is one of the most popular entry points into Poland, thanks to the passenger ships which sail there from Sweden, Denmark and Germany. The international ferry terminal, together with the bus and train stations, lie on the right bank of the River Świna, part of the Odra delta, just before it opens out into the Gulf of Pomerania.

The town centre, on the other hand, lies across the water on the quite separate island called Uznam in Polish, but far better known by its German name of Usedom. In 1945, the victorious allies decided to allocate all of Świnoujście to Poland, rather than use the more obvious river boundary, with the result that the town was left as a tiny enclave at the end of an otherwise German island. Regular car ferries link the two parts of the town, but, once across, it is not possible to drive much further afield. Although Ahlbeck, the first of a chain of German beach resorts, is only 1 mile (2km) away, the only means of getting there by car is to make a 62 mile (100km) detour via Szczecin. Since the fall of Communism, however, this frontier has been opened to pedestrians; local buses run to it on both sides of the border, and the whole area is inundated with market traders.

Other than this, Świnoujście's only attractions are a spacious spa park and the lovely white sandy beach which attracts throngs of sunseekers in summer. In the Communist era, the villas along the seafront were holiday homes for trade unions and other organizations, but most of these have since been thrown open to the general public, with the result that the town has the largest choice of accommodation along the entire Pomeranian coast.

However, a much better base for exploring Wolin is **Międzyzdroje**, 9 miles (15km) east, which has a superior beach (and one less subject to pollution), as well as ready access to the finest of the island's scenery. A favourite Baltic resort with the pre-war German middle class, Międzyzdroje inevitably went downmarket with its transferral to Poland. Now, in an almost indecently quick about-turn, the town has turned to Western developers. Already the skyline is dominated by the white bulk of a luxury hotel at the eastern end of the 2 mile (4km) long promenade, rapidly thrown immediately after the fall of Communism to cater for well-heeled Germans and Scandinavians.

In 1994, the first part of the new pier was opened; when complete, this will stretch for 394ft (120m) into the Baltic, and will feature landing stages for yachts and passenger steamers plus an outlook tower in the form of a lighthouse. Yet the resort has not entirely sold its soul to outsiders: it remains a busy fishing port, and the fisherfolk can often be seen at work on the beach, mending their nets and sorting the latest catch. For the best view over the town and the coast, climb the hump known as Kawcza ('Coffee Hill') at the resort's north-eastern extremity.

The **Wolin National Park** (Woliński Park Narodowy), which occupies a sizeable portion of the island, is an area of outstanding natural interest. Apart from its richly varied landscapes, it is the habitat of over 200 different types of bird — the rare sea-eagle is its emblem — as well as numerous animals such as red and fallow deer, wild boar, badgers, foxes and squirrels. Full documentation about the flora and fauna is to be found in the National Park Museum in Międzyzdroje. While it would take several days to cover all the park's many delights, a good cross-section of scenery can be seen without venturing too far from Międzyzdroje. As so often, the best can only be seen on foot via the colour-coded trails. None of these is strenuous, and all have easy access to public transport routes.

By far the most spectacular scenery in the park is to be seen by following the red trail along its eastward stretch from Międzyzdroje. One curiosity is that the shoreline has been retreating inland, by an average of as much as 262ft (80m) per year. The route passes for a while directly along the beach, below some truly awesome-looking dunes, where the sand has been swept up into cliff-like formations up to 312ft (95m) in height — the highest to be seen anywhere on the Baltic. Trees crown the summits, while other vegetation, most prominently the sea holly, which resembles the thistle, grows on the slopes. Quite apart from its visual impact, much of this secluded stretch is ideal for a spot of swimming or sunbathing away from the crowds. After a few kilometres, the markers point the way upwards into the forest, and the path skirts the tiny Lake Gardno before arriving at the village of Wisełka, set by the lake of the same name, and above a popular stretch of beach. The trail continues eastwards through the woods and past more small lakes to its terminus at Kołczewo, set at the head of its own lake.

Also terminating at Kołczewo is the green trail, which could be combined with the red trail in a day-long circular trip. The path, which is best picked up near Międzyzdroje's train station, ascends gently through the woods to a small bison reserve, set up a couple of decades ago to reintroduce these animals to this habitat. The trail continues its forest course, emerging at a group of glaciary lakes around the village of Warnowo (which can also be reached directly by train), where there is another reserve, this time for mute swans. Five lakeshores are then skirted en route to Kołczewo.

The third route, the blue trail, follows a southward course from Międzyzdroje's train station, again passing through wooded countryside before arriving at the secluded Turquoise Lake (Jezioro Turkosowe), which takes its name from the unlikely colour of its waters. It continues to the village of Lubin at the mouth of the Szczecin Lagoon, which is being developed as a watersports centre and yachting marina. From there, the route takes an easterly direction, traversing the heights of the Mokrzyckie Góry, then descending to the town of Wolin.

Finally, the western section of the red trail follows the coast for 1 mile (2km), then cuts straight down the narrow peninsula at the end of the island to the shore of the islet-strewn Lake Wicko Wielkie, finally cutting inland to Świnoujście.

The Baltic Towns

The route eastwards from Wolin is punctuated at fairly regular intervals by historic towns, most of which are set slightly inland from the Baltic. These have endured a variety of fates: some have grown into bustling examples of modern urban life, while others have decayed, or at least grown no bigger than they were during the Middle Ages.

A striking example of the latter phenomenon is **Kamień Pomorski**, which has a picturesque setting on a little headland on the Kamień Lagoon, across the water from the east coast of Wolin. It was for several centuries the spiritual capital of Pomerania, the bishopric having moved from Wolin when the latter was captured by the Danes in 1175. Despite suffering predictably heavy damage in World War II, Kamień has preserved many of its showpiece monuments, which now look highly exaggerated in scale for a place that is now little more than an outsized village. Kamień is in every sense off the beaten track, by-passed by the main road along the Baltic, and with the only rail link being that south to Szczecin.

Predictably, the cathedral still dominates the town. It was begun in granite, but only the lower parts of the walls plus the northern doorway were built before it was decided to change to using bricks instead. The building was substantially complete by the mid-thirteenth century, and displays elements of both Romanesque and Gothic. This originally plain and simple design was beautified in the late fourteenth and early fifteenth centuries by the addition of the south aisle. Inside, this features elaborate star vaults, while outside are wondrously decorative gables, fashioned from both glazed and unglazed handmake bricks. A number of frescos from the time of construction have been uncovered, while the high altar has a fine sixteenth-century carved retable modelled on its famous counterpart in the Mariacki in Cracow. However, the most precious adornment is the Baroque organ, set in a gloriously ornate case complete with figures of angel musicians and a portrait of the bishop who donated it. It can be heard during the Friday evening recitals held in July and August; shorter demonstrations are given twice daily throughout the summer months. On the north side is the only cloister in Pomerania, its walls lined with tombstones brought from their original position in the cathedral pavement. The twelfth-century font, the oldest surviving furnishing, is now kept in the garth, while one of the upstairs chambers houses the treasury.

Opposite the south side of the cathedral is the former Bishop's Palace, now the public library, which is distinguished by a large Renaissance gable. To the west is the Rynek, in the middle of which is the late Gothic Town Hall, whose open porch was formerly used as a public law court. Substantial sections of the former wall can be seen, the most notable being the intact Wolin Gate overlooking the lagoon to the west. South of the fortification system is a shady park with the former church of St Nicholas, the only surviving part of the fourteenth-century hospital. Now the home of the local museum, it has a striking modern tower, while outside stand stylized wooden statues of the Slav warriors who originally settled in the region.

On the banks of the Baltic-bound River Rega, just over 19 miles (30km) to the south-east, is **Gryfice**, another former Hanseatic town, but this time one with rather more of a modern urban feel to it. Though taken undamaged by the Red Army in 1945, it was set ablaze soon afterwards, then used as the site of a penal camp in which many civilians were detained. The Gothic church of St Mary is a copybook example of the Baltic style, notable chiefly for its sturdy single western tower, and its finely detailed portals; inside are some good Baroque furnishings, notably the pulpit and the high altar. Significant surviving parts of the fortifications — the Stone Gate, the High Gate and the Powder Tower — can be seen towards the river to the east.

Some 12 miles (20km) down the Rega, back on the main road along the Baltic, but a good 6 miles (10km) from the sea itself, is **Trzebiatów**. Like Kamień, it is a place where time seems to have gone backwards: nowadays it is a straggling agricultural village, rather than the prosperous trading town it formerly was. A good deal of imagination is required to visualise this sleepy Polish backwater as the dynamic community it was in the sixteenth century when it played a leading role in the German Reformation. Johannes Bugenhagen, who spent nearly two decades as rector of its Latin School, became one of Luther's leading chief lieutenants, returning in 1534 to persuade the Pomeranian assembly which had specially convened there to adopt the new faith throughout the province.

Trzebiatów's skyline is dominated by the magnificent tower — crowned with the unusual combination of a brick octagon and a lead spire — of St Mary, one of the most accomplished Gothic churches of the Baltic region. In it hang two historic bells — one, named Gabriel, is from the late fourteenth century, the other, known as Mary, dates from the early sixteenth century. The building's interior is chiefly notable for its clear architectural lines and uncluttered appearance which, like the German epitaphs on the walls, are evidence of the four centuries it spent in Protestant hands.

Uphill from the church is the Rynek, in the centre of which stands the Town Hall, constructed in the sober Baroque style favoured in northern German lands. A few restored Gothic houses line the square, though their appearance is diminished by the presence of so many undistinguished newer buildings. Just off the southern side is the chapel of the Holy Ghost, another brick Gothic structure, and the setting for the assembly which decided to introduce the Reformation into Pomerania. Substantial sections of the town walls also survive, particularly along the Rega, which is overlooked by the impressive Kaszana Tower.

The only town of any size actually on the Pomeranian coast is **Kołobrzeg**, situated at the mouth of the River Parsęta, about 30km from Trzebiatów. It has had an eventful history: in 1000 it was chosen as the first site of the Pomeranian bishopric and, although it lost this role the following century, it prospered as a port and trading town. In the seventeenth century, the Margraves of Brandenburg transformed it into a redoubtable fortress. Following its destruction during the Napoleonic Wars, it developed as a spa, later as a beach resort, and it still ranks as one of Poland's most popular holiday destinations.

The Old Town lies about half a mile (1km) back from the sea, and now separated from it by the railway tracks. Nine-tenths of it was lost in 1945, when the Germans mounted a futile last-ditch resistance against the advancing Red Army. Modern concrete flats were erected to fill many of the gaps left between the surviving burghers' houses, but since the fall of Communism attempts have started at re-creating a townscape in keeping with Kołobrzeg's illustrious past.

The collegiate church of St Mary was originally built as a simple Gothic hall, but was extended in the fifteenth century with the addition of star-vaulted aisles which give the building an impression of depth and spaciousness.,A particularly striking effect was achieved with the façade, whose twin towers were moulded together into one vast solid mass of brick. Many of the furnishings perished in the war, but some significant items remain. These include a seven-branched candelabrum, a bronze font, and a set of choir stalls, all from the fourteenth century, and a sixteenth-century chandelier with figures of the Madonna and St John. To the north of the church stands the other key public building, the Town Hall. A castellated Romantic creation incorporating some of its fifteenth-century predecessor, which was left as a ruin by Napoleon's troops, it was built from designs provided by the great Berlin architect Karl Friedrich Schinkel.

At the far end of Kołobrzeg's long sandy beach, which still preserves its old pier, is a late eighteenth-century lighthouse which can be ascended for a view over the town and the coast. Nearby is a monument, *Poland's Reunion with the Ocean*, which commemorates a spontaneous event in 1945. After the defeat of the German garrison, a group of Polish patriots gathered at the spot, swearing that forever after this coast would belong to Poland. One of the women present threw her ring into the sea, symbolising the eternal 'marriage' thereby contracted.

Koszalin, 28 miles (45km) east, is the largest town in the vicinity of this part of the Baltic, its medieval centre now engulfed in a modern urban sprawl. Once again, the dominant monument is the Gothic church of St Mary, which is much simpler in style than its counterpart in Kołobrzeg. The Rynek opposite had to be rebuilt following destruction in World War II, but downhill to the north are several sections of the town walls. Nearby, an old mill houses the Regional Museum; outside is a small *skansen* with traditional farm buildings of the Pomeranian countryside. Round the walls to the north-east are the ruins of the castle, along with its Baroque chapel, which was allocated after the war to Orthodox immigrants from the lost Eastern Territories, and decked out with icons. South-east of the Rynek is St Gertrude, a fine example of the highly distinctive Gothic cemetery chapels found in several Pomeranian towns. Octagonal in shape, it has a tapering pyramidal spire and a graceful star-vaulted interior.

On the coast just north of Koszalin are several small beach resorts. Closest to town is the fishing village of **Mielno**, 6 miles (10km) north, lying at the western end of Lake Jamno, which is much used by sailing and watersports enthusiasts. A couple of kilometres along the narrow spit of land dividing the lake from the Baltic is **Unieście**, a tiny fishing port given ample shelter by trees and high dunes. Back in the direction of Kołobrzeg are **Chłopy**, which has traditionally been patronised by artists, and **Sarbinowo**, with a pretty village church.

Darłowo, 22 miles (35km) north-east of Koszalin, is one of the few Pomeranian towns which came through the last war virtually undamaged, and the lack of obtrusive modern buildings in the chessboard-plan town centre makes for a refreshing change. A favourite seat of the Pomeranian dukes, and a capital in its own right on occasions when the ruling family partitioned its territory, Darłowo was the birthplace in 1382 of Erik I, the most colourful figure in the ducal panthcon, and the only one who gained royal status. Erik was adopted by his great-aunt, Queen Margaret of Denmark, who appointed him joint ruler in 1397. Later the same year, following the Kalmar Union, he gained the thrones of Norway and Sweden as well. Never very popular with his Scandinavian subjects, Erik, who had already fled to the Swedish island of Gotland, was deposed by the Danes and Swedes in 1440, and by the Norwegians 2 years later. From his exile, he mounted raids against trading ships, gaining the nicknames 'The Pirate King' and 'The Last Viking of the Baltic'. In 1449, he returned to his home town, where he spent the last 10 years of his life.

Erik's residence, the Castle of the Pomeranian Dukes, is set at the confluence of two arms of the River Wieprza in the southern part of town. Originally built in the mid-fourteenth century, it has been altered on various occasions, and only part of the complex survives to this day, now restored to house the Regional Museum. There are a few reconstructed Gothic interiors, notably the Knights' Hall by the entrance, which contains the elaborate Baroque pulpit from the former chapel. Elsewhere, the exhibits range from portraits of the Pomeranian dukes via some fine Renaissance furniture to a collection of African ethnololgy. Additionally, the outlook tower can be climbed for a view of the town.

Plac Kościuszki, the central market square, is dominated by the Town Hall, which dates from the early eighteenth century, a time when Darłowo's prosperity revived after more than two centuries in the doldrums. There are also some colourful arcaded burghers' house from the same epoch. Behind rises the church of St Mary, a fairly plain example of the Baltic Gothic style, distinguished mainly by its 197ft (60m) tower. Under this stands the sarcophagus of Erik I, commissioned in 1882 as a very belated tribute by Kaiser Wilhelm II of Germany. In terms of artistry, it is overshadowed by its two older companions, which contain the remains of two female members of the local ducal house.

A block north of the square is the mighty Stone Gate, the only surviving part of the fortifications. Despite its name, it is another typical example of Baltic brickwork. A little further north is the cemetery, in which stands the chapel of St Gertrude, the town's most distinguished and unusual building. It is built to a centralised groundplan, with the vault resting on a single pillar, around which is a hexagonal chancel surrounded by a dodecagonal ambulatory. The shingle-roofed exterior, with its tall, twisting spire, is equally dapper.

At the mouth of the Wieprza, less than 2 miles (3km) from Darłowo, is **Darłówko**, whose development as a beach resort, the first in Pomerania, began immediately after the Napoleonic Wars. It is also an active fishing harbour, boasting a 1,640ft (500m) long dyke, a lighthouse, and a drawbridge over the river whose regular raising and lowering to let members of the fleet in and out forms one of the main tourist attractions. The beach to the east of town is particularly fine, and becomes ever more secluded, eventually occupying a narrow strip of land, accessible only on foot, between the sea and Lake Kopań behind.

Indeed, the 25 miles (40km) of coast between Darłówko and **Ustka**, the next coastal town of any size, are circumnavigated by the main road, which passes well inland. Ustka, which lies at the mouth of the River Słupia, preserves nothing from its Hanseatic past, but it ranks second to Kołobrzeg as the busiest resort on the Pomeranian coast, thanks to to the fine sandy beaches on either side of the river, and is also an important fishing port.

Słupsk, 11 miles (18km) downstream, was formerly the residence of a scion of the Pomeranian ducal house. Like Koszalin, it was badly damaged in the last war, and has since grown into a sizeable modern city. Even though its sights can be seen in a few hours, it is worth considering as a touring base for the Baltic area, as it has plenty of accommodation which does not tend to get oversubscribed, as can happen in places nearer the coast. Nationally, it is best known as the home of the Polish Piano Festival, held annually in September, featuring recitals by many of the country's leading pianists.

By far the most attractive part of Słupsk is the south-east corner of the Old Town, which retains a significant cluster of historic monuments centred on the Renaissance Castle of the Pomeranian Dukes, of which only a tower and one wing survive. The pride of the Regional Museum housed inside is a room containing several dozen pastel portraits by Stanisław Ignacy Witkiewicz, otherwise known as Witkacy, one of the great figures of twentieth-century Polish culture. He is best known for his literary achievements: he invented the Theatre of the Absurd long before the term came to be used in conjunction with the plays of Beckett and Ionesco, while his epic novel *Insatiability* is a key work of modern experimental fiction. However, this display amply proves that he was no less accomplished as an artist — even if his work in this field was often undertaken after he had deliberately put himself in a drug-influenced state.

Alongside the castle is its mill, still in full working order and now devoted to the museum's ethnographic section. Behind it rises the Mill Gate, part of the fifteenth-century fortification system. Another rare survivor of this is the Witches' Tower just to the north, which takes its name from having been the place where women suspected of sorcery were imprisoned.

On the opposite side of the castle is the Gothic church of St Hyacinth, which was originally part of a Dominican monastery. It has an unusual interior arrangement, divided into two unequal chambers. The larger of these is the main place of worship, and contains the black and white marble funerary monuments of the last members of the Pomeranian ducal house. There is also an outstanding Baroque organ in a handsome case, on which recitals are given every Thursday evening in July and August. In a small area of greenery just to the south is the former cemetery chapel of St George, which was brought stone by stone from its original location.

The dominant building in the heart of the old town is the church of St Mary, a typical example of Pomeranian Gothic remodelled in the nineteenth century. To its west is the New Gate, the last remaining part of the fortifications, now used as a commercial art gallery. Facing it across plac Zwycięstwa, the square which forms the modern commercial centre, is the Town Hall, a typically self-confident example of German neo-Gothic from the turn of the century.

The Slovincian National Park

Undoubtedly the most impressive stretch of coast anywhere on the Baltic is the **Slovincian National Park** (Słowiński Park Narodowy), which occupies a 20 mile (33km) stretch at the far eastern end of Pomerania, taking its name from the Slav tribe which originally settled in the area. Like the Kashubians to the east, the Slovincians struggled to maintain a separate language and identity throughout centuries of enforced Germanisation and Polonisation. Nowadays, their culture is little more than a memory, though their descendants still live in the villages in the south of the park, the only part which is inhabited.

The Slovincian National Park is included in UNESCO's list of World Biosphere Reserves, and within its relatively small area is a unique combination of aquatic and terrestrial ecosystems, the former represented by sea, rivers and lakes, the latter by dunes, marshland, peat bogs and forests. It is best known for the huge sand dunes, which are among the most bizarre natural features to be seen anywhere in Europe. Formed from sand thrown up on to the beach which is dried by the wind and the sun, they offer the uncanny illusion of being a desert. Indeed, during World War II, they served as a simulated Sahara for training exercises by Rommel's Afrika Corps.

The dunes have been moving for the last 5,000 years, by anything from 7 to 33ft (2 to 10m) annually. As they shift, they obliterate whatever lies in their path, leaving it to re-emerge in a changed state once they have passed over; hence the presence of such weird scenery as woods half-submerged in sand. Many of the dunes reach a height of 98ft (30m), and the highest is currently 138ft (42m). However, they are gradually becoming lower as the wind spreads the sand over an ever larger area. The wind constantly alters their appearance in other ways — for example changing their physical formations, and by carrying the seeds of plants which take root in the sand, and have a stablising effect.

Originally, the lakes in the park were Baltic bays, but they were cut off from the sea by the formation of the dunes. As a result of the continuing encroachment of the sand, they are contracting all the time. Although Lake Łebsko at the eastern end of the park is still the third largest stretch of inland water in Poland, it is 5 per cent smaller than it was just 60 years ago. Further west, Lake Dołgie Małe and the minute Lake Dołgie Wielkie were once part of the much larger Lake Gardno at the western end of the park. These lakes all have reedy shorelines which are difficult of access. However, in a rare departure from the otherwise strict conservation policies, yachting is permitted on Lake Gardno.

Because of the unusual conjunction of very low human habitation, the protection offered by the marshland and the shores of the lakes, and the fact that the area lies on the southern migratory route, the park is inhabited by around 75 per cent of all the birds which have been recorded in Poland. Of these, some 200 nest there, including white-tailed eagles, eagle-owls, mute swans, ruffs, cranes, black storks, as well as such rare species as the white-winged lark and the king eider. There is a sizeable otter colony in Lake Łebsko, while red deer, roe deer, wild boar, foxes, badgers and raccoons all live in the forests.

Careful advance planning is advisable before making a trip to the Slovincian National Park, and logistics dictate that this is best spread over two days. The only roads, which are serviced by occasional buses from Słupsk, are those linking the villages strung along its surrounding boundary. Elsewhere, motorised transport is banned and access is allowed from May until September only.

By far the most convenient jumping-off point for a visit is the fishing village and seaside resort of **Łeba**, which has good bus and train links with the main routes to the south. It lies just outside the park's eastern boundary, at the confluence of two little rivers — the Łeba, which flows from Lake Łebsko, and the Chełst, which arrives via Lake Sarbsko to the east of town. The shifting dunes have caused the inhabitants of Łeba problems in the past, necessitating the removal of the original settlement, whose parish church can be seen half-buried in the sand, to a more secure site back from the coast.

Łeba is the starting-point for the two long coloured-coded trails which are, apart from a few linking sections with each other or with the beach, the only officially sanctioned means of passage through the park. Much the more enticing of these is the red or sea-shore path. This first travels 1 mile (2km) east to the hamlet of Rąbka, which has a large car park plus a wooden observation platform offering a view over Lake Łebsko. Once inside the gates of the park, there is the option of taking one of the tourist buggies along a 2 mile (3km) stretch of paved road. After this, there is a 1 mile (2km) walk through the woods to Łacka, the first and highest of the shifting dunes. From the top is a marvellous panorama over the sea, the lake, the forest and the vast expanse of dune to the west, which is out of bounds for conservation reasons.

Most visitors then go down to relax on the beach, which in turn has a wonderful view back to Łacka. They then return the same way they came, or else double back along the beach all the way to Łeba. Those wishing to continue following the red trail, which is a strenuous full day hike, follow the beach westwards for 4 miles (6km), before cutting inland to the Czołpińska Hill observation tower, the highest point within the park. From there, the trail skirts the end of Lake Dołgie Wielkie, then passes through the forest all the way along the northern shore of Lake Gardno which is, however, only visible from a platform located towards its western end. Just beyond lies **Rowy**, a smaller version of Łeba located in an equivalent position at the opposite edge of the park, and with a regular bus service to Słupsk, just 12 miles (20km) south.

The villages along the park's southern border have more sporadic bus connections with Słupsk. They are also linked by the other hiking trail, the yellow route, which goes from Łeba to **Gardna**, a boating resort at the south-eastern end of Lake Gardno. Around 3 miles (5km) north-west of here is **Smołdzino**, which lies outside the park boundaries, but is home to the National Park Museum, with displays on the local flora and fauna. At the edge of the village is the Rowokół Hill, at the top of which is a tall wooden observation tower commanding a truly grandstand panorama over virtually the entire extent of the park.

Kluki, 5 miles (8km) west, is the most characterful of the Slovincian villages, one where the local language is still spoken by the oldest residents. A cemetery with idiosyncratic iron crosses at the entrance to the village is one legacy of their distinctive culture. Another is the Slovincian Open-Air Museum, which differs from most other *skansens* in Poland in being based largely on buildings remaining in situ, rather than on those reassembled from a variety of other locations. In addition to a couple of sizeable farmsteads, there are several smaller agricultural structures which, apart from being extremely practical, often evince a surprisingly inventive streak.

The Pomeranian Lake District

Despite its indelible associations with the sea, Pomerania also has an extensive Lake District, which stretches over most of its interior. Formed during the last phase of Baltic glaciation, its landscape is very similar in character to that of the Great Masurian Lakes to the east, with over a thousand lakes of varying sizes, many of them linked by slow-flowing rivers. These are ideal for exploring by kayak or canoe, and are consequently popular with Polish sailing enthusiasts. However, few other visitors penetrate the area and tourist facilities remain rudimentary.

At the far eastern end of the Lake District, 34 miles (55km) south-east of Słupsk, is **Bytów**, a town founded by the Teutonic Knights on territory purchased from the Pomeranian dukes. The castle, built at the turn of the fifteenth century, became the westernmost outpost of their domains. It is simpler than most of the castles they had built in their strongholds to the east, characterised by four sturdy corner towers which are among the earliest in Europe to have gunloops. Left as a ruin in the seventeenth-century Swedish wars, the castle has been rebuilt, with part of it now converted to serve as a hotel.

The main concentration of lakes lies just over 62 miles (100km) south-west of Słupsk; the main gateway to the region, as well as its largest town, is **Szczecinek**, which was likewise founded in the fourteenth century as a frontier post, this time by the Pomeranians themselves. It lies on the north shore of Lake Trzesiecko, on the narrow strip of land separating it from the much larger Lake Wielimie — a once strategically important position which has been of enormous benefit in its modern development as a holiday centre. Unfortunately, only a few historic buildings survive. These include the tower of the fifteenth-century church of St Nicholas, which currently serves as the Regional Museum, and the lakeside castle, rebuilt in the eighteenth century as a Baroque palace for a dowager duchess, and nowadays a hotel. There are also a fair number of imposing turn-of-the-century buildings in the town centre, some in the bloated Historicist style, others examples of the Secessionist movement.

West of Szczecinek, the road and railway pass by a string of tranquil lakes along the 28 miles (45km) route to the little town of **Czaplinek**, the most popular resort in the district. Again, it is sandwiched into a narrow stretch of land, with Lake Czaplino to the south-east and the southern shore of Lake Drawsko to the north. The latter, with its strange, almost cruciform shape, is the most picturesque lake in Pomerania; its clear blue waters reach a depth of up to 272ft (83m), while its sharply indented shoreline stretches for all of 47 miles (76km). Czaplinek itself boasts a startlingly colourful array of houses on plac 3-go Maja, the huge open square where the buses stop. On the smaller Rynek in the heart of town are some Secessionist buildings plus the eighteenth-century parish church, which has some fine Baroque and neo-Classical furnishings.

On a narrow isthmus separating Lake Drawsko from Lake Zerdno, some 4 miles (6km) north of Czaplinek, and reached either by road or by the marked footpath skirting the eastern shore of the former, is the hamlet of **Stare Drawsko**. The castle of the Knights Templars still survives in a ruinous state, offering one of the best viewpoints in the region. Further north, the same main road has gained the nickname of the Road of a Thousand Curves for the final stages of its journey to the spa town of **Połczyn-Zdrój** some 22 miles (35km) away. In addition to the standard parks and recuperative facilities, Połczyn preserves some fragments of its medieval walls, plus a castle rebuilt in the eighteenth century which now houses a theatre, library and hotel.

The most beautiful part of the Pomeranian Lake District is also one of the least known, despite its designation a few years ago as the **Drawa National Park** (Drawieński Park Narodowy). This is centred on the stretch of the River Drawa — a navigable canoe route rising just west of Lake Drawsko — between the villages of Drawno, some 34 miles (55km) south-east of

Czaplinek, and Stare Osieczno. Within the park are thirteen lakes, the largest being Lake Ostrowieckie; other characteristic features of the landscape are kane hills, gulleys and peat bogs. A rich wildlife includes the otter, the park's symbol, and the beaver, which has been re-introduced following a long absence. There are also around 150 bird species, including eagles, ospreys and storks.

Further Information
— Pomerania —

Places to Visit

Darłowo
Castle of the Pomeranian Dukes
ul. Zamkowa
Open: Tuesday to Sunday 9am to 4pm.

Kluki
Slovincian Open-Air Museum
Open: 15 May to 15 September
Tuesday to Sunday 9am to 4pm,
16 September to 14 May Tuesday to
Sunday 9am to 3pm.

Koszalin
Regional Museum
ul. Myłńska 27-29
Open: Tuesday to Sunday 10am to 4pm.

Międzyzdroje
Wolin National Park Museum
ul. Niepodległości 3
Open: Tuesday to Sunday 10am to 3pm.

Słupsk
Castle of the Pomeranian Dukes
(Regional Museum)
ul. Dominikańska 5
Open: June to August Tuesday to
Sunday 10am to 4pm, September to
May Tuesday to Sunday 10am to 3pm.

Smołdzino
Outlook Tower
Rowokoł Hill
Open: May and September Tuesday to
Sunday 9am to 4pm, July and August
Tuesday to Sunday 9am to 6pm.

Slovincian National Park Museum
ul. Bohaterów Warszawy 1
Open: Tuesday to Friday 8am to 4pm,
Saturday and Sunday 9am to 4pm.

Szczecin
Castle of the Pomeranian Dukes
ul. Korsarzy
Open: Tuesday to Sunday 10am to 4pm.

National Museum (fine and applied arts)
ul. Staromyłńska 27-28
Open: Tuesday and Thursday 10am to
5pm, Wednesday and Friday 9am to
3pm, Saturday and Sunday 10am to 4pm.

National Museum (maritime and
ethnology)
Wały Chrobrego 3
Open: Tuesday and Thursday 10am to
5pm, Wednesday and Friday 9am to
3pm, Saturday and Sunday 10am to 4pm.

Old Town Hall (Historical Museum of
Szczecin)
Stary Rynek
Open: Tuesday to Sunday 10am to 4pm.

Szczecinek
Regional Museum
ul. Księżnej Elżbiety 6
Open: Wednesday to Sunday 10am to
3pm.

Tourist Office
Szczecin
ul. Wyszyńskiego 26
☎ 340-440

4 • Royal Prussia

Although its name no longer appears on modern maps of Poland, the old province of **Royal Prussia** (Prusy Królewski) is a coherent and well-defined unit. Geographically speaking, it consists of the lower basin of the Vistula, a varied if visually undramatic landscape in which rich farmland gives way to an enormous marshy delta as the river divides into several channels before disgorging itself into the Baltic. Since the early Middle Ages, the area has also had a common historical heritage, though this sprang from diverse and complex origins.

The province takes its name from the Prussians (or Pruzzi), a Baltic people who first settled in the lands east of the Vistula in the second or third century AD. During the Dark Ages the Pomeranians gradually spread from their original western Baltic base towards the Vistula, and eventually the eastern part of their territory became a separate duchy in its own right, known as Pomerelia (literally, 'Little Pomerania'), or as Gdańsk-Pomerania after its capital. Simultaneously, the duchy of Mazovia expanded its boundaries northwards, establishing a county named Chełmno immediately to the south of Pomerelia. Whereas the early Polish state, with which Pomerania and Mazovia were both associated, fervently embraced Christianity, the Prussians were still defiantly pagan more than two centuries after they had given Poland its first martyr by murdering St Adalbert in AD997. In 1226, Duke Konrad of Mazovia made the fateful decision to grant Chełmno county as a fief to the Teutonic Knights, a quasi-monastic German military order which had been founded in Palestine during the Third Crusade, in the hope that they would finally subjugate and convert the Prussians, thereby securing Poland's borders.

Unfortunately for the Poles, the Knights nourished the far grander ambition of establishing a theocratic state of their own. Within a few decades, they had taken over the lands of the Prussians and their eastern neighbours the Jatzvingians, exterminating both tribes in the process. In 1308 they seized Pomerelia when the local dukes died out, an action which left them in control of a large tract of the Baltic. German settlers poured into the areas conquered by the Knights, which were protected by some of the most awesome castles the world had ever seen, most notably Marienburg (now Malbork). Within a very short period, the towns they established along the Vistula had grown rich from the profits of the grain trade.

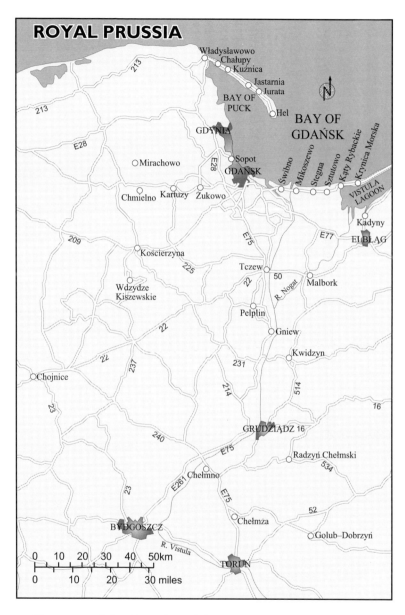

The power of the Teutonic Knights waned following their defeat at Grunwald in 1410 by the combined armies of Poland and Lithuania, but was not decisively broken until the Thirteen Years' War of 1454-66, when their two traditional enemies joined forces with the German settlers, organised into the Prussian League, who resented the crippling taxes levied on them. Following the Knights' defeat, Royal Prussia, the western half of the

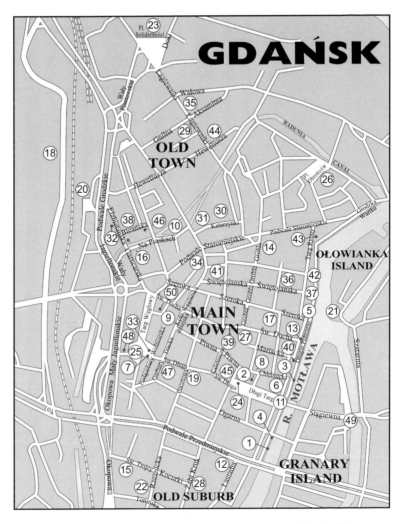

Teutonic state, was placed under the direct protection of the Polish crown. However, it was not fully integrated into Poland — indeed it later became one of the four constituent parts of the Polish-Lithuanian Commonwealth — and ethnic Germans continued to account for a large percentage of its population. Danzig (as Gdańsk was then known) gained the effective status of an independent city-state, while Elbing (now Elbląg) and Thorn (now Toruń) also achieved considerable municipal autonomy.

During the Partitions of Poland, all of Royal Prussia was annexed by the misleadingly-titled Kingdom of Prussia, the military state centred on Berlin. Extended slightly to the east, it was re-christened as West Prussia, and survived as such until 1919, when the lands west of the Vistula (other than Danzig, which regained its role as a city-state), were ceded in order to create

KEY

1 Anchormakers' Tower	26 Polish Post Office
2 Artus Court	27 Royal Chapel
3 Bakers' Gate	28 SS Peter and Paul Church
4 Cow Gate	29 St Bartholomew's Church
5 Crane Gate	30 St Bridget's Church
6 English House	31 St Catherine's Church
7 Golden Gate	32 St Elizabeth's Church
8 Golden House	33 St George's Court
9 Great Arsenal	34 St Hyacinth's Tower
10 Great Mill	35 St James' Church
11 Green Gate	36 St John's Church
12 Gymnasium	37 St John's Gate
13 Holy Ghost Gate	38 St Joseph's Church
14 Holy Ghost Hospital	39 St Mary's Church
15 Holy Trinity Church	40 St Mary's Gate and
16 House of the Abbots of Pelplin	Archaeological Museum
17 House "Under the Salmon"	41 St Nicholas' Church
18 Main Bus Station	42 Stall Gate
19 Main Post Office	43 Swan Tower
20 Main Railway Station	44 Tourist Office
21 Maritime Museum	45 Town Hall of Main Town
22 National Museum	46 Town Hall of Old Town
23 Monument to the	47 Uphagen House
Shipyard Workers	48 Upland Gate
24 Neptune's Fountain	49 Vat Gate
25 Outer Gate	50 Wybrzeże Theatre

the notorious Polish Corridor, which gave the otherwise landlocked Poland access to the sea. The small rump on the opposite side of the Vistula was then transferred to the province of East Prussia, which was left cut off from the rest of Germany. Such a complicated mosaic ended up satisfying no-one, and it was the Nazis' conquest of these lost territories which directly triggered off World War II. Their eventual defeat led to all of Royal Prussia being ceded to Poland, so bringing to an end seven centuries of German domination — and of place-names, which were all Polonised.

The province's principal tourist magnet is the re-named Gdańsk, which has arisen from wartime rubble to take its place among the driving forces of modern Poland. In terms of visual appeal, it is the only one of the country's larger cities which comes near to rivalling Cracow — and is arguably even more photogenic, although its historic monuments are fewer in number and not so authentically preserved. Most other destinations in Royal Prussia are easily accessible on day trips from the city, but it is best to explore the Vistula itself, with its spectacular legacies of the Teutonic Knights, by means of a continuous journey lasting several days.

Gdańsk

Gdańsk (which is still more familiar to many under its German name of Danzig) is surely the ultimate of Poland's many paradoxes. In recent times, its dockyards attracted worldwide media attention as the focal point of the national struggles against Soviet-imposed Communist rule, which eventually crystalized around Solidarity, the free trade union founded there in 1980. Yet in 1939 only 7 per cent of the local population was Polish, and the city's incorporation into Poland in 1945, which was accompanied by the expulsion of most of the remaining German inhabitants, was the first occasion it had, strictly speaking, officially formed part of a nation with which it had often been in close alliance.

Having shaken off the feudal overlordship of the Teutonic Knights in the Thirteen Years' War, the city agreed to pay homage and an annual tax to the Polish monarch, but otherwise functioned as an independent state in its own right. It took full advantage of its favourable location at the point where the Dead Vistula (Martma Wisła), the westernmost arm of the great river, flows into the Baltic, to establish itself as one of the largest and richest cities in Europe, one which quickly assumed the dominant role in the Hanseatic League. Settlers from all over Europe came to the city to make their fortunes. A sizeable Scottish presence is indicated by the districts of Old Scotland (Stare Szkoty) and New Scotland (Nowe Szkoty), whose names survive to this day. However, it was the Dutch and Flemings who left the most profound mark on the face of the city, designing a host of magnificent public and private buildings in the Renaissance and Mannerist styles of Amsterdam and Antwerp. These make perfect foils to the older Germanic brick Gothic churches, creating an appropriately cosmopolitan cityscape.

What can be seen today is not always absolutely authentic, as most of the city centre was devastated in World War II. However, it was lovingly re-created by Polish restorers in an exercise which made even the rebuilding of Warsaw seem almost straightforward and mechanical by comparison. For the restorers did not content themselves with re-instating what had been lost: they set out to improve the pre-war appearance of the city, resorting to old pattern books to create a vision of the historic centre as they imagined it must have looked in its mercantile heyday. The result might have turned out as kitsch, but it was executed with such assurance and aplomb that it is almost impossible to regard it as anything less than a total success, particularly now that the passage of time has creating a mellowing effect.

Gdańsk's attractions are more concentrated than those of Warsaw or Cracow, and hence can be seen in a shorter time. The historic centre divides into several distinct parts, the most important being the Main Town, the Old

Town and the Old Suburb, each of which is described separately below. Much of what lies beyond is a typical modern urban sprawl, though a few of the environs are worthwhile destinations in their own right.

The Main Town

By far the largest and most imposing part of Gdańsk's historic core is the **Main Town** (Główne Miasto), which was chartered in 1343, and occupies the site of the original Pomeranian settlement. Unlike the Old Town to the north, it was completely enclosed within a powerful system of fortifications. Only a few fragmentary stretches of the walls remain, but many of its towers and gateways survive intact, providing a potent reminder of the strength of the defences as well as being handy delineators of the Main Town's boundaries.

The most strongly guarded approach to the city was that on the vulnerable inland side to the west, where three consecutive gateways can still be seen. These mark the start of Gdańsk's Royal Way, the processional route taken by Polish kings on their annual visits to the city. The outermost building, the **Upland Gate**, was erected in the 1570s by a Dresden architect, Johann Kramer, as part of a general strengthening of the medieval walls. A decade later, it was decorated by Willem van den Block, a member of an artistic dynasty of Dutch origin which left a profound mark on the face of the city. On the frieze, two angels are shown bearing the coats-of-arms of Poland, two lions those of Gdańsk, and two unicorns those of Royal Prussia. This armorial grouping is a recurrent motif in the historic part of the city.

Immediately to the rear of the Upland Gate is the considerably larger **Outer Gate**, which dates back to the early fifteenth century. Once the Upland Gate had been completed, the western section of this was remodelled as a torture chamber, while the tower behind, which had been heightened at the beginning of the sixteenth century, became the town gaol. It is now open as a branch of the Historical Museum, displaying a gruesome collection of old torture instruments.

Next in line, framing the entrance to ul. Długa, the Main Town's principal thoroughfare, is the **Golden Gate**, which was built between 1612 and 1614 by Abraham van den Block, the son of Willem. Although it replaced a medieval gateway, it had no defensive function, being instead a Mannerist re-interpretation of the Roman triumphal arch, to which its articulated columns directly allude. To celebrate the Peace of Westphalia of 1648, which brought to an end the disastrous series of European conflicts known as the Thirty Years' War, it was embellished with a series of allegorical statues: those on the west side represent Peace, Freedom, Wealth and Fame; those on the east Wisdom, Godliness, Justice and Concord. Because of the effects of erosion and pollution, the originals have had to be replaced by copies. Adjoining the north side of the Golden Gate is **St George's Court**, a two-storey brick building from the end of the fifteenth century. Originally the headquarters of a shooting fraternity, it nowadays fulfils the same function for the local society of architects.

Despite its name, which literally means 'Long Street', ul. Długa stretches for no more than 984ft (300m). Nonetheless, it contains many of Gdańsk's most splendid mansions. The **Uphagen House** (number 12), a typical example of a burgher's residence of the last quarter of the eighteenth century with furnishings and fittings from the same era, was formerly open as a museum, and will hopefully be re-instated as such before long. Also worthy of special mention are three Mannerist mansions from the 1560s — the Feber House (number 28), the Lion Castle (number 35) and the Szuman House (number 45).

At the point where ul. Dluga widens out to form the rather more appropriately named 'Long Market', Długi Targ. stands the **Town Hall** of the Main Town. In contrast to its counterparts in many of the other great Hanseatic cities of the Baltic, this was not used for trading purposes, serving only to house the municipal administration. For this reason, it was initially fairly modest in size, but in the mid-sixteenth century an extra storey was added and the slender tower was heightened and crowned with a statue of King Zygmunt August. At the end of the same century, a team of Netherlandish artists and decorators began transforming the interior, creating a spectacular suite of Mannerist chambers.

These now house the Historical Museum of Gdańsk, though the exhibits seem of incidental importance to the rooms themselves. By far the most opulent of these is the Great Council Chamber, usually known as the Red Hall because of the damask lining the walls. Its fittings, which were spirited away to safety during World War II, include a huge fireplace carved by Willem Bart; a cycle of wall paintings by Hans Vredeman de Vries, who is better known as the leading architectural theorist of the Northern European Renaissance; and an elaborate comparmentalised ceiling by Anthonis van Opbergen. The oval central panel of the last-named was painted by Isaak van den Block, and is an allegory entitled *The Glorification of the Unity of Gdańsk with Poland*, featuring a detailed view of the city. In the modest rooms on the second floor is a permanent exhibition of photographs showing the city's destruction in 1945. During the summer months, it may be possible to ascend from there to the top of the tower.

A few paces from the Town Hall is the **Artus Court**, which served as the main meeting-place and ceremonial hall for the city's patrician class during its mercantile heyday. It is vividly described in the short story of the same name by the German Romantic writer and master of the macabre, Ernst Theodor Amadeus Hoffmann. The present structure, the second on the spot, was erected in the late fifteenth century, but the façade was remodelled by Abraham van den Block, who added a rich sculptural programme which includes statues of the Virtues and antique heroes as well as roundels of King Zygmunt Waza and his son, the future King Władysław Waza. Inside is a single chamber with a magnificent star vault held aloft by four sturdy columns which were, according to tradition, salvaged from the destroyed Castle of the Teutonic Knights. Once restoration work is complete, this will house a branch of the Historical Museum.

In front of the Artus Court is **Neptune's Fountain**, which was erected to provide a focal point for the great municipal festivities held on the square. The bronze figure of the sea god is the oldest secular monument in Poland: it was designed by a Dutch sculptor, Peter Husen, and completed in 1613. A couple of decades later, it was surrounded by an iron grille, but it was not until the middle of the following century that the monument was finished off by the addition of a rococo basin surrounded by a shoal of acquatic creatures.

Three doors down from the Artus Court is the **Golden House**, the most elaborate mansion in the city, named after the gilding used on its façade. It was built for Mayor Johann Speimann by Abraham van den Block, and festooned with carvings by Johann Voigt, a sculptor from Rostock, another of the Hanseatic ports on the Baltic. In addition to delicately carved friezes depicting historical scenes, there are statues representing the Three Theological Virtues and the Four Cardinal Virtues.

Closing the eastern end of Długi Targ is the monumental **Green Gate**, built in the 1560s by an Amsterdam architect known only by the name of Regnier. It was intended to serve as the residence of the Polish king during his visits to the city. However, it proved too uncongenial for this role, and the courtly retinues preferred to stay in the nearby houses (numbers 1 to 4) on the southern side of the square. It has served instead as an arsenal and as a reception hall, and is currently occupied by the municipal offices for architectural preservation.

The eastern façade of the Green Gate overlooks one of the channels of the River Motława which flow around Granary (Spichlerze) Island. Prior to World War II, there were 175 historic granaries in Gdańsk. Only one survived without significant damage; of those which were rebuilt, some are accurate reproductions, while others adopt a recognizably modern idiom. Despite the losses, the waterfront remains the most photogenic of all Gdańsk's many picturesque corners. There is a particularly beautiful view over it from the little bridge leading from the Green Gate to Granary Island. Overlooking the other channel of the Motława at the opposite side of the island is the unfinished **Vat Gate**. This consists of two towers, the higher of which was used as a terrace for cannon.

By following the promenade southwards from the Green Gate, two more fragments of the medieval fortifications can be seen. The fifteenth-century **Cow Gate** is named after the bridge opposite, which was used for driving cattle between the Main Town and Granary Island. Beyond is the **Anchormakers' Tower**, which is late fourteenth-century by origin, but rebuilt in Renaissance style in the sixteenth century.

Each of the Main Town's parallel eastward-running streets terminates at the waterfront, from which it is separated by a fortified gateway. The first and oldest of these, the mid-fifteenth-century **Bakers' Gate**, still bears the paired crosses of the Teutonic Knights, though the Polish royal crown was added shortly afterwards to mark the city's change in allegiance. It guards ul. Chlebnicka, whose finest mansion is number 16, a Mannerist building usually known as the English House. Whether or not it ever had any connection with the once-sizeable community of merchants from England remains a matter of dispute: its original owner was a German, and it may be that its name is actually a corruption of Angel House. The late Gothic **Schlieff House** next door (number 14) is a copy of the original, which so enchanted the future King Friedrich Wilhelm IV of Prussia that he had it dismantled stone-by-stone and transported to Berlin, where it was re-erected on Peacock Island.

A block further north is ul. **Mariacki**. This is a particularly charming street, as it is the only one where all the houses — many of which are now boutiques selling handicrafts, and in particular amber jewellery — are separated from the street by highly distinctive raised stone platforms. These terrace-like constructions (known as *Beischlage* in German, or *przedproży* in Polish), are found in other Hanseatic cities, but were something of a Gdańsk trademark. They were prevalent throughout the Main Town right up until World War II, but unfortunately few others, save those on Długi Targ, have been rebuilt. Guarding the waterfront entrance to the street is the late fifteenth-century **St Mary's Gate**. Alongside it is a tall Renaissance mansion known as the House of the Scientists. This currently houses the **Archaeological Museum**, which specializes on the prehistory of the Gdansk region.

At the opposite end of ul. Mariacki is the gargantuan **St Mary's church**, the dominant landmark of the Main Town's skyline. This is reckoned to be the largest brick-built church in the world, one capable of accommodating a congregation of 25,000 — more than the entire population of the city during its Hanseatic heyday. In its size and austerity of appearance, it stands as a direct ecclesiastical counterpart to the contemporary castles of the Teutonic Knights. When work began in the 1340s, the intention was to construct a lofty but otherwise conventional basilica. A generation later, it was decided to convert this into a hall church. Nearly 130 years elapsed before the project, which pioneered the technique of building huge side chapels between the buttresses, finally reached completion in 1502. A really magnificent bird's-eye view over the church, the whole city centre and the famous dockyards can be enjoyed from the platform on top of the tower, amply rewarding the steep climb up via an old wooden stairway.

The large windows give St Mary's interior a bright and spacious feel, an effect accentuated by the whitewash which covers the walls and the intricate cellular and network vaults. Prior to World War II, the church was filled with works of art, but many of the altarpieces have been moved to the National Museum in the Old Suburb, or to its counterpart in Warsaw. Nonetheless, some valuable pieces remain, including the early fifteenth-century *Beautiful Madonna* in the third chapel of the north aisle; the slightly later Crucifixion group in the chapel of the Eleven Thousand Virgins to the right of the choir; the tall, tapering tabernacle from later the same century; the early sixteenth-century rood beam over the crossing; and the roughly contemporary high altar by Master Michael of Augsburg, which has a carved central panel of the Coronation of the Virgin and painted wings. Most conspicuous of all is the astronomical clock in the north transept, which was made in the 1460s by Hans Düringer. It showed not only the time, date and year, but also the phases of the sun and moon, the zodiacal cycle and the calendar of the saints. The organ, a fine Baroque instrument of the 1620s, was brought from the disused church of St John.

To the rear of St Mary's is the **Royal Chapel**, which was built between 1678, and 1681 under the patronage of King Jan Sobieski to provide a permanent place of worship for the local Roman Catholic minority in what was, from the onset of the Reformation until the explusion of the German population in 1945, a predominantly Protestant city. Sobieski's court archi-tect, the Dutch-born Tylman van Gameren, was responsible for the design, while the carved deocation was entrusted to a young local mason, Andreas Schlüter. In due course, the latter became the pre-eminent sculptor and architect of Northern European Baroque, but this is the only major building in this style in his native city.

The Royal Chapel faces ul. św. Ducha, whose waterfront side is protected by the reconstructed **Holy Ghost Gate**. A block further north is the mid-fifteenth century **Crane Gate**, a remarkable technical monument that has became something of a symbol of the city. Sturdy twin defensive towers flank the wooden crane, the largest ever built in medieval Europe. It was used for loading and unloading cargoes from ships docked in the harbour below, and was capable of hoisting up to 2,000kg at a time. Nowadays, it forms part of the **Maritime Museum**, and houses a material on the history of Polish shipping, as well as shells and corals from around the world. However, the exhibts are overshadowed by the interior mechanisms of the crane itself, and in particular the two giant wheels round which the hoisting rope was wound.

The rest of the museum is housed in three restored granaries on Ołowianka Island on the opposite side of the Motława. A complimentary ferry service shuttles between the two at regular intervals, though it is worth making at least one leg of the journey on foot, as the 10-minute walk via the Vat Tower offers some wonderful views of the waterfront. Within the spacious halls of the granaries are copious displays on all aspects of Poland's relationship with the sea from prehistoric times to the present day. Highlights include a dugout canoe from the Dark Ages and a number of perfectly preserved bronze cannon retrieved from the wrecks of seventeenth-century Swedish vessels which sank in the Bay of Gdańsk. Moored outside is the museum-ship *Sołdek*, the first freighter built in the city after World War II.

At number 54 on ul. Szeroka, the street leading to the Crane Gate, is the **House 'Under the Salmon'** (Pod Łososiem), nowadays Gdańsk's most elegant restaurant. The famous Goldwasser liqueur, so called because it has flakes of gold leaf floating in it, was first produced there in 1598. A block further north is ul. Świętojanska, which takes its name from the Gothic hall **church of St John**. This has a pronounced tilt, caused by the sinking of the foundations into the soggy ground beneath. It is no longer used for worship and has yet to be given an appropriate new role. Just to the east is **St John's**

Gate, which was remodelled in neo-Classical style at the turn of the nineteenth century.

Next in line along the waterfront is late fifteenth-century the **Stall Gate**, which differs from its counterparts in having a side wing. The set of coats-of-arms of Poland, Gdańsk and Royal Prussia is the oldest in the city. Further north is the slightly older **Swan Tower**, which overlooks the fish market, the Targ Ryby. A short distance west is the **Holy Ghost Hospital**, which was founded in the fourteenth century, but rebuilt on several occasions, latterly to serve as a school.

At the north-western edge of the Main Town is the late fourteenth-century **St Hyacinth's Tower**, which was an outlook post as well as part of the defences. Immediately to the south are the few surviving fragments of the **Castle of the Teutnonic Knights**, including a tower which has been converted into a house. Directly opposite, at the head of ul. Świętojanska, is the Dominican **church of St Nicholas**, which somehow came through World War II with only minimal damage. Although built in the severe form of Gothic favoured by the mendicant orders of friars, the exterior has some unexpected flourishes, such as the steep gables, the large blind arcades, the octagonal turret over the east end and the battlemented sacristy extension. Inside are some fine furnishings, including a limpid fifteenth-century Pietà in the nave, the Crucifixion group on the rood beam, and the Gothic choir stalls, whose Baroque backs are painted with New Testament scenes.

Three blocks south, facing down ul. Piwna to the east and the old coal market, the Targ Węglowy, to the west, is the **Great Arsenal**. The showiest of all the city's Netherlandish-inspired setpieces, it was built during the first half of the seventeenth century to plans by Anthonis van Opbergen. Most of the decoration is concentrated on the eastern façade, which has octagonal staircase towers, florid gables crowned with figures of soldiers, elaborate portals topped with armorial bearings, a pretty well-house which doubled as a lift for hoisting heavy ammunition, and a central niche with a statue of the goddess Pallas Athene. Nowadays, the ground floor serves as a shopping mall, while an art college occupies the upper storeys.

The Old Town

The **Old Town** (Stare Miasto) lies immediately beyond the northern range of the Main Town's fortification system. There seems to have been a settlement on the site as early as the tenth century; it was granted a charter in 1375, and functioned as a separate municipality until the Second Partition of 1793. For all but the early part of this period, it was a poor relation of its neighbour, the most obvious evidence of this being the lack of a town wall. Nonetheless, it was still imbued with the cosmopolitan imprint characteristic of the city as a whole, with clear German and Netherlandish influences. These are still evident, even although the post-war restoration has been far less assiduous and inventive than that of the Main Town.

Across the inner ring road from the m^c[ain railway station, a typical example of the Historicist architectural tastes of late nineteenth-century

Prussia, is the little Gothic **church of St Elizabeth**, which was erected around 1400 as part of a hospital complex, the rest of which was rebuilt in the mid-eighteenth century. To its rear is the Carmelite **church of St Joseph**, which has a beautiful star-vaulted late Gothic choir, though lack of funds meant that the nave was not added until the Baroque era. A few paces to the south, at number 3 on ul. Elżbietanska, is a Mannerist mansion fully worthy of comparison with those in the Main Town, especially as it survived the war intact. It was built by Abraham van den Block, probably for a wealthy burgher, but later became a town house for the abbots of the Cistercian monastery of Pelplin, which is described later in this chapter.

The house overlooks the **Radunia Canal**, which was dug in the mid-fourteenth century by the Teutonic Knights in order to service a series of industrial concerns they established along its banks. A little further along the canal is the **Town Hall** of the Old Town, designed at the end of the sixteenth century by Anthonis van Opbergen in the dignified Renaissance style of the Low Countries, as opposed to the ornate Mannerism he later employed for the Great Arsenal in the Main Town. The façade has the usual frieze of coats-of-arms of Poland, Gdańsk and Royal Prussia. A number of lapidary fragments from demolished buildings have been assembled in the interior, which is the headquarters of a cultural institute.

On the island beyond is the **Great Mill**, a unique piece of industrial architecture which ranks as the largest of its type in Europe. It is the only survivor of the enterprises established as the Teutonic Knights, and functioned without interrpution until 1945, the only major change in this period being the replacement in 1880 of its eighteen giant water wheels with turbines. As well as grinding flour, it served as a bakery, the chimney of this being visible above the east gable. Badly damaged during the war, it has been faithfully restored, albeit minus the machinery, and it is now occupied by shops and offices.

A little further to the east is **St Catherine's**, the parish church of the Old Town. Having been founded in the thirteenth century, it is also the oldest church in Gdańsk, though the present Gothic hall design is from the following two centuries. Outside, the most interesting feature is the east end, which has three elaborate gables of differing shape. Inside, some elements of the original fifteenth-century mural decoration have been preserved. The high altar has a painting of the Crucifixion by the local seventeenth-century artist Anton Moeller which incorporates a background view of Gdańsk. Also in the chancel is a monument to the great astronomer Johannes Hevelius, who is buried there along with other members of his family. The church's tower houses a carillon of thirty-seven bells, modern replacements for the celebrated set melted down during the war.

To the rear of St Catherine's is another Gothic church, dedicated to **St Bridget** and originally part of a convent. It is mainly of interest because of its prominent role in recent history: the parish priest, Henryk Jankowski, was a spiritual advisor to the Solidarity trade union, whose leader, the shipyard electrician Lech Wałęsa, regularly worshipped there prior to his election as the country's first post-Communist president in 1990. Several art works bear witness to the heady days of the alliance between Solidarity and the Catholic church, a combination which was ultimately responsible for the overthrow of Communism.

Another key monument from the city's not-so-distant past, the **Polish Post Office**, lies several blocks to the west on plac Obrońców. This mid-nineteenth century building, originally part of a garrison hospital, was allocated in 1925 to the Polish postal authorities in the Free City of Danzig. It was attacked by the Nazis on 1 September 1939, and thus saw some of the very first fighting of World War II, an event described in Günter Grass' famous novel *The Tin Drum*, the first of a trilogy set in his native city. A small memorial museum to the defenders, most of whom were either killed in the fighting or summarily executed afterwards, has been established inside; there are also general displays on postal and telecommunications history. There is also a commemorative monument on the square.

In the northernmost part of the Old Town are two more Gothic churches: **St Bartholomew's**, which is currently occupied by the Jesuits and has typical cellular and stellar vaulting; and **St James'**, a modest little building with an old timber ceiling. Just beyond the latter lie the vast **Gdańsk Shipyards**, which have operated continuously since the fourteenth century. In 1970, they were the scene of riots which toppled the longstanding government of Władysław Gomułka; 10 years later, they were the setting for the strikes which led to the birth of Solidarity. One immediate consequence of the latter was the erection of a monument to the thirty shipyard workers who were killed during the suppression of the earlier dispute. The first-ever memorial to the victims of a Communist state, it stands just outside the entrance to the shipyards on plac Solidarności.

The Old Suburb

The third main component of the historic core of Gdańsk is the **Old Suburb** (Stare Przedmieście), which grew up south of the Main Town in the late fourteenth and early fifteenth centuries. Unlike the Old Town, it had its own set of walls, though most traces of these had already disappeared by the seventeenth century, when the southern part of the district was endowed with a modern set of fortifications on the Italian model.

The old suburb is nowadays separated from the Main Town by a busy boulevard, Podwale Przedmieście. Overlooking this from the top end of ul. Lastadia is the city's finest nineteenth-century building, the former **Gymnasium**. This was designed by the great Berlin architect Karl Friedrich Schinkel, and in order to blend in with the city's other buildings is in his Romantic, mock-medieval manner, rather than in the neo-Classical style for which he is best known. A little to the south-west is **St Peter and St Paul**, the original parish church of the old suburb. Its massive tower provides the main focus of interest; the church served for several centuries as the main place of worship for the local Calvinist community, and therefore retains almost no historic furnishings of note.

Two blocks to the west is the former Franciscan **church of the Holy Trinity**. Apart from St Mary's, this is the most satisfying and inventive of the city's brick churches. It belongs to the last and most highly decorative period of the style, and has a particularly picturesque façade with three fantastical gables and a protruding chapel which pre-dates the church itself. Inside are several notable Gothic furnishings, including two winged altars, a font, a set of stalls and the oldest surviving pulpit in the city.

The adjoining monastic buildings now house the **National Museum**. Its star exhibit is the fabulously detailed *Last Judgment* triptych by Hans Memling, the earliest surviving work by the artist. It was painted in Bruges in the early 1470s for the Medici representative, Angelo Tani, who is portrayed opposite his wife on one of the outer wings. He shipped it to his native Florence, but it was captured en route by a caravel from Gdańsk and donated to the church of St Mary. Other highlights include the original statue of St George from St George's Court, an elaborate tiled stove from the Artus Court, several fine examples of the giant Baroque wardrobes which were the speciality of the city's cabinetmakers, and a collection of seventeenth-century Dutch and Flemish paintings.

South of the Franciscan monastery, at the end of ul. Rzeźnicka, is the **White Tower**, the most significant survivor of the old suburb's medieval fortifications. A short distance beyond is the **Little Arsenal**, built in the 1640s by the municipal architect, Jan Strakowski. At the southernmost end of the Old Suburb, the crumbling remnants of the seventeenth-century bastions can be seen. Among them stands the **Lowland Gate**, an earlier work by Strakowski, built in the form of a triumphal arch. To its east, bridging the artificial channel of the Motława, is the **Stone Lock**. The only one of its type in Poland, it regulated the flow of water to the moats all around

The Outskirts

After the riches of the city centre, the outskirts of Gdańsk cannot but seem very thin on sights. One obvious destination, however, is **Westerplatte**, which occupies a promontory overlooking the Bay of Gdańsk on the eastern bank of the Dead Vistula, 4 miles (7km) north of the city centre. Throughout the summer, several excursion boats run there every day from the wharf below the Green Gate, and this trip is well worth making in its own right, as it offers plenty of views of the shipyards and the sprawling port beyond.

The interest of Westerplatte itself is primarily historical, as it was the place where the very first shots of World War II were fired at daybreak on 1 September 1939. Hitler's demand that the Free City of Danzig, which was already under Nazi control, be incorporated into the German Reich served as his pretext for launching an all-out war on Poland, whose elimination and partition had already secretly been agreed with Stalin. The battleship *Schleswig-Holstein* was despatched to attack the garrison at Westerplatte, the part of the port which then lay under Polish jurisdiction. Although hopelessly outnumbered and possessing greatly inferior weapons, the defenders held out for 7 days, by which time the dispute had already grown into a European-wide war. In 1966, a typical Communist-era monument commemorating their heroism was raised on top of a 72ft (22m) high mound overlooking the river. One of the surviving barracks in the park to the east has been converted to house a small museum containing documentary material on the siege.

En route to Westerpatte, the excursion boats pass **Wisłoujście**, just over ¹/₂ mile (1km) to the south. This preserves a far more tangible survivor of the port's defences in the shape of the Fortress Wisłoujście, which is set on a small island in the Dead Vistula, linked to the mainland by a short causeway. It dates back to the fourteenth century, though the oldest significant surviving section is the tower, which was built in the 1480s to serve both as a lighthouse and for defensive purposes, and which can be climbed for a fine view over the port. The main ramparts were rebuilt in the early seventeenth century by Anthonis von Opbergen, using the system of protruding bastions that was then much in vogue.

By far the most attractive and worthwhile of Gdańsk's suburbs is **Oliwa**, which lies 6 miles (9km) north-west of the city centre. Although now densely populated and incorporating a number of large modern housing estates, the Cistercian monastic complex from which the settlement derives still stands within a landscaped park with ponds and formal gardens. The monastery was founded in 1186 under the patronage of Duke Sambor of Pomerelia, and settled by monks from Kołbacz near Szczecin. Despite being damaged in a variety of wars, fires and conflicts, it enjoyed a distinguished history, the highpoint being the signing in 1660 of the Peace of Oliwa, which brought to an end the long and costly wars between Poland and Sweden.

Although the monastery was secularized by the Prussians in 1831, the church, initially demoted to parish use, was given a new lease of life in 1925, when it was raised to the status of a cathedral. Most of the fabric dates from the fourteenth century, and is in an austere, unadorned Gothic style. The façade, however, was twice remodelled in the Baroque era, and now has a decorative central section sandwiched between the two towers, which are crowned with fancy lead steeples.

One curiosity of the interior is that its floor level is more than 3ft (1m) below that of the ground outside. The proportions of the building are also idiosyncratic: not only is it more than 10 times as long as it is broad, the southern aisle, in order to accommodate the cloister walk behind, is reduced to the dimensions of a narrow passageway. A sixteenth-century fire destroyed the vaults, which were rebuilt as extravagant late Gothic star shapes; the old furnishings were also lost, hence the profusion of Baroque replacements. Of these, the most notable are the illusionist high altar and the organ. The latter, probably the most famous instrument in Poland, is set in a dazzling Rococo case and equipped with mechanical angel musicians which can be activated by the organist to provide an accompaniment. It was begun in 1765 by Jan Wulf, and not finished until 25 years later, by which time the builder had taken monastic vows and assumed the name Brother Michael.

The River Motława waterfront in Gdańsk with the Crane Gate (Chapter 4)

The Sołdek museum-ship and the River Motława waterfront, Gdańsk (Chapter 4)

Horses and riders at the Imperial Stables of Kaiser Wilhelm II of Germany in Kadyny (Chapter 4)

The Grand Master's Palace in the Castle of the Teutonic Knights in Malbork (Chapter 4)

During the summer, there are recitals every week, while short demonstrations are held at least twice daily.

The handsome interiors of the eighteenth-century Abbots' Palace to the rear of the cathedral are home to the Modern Art Gallery, a branch of the National Museum in the Old Suburb. Directly opposite is the monastery granary, which now contains the Ethnographic Museum. This has displays of crafts and everyday objects from throughout the region.

Gdańsk's Zoo occupies a pretty hillside location, about $^1/_2$ mile (1km) east of the cathedral. In the far south of Oliwa, at the junction of ul. Abrahama and ul. Polanki, is the new mosque of the small local Tatar community. It is the first Muslim place of worship to have been erected in a Polish city, and is one of only three in the country, the others being the eighteenth-century wooden mosques in the Podlasian villages of Kruszyniany and Bohoniki, which are described in Chapter 6.

The Coast North of Gdańsk

The coast north of Gdańsk has a nicely contrasted choice of destinations, all of them within easy day excursion range of the city. **Sopot**, 7 miles (12km) to the north, has been one of Poland's most popular holiday resorts ever since Johann Georg Haffner, who had been a physician in Napoleon's army, first established bathing facilities there in 1823. The town's heyday as a meeting-place for the internationally rich and famous came during the era of the Free City of Danzig, of which it formed a part. During this period, it was equipped with a 1,679ft (512m) long pier, which is still the longest on the entire Baltic coast, and with the appropriately-named Grand Hotel, which maintains its reputation as classiest place to stay in the entire region.

Inevitably, Sopot went downmarket during the Communist era, and now has a somewhat dated feel. In recent years, there have been widespread fears about the effects of pollution on the sea water and the beach, though the scare stories do not seem to deter the crowds of summertime holidaymakers. During the month of August, Sopot assumes a cosmopolitan air for the Festival of Song. Performances take place in the Opera in the Woods (Opera Leśna) in the hilly western part of the resort. This amphitheatre was built in 1909 and modernised in the 1960s; it can seat 5,000 and has a folding roof in case of inclement weather.

Both Sopot and **Gdynia**, a further 6 miles (9km) north, are gradually merging with Gdańsk to form a single conurbation known as the Tri-City (Trojmiasto), though the latter is a major city in its own right, and Poland's largest port after Szczecin. Founded in medieval times, Gdynia was an insignificant fishing village right up until the early 1920s. Crucially, however, it lay within the narrow strip of coastline allocated to Poland by the victorious allies of World War I, and the new authorities decided to develop it as their major sea outlet. It duly grew by leaps and bounds, a process which continued apace after World War II.

For the most part, Gdynia is an ugly sprawl, but the harbour area contains a number of tourist attrctions. Among these are two museum-ships: the

Błyskawica, a destroyer which spent part of the war defending Cowes on the Isle of Wight; and the triple-masted *Dar Pomorza*, which was built in Hamburg in 1909 and served for over 50 years as the training vessel of the Polish merchant navy. On the quayside opposite is the Oceanographic Museum, which incorporates an aquarium, while just to the south its the Maritime Museum, which traces Poland's seafaring history from the Dark Ages to the present day. A fine view over the port can be had from the 171ft (52m) high Kamienna Góra (literally, 'Stone Mountain') to the east.

Jutting out from the coast north of Gdynia is a curious 21 miles (34km) long crescent-shaped sandbank known as **Hel Peninsula** (Mierzeja Helska). For most of its length, it is no more than 1,640ft (500m) wide: only towards its eastern tip does its width increase to 2 miles (3km). The peninsula was formed by sand thrown up by the wind and the sea, and it is only in the last few centuries that it has evolved into an uninterrupted stretch of land, with trees and other vegetation helping to ensure its continued stability. All along the northern coast are marvellous white sandy beaches; those in the immediate vicinity of the villages tend to get overrun with beachcombers, but the rest of the shore is remarkably unspoilt. The southern coastline, on the sheltered Bay of Puck, unfortunately suffers from the same pollution problems as Sopot.

Most visitors head for the fishing port of **Hel** at the southern end of the peninsula. Throughout the summer, steamers run there every day from Gdańsk, Sopot and Gdynia: the crossing takes about 2$^1/_2$ hours, and it is possible to return the same day. The journey can also be made by rail or bus, but only permit-holders can take private cars along the eastern part of the peninsula. Hel is probably as old as Gdańsk itself, but the geographical vagaries of its position always mitigated against its development, and the ban on cars has stifled the possibility of it developing into a major resort. It was able to hold out for over a month against the Nazis in 1939, and by the same token was also the last place in Poland to be liberated from them in 1945. On the main street are a number of quaint wooden fishermen's cottages from the nineteenth century. The former parish church, a fifteenth-century brick Gothic building with a wooden tower, now houses the Museum of Fishing. which includes an open-air section in the graveyard outside.

There are four other villages on the peninusula. Those immediately to the east of Hel, **Jurata** and **Jastarnia**, are quite lively resorts, whereas **Kuźnica** (situated at the narrowest point on the peninsla, with only 656ft (200m) of land separating the two coasts) and **Chałupy** are sleepier and more tradi-tional in feel. Accommodation is available in a fair number of holiday homes, private houses and campsites, but there are as yet no hotels.

The mainland gateway to the peninsula is **Władysławowo**, a somewhat larger port and holiday resort than those on Hel itself. About 5 miles (8km) west is Cape Rozewie, Poland's northernmost tip. A lighthouse was first built on its clifftop in the fifteenth century, and the late eighteenth-century successor to this can be ascended for a grandstand view over the coast.

Kashubia

Between the Gdańsk conurbation and Pomerania is an area known as **Kashubia** (Kaszuby), a land of forests, moraine hills and post-glacial lakes where a traditional rural lifestyle is still the norm, with no major industries and only a few modest-sized market towns. Like the Slovincians immediately to the west, the Kashubians resisted centuries of attempts at enforced Polonisation and Germanisation to preserve a very distinctive identity. However, in contrast to the Slovincians, they have kept their culture very much alive to the present day. This is most evident with regard to their language, which is still in everyday use throughout the region, particularly among the older generation, and is not readily intelligible to native Polish speakers. Local handicrafts, particularly weaving, pottery and basket-making, are still important to the economy, while a distinctive musical tradition also flourishes. Kashubia is very much off the beaten tourist track, though its few towns all have good transport links with Gdańsk, and most places described below are feasible half- or whole-day excursions from the city. Only a few buses penetrate the farther reaches, which really need to be explored by car.

Żukowo, just 12 miles (20km) west of Gdańsk, is centred on a Premonstratensian convent founded in 1209. The church was built in Gothic style during the following century, and was given a Baroque remodelling in the seventeenth century, when it also acquired many fine furnishings, including the high altar, the choir stalls and a nuns' gallery linked by a stairway to the pulpit. Several older works of art were retained, including the richly carved late Gothic triptych from Antwerp depicting scenes from the life of Christ.

A further 7 miles (12km) west is **Kartuzy**. Its name literally means Charterhouse, and from 1381 until 1826 the site was occupied by an isolated Carthusian monastery. Only after this was secularised by the Prussians did a town grow up, with the former monastic church being taken over for parish use. It is an imposingly large and spacious Gothic building, completed within a couple of decades of the arrival of the first monks from Bohemia. The Carthusians, the most austere of all monastic orders, were preoccupied by the concept of death, and reflected this in their choice of artistic motifs. Below the sundial is a representation of a skull inscribed *Memento Mori* (Remember Death), while the clock on the balustrade of the organ gallery has a pendulum in the shape of the grim reaper armed with a scythe. Most strikingly of all, the roof was replaced in the 1730s by an extraordinary new construction shaped like a coffin. However, the morbid air is far from being all-pervasive: the furnishings also include a carved and gilded fifteenth-century triptych in the south chapel, a set of early Baroque stalls in the nave and some unusual stamped leather decoration in the chancel.

Alongside the church there were formerly 18 hermitages, where each monk lived in solitude, but only one of these remains; opposite it is the refectory, the only other surviving part of the original complex. A short walk to the north is the Monastery Lake, surrounded by a beechwood forest. South of the town centre is the Kashubian Museum, with exhibits ranging over all aspects of local culture, including agricultural implements, applied arts and crafts, costumes, furniture and musical instruments.

Just to the east of Kartuzy is the **Kashubian Landscape Park** (Kaszubski Park Krajobrazowy), which was set up to provide protection for some of the finest scenery in the region. Control is far less strict than in a national park, so the area has undergone a certain amount of development, and is well equipped with holiday homes. The main base is **Chmielno**, a sailing and canoeing centre on Lake Radunia. At the northern end of the park is **Mirachowo**, which preserves many characteristically Kashubian half-timbered houses.

Some of the best examples of the regional vernacular architecture have been collected together in the Kashubian Ethnographic Park in **Wdzydze Kiszewskie**, which lies about 31 miles (50km) south-west of Kartuzy via the other Main Town of central Kashubia, Kościerzyna. This is the oldest *skansen* in Poland, founded by a local schoolmaster in 1906, and it remains one of the best, if not the largest, in the country, given added appeal by its peaceful lakeside setting. The main exhibit is an eighteenth-century wooden church brought from the village of Swornigacie, which has charming folk decoration inside, including a stylized depiction on the ceiling of the all-seeing eye of God. Other buildings include a school, a windmill, a sawmill, a manor house and several thatched cottages and barns.

At the extreme end of Kashubia, another 31 miles (50km) south-east of Wdzydze Kiszewskie, is **Chojnice**, which makes an obvious stopping-point for those wishing to travel on to the Pomeranian Lake District. The town, which has considerably more bustle than those in central Kashubia, was the westernmost outpost of the Teutonic Knights, and preserves a few medieval monuments as reminders of the period. Of these, the most impressive is the five-storey Człuchowska Gate. This now contains the Regional Museum, which has displays on local history and ethnography. Fragments of the walls which enclosed the Old Town can be seen outside; the monuments within their perimeter include the fourteenth-century parish church and the seventeenth-century Jesuit church and college.

The Vistula Lagoon and Vistula Spit

Before the Vistula flows into the Baltic, it forms an marshy delta with two main channels. The eastern of these, known as the River Nogat, connects with the vast **Vistula Lagoon** (Zalew Wiślany), which stretches 43 miles (70km) eastwards to the Russian city of Kaliningrad, as the former East Prussian capital of Königsberg is now known. Across the water from the city is the lagoon's only outlet to the Baltic. The lagoon is otherwise separated from the sea by a narrow sandbar, which is generally around 1 mile (2km) wide. Together with the coastal headland to the west, this is known as the **Vistula Spit** (Mierzeja Wiślana), and is under permanent protection as a landscapse park. It was formed immediately after the last Ice Age from a mixture of sand drifts thrown up by the wind and coastal currents and silt deposits from the river. Until the late eighteenth century, there were shifting dunes similar to those which can still be seen in the Slovincian National Park in Pomerania, and these buried many buildings and even whole villages. They were successfully stabilised by extensive tree plantations, mainly of pines, and these now cover a quarter of the whole area.

Coming from Gdańsk, the main course of the Vistula is crossed at **Świbno**, which is linked by an old-fashioned chained car ferry to **Mikoszewo**, the westernmost village on the Vistula Spit. The area between the two villages and the river mouth has been designated the Mewia Łacha Nature Reserve, and is an important breeding ground and migratory resting place for various species of tern. These can best be observed, albeit from a distance, around Lake Mikoszewskie, which can be reached by various footpaths from Mikoszewo. This reed-strewn lake, formed by marsh and flood waters and separated from the sea by a terminal dune, is also the habitat of gulls, grebes, ducks and cormorants.

The first important holiday resort on the spit is **Stegna**, 7 miles (11km) east of Mikoszewo, which falls into two clearly defined parts, with the beach and fishing port lying about $1/2$ mile (1km) north of the village centre. At the eastern edge of the latter is the parish church, a striking half-timbered construction of the 1680s. It has rustic Baroque decoration from the same period, including a painted ceiling and a pulpit, as well as an organ from the following century which is regularly used for recitals during the summer.

Stegna is also the hub of a T-shaped network of narrow-gauge railways. These lines helped open up the Vistula Spit in the early years of the century, but are now kept in service for tourist purposes only, operating from June to September inclusive. They have rather a toytown feel, but are a good way of seeing the countryside at a sedate pace. Passengers can opt to travel in either enclosed or open-sided carriages, which may be pulled either by diesels or steam trains. One line goes all the way across the headland, its western terminus being in open countryside midway between the built-up part of Mikoszewo and the car ferry; the other links up with the mainline railway at Nowy Dwór Gdański, 7 miles (12km) south of Stegna on the main road between Gdańsk and Elbląg.

The eastern terminus of the headland line is **Sztutowo**, 2 miles (4km) beyond Stegna. This village first came into existence as a stud farm of the Teutonic Knights, but its name, at least in its German form of Stutthof, is synonymous with the concentration camp at the western fringe of the village. It was set up by the Nazi authorities of the Free City of Danzig just before war broke out, the first prisoners being 'undesirable' Polish elements rounded up on the first day of hostilities. In 1944, the original camp was greatly expanded in order that it could be used for the extermination of Jews, though it never became one of the major death factories. Stutthof operated until virtually the end of the war, by which time an estimated 65,000 prisoners had lost their lives. Much of it was demolished by the Soviet soldiers who liberated it, though a fair amount survives, including the administration buildings and some prisoners' barracks near the entrance — which contain displays on the camp's history — and the gas chambers and crematorium at the far end of the complex.

Kąty Rybackie, a further 2 miles (3km) east, is a small port at the north-eastern end of the Vistula Lagoon founded by a group of fisherfolk in the eighteenth century in the vicinity of a manor house of an English merchant. Tucked away in the woods 1 mile (2km) north-west is Europe's largest cormorant reserve. Although poorly signposted, it is fairly easy to locate, as the birds themselves are directly responsible for creating a desolate pocket landscape of bare trees and barren vegetation within the otherwise luxuriant forest. The best time to visit is during the summer: the cormorants nest, often several to a tree, in May and June, hatching the eggs a month later, and flying away to sunnier climes in the autumn.

Krynica Morska, 10 miles (16km) along the sandbar, is one of Poland's leading beach resorts. It was first developed in the 1820s as a rather exclusive destination. None of the Grecian-style villas from this period survive, though there are several examples of the second generation of holiday homes, hybrid constructions with elements copied from Swiss chalets and traditional fishermen's cottages. The classiest of these are on ul. Robotników, in the north of the village, just before the beach; the others are on ul. Gdańska and ul. Rybacka, which both overlook the harbour on the Vistula Lagoon. After World War I, the resort began to cater to a wider audience, and is now of a mixed character, with a yachting marina counter-ing the downmarket tendencies evident elsewhere.

In summer, steamers run across the Vistula Lagoon, linking Krynica Morska with both Frombork, which is described in the following chapter, and **Elbląg**, which lies 40 miles (65km) south-east of Gdańsk by road or rail. The latter was established by the Teutonic Knights in 1237 as their first port. At that time, it lay directly on the lagoon shore, which has since retreated dramatically as a result of silting. Nonetheless, the city prospered as a member of the Hanseatic League, developing particularly strong ties with England. Like Gdańsk, it became to all intents and purposes an independent city-state after Royal Prussia came under Polish jurisdiction in 1466. When it was fully integrated into Poland for the first time in 1945, it was in a sorry state, its Old Town having been all but totally destroyed by the Red Army. The Communists left this as a wasteland surrounded by modern suburbs, but in 1991 a programme of re-creating the pre-war appearance of the quarter was begun, inspired by the success of similarly belated rebuilding schemes in Germany. Work on this is likely to continue for many years yet.

The Old Town's skyline is dominated by the tall tower of the Gothic church of St Nicholas, one of the few historic buildings in Elbląg which was restored imediately after the war. It has recently been promoted to the status of the cathedral of the revived diocese of Pomesania, one of the four bishoprics founded by the Teutonic Knights. The streets to the south, ul. Mostowa and ul. św. Ducha, are now lined with accurate reproductions of the old mansions which formerly stood there, while at the western end of the latter is a reconstruction of the thirteenth-century Hospital of the Holy Ghost. A little further south via the waterside promenade are the surviving parts of the Castle of the Teutonic Knights, including a granary which now houses the local museum. In addition to archaeological and historical artefacts, this has a large display of old photographs of the city. At the northern end of the Old Town is the deconsecrated Dominican church of St Mary, now a gallery of modern art. The adjoining cloister walk is lined with epitaphs, some of which are to English merchants. To the rear is the Market Gate, the only surviving part of the medieval fortifications.

The wharf between the cathedral and St Mary's is the departure point for the summer cruises which are the principal reasons for Elbląg's increasing popularity with tourists, particularly Germans. In addition to the sailings to Krynica Morska, there are regular trips along the famous Elbląg-Ostróda Canal, a journey described in detail in the following chapter, and to Kaliningrad, for which a visa, obtainable on the spot, is required.

Kadyny, 11 miles (18km) north-west of Elbląg on the road and railway lines to Frombork, was a favourite summer residence of Kaiser Wilhelm II of Germany. His Royal Palace stands forlorn and semi-derelict in the centre of the village, and may be beyond meaningful repair. However, the ancillary buildings to the rear were converted into a luxury hotel a few years back, with the old distillery, easily recongnisable from its chimney, serving as its restaurant. The hotel is principally geared to visitors wishing to avail themselves of the facilities of the adjoining stables and stud farm, which were once the personal property of the Kaiser but are now open to all, with some 160 horses available for hire.

The Route of the Teutonic Knights

One of the most fascinating touring routes in Poland is that between Elbląg and Toruń. This passes through a string of small and medium-sized towns which between them preserve some of the greatest medieval monuments to be seen in the country. Most of these are intimately associated with the Teutonic Knights, whose indelible imprint on the face of the region remains obvious, even although more than half a millennium has elapsed since their rule over it was ended.

Malbork, which lies 22 miles (35km) south-west of Elbląg, was founded by the Knights in around 1274 under the name of Marienburg, which literally means Fortress of St Mary. It was intended from the outset to be the monastic headquarters of the Order, but the acquistion of Pomerelia in 1308 recommended it, on account of its central position within the Knights' ever-expanding territories, for the much grander role of capital of their theocratic state. A year later, the Grand Master moved his residence there from Venice, and a flurry of construction work was undertaken, which continued for most of the rest of the century. The result is the largest, most magnificent and most architecturally innovative castle built during the European Middle Ages, though it is hardly adequate to characterise it as a mere castle, as there are three separate but interconnected fortresses, which together contain a host of buildings whose diverse functions reflect the mixed military, religious and political facets of the Order. The castle is far larger than many medieval towns; indeed, it completely dwarfs the municipality alongside, which was chartered in 1276 and later enclosed within its own set of walls.

While Malbork Castle is rightly regarded as one of Poland's supreme tourist attractions, the irony is that, far from being Polish, it was the main bulwark of the Teutonic state in its ever more bitter rivalry with Poland. What is perhaps surprising, given its awesome size, is how short-lived, in a relative sense, this role was. Although the Poles failed to take the castle in the immediate aftermath of their stunning victory at Grunwald in 1410, they managed to capture it in 1457, in what were still the early stages of the Thirteen Years' War. Thereafter, the Knights moved their base to Königsberg, while Malbork served as the seat of the legislature and regional administrator of Royal Prussia, as well as an occasional residence for Polish kings. After it passed back into German hands in 1772, it initially looked set for demolition and replacement by a more modern fortress. Thankfully, it was saved by the Romantic infatuation with all things medieval, and was given a thorough, indeed slightly over-enthusiastic, restoration. It sustained a certain amount of damage in World War II, but nonetheless survives in quite remarkably complete shape. Because of its sheer size, restoration work is an ongoing process, so at any time at least part of the complex is likely to be closed to visitors.

By far the best view is from the opposite side of the River Nogat: this shows the distinctive and contrasting bulks of the Middle and Upper Castles rising high behind the waterfront wall, the outermost of a set of three, which is guarded by the most formidable of the gateways, the twin-towered Bridge Gate. This scene is particularly memorable in the late afternoon, as the setting sun deepens the colours of the brickwork and casts long shadows over the water.

The largest part of the whole complex is the Lower Castle, which was built to the north and east of the two existing parts in order to provide extra protection and to cater for a variety of utilitarian functions. It is also the least prepossessing and least well-preserved part, and is now virtually contiguous with the Old Town. Most visitors overlook it altogether, though it is definitely well worth walking around it, if only for the sake of the views, particularly along the eastern side, which offers the inland counterpart to that from across the Nogat. From the south, the buildings lining its perimeter wall are the Bakery Tower, the residence of the manual workers, the High Gate, the combined Arsenal and Coach House, the Powder Tower, the Hexagonal Tower and the Octagonal Tower. Facing the Arsenal across the courtyard is a long block which formerly contained St Lawrence's chapel, an infirmary and storerooms. All of this has recently been converted into a luxury hotel, with the chapel serving as its restaurant. Further north are the interconnected Blunt Tower and the Buttermilk Tower. Before visiting the rest of the complex, entrance tickets have to be obtained from the booth adjoining the Arsenal.

The Middle Castle, which served the affairs of state, is entered via a reconstructed covered wooden bridge, which leads directly into the courtyard, where *son et lumière* performances are held throughout the summer. To the right of the gateway is the original infirmary, whose magnificent gabled façade is linked by a sentry walk to the Henfoot Tower, which has a picturesque half-timbered upper storey. The wing on the opposite side of the entrance gateway was the residence of the commandant. Running south of the latter is a rather plain long construction whose lower storey was used as cellars, while the upper served as the guest house for visiting dignatries. This wing now contains a number of permanent exhibitions, including what is claimed to be the world's largest collection of amber, a key commodity in the trade along the Vistula since Roman times. The displays range from uncut specimens of the mineral, via lumps with insects or plants preserved inside, to jewellery and objets d'art from ancient times from the present day, the most beautiful piece being a cabinet made for King Stanisław Poniatowski.

On the opposite side of the courtyard is the Knights' Hall or Great Refectory, which was reserved for the most splendid state occasions. Nowadays, it displays a splendid array of medieval arms and armour. Its spectacular ribbed vault rests on slender marble columns with delicately carved capitals; the walls were formerly covered with murals, but of these only *The Coronation of the Virgin* survives.

Adjoining this to the south is the Grand Master's Palace, the most splendid and original part of the whole complex. It probably dates from the last quarter of the fourteenth century, and was built by an architect of rare genius, who is generally assumed to be a Rhinelander named Nicolaus Fellensteyn. The turrets and battlements are of such refined craftsmanship that it seems certain they were employed for decorative effect, though they look formidable from afar. Inside, all kinds of architectural tricks are employed to create unexpected effects of light and shade, some of them almost Oriental in their patterns and texture. These reach a climax in the Winter Refectory, the similar but slightly larger Summer Refectory, and the passageway linking the two. Likewise on the first floor are the private apartments of the Grand Master, including the living room, which has floral decoration on its vault and trompe l'oeil paintings of curtains on its walls. The ground floor rooms served as the state chancellery.

A high wooden bridge leads to the Upper Castle, the oldest part of the complex. It is entered via a gatehouse and passageway set at a sharp diagonal to the courtyard beyond, in the middle of which stands a well with a wooden canopy. This courtyard can more accurately be described as a cloister, as the upper castle is essentially a fortified monastery which served as the spiritual heart of the Teutonic state. The undercroft of the two-tiered church is dedicated to St Anne. It served as the burial chapel of the Grand Masters and has a beautiful portal illustrating the Legend of the Cross. Perched above it is the church of St Mary, an archetypal High Gothic design entered via the Golden Gateway, which takes its name from its gilded statues of the Wise and Foolish Virgins. To the west is the Chapter House, where the Grand

Masters were elected. From there, it is possible to take a guided tour up the 216ft (66m) high tower, which commands a sweeping view over Malbork and the Vistula.

The west wing of the cloister has the conventual bakery and kitchens on the ground floor and the treasury upstairs, while the east and south wings have storerooms on the ground floor and the Knight' dormitories above. These now house yet more permanent exhibitions, including a fine collection of medieval sacred art. On the second floor, the Knights' Refectory, a graceful large hall, has displays on the castle's relationship with Poland. From the south-western corner of the Upper Castle, an arched walkway leads to the Dansker, a latrine tower. This curious architectural arrangement is a recurrent feature of Teutonic castles, and is thought to be a direct consequence of an obsession with cleanliness acquired during the Order's early years in the Holy Land.

Malbork's Old Town was devastated in World War II, and replaced in the 1960s with a residental quarter of standard modern apartment blocks, though a few notable monuments survive among the concrete. Just to the south of the castle is the hall church of St John, which was rebuilt soon after the departure of the Teutonic Knights. Its proportions are unusual, being both very broad and rather squat, and the same applies to the tower, which has a wooden superstructure. A little further south is the Town Hall, a perky little late fourteenth-century building with fine decorative details. Two gateways, the Potters' Gate and St Mary's Gate, can be seen to the east and south, while a section of the town wall survives along the waterfront.

From Malbork, one option is to continue directly southwards to Kwidzyn, which is described in the next chapter; the alternative is to travel southwards via the left bank of the Vistula. **Tczew**, which is 12 miles (20km) west of Malbork, is the last significant town on the main channel of the river, which is forded by an 2,912ft (890m) long trussed iron bridge, Europe's largest at the time of its opening in 1857. Nowadays Tczew is an industrial town, with only a few reminders of its medieval past. These include the thirteenth-century Dominican church, which has a monumental west porch with an off-centre turret; the largely fourteenth-century parish church, which has predominantly Baroque decoration; and a fragment of the walls.

Some 12 miles (20km) south, on the banks of the Wierzyca, a Vistula tributary, is **Pelplin**, an unassuming small town which nonetheless posseses, in its former Cistercian monastery, one of the greatest masterpieces of European brickwork, a worthy ecclesiastical counterpart to Malbork Castle. The site was settled in 1276 by monks from Doberan in northern Germany, at the invitation of successive Dukes of Pomerelia, and building work began shortly afterwards. Monastic life continued until its suppression by the Prussian authorities in 1823. Just one year afterwards, the church was given a new lease of life as the cathedral of the recently-expanded Chełmno diocese, while the monastic buildings subsequently became a seminary.

The cathedral, which since 1992 has been the headquarters of the new bishopric of Pelplin, looks as solid and formidable as any of the Teutonic castles, and its imposing length and height both create an immediate impression. Exterior decoration is confined to the gables above the main window and flanking octagonal turrets of the façade, and to the south doorway, which preserves a few medieval carvings as well as a nineteenth-century tympanum. The majestic interior possesses some of the most spectacular vaults ever built, forming a virtual encyclopaedia of the various forms used during the Gothic period. Tierceron vaulting — a standard feature of English cathedrals, but seldom encountered elsewhere — covers the aises. Various stellar shapes, which become progressively more elabo-rate towards the west, are to be seen above the nave and choir. Best of all is the extravagant sixteenth-century vaulting of the two transepts, which were perhaps added as afterthoughts: each rests on a single central pillar, which sprouts into cellular shapes on the north side, and a network pattern to the south. The latter transept is particularly idiosyncratic, as it uses the north-east corner of the cloister as its lower storey and support for the organ gallery above.

Of the cathedral's original Gothic furnishings, only the stalls survive. Sections of these can be seen in the end bays of the nave aisles and in the north transept, as well as in the choir. Their carvings illustrate a complicated iconographic programme, and include several unorthodox representations: the Holy Ghost, for example, is depicted as a youth holding a dove, while the Crucifixion scene shows Christ being crucified by three female figures representing the Virtues. The late Renaissance high altar is 85ft (26m) in height, making it the tallest in Poland. Its central panel of *The Coronation of the Virgin*, by the Silesian painter Hermann Hahn, is a Counter-Reforma-tion allegory which incorporates portraits of leading personalities of the day. Hahn also painted the altar at the extreme south-east corner of the church, which has a main panel of *The Assumption* and a beautiful nocturnal *Adoration of the Shepherds*. Other altarpieces of note are those dedicated to St James in the south choir aisle, which was painted by Bartholomäus Strobel, the most accomplished Polish-based painter of the seventeenth century, and to St Philip in the north choir aisle by the Gdańsk artist Andreas Stech, whose scene of *The Conversion of the Egyptian Chamberlain* is based on an engraving by Rembrandt.

In order to visit the cathedral, it is usually necessary to go first to the seminary for a guide. Many of the students speak English, and are pleased to show visitors around other parts of the former monastery, such as the cloisters, the chapter house, the summer and winter refectories and the library. The last of these is among the richest in Poland, with the only copy of the Gutenberg Bible in the country. Across the road from the cathedral are the only other historic buildings in the town: the pretty little brick Gothic parish church, and the neo-Classical Bishop's Palace.

Gniew, which has an exhilarating position high above the confluence of the Wierzyca with the Vistula 7 miles (12km) south, was originally the property of the Cistercians of Pelplin. However, the Teutonic Knights staked a claim to the town in 1276, and quickly established overall control.

Although not among the largest, the castle they constructed soon afterwards proved to be one of the most strategically important they ever built: it was the last to capitulate during the Thirteen Years' War, and its capture quickly led to an end to the conflict, and the departure of the Knights from the western half of their realm. The castle is built to a square groundplan, with slim corner towers and a more substantial keep at the north-east corner. All the historic interiors were destroyed in a fire in 1921, though the main fabric of the building has since been restored.

Perched directly above the Vistula escarpment alongside the castle is the so-called Marysieńka Palace, which is now a hotel and conference centre. According to tradition, it was built by the future King Jan Sobieski, in his capacity as sub-prefect of Gniew, as a present for his wife. However, it is probable that this building was later destroyed, and the one which bears its name is in reality a converted granary. On the other side of the castle, the regular chessboard pattern of streets of Gniew's miniature Old Town can still be seen. The Rynek is still lined with some imposing mansions, though these are all Baroque or neo-Classical remodellings of the medieval originals. Just off the square is the fourteenth-century church of St Nicholas, a typical example of the Gothic brickwork of the region.

From the marshy meadows beside the Vistula there is a fine view of the town's skyline. The river itself is forded by a decrepit chain ferry which carries cars and pedestrians to the other bank without charge. Another ferry operates 18km south, but its operation is sometimes curtailed when water levels become too high. Either of these offer drivers an easy route to Kwidzyn, a journey that cannot be made directly by public transport.

Grudziądz, the next former Teutonic stronghold, lies about 31 miles (50km) up the Vistula from Gniew, or 22 miles (35km) south-west of Kwidzyn. Nowadays it is a large industrial centre with ugly modern suburbs, but its Old Town, despite the loss of many significant monuments down the centuries, nonetheless has one of the most arresting and distinctive skylines in Poland. It is seen to most dramatic effect from the west bank of the river, north of the road bridge. However, this is a long walk or drive from the city centre, and the view is only marginally less impressive from the grassy eastern bank.

The picture is dominated by a row of multi-storey fortified granaries, an intact ensemble which is broken only by the stairway giving pedestrian access to the streets behind. These granaries are the most potent surviving evidence of the importance of the Vistula grain trade in medieval times; they served not only as storerooms but also as the western bulwark of the town's defences. They were built between the fourteenth and sixteenth centuries, though have been subject to subsequent remodellings, with many converted into houses in the eighteenth century.

At the southern end of the row of granaries is the Water Gate, the only one of the fourteenth-centuries gateways to have survived. Immediately to the right is the former Benedectine convent, a Baroque complex which is now home to the paintings and decorative arts sections of the local museum. The archaeological and local history collections are housed in two granaries which lie diagonally opposite. A couple of blocks to the north is the Rynek, whose buildings are mostly nineteenth-century, an exception being the sixteenth-century Swan Pharmacy (number 20).

Just to the west is the church of St Nicholas, a typical if rather heavily restored example of Gothic brickwork. To its rear is the bulky former Jesuit college, which now houses the offices of the municipal administration. The Jesuit church alongside has far more ornate decoration than is normal for this order, including some unexpected Chinoisserie under the organ gallery. Further north is Castle Hill, which is now a shady promenade. A modern obelisk marks the site of the Teutonic Knights' castle, which fell into ruin in the eighteenth century and was razed altogether in 1801. The magnificent Gothic polyptych which hung in its chapel still survives, however, and can be seen in the National Museum in Warsaw.

From Grudziądz, it is worth making an 11 miles (18km) detour to the south-east to the now insignificant village of **Radzyń Chełmski**, which preserves the substantial ruins of a Teutonic castle. Originally, it must have been similar in appearance to its smaller and older counterpart in Gniew, with corner turrets and a keep at the north-east end. The parish church also dates back to the time of the Knights; its main features are the elaborate gabled façade, the single massive tower, and the unconventional flat ceiling covering the interior.

Chełmno, 25 miles (40km) south-east of Grudziądz, is the best-pre-served example of a small medieval town to be seen anywhere in Poland, and is fully worthy of comparison with more famous counterparts elswhere in Europe, such as Carcassonne in France or Avila in Spain. The original Mazovian settlement, a missionary outpost against the heathen Prussians, lay directly on the Vistula, but the risk of flooding led the Teutonic Knights, who Germanised its name to Kulm, to relocate it to its present position on a hilltop about 1 mile (1¹/₂km) back from the river. It was chartered in 1233, soon after Toruń had become the first town in the Knights' territory to receive this honour, and laid out on a chequer plan.

The town's heyday came in the following century, when it grew rich from trade, and all but one of its major buildings, which include a virtually complete set of walls and six brick Gothic churches, date from this time, making it a truly remarkable period piece. However, its setting away from the river mitigated against its economic development, and it went into irreversible decline. By the time it was annexed by Frederick the Great's Prussia in the First Partition of 1772, only one in eight of its bouses was occupied. Although it has recovered a little in the past two centuries, it is no more than a modest-sized county town whose medieval showpieces — which have come through the wars which have wracked the region relatively unscathed — seem highly exaggerated in relation to its present size.

The walls, which are rivalled for completeness only by those of Paczków in Silesia, stretch for a total length of over 1 mile (2km), and it is possible to walk all the way round them, except for a short section to the north-west which is perched over a sheer drop. A total of seventeen towers and bastions survive, but only one gateway, the Grudziądz Gate on the east side. A chapel was appended to this in the early seventeenth century, together with a niche bearing a sculpture of the Pietà. Private cars have to be left at the car park outside, as the Old Town is pedestrianised.

In the middle of the central Rynek is the Town Hall, a gleaming white building in a playful late Renaissance style which was erected during a brief upturn in the town's prosperity in the second half of the sixteenth century. Although it seems a total anomaly in this otherwise very sober Gothic town, it is a beautiful design in its own right. The decoration on the two lower floors is confined to door and window frames, but the third storey has a highly mannered Ionic frieze, while the roofline erupts into a fantastical array of scrollwork and finials. A two-tier lantern was added to the plain clocktower in the 1720s. The Regional Museum housed inside is devoted to the history of Chełmno and the surrounding countryside, though the interiors them-selves are of more interest than the exhibits.

Off the south-western corner of the Rynek is St Mary's, the town's parish church, and the only one of the first generation of Gothic churches built in the region to have survived without major alteration. It is built at a sharp diagonal line to the street, an ingenious solution which not only means that the chancel is orientated precisely towards the east, but also enables the whole of the massive façade to be seen in one glance. Although only one of the two towers reached its intended height, it is still an impressive sight. The same is true of the long elevations of the church, each aisle of which has its own saddleback roof. Inside, the plain rib vault rests on slender octagonal pillars, some of which bear expressively carved fourteenth-century statues of the Apostles. A number of Gothic frescos have also survived, while the furnishings include a Romanesque font made of Gotland stone and a much-venerated seventeenth-century painting, *Our Lady of Chełmno*.

At the north-western edge of the town, built right up against the forifications, is the Sisters of Mercy convent. The conventual buildings, which serve as a hospital for the handicapped, are in the bloated Historicist style of nineteenth-century Prussia. However the church behind, which is dedicated to St John the Baptist and St John the Evangelist, is authentically medieval and has an unusual and highly distinctive design, lacking aisles but having a large overhanging gallery. Most of the furnishings, including the choir stalls, the organ and the altars, are late Renaissance in style, but there is also a tomb slab made in 1275 for a burgher named Arnold Lieshorn, who is depicted with an abbess serving as his intercessor.

Chełmno's other four churches are only used for worship periodically and in rotation. It is therefore not easy to gain access to them, though it is still worth seeing them from the outside. Immediately in front of the convent is the former Franciscan church of St James, which has richly ornamented gables at either end, a pretty turret and an eccentrically-designed nave whose middle bay is wider and taller than those flanking it. Its Dominican counterpart at the north-eastern end of town, dedicated to St Peter and St

Paul, is chiefly remarkable for its imposing façade, and in particular for the fine brickwork of its outsized gable. In the southern part of town are St Martin's, a tiny box-like church with two gables, and the former hospital church of the Holy Ghost, which has a dignified tall tower.

Chełmno was chosen as the seat of one of the four bishoprics established by the Teutonic Knights in association with the Archbishopic of Riga, an alliance which ensured they were free from the control of the Primates of Poland. Curiously, the cathedral was not built in Chełmno itself, but in a little lakeside village subsequently rechristened **Chełmża**, 14 miles (23km) to the south. The choir and transepts were begun in Romanesque style, but the bulk of the building is Gothic, the main external features being the gable over the east end, and the four towers, only one of which was completed. Of the furnishings, pride of place goes to the red marble tomb of Bishop Kostka, which was probably made by one of the Italian Renaissance sculptors of Cracow. In 1823, the cathedral was demoted to the status of a parish church when the bishops moved their base to Pelplin, and Chełmża has languished in provincial obscurity ever since.

Some 22 miles (35km) east, and a similar distance south of Radzyń Chełmski, is **Golub-Dobrzyń**, a double town straddling a bend on the Drwęca, a Vistula tributary. The castle was built by the Teutonic Knights at the beginning of the fourteenth century to a square groundplan around a central courtyard, and a century later buttressed with two great round towers, one of which survives. In the early seventeenth century, it came into the possession of Anna Waza, the sister of King Zygmunt Waza, who had it transformed into a splendid Renaissance palace. Nonetheless, many Gothic interiors are preserved, and these now house the Regional Museum. The highlight is the star-vaulted chapel, which contains a collection of cannon and copies of the standards carried at the Battle of Grunwald. Another part of the castle has been converted into a hotel, and a mock-medieval tournament is held in the grounds in mid-July each year. Golub's other notable monument is the fourteenth-century church of St Catherine, which has a number of wall paintings from the same period.

Toruń

Toruń, located on the banks of the Vistula 12 miles (20km) south of Chełmża, is, after Cracow, the best-preserved large city in Poland. Its rapid rise to prominence in the early Middle Ages was a direct consequence of the arrival of the Teutonic Knights in Chełmno county in 1226: it lay at the extreme southern end of their fiefdom, and they set about developing the small existing settlement into a major fortress and trading centre. A municipal charter was granted as early as 1233; another followed in 1264 for the New Town which grew up immediately to the north-east, and by around 1280 Toruń had become an active member of the Hanseatic League. By the fifteenth century, the local citizens had become rich and powerful enough to challenge the rule of the Knights, playing a leading role in the Thirteen Years' War which culminated in the Peace of Toruń of 1466, which saw the partition of the Order's territories, with Royal Prussia coming directly under the protection of the Polish crown. Like Elbląg, Torun functioned as a quasi-autonomous city-state until annexed by Prussia in the Second Partition of 1793. Largely spared from destruction since the seventeenth-century Swedish wars, it followed a steady growth pattern, and therefore has plenty of grand nineteenth-century buildings in the centre as well as rings of modern industrial and residential suburbs.

Much the best way to approach the city is from the south: the road bridge over the Vistula offers a marvellous panoramic view of the Old Town. The waterfront stretch of the medieval walls survives virtually intact, and a promenade has been laid out along the narrow strip of land separating it from the sandy bank of the river. At the western end is the 49ft (15m) high Leaning Tower, which now stands 5ft (1.4m) out of true as a result of having been built on insecure foundations on marshy ground. Next in line is the Monastery Gate, which is named after the now-vanished Monastery of the Holy Ghost which stood behind. Its lower storey dates back to the fourteenth century and is thus one of the oldest surviving parts of the fortifications. The upper section was added the following century and, like the Leaning Tower, has been converted into a residence. Further along are the plain Sailors' Gate, which gives access to the very heart of the city, and the much grander Bridge Gate, named after the medieval bridge it originally guarded.

Further east is a double set of fortifications protecting the Castle of the Teutonic Knights. This was once among the most imposing of their strongholds, but has been a ruin since 1454, when most of it was sacked by the local townsfolk. The most significant surviving part is the Dansker, the latrine tower at the extreme eastern end of the complex, which is linked to the main buildings by a bridgeway over what was formerly a stream. Elsewhere, only the lower parts of the walls and the cellars survive; the latter now house an exhibition on the castle's history. Towards the top end of ul. Podmurna, the street running northwards from the western side of the castle, is the octagonal Monstrance Tower, the sole relic of the other three sides of the municipal fortifications.

In the very heart of Toruń, occupying the entire central space of the main square, the Rynek Staromiejski, is the Town Hall. The biggest medieval building of its type anywhere in Europe, it was not only the seat of the local administration offices and the civic reception chambers, but also of all the main trading functions, which many other cities preferred to confine to a separate building. Its severe brick Gothic architecture directly mirrors that of the Teutonic Knights' castles, yet its sheer size and self-confidence were intended as a direct expression of municipal independence from the order's control. The oldest surviving section is the square tower at the south-eastern corner, which can be ascended for a wonderful view over the city and the Vistula. Soon after it was completed in 1385, work began on replacing the jumble of buildings around it with a symmetrical construction grouped around a central courtyard. The only major subsequent alteration was carried out in the early seventeenth century, probably under Anthonis van

The Water Gate and the old waterfront granaries in Grudziądz (Chapter 4)

The Cathedral Hill in Frombork viewed from the south (Chapter 5)

The Castle of the Warmian Bishops in Lidzbark Warmiński (Chapter 5)

Opbergen, when the building was raised by a storey, and decorative turrets placed on the corners.

Many of the Town Hall's splendid Gothic interiors are now used to house the Regional Museum. This has notable collections of medieval sculpture and stained glass, and a gallery of portraits of Polish kings and wealthy bughers of Toruń, including a rare contemporary likeness of the city's most famous son, Nicolaus Copernicus. On the square outside is a mid-nineteenth-century commemorative monument to the great astronomer, who is shown holding a model of the heliocentric cosmos; it was designed by Christian Friedrich Tieck, a prominent neo-Classical sculptor from Berlin.

Set behind a wall off the north-western corner of the Rynek Staromiejski is St Mary's, one of three surviving Gothic churches in Toruń, all of which are primarily notable for their sense of mass. St Mary's originally belonged to the Franciscans, who established themselves in the town soon after its foundation, and hence were able to obtain a more prominent position for their church than normal. The present building was constructed in the fourteenth century, and outwardly consists of two huge brick boxes pierced by tall narrow lancet windows, the only decorative note coming from the trio of bell gables at the east end. Inside, however, the impressively lofty space has many adornments, including late fourteenth-century murals by Bohemian artists in the south aisle; a vigorously carved set of fifteenth-century choir stalls; a large number of epitaphs, including a memorial monument in the chancel to Anna Waza; and a resplendent Renaissance organ case (the instrument itself is more recent), which is placed on the north wall, instead of in the usual position to the west.

At the south-western corner of the Rynek Staromiejski is the church of the Holy Ghost, which was built in the mid-eighteenth century for Protestant worship in the sober Lutheran Baroque style, but is now in the hands of the Jesuits. Of the mansions on the square, the most imposing is the House Under the Star (Pod Gwiazdą) at number 35. Although Gothic by origin, it was remodelled at the very end of the seventeenth century in the short-lived but highly distinctive local Baroque style, which favoured façades festooned with stuccowork, in this case garlands of fruit and flowers. The interior now houses a small but unexpected Museum of Oriental Art, with objects from China, Tibet, Japan, Vietnam and India. A spectacular wooden spiral staircase, with carvings of Minerva and a lion, can also be seen inside, as well as a later wrought-iron counterpart.

A block south of the Rynek Staromiejski is ul. Kopernika, named after Copernicus (Kopernik in Polish), who was born at number 17 on the street in 1474. However, it seems that the present late Gothic house on the site is a rebuilding from the following decade commissioned by the astronomer's father. Now designated the Copernicus Museum, it contains old editions of his books, models explaining his theories, replicas of the astronomical instruments he used, and all kinds of objects — ranging from medals to matchbox labels — bearing his likeness. The adjoining house is furnished as a prosperous burgher's residence of the time, and contains a scale model of Toruń as it was at the time.

On ul. Żeglarska, the next street to the east, is St John's, the parish church of the Old Town, which has recently been raised to the status of a cathedral. Its chancel was built in the thirteenth century, and boasts one of the earliest-known star vaults, as well as large fourteenth-century murals of St John the Baptist and St John the Evangelist. The rest of the building is a fifteenth-century hall design which is even more spectacularly vertiginous than St Mary's in Gdańsk. Unfortunately the tower never reached its intended height, being roofed over immediately above the level of the clock and bells, among which is the Tuba Dei, the second biggest in Poland. Nonetheless, it is an extraordinary composition, with porches on the north and south sides and two gigantic protruding buttresses flanking a deeply recessed entrance on the main west front. Copernicus was baptised at the bronze font which still stands in the westernmost chapel of the south aisle. A memorial painting to him was placed above it in 1589, and was later joined by a Baroque bust.

Just south of St John's, at number 8 on the same street, is the Palace of the Bishops of Kujawy, which has a richly decorative façade similar to that of the House Under the Star. The only other surviving mansion in this style lies two blocks to the west, at number 37 on ul. Piekary. To the rear of St John's is the Esken Palace, a Gothic mansion which was later converted into a granary and is now a branch of the Regional Museum, one mainly used for temporary exhibitions.

Toruń's New Town was always far more modest than its Old Town, being inhabited in the main by craftsmen rather than merchants. Its main square, the Rynek Nowomiejski, formerly had a Town Hall in the middle, but this was converted into a Protestant church and then demolished in the early nineteenth century to make way for a new place of worship designed by the Prussian court architect Karl Friedrich Schinkel. Other than this, the most notable buildings on the square are the former Blue Apron Inn (number 8) and the still-functioning Lion Pharmacy (number 13).

Just off the eastern corner of the square is the New Town parish church of St James. Largely fourteenth-century in date, it differs from its Old Town counterparts in adopting the basilican format. Its west tower is a worthy rival to St John's and is likewise built to a highly idiosyncratic design. The rest of the exterior is equally impressive, with a profusion of elaborate gables, and a curious little pepperpot turret on the north side. A number of Gothic murals have been uncovered inside; the furnishings are mainly Baroque, though one of the altars incorporates a fourteenth-century Crucifix.

The former Arsenal in the park immediately north of the historic part of the city has been converted to house the Ethnographic Museum, which has displays of local crafts, folklore and industries, including a sizeable section on fishing. This also incorporates a small *skansen* to the rear, which has traditional farmsteads brought from three nearby regions — Kujawy, Kashubia and the Bory Tucholskie.

Further Information
— Royal Prussia —

Places to Visit

Chełmno
Town Hall (Regional Museum)
Rynek
Open: Tuesday to Saturday 10am to
4pm, Sunday 10am to 1pm.

Elbląg
Elbląg Museum
Bulwar Zygmunta Augusta 11
Open: Tuesday to Saturday 9am to
4pm, Sunday 10am to 4pm.

Modern Art Gallery
ul. Studzienna 6
Open: Tuesday to Saturday 10am to
5pm, Sunday 10am to 4pm.

Gdańsk
Archaeological Museum
ul. Mariacka 25-26
Open: Tuesday, Wednesday and
Friday to Sunday 10am to 4pm.

Ethnographic Museum
Park Oliwski
Open: Tuesday to Saturday 9am to
3pm, Sunday 9.30am to 3pm.

Maritime Museum
ul. Szeroka 67-68
Open: Tuesday to Sunday 10am to 4pm.

Modern Art Gallery
Park Oliwski
Open: Tuesday to Saturday 9am to
3pm, Sunday 9.30am to 3pm.

National Museum
ul. Toruńskal
Open: Tuesday 11am to 5pm,
Wednesday to Sunday 9am to 3pm.

Outer Gate (Historical Museum)
Targ Węglowy
Open: Tuesday to Thursday, Saturday
and Sunday 10am to 4pm.

Polish Poast Office
plac Obrońców 1-2
Open: Tuesday to Saturday 10am to
4pm.

Town Hall and Historical Museum
ul. Długa
Open: Tuesday to Thursday, Saturday
and Sunday 10am to 4pm.

Westerplatte Museum
Open: Tuesday to Sunday 10am to 4pm.

Wisłoujście Fortress
Open: May to September Tuesday to
Sunday 9am to 3pm.

Gdynia
*Museum-ships Błyskawica and Dom
   Pomorza*
Open: Tuesday to Sunday 10am to
3.30pm.

Naval Museum
Bulwar Nadmorski
Open: Tuesday to Sunday 10am to 4pm.

Oceanographic Museum and Aquarium
Molo Południowe
Open: Tuesday to Sunday 10am to 5pm.

Gniew
Castle of the Teutonic Knights
Open: Tuesday to Sunday 10am to 4pm.

Golub-Dobrzyń
Castle of the Teutonic Knights
Open Tuesday to Sunday 9am to 3pm.

Grudziądz
Grudziądz Museum
ul. Wodna 3-5
Open: Tuesday 10am to 6pm,
Wednesday, Thursday and Saturday
10am to 3pm, Friday 1pm to 6pm,
Sunday 10am to 2pm.

Hel
Fishing Museum
Open: Tuesday to Sunday 10am to 4pm.

Kartuzy
Kashubian Museum
ul. Ludowa Polskiego 1
Open: Tuesday to Saturday 9am to 4pm,
May to October also Sunday 9am to
3pm.

Malbork
Castle of the Teutonic Knights
ul. Hibnera 1
Open: May to September Tuesday to
Sunday 8.30am to 4.30pm, October to
April Tuesday to Sunday 9am to 3pm.

Sztutowo
Stutthof Concentration Camp
Open: May to September daily 8am to
6pm, October to April daily 8am to 3pm.

Toruń
Castle of the Teutonic Knights
ul. Przedzamcze
Open: May to September Tuesday to
Sunday 10am to 4pm.

Copernicus Museum
ul. Kopernika 15-17
Open: Tuesday to Sunday 10am to 4pm.

Eskew Palace
ul. Łazienna 16
Open: Tuesday to Sunday 10am to 4pm.

Ethnographic Museum
Wały Sikorskiego 19
Open: Tuesday 10am to 5pm,
Wednesday to Sunday 10am to 3pm.

Star House (Museum of Oriental Art)
Rynek Staromiejski 35
Open: Tuesday to Sunday 10am to 4pm.

Town Hall (Regional Museum)
Rynek Staromiejski 1
Open Tuesday to Sunday 10am to 4pm.

Wdzydze Kiszewski
Kashubian Ethnographic Park
Open: 15 April to 15 October Tuesday
to Sunday 9am to 4pm, 16 October to 14
April Tuesday to Sunday 10am to 3pm.

Tourist Offices

Gdańsk
ul. Heweliusza 27
☎ 31-43-55 or 31-66-37

Toruń
Rynek Staromiejski 1
☎ 10-931

5 • Warmia and Masuria

The two provinces known as **Warmia** and **Masuria** are almost invariably bracketed together. Prior to 1945, both lay within the German prövince of East Prussia, which was partitioned at Stalin's behest by an almost straight horizontal line. Its northern half, including the capital and strategic port of Konigsberg (re-named Kaliningrad) became an administrative district of the Russian Federation, and remains so today, though it faces an uncertain future, now that it is cut off from the rest of the country by the independent republics of Lithuania and Belarus.

Warmia (also known by its German name of Ermeland or Ermland) has a very coherent identity, dating back to 1243, when the Teutonic Knights established four bishoprics within the land they had recently conquered from the heathen Baltic tribes. Each was vested with full temporal rights over about a third of the total area of its spiritual realm, and this in turn was apportioned between the bishop and the chapter in a ratio of two to one. The largest of these new ecclesiastical states was Warmia, whose territory was shaped like a trapezoid, with its apex in a 9 mile (15km) long coastal strip on the Vistula Lagoon.

In time, the bishops and chapter established virtual autonomy from the jurisdiction of the Knights; they also fostered a highly distinctive form of brick Gothic architecture which dominates many of the townscapes to this day. Following the Knights' defeat in the Thirteen Years War of 1454-66, Warmia transferred its formal political allegiance to the Polish king, while remaining directly subject to the pope in Church affairs. For the next three centuries, it functioned as a quasi-independent theocratic state, populated by a mixture of ethnic Germans and Poles. The most significant period in its history began in 1496, when Bishop Lucas Watzenrode secured a position in the chapter for his multi-talented nephew Nicolaus Copernicus, whose nominal duties left him with plenty of time for his mould-breaking astronomical researches. Warmia later became a stout promoter of the Counter-Reformation, during which time several spectacular Baroque pilgrimage churches were constructed. It finally lost its special political status when it was forcibly incorporated into East Prussia in 1772, but has retained its episcopal role to the present day.

Masuria (Mazury in Polish, Masuren in German) is altogether more difficult to define, as at no time has it functioned as a political unit. The term is sometimes loosely used in connection with the whole of north-eastern

117

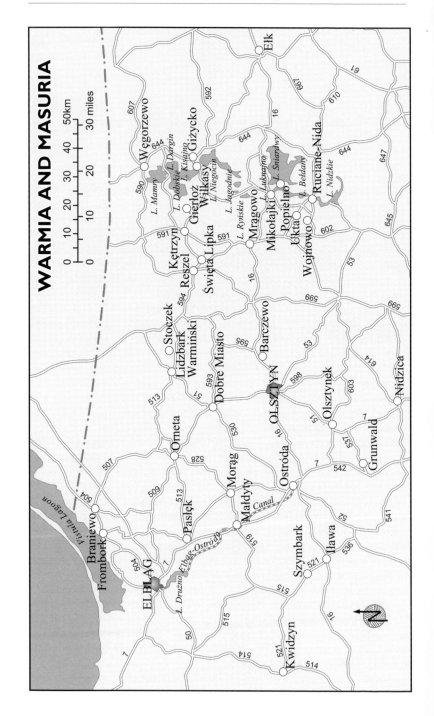

Poland, though in its narrowest sense it refers only to the remarkable lakeland immediately east of Warmia, which is dotted with several thousand separate stretches of water. Most commonly, it is applied to the Polish parts of the former East Prussia, other than Warmia and Powiśle. The latter, a narrow strip of land in the eastern basin of the River Vistula, was transferred to the province of West Prussia during the period when Poland was partitioned, but reverted to East Prussia after World War I.

Originally known as Ducal Prussia, East Prussia was the rump state retained by the Teutonic Knights after their defeat in the Thirteen Years War. Following their mass conversion to Protestantism in 1525, it was transformed into a secular duchy under the rule of the last Grand Master, Albrecht von Hohenzollern. Although nominally subject to the Polish monarch, it had full control over its internal affairs, and Lutheranism was adopted as the only officially sanctioned religion. It was inherited by the Berlin-based branch of the Hohenzollern dynasty in 1618, who merged with their other holdings to form the state of Brandenburg-Prussia, and it had no further connection with Poland until 1945.

Both Warmia and Masuria are predominantly rural, and this inevitably means that the attractions are well spread out. Warmia's are almost entirely historical, with a notable legacy of both churches and castles. Masuria's are largely scenic, and are chiefly associated with water: it is a mecca for sailing and watersports enthusiasts, and offers the most enticing boat trips in Poland.

Warmia

Warmia's sparse allocation of coastline lies on either side of **Frombork**, which is idyllically located on the southern shore of the Vistula Lagoon, 19 miles (31km) from Elbląg by road, or about 25 miles (40km) via the scenic coastal railway. Despite its tiny size, and its repeated devastation in wars, Frombork is undoubtedly one of the most atmospheric and interesting places in Poland: not only was it the spiritual capital of the Warmian bishopric for five and a half centuries, it was also Copernicus' home for most of the last thirty-odd years of his life, and formed the backdrop to his researches into planetary movements. This culminated in the publication of *De Revolutionibus Orbitium Coelestium* in 1543, the first printed copies of which were delivered to the astronomer just hours before he died. By proving that the earth moves round the sun, rather than vice versa, he overturned the conventional wisdom about the universe that had been accepted since the time of Ptolemy, and so changed the whole course of astronomy. Nowadays, Frombork is a somnolent backwater — it lost its episcopal role in 1945 and was deprived of its town rights in 1959 — and its sense of quiet is disrupted only by the flapping wings of the storks which nest on so many of its towers and chimneys.

Frombork, a Polish variant of its original German name of Frauenburg, means Fortress of Our Lady. This refers to the strongly fortified Cathedral Hill high above the lagoon, whose spiky silhouette is visible for miles around, most dramatically from the steamers which in summer ply across the water to the resort of Krynica Morska on the Vistula Spit. Although the Warmian chapter and the first German colonists first established a presence in 1278, work on the present walled enclosure did not begin until the following century, and the defences were continually strengthened and improved over the following 200 years. As the north side of the complex overlooks a sheer drop, the only entrance is via the gateway on the south side, which is flanked by two semi-circular bastions erected around 1530.

The cathedral itself, in the heart of the enclosure, was built between 1329 and 1388. It served as a model for all but one of the churches built in the Warmian diocese during the Middle Ages, taking its own inspiration from the severely geometric brick architecture of the Cistercians. The highly distinctive outline is due above all to the slender octagonal turrets topped with sharply pointed steeples, which feature on all four corners of the building. Otherwise, the exterior decoration is concentrated on the facade, whose main gable, with its intricate blind arcades, is a dazzling exercise in patterned brickwork. The porch below bristles with smaller gables and is framed by a stone doorway with carvings of beasts, vines and other patters. This gives access to the main doorway, which has tiny figures depicting the Last Judgment, and a tympanum illustrating the parable of the Wise and Foolish Virgins.

Inside, the cathedral looks rather low in relation to its length. The reason for this is that the aisleless chancel, the first part to be built, adopted the traditional formula of the height being twice the width. Thus when the unusually long nave was added, it had to be vaulted at the same level, rather than rising to a loftiness commensurate with its length. Only a few Gothic furnishings remain, such as the sedilia in the chancel and the polyptych commissioned by Lucas Watzenrode for the high altar, which has been in the north aisle since being displaced in the mid-eighteenth century by a monumental Baroque creation. Most of the numerous altars and funerary monuments are likewise Baroque: among the latter are two bearing grim representations of Death, who is depicted as a skeleton bearing a skull. Copernicus is known to be buried in the cathedral, but the exact place has never been identified, and the plaque bearing his portrait is a belated tribute. Off the southern aisle, and separated from it by a beautiful iron grille, is the ornate Szembek chapel, named after the bishop who commissioned it in the 1730s to house the cathedral's collection of holy relics. However, the proudest Baroque adornment is the organ, made in the 1680s by Daniel Nitrowski of Gdańsk. Although subsequently much altered, it ranks among the finest instruments in Poland. In summer, short demonstrations are given three times daily, with full recitals on Saturdays.

At the south-west corner of the cathedral fortifications is the belfry, otherwise known as the Radziejowski Tower after the bishop who remod-elled it by adding a Baroque superstructure and helmet to the original Gothic base. It can be climbed for a truly breathtaking panorama over the cathedral, the town and the lagoon. There is also a small Planetarium inside, which gives regular shows, albeit in Polish only. In the corresponding position at the north-west corner is the oldest-surviving part of the defensive system; this is known as the Copernicus Tower, and is popularly supposed to be where the astronomer conducted his experiments. However, there is no hard evidence to support this, and scholars believe that he is more likely to have worked from his house, a predecessor to those on the next hill to the west: now a tourist lodge, these were formerly the official residences of the canons. At the eastern side of Cathedral Hill is the Bishop's Palace, which is now a museum. The ground floor has archaeological finds, while the second floor is devoted to Copernicus, and includes early editions of his main treatises, scale models explaining his theories, and works of art inspired by his life and discoveries.

Whereas the Cathedral Hill came through World War II with only minimal damage, 80 per cent of the little town which lay below was destroyed. Most of it has been rebuilt in soulless concrete; a large statue of Copernicus was added in 1973 in commemoration of the 500th anniversary of his birth. A few historic monuments remain, notably the sixteenth-century Water Tower, one of the oldest of its kind in existence. It was linked by a 3 mile (5km) long canal to the River Bauda, and pumped water up to the Cathedral Hill by means of an ingenious system of wooden pipes. In summer, the summit is open as an observation platform, offering a view, particularly of the north side of the cathedral and its fortifications, which nicely complements that from the Radziejowski Tower. Just to the east, the fourteenth-century parish church of St Nicholas has been restored following wartime damage, but is no longer used for worship. A few minutes' walk east of Cathedral Hill, beyond the neo-Gothic New Bishop's Palace, erected after Frombork became the main residential seat of the bishopric in 1837, is the fifteenth-century Hospital of the Holy Ghost. The latter's chapel, dedicated to St Anne, has a fresco of the Last Judgment, while the wards have recently been fitted out with a small Museum of the History of Medicine.

The original seat of the Warmia bishopric was **Braniewo**, which is located slightly inland in the delta of the River Pasłęka, 6 miles (10km) east of Frombork. It lost its role because it was considered too difficult to defend, but it continued to play an important part in the history of the diocese, particularly during the Counter-Reformation spearheaded by the Jesuits, who established their first Eastern European outpost in the town. Sadly, Braniewo was almost totally destroyed in 1945, and it was not until the changed political climate of the 1980s that much was done about restoration. The main focus of this has been the rebuilding of the fourteenth-century church of St Catherine, which stands high above the river. This is, for the most part, a typical example of Warmian Gothic, with a massive west tower and elaborate star vaults, though its pentagonal chancel is a variant on the standard groundplan. Many wish it had been left in its ruined state as a war memorial, but it has been returned to pristine condition and serves once more as the main place of worship in town. The photographs displayed inside offer a chance to assess the success or otherwise of the project. Near the church are fragments of the town walls and the tower which is the sole surviving relic of the Bishop's Palace.

Through the rolling Warmian countryside, some 31 miles (50km) south-east of Braniewo by road or rail, is **Orneta**, one of a number of small market towns founded by the bishopric at the beginning of the fourteenth century. Unusually for this region, it came through World War II relatively unscathed, and life still revolves around the characterful little Rynek, which has arcaded houses along its sides, and a gabled fourteenth-century Town Hall in the middle. However, the chief joy is the church of St John just off the square. Dating back to the mid-fourteenth century, it differs from all its counterparts in Warmia in its decisive rejection of the hall church format, the aisles being built at only half the height of the nave. At the end of the fifteenth century, the simple original structure was completely remodelled. A regular set of outsized chapels crowned with giant gables was added to the north and south sides, friezes of vegetable motifs and grotesque heads were placed above and below the windows, and the whole building was given elaborate new vaults. The result is one of the most ornate and distinctive brick churches to be found anywhere in Europe.

Just 2 miles (3km) north-east of Orneta is the hamlet of **Krosno**, home to one of several Baroque pilgrimage churches erected in Warmia during the Counter-Reformation. Closely modelled on its great predecessor at Święta Lipka, described below, it attracts huge crowds of believers for its big annual pilgrimage on the last Sunday in May.

Dobre Miasto, 15^1/$_2$ miles (25km) south-east of Orneta, was likewise founded in the early fourteenth century. The town is centred on a collegiate church which is generally considered to be the classic example of the Warmian Gothic style, with all the most characteristic features — a sturdy square tower above the façade, tall gables at both east and west ends, a single massive roof, a hall church design without a separate chancel, and, inside, star vaults springing from octagonal pillars. Most of the furnishings, including the high altar, the pulpit, the canopied font and the stalls are Baroque, though the last of these incorporates carved lions from its Gothic predecessor. The adjoining collage, based around a simple cloister, is now a seminary. From the first floor, there is direct access to the church, and this is the easiest way to gain entry, as the main door is normally only open around the time of masses.

Just as Frombork was historically the ecclesiastical capital of Warmia, so was **Lidzbark Warmiński**, situated on a bend of the River Łyna 12 miles (20km) north-east of Dobre Miasto and 22 miles (35km) east of Orneta, its temporal equivalent. It became the main residence of the bishops in 1350, and retained the role until the prince-bishopric was absorbed into Prussia. Lidzbark had a distinguished courtly life: Copernicus lived there between 1503 and 1510 in the official capacity of physician and advisor to his uncle, while the last and most distinguished holder of the prince-bishopric was Ignacy Krasicki, one of Poland's leading men of letters, an author of a pioneering novel in Polish as well as verse fables and satires, including

Monomachia, which attacked the dissolute lifestyle of monks.

Although the town centre was badly damaged in World War II, with the loss of almost all its historic dwellings, the castle of the Warmian Bishops immediately to the east emerged virtually unscathed. A masterpiece of military architecture of the first rank, it shows an obvious debt to the great fortresses of the Teutonic Knights, as well as forming a secular counterpart, in its austere geometricity, to the province's churches. Surrounded by now ruinous walls as well as a moat, the castle is in two distinct parts. The outer area, consisting of three wings facing an open courtyard, was remodelled as a palace in the eighteenth century, but subsequently fell into decay and is currently the object of major renovation works.

The castle proper, erected throughout the second half of the fourteenth century, has a square ground plan, massive brick walls, an octagonal tower to the north-east and square turrets at the other three corners. At its heart is a graceful two-storey patio reminiscent of a monastic cloister. Steps lead down to the vaults, where a number of cannon, the main weapons of medieval Warmia's tiny army, are on view. On the first floor are the main public rooms, the most impressive being the refectory, which now forms an apt setting for an excellent display of medieval sculpture collected from churches throughout Warmia, Masuria and Royal Prussia. It also preserves some of its original mural decoration; another cycle is in the adjoining tower room. The neighbouring chapel retains its pure Gothic shape, but was given a Rococo decorative scheme in the eighteenth century, when the vault was painted and an organ and gallery added. On the second floor is a display of contemporary Polish painting and a roomful of eighteenth- and nineteenth-century icons brought for safekeeping from the Old Believers' convent at Wojnowo described later in the chapter.

Lidzbark's other main landmark is the church of St Peter and St Paul overlooking the loop in the river. It is exactly contemporary with the castle, but was only remodelled into a typical Warmian hall church following a fire at the very end of the fifteenth century. In the Baroque period, the handsome tower was crowned by a three-tier lantern. The chancel was only added in the nineteenth century, and most of the furnishings date from the same period. On the hill directly across the river is the former Winter Garden of the bishops, of which the only significant reminder is the eighteenth-century orangery.

The massive High Gate, which served as the western entrance to the town but is nowadays a basic tourist hotel, is the only reminder of the once formidable municipal fortifications. A few minutes' walk to the west is the wooden Protestant church, built in the 1820s to designs by the great Prussian architect Karl Friedrich Schinkel as the first-ever Lutheran place of worship in Warmia. Nowadays, it serves the small local Orthodox community, and has, rather unfortunately, been given a coat of green paint.

Kierwiny, 5 miles (8km) east of Lidzbark on the main road towards the Great Masurian Lake District, is the turning-off point for visiting **Stoczek**, another of Warmia's leading places of pilgrimage: the monastery is located at the very end of the straggling village, 2 miles (3km) to the north. Founded in 1639 to house a copy of a devotional image known as The Madonna of Peace, it holds a special place in the affections of pious Poles, as the country's great post-war Primate, Cardinal Stefan Wyszynski, spent the first of his 3 years of internment there between 1953 and 1954, having been placed under house arrest by the Communist authorities on account of his outspokenness. Not long after his release, an event which marked the abandonment of attempts to subdue the power of the Church, the Order of Marian Fathers was allowed to re-establish monastic life at Stoczek.

Entry to the monastery is via the three-sided cloister, which has two corner chapels and a pretty garden with a pair of shrines. The church has a circular nave and a small presbytery, above which is a tower forming a link with the conventual buildings behind; the miraculous image is the centrepiece of the high altar. In the company of one of the monks, it is possible to visit the monastic quarters, including the cell where Wyszyński was imprisoned, which is filled with memorabilia of his stay and subsequent career.

Reszel, about 25 miles (40km) east of Lidzbark, has a tiny but exceptionally atmospheric and well-preserved Old Town which still conforms to its medieval layout. The Castle of the Warmian Bishops was begun at the same time as its counterpart in Lidzbark, but was completed in a much shorter time and has none of the latter's strict geometricity. Instead, it has a varied outline which includes a circular keep resting on a square base, a watchtower over the main entrance, and a row of machicolations beneath the sentry walk. This silhouette was made yet more picturesque in the nineteenth century, when the south wing was rebuilt to serve as a Protestant church, with a tall gable placed over its façade. In recent years, this has been converted once again to serve as a gallery for exhibitions of contemporary art, both home-grown and foreign. None of the castle's medieval interiors survives, so the west wing has been converted into a hotel, while part of the east wing is a café. A small archaeological museum has been set up in the keep, which commands a fine view over the town.

The other main monument, the church of St Peter and St Paul, is only a few paces away. It likewise dates back to the mid-fourteenth century, though it did not gain its characteristically Warmian star-shaped vaults until more than a hundred years later. Badly damaged in the early nineteenth century in a fire which ravaged the whole town, much of the exterior, and in particular the tower, was rebuilt in a rather austere manner. The interior is altogether lighter in feel: its Renaissance polychromy, with plant and animal motifs, is still in evidence, while the furnishings include a playful Rococo font with baldachin. From the church, steps lead down to a surprisingly deep and narrow gulley, with a footpath running parallel to the stream. This is forded by a bridge, the Most Rybacki, which dates back to the fourteenth century. Its once broad archway was gradually filled in over the years, eventually serving, improbably but effectively, as the town prison.

Święta Lipka (whose name literally means Holy Linden Tree) lies

4 miles (6km) east of Reszel, right on the traditional boundary between Warmia and Masuria. The tiny hamlet situated between two lakes is no more than an appendage to the magnificent Baroque pilgrimage church, one of the most ornate and exotic-looking buildings in Poland. This swarms with the faithful for the big annual pilgrimages which occur on the last Sunday in May (the Feast of the Visitation), 11 August (the Feast of Our Lady of Święta Lipka) and 15 August (the Feast of the Assumption). On the day prior to the last-named, there is a special pilgrimage for disabled people.

According to legend, Święta Lipka became sanctified in the year 1300, when the Virgin Mary appeared to a condemned prisoner in the castle at Rastenburg (present-day Kętrzyn) on the night before his sentence and gave him a piece of wood and a chisel with which to fashion her image. The sculpture he created so astonished the judge that he was immediately granted his freedom. He then set out to walk to Reszel, leaving the carving, in accordance with the Virgin's wishes, on the first linden tree he encountered on the way. This spot soon came to be associated with miracles, and in time a chapel was built was built to house the figure. In 1519 the last Grand Master of the Teutonic Knights, Albrecht von Hohenzollern, made a barefoot pilgrimage there, but 6 years later, having converted to Protestantism, he ordered that the chapel be raised and the image destroyed. Pilgrims were banned under pain of death, though many reputedly took the risk under cover of darkness, before escaping over the frontier to Catholic Warmia, which lay around 650ft (200m) away.

In 1618, the land where the chapel had stood was acquired by Stefan Sadorski, secretary to King Zygmunt Waza, and placed under the jurisdiction of the Warmian bishops. A new chapel was erected, which in 1631 was entrusted to the Jesuits who had recently established themselves in Reszel. In 1687, work began on replacing this with the present church. The initial plans were entrusted to Georg Ertli, an Austrian architect who was a resident of the Lithuanian capital Vilnius, a connection which explains Święta Lipka's close affinity with the highly distinctive Baroque architecture of that city.

Surrounding the church is a cloister whose outer wall is topped with forty-four statues illustrating the genealogy of Christ carved by another Austrian, Christoph Pervanger. Entry to the complex is via a truly splendid wrought-iron grille designed by Johann Schwarz of Reszel. His fellow Warmian, the painter Matthias Johann Meyer of Lidzbark, began an ambitious programme of frescoing the cloister walk in the trompe l'oeil manner he had learned as a student in Rome, depicting the *Old Testament* on the vaults and the *New Testament* on the walls. Unfortunately, he only completed a small part of this before his death, and the project was abandoned.

From the cloister, there is a wonderful view of the church's yellow and white stucco façade, with its twin clock towers and deeply recessed niche with a representation of the Madonna of the Linden Tree. Another version of the latter, incorporating a silver statue of the Virgin, can be seen in the

sumptuous interior, almost every square centimetre of which is a proclama-
tion of the cult of the Virgin. Matthias Meyer depicted her Assumption and
Glorification on the ceiling; between the windows and in the presbytery he
painted scenes from her earthly life, while on the aisle vaults he interpreted
the Mysteries of the Rosary. The triple-tiered high altar, which is made of
walnut but painted to resemble marble, has as its focal point a much revered
devotional painting, known as the *Mother of God of Święta Lipka*. This was
adorned with a crown in 1968 at a ceremony conducted by Cardinal
Wyszyński and his protege Cardinal Karol Wojtyła, the future Pope John
Paul II.

The church's most celebrated adornment is the organ, made by Johann
Josue Mesengel of Königsberg. Almost all the original case survives,
including the angel musicians; these have moving parts which can be
activated by the organist to serve as an accompaniment to his playing.
Although most of the original pipework has been replaced, it remains one
of Poland's great musical treasures. Short demonstrations are given hourly
in summer, while in July and August recitals are held every Friday at 8pm.

Barczewo, which is about 25 miles (40km) south-west of Reszel and a
similar distance south of Lidzbark, is a typical small Warmian town which
boasts two notable churches. The riverside St Anne's, with its imposing
tower, is another of the fourteenth-century hall churches so characteristic of
the region, though it was partially rebuilt in the nineteenth century, having
been damaged by fire. Just of the Rynek is the much-altered Franciscan
church, which contains the black and white marble tomb of Cardinal Andrej
Batory, the nephew of King Stefan Batory, and his brother Baltazar: the
former is depicted at prayer, the latter in a reclining position. This fine
example of Renaissance sepulchral art was carved at the end of the sixteenth
century by the Gdańsk-based Dutch sculptor, Willem van den Block. Until
his death in 1986, the adjoining monastery served as the prison of the
notorious Nazi Gauleiter of Masuria, Erich Koch. South of the Rynek, on ul.
Kościuszki, is the mid-nineteenth-century synagogue, now housing the
local cultural centre and crafts workshops.

Olsztyn, 11 miles (18km) south-east of Barczewo, was established in the
fourteenth century as the southern outpost of the Warmia bishopric. It is the
only place in either Warmia or Masuria which has developed into a city, and
also the only one with much in the way of manufacturing industry. Whereas
most other settlements in the former East Prussia have fewer inhabitants
than they did before the war, Olsztyn has trebled its population since it
passed from German to Polish control. Inevitably, this means that most of
it is now a featureless urban sprawl, though it does have a fine setting with
a number of lakes on both its eastern and western borders. With a wide range
of accommodation and excellent transport links, it also makes a good
touring base.

The compact Old Town is entered via the High Gate, the only surviving
part of the medieval fortifications. Its outer side is adorned with blind arches,
while the inner has diamond patterned brickwork. Beyond lies the central

Rynek, with the plain Baroque Town Hall in the centre. Most of the original gabled houses which lined the square were destroyed in 1945, and a controversial rebuilding scheme was adopted after the war. This rejected both of the drastic solutions which other Polish towns chose between — faithful reconstruction or else replacement by totally new buildings. Instead a middle course was taken, whereby the architects were encouraged to re-interpret the idiom of the old houses in a modern manner. Just west of the Rynek is the neo-Gothic Protestant church, which is still used by the tiny rump of the ethnic German community who still live in the city.

A little further west, commanding the high ground above the gentle valley of the River Łyna, is the castle. This is contemporary with those in Lidzbark and Reszel, but differs from them in having been the property of the Warmia chapter, rather than of the bishops. It has been much altered down the centuries, and so has a nicely varied silhouette. One of the oldest surviving parts is the round tower at the south-west corner, which can be ascended for a view over the city. In the courtyard are three rudely carved granite blocks which are thought to have been cult objects of the Baltic Prussians who first settled the area.

Copernicus, in his capacity as an administrator of the estates of the Warmia chapter, lived in the castle from 1516 to 1519 and again from 1520 to 1521, taking part during the latter period in its defence against a siege mounted by the Teutonic Knights. While there, he wrote the first part of *De Revolutionibus* and drew a map of the Vistula Lagoon, as well as undertak-ing more mundane work such as the compilation of land registers and treatises on currency reform in the Kingdom of Poland. The most intriguing reminder of his stay is the experimental diagram he painted on the courtyard wall to record the equinox and so determine the exact length of the year. During his sojourn, he occupied the star-vaulted chambers in the north-west part of the castle, and these now contain a permanent exhibition on his life and work. Other rooms are devoted to the history of Warmia and Masuria. This is presented from an unashamedly partisan Polish perspective, but has a good section on costumes and folklore.

East of the Rynek is the former parish church of St James, which since 1945 has been the cathedral. As such, it is the spiritual hub of present-day Warmia, which has been promoted to the rank of an archbishopric. A particularly large-scale example of the Warmian Gothic style, the cathedral boasts beautiful network vaults in the nave, with star-shaped counterparts in the aisles. The 197ft (60m) high tower, which was only added in the sixteenth century, varies the traditional redbrick appearance by the inclu-sion of green and yellow glazed bricks.

In the wake of the celebrations commemorating the 500th anniversary of Copernicus' birth, two new astronomical attractions were opened to add lustre to Olsztyn's tourist appeal. On al. Piłsudskiego, to the east of the Old Town, is a purpose-built Planetarium with the usual dome-shaped roof. Just to the south on ul. Zolnierska, an old water tower has been converted to house the Observatory.

Powiśle and Western Masuria

Kwidzyn is the modern Polish name of the longtime German town of Marienwerder, which lies 2 miles (4km) back from the River Vistula on a loop of an insignificant tributary, the Liwa. Being on the main road and rail lines between Malbork and Grudziądz (both described in the previous chapter), it is most conveniently visited in conjunction with them. However, it was the only one of the fortified towns established by the Teutonic Knights in the vicinity of the Vistula which did not fall to Poland in the sixteenth century, and it thereafter served as the western outpost of the Teutonic state and its successor, Ducal Prussia. Not until 1945 was the German link, which stretched unbroken back to 1233, finally ended. Unfortunately, this lack of a Polish pedigree meant that the newly acquired and battle-damaged town was treated ruthlessly by the post-war authorities, with the masonry of its ruins, and even of its pavements, carted off to help with the rebuilding of Warsaw.

Although most of Kwidzyn is totally nondescript, it does possess a truly remarkable double monument in the contiguous cathedral and castle which together completely dominate the town. These were built by the chapter of Pomesania, one of the four bishoprics founded by the Teutonic Knights. The town was chosen as the seat of the prince-bishop in 1254, and the chapter, made up of priests who were also members of the Teutonic Order, was formed a generation later. Architecturally, the complex, almost all of which was erected in a sustained burst of building activity in the early fourteenth century, mirrors that of the great fortress at Malbork. Unlike their Warmian counterparts, the Pomesanian bishops and chapter maintained a close association with the Knights, eventually joining them in adopting the Reformation in 1525.

The relentless redbrick appearance of the cathedral's exterior is broken by the white limestone porch on the south side which was added at the end of the fourteenth century. Above it is one of only three medieval mosaics in the whole of Central Europe: it depicts St John the Evangelist, under torture in a vat of burning oil, being adored by a Pomesanian bishop. An eccentricity of the building's design is that, although it adopts the basilican format, the nave has no clerestory, and light only comes from the low windows in the aisles, as in a hall church. Between these windows are several cycles of much-retouched fourteenth-century frescos, depicting scenes from the lives of Christ, the Virgin Mary and the saints. In the elevated part of the chancel are more frescos, this time from the early sixteenth century, showing three Grand Masters of the Teutonic Knights and seventeen Pomesanian bishops in the company of the Virgin and St John. A rather folksy bishop's throne is one of the few original Gothic furnishings; most of its counterparts are Romantic imitations from the nineteenth century. Off the north aisle is a spectacular memorial chapel to the early eighteenth-century soldier of fortune Otto Friedrich von Groebben, who served as a general in the armies of both Brandenburg-Prussia and Poland, and also established Brandenburg's first African colony on the Gold Coast. Episodes from his colourful life are depicted on the doorway, while inside are Rococo statues of the general, his three wives and two negroes.

Façade and gateway of the pilgrimage church of Święta Lipka (Chapter 5)

The Castle of the Pomesanian Chapter in Kwidzyn (Chapter 5)

Men working on the Elbląg-Ostróda Canal (Chapter 5)

Winding gear used to haul boats along an overland stretch of the Elbląg-Ostróda Canal (Chapter 5)

The cathedral's belfry doubled as the keep of the castle, which is built round a square courtyard, high above the former course of the Liwa. Unfortunately, two of the wings were demolished at the end of the eighteenth century, but it is still an impressive and formidable sight, with a showier exterior than normal for what was essentially a defensive structure. Especially imposing is the Dansker, a tall tower located 197ft (60m) west of the main body of the castle, and linked to it by a covered passageway carried over the old river bed by five massive arches, rather in the manner of railway viaducts of five centuries later. Although the Dansker served as a first line of defence, its primary purpose was as a latrine, and it has been described as the most magnificent sewage system ever built. The interior of the tower and the walkway form part of the tourist circuit round the castle, though the most beautiful chamber is the so-called Palm Tree Hall, named after its spectacular vault which springs from a single central column. Spread throughout the various floors of the building are various displays, including a gruesome collection of torture instruments as well as the expected exhibits on local archaeology, history, folklore and fauna.

One other place associated with the Pomesanian diocese is **Szymbark**, which is about 31 miles (50km) east of Kwidzyn, 3 miles (5km) before the small industrial town of Iława. The castle, begun in the late fourteenth century, served as the summer residence of the bishops. Perched atop a small hillock, it is an impressively angular construction, whose main wall is some 328ft (100m) long. It was later modified into an aristocratic country house, but was badly damaged in World War II and is now a ruin, albeit an impressive one.

From Iława, it is a journey of 20 miles (32km) north-east to **Ostróda**, a commercial and resort town situated at the south-eastern end of Lake Drwęckie, which is shaped like a reverse L and has a shoreline of 24 miles (39km). Ostróda was the site of another of the Teutonic Knights' castles, but the building has been so frequently altered that it is unrecognisable as such today. There are no other monuments of note, and the town's tourist standing is due entirely to its sailing and cruising facilities.

Above all, it is the southern terminus of the **Elbląg-Ostróda Canal** (also known as the **Oberland Canal** after the German name for the district it traverses), which is one of the world's most unusual waterways as well as one of Poland's most outstanding technical monuments. Since the Middle Ages, merchants had dreamt of forging a suitable transport link for the movement of heavy goods between Ostróda and the Baltic, utilising the chain of lakes which lay along the route. As it was, they were forced to use the River Drwęca, which flows south-westwards to its confluence with the Vistula at Toruń, resulting in a journey that is five times longer than as the crow flies. For centuries, it seemed that there was an insuperable technical obstacle to the construction of a canal: the lakes near Ostróda are at an altitude of more than 328ft (100m) above their counterparts near Elbląg. an amount far too great to counteract by means of conventional locks.

In 1825 Georg Steenke, a young engineer from Königsberg, came up with an ingenious solution to this problem. He proposed a canal interrupted by a series of slipways, dry stretches where the boats would be hauled overland. This was rejected unconditionally by the authorities as being unsound and too costly. Undeterred, Steenke eventually managed to gain an audience with King Friedrich Wilhelm IV who was unimpressed by the economic arguments but won over by the idea of his country gaining a facility that would be unique in Europe. Accordingly, construction work, funded almost exclusively out of the Prussian state coffers, began in 1848. The process was long and complicated: in addition to digging the channels, building embankments and constructing the slipways, it involved lowering the water level of the lakes along the route to a uniform 99.5 metres. By 1870, the first boats were able to sail between Elbląg and Miłomłyn to the north of Ostróda. Six years later, the entire system was complete. In addition to the main 49.6 miles (80.4km) stretch between Elbląg and Ostróda, it included a 19.9 miles (32.2km) branch from Miłomłyn to Iława, and 10.4 miles (16.9km) extension from Ostróda to Stare Jabłonki. Although initially used by commercial barges, the advent of the railways quickly put an end to any economic value the canal might have had. Nowadays, it is purely a tourist attraction.

The entire canal system is open to yachts, canoes and rowing boats. Larger craft are banned from the eastern extension for conservation reasons, and only very occasion services are run along the branch to Iława. However, between mid-May and mid-September, two pleasure boats are scheduled to make daily journeys between Elbląg and Ostróda, which is a truly memorable experience as well as a remarkable bargain. The boats depart from each town at 8am and arrive at the other just under 12 hours later — but note that this is dependent on there being at least twenty passengers. At weekends and during the height of summer, there is little chance of the trip being cancelled, though it can happen at other times, despite its ever-increasing popularity with German tour groups. As there is no direct rail link between the two towns, it is not usually possible to return to the departure point on the same day, but luggage can be taken aboard on payment of a small supplement. There is also the option of taking the boat from Elbląg to Małdyty, the only stop on the way: this is the more picturesque and interesting half of the route, and allows for a return by train in the afternoon. One other point to note is that the boats serve drinks but not food.

An amazing variety of landscapes are passed, including rich open farmland, dank woods and the full length of six lakes; from south to north these are Drwęckie, Jelonek, Ruda Woda, Sambród, Piniewo and Drużno. The last of these is unquestionably among the most beautiful in Poland. It was originally a southward extension of the Vistula Lagoon, and in the thirteenth century measured 77sq miles (200sq km). During the summer, parts of the lake dry up, leaving swampy marshes and rings of vegetation reminiscent of those found in oceans. Lake Drużno is inhabited by a rich variety of birdlife, some of which can be observed at quite close quarters from the boat, particularly when its imminent approach inspires a whole flock to take flight.

Between Ostróda and Miłomłyn there are two conventional locks, but these are overshadowed by the five slipways which are the most abiding memory of the canal. They all lie between Lakes Piniewo and Drużno, and together bridge a 326ft (99¹/₂m) difference in level over a course of 6 miles (10km). The most spectacular is Jelenie, the middle one of the quintet, which is the shortest in length at 1,148ft (350m), but also bridges the highest gap of 80ft (24¹/₂m). Just before leaving the water, the boats are loaded on to high-sided platform cars with eight wheels. With the help of rope pulleys, these vehicles transport the boats overland along rail tracks, then deposit them in the water at the other end. Halfway along, an empty platform passes along the parallel rails in the opposite direction. The slipways, which are very economical to operate, are each powered by a water wheel at the upper level which is fed by a tank connected to the canal by pipeline.

As passengers cannot disembark, they are deprived of the surrealistic sight of the ships trudging up or downhill. To see this, it is necessary to visit one of the slipways, which all lie well away from the main Ostróda to Elbląg road. Jelenie can be reached by branching off in the direction of Jelonki and Dzierzgoń, a road serviced by occasional buses. It should be possible to see the southbound boat going uphill at around 11am, or the northbound travelling downwards at around 4pm, but these are only approximate timings.

The turn-off to Jelonki is near the hilltop town of **Pasłęk**, 15¹/₂ miles (25km) south-east of Elbląg, whose pre-war German name of Preussich Holland indicates that it was once settled by Dutch refugees. Until 1945, it was regarded as something of a medieval showpiece, but the destroyed gabled houses for which the town was renowned have been replaced by ugly concrete apartments, creating a somewhat uncomfortable mix of old an new. Substantial sections of the walls still survive, as well as two gateways, including the impressive High Gate which is still the main entrance to the historic quarter. The brick Gothic church of St Bartholomew, whose interior was partially remodelled in the nineteenth century, contains rich Baroque furnishings. Alongside, and likewise Gothic, is the Town Hall, a handsome structure endowed in the fifteenth century with an arcaded extension bridging the street, and topped with a pilastered Renaissance gable another century later. A little further along is the three-winged Castle of the Teutonic Knights, which was modified to form a private residence, then plastered over in the course of its conversion to form local government offices.

Morąg, a further 15¹/₂ miles (25km) south-east, is best-known as the birthplace of Johann Gottfried Herder, the literary theorist, poet, philosopher and pastor who was one of the leading figures of the German Enlightenment. The house where he was born was destroyed in the war, but his life and career are documented in the museum housed in the Dohna Palace, an eighteenth-century aristocratic mansion located just off the Rynek. Displays of eighteenth- and nineteenth-century decorative art and seventeenth-century Dutch paintings are also featured. Nearby are three notable medieval monuments: a single surviving wing of the Castle of the

Teutonic Knights, a pretty step-gabled Town Hall, and the church of St Peter and St Paul, which contains late Gothic murals. Some 3 miles (5km) east of town is Lake Narie, undoubtedly one of the loveliest in the region: it has a heavily indented shoreline and no fewer than seventeen islets in its clear, deep waters.

Olsztynek, 29 miles (33km) south-east of Ostróda and 18 miles (29km) south-west of Olsztyn, was also the site of one of the Knights' castles, but the remains of the fortress are now embedded within a nineteenth-century school building. The town's only real tourist attraction is the Museum of Folk Architecture, an excellent *skansen* located in the outskirts, close to the Olsztyn road. It was originally founded in the East Prussian capital of Königsberg, but was transferred to this specially acquired site just before the outbreak of World War II. The buildings, mostly wooden, date from the late seventeenth to the early twentieth century, and include characteristic examples of rural buildings from all over Warmia, Masuria and Powiśle, as well as from Lithuania and what is now the Russian part of the former East Prussia. Among the exhibits are a thatch roofed wooden church, a water mill, an oil mill, a gypsy caravan, a fire station and three beautiful windmills; there are also numerous farmhouses, barns and cottages.

On a hill about $^1/_2$ mile (1km) from the *skansen* can be seen the scanty ruins of the once spectacular Tannenberg Monument, which was erected to commemorate the victory of the German Eighth Army under Paul von Hindenburg over the Russians at the eponymous 3-day battle in August 1914. In 1934, it also became the mausoleum of Hindenburg, who had been President of Germany since 1925, though for the last year of his life he had been reduced to figurehead status by Hitler, whom he had himself appointed, albeit reluctantly, as Chancellor. Hindenburg's remains were removed in 1945 by the retreating Nazis, and the monument was later blown up by the Soviets, who carted off the masonry for use elsewhere.

The 1914 battle, which ranged over a huge area, was so named by the Germans because it was seen as revenge for another battle of the same name in 1410, one of the epic contests of the Middle Ages, in which the Teutonic Knights were defeated by a combined force commanded by King Władysław Jagiełło and consisting of the national armies of Poland and Lithuania boosted by contingents of Ruthenians, Tatars, Hungarians, Czechs and others. In Poland, this battle is known as **Grunwald**; the site and the village of the same name lie 12 miles (19km) south-west of Olsztynek. As the event and the date are sharply etched on the national consciousness, Grunwald is something of a patriotic tourist magnet. Impartial historians tend to be more sceptical about the true significance of the event: although it was the first major reversal suffered by the Knights in 150 years of dominance of the Baltic lands, it was not until more than 50 years later that their territorial base was eroded. Indeed, the Knights returned to the battlefield a year later and erected a memorial chapel to their Grand Master, Ulrich von Jungingen, one of several thousand of their number to have been slain. The foundations of this can still be seen; there is also a huge steel monument erected by the Poles to commemorate the 550th anniversary of the event. Behind the latter is a museum, which features a few original weapons from the time plus a number of copies.

Nidzica, 19 miles (30km) south of Olsztynek by road or rail, still offers telling visual evidence of the awesome military power of the Knights. This was their southern outpost, located in a marshy, lake-strewn landscape right on the boundary with Mazovia. The castle, which now houses a cultural centre and a basic tourist lodge, is the finest of the last generation of fortresses that they built. It was begun in the 1370s, and completed in around a decade, with the town laid out below in an axial relationship that is still clearly apparent.

The Great Masurian Lake District

The Great Masurian Lake District is popularly known as 'The Land of a Thousand Lakes'. In actual fact, there are several times that number, though estimates of the total vary widely, as so many of the lakes are tiny, while the arms of many of the larger stretches of water are usually classified as individual lakes in their own right. Whatever the case, the density of lakes is by far the highest in Poland, amounting to some 15 per cent of the total land area, and both of the country's largest lakes, Śniardwy and Mamry, are in the region. The deep clear waters once teemed with fish, though stocks have diminished in recent decades as a result of excessive exploitation and the encroachment of pollution, though the latter is of minor consequence in the context of the country as a whole.

Where the lakes do not themselves interconnect, they are often joined by rivers or canals. This makes them ideal for yachting and canoeing, the more so as there are plenty of sheltered areas along the shores, and it is possible to explore the entire region without leaving the water. The almost limitless possibilities for sailing and watersports has made Masuria one of the most popular summer destinations with vacationing Poles, and in recent years with increasing numbers of Germans and Scandinavians as well. During this period, the lakes are awash with sails, which add a welcome dash of colour to the verdant landscape. Excursion steamers ply the main lakes between mid-May and mid-September and are the most relaxing way of seeing the region. However, the overwhelming majority of visitors choose to pilot themselves. All kinds of sailing craft are available for hire, though demand often exceeds supply in July and August. It can also be difficult to find somewhere to stay during these two months, though it is correspondingly easy at other times. There are, in any case, very few hotels: most of the available accommodation is in pensions, holiday homes, chalets and camp-sites.

The Great Masurian Lake District had no permanent settlements prior to the establishment by the Teutonic Knights of a few strongholds in the fourteenth century. Even now, it remains a sparsely populated area, though the advent of tourism has led to the development of a number of resort towns. It has to be said that only one of these can be regarded as attractive in itself, and that there are very few historic monuments of note in the entire region.

Another important point to note is that this is one part of Poland where having a car is a definite advantage. Although three roughly parallel railway lines traverse the district from west to east, they are of limited use other than for getting to or from a particular resort. Buses are an altogether better means of communication, but the frequency of services is well below the national average, and some of the finest scenery lies outside the network.

The main gateway to the district is **Kętrzyn**, which is 8 miles (13km) north-east of Święta Lipka. Like several other Masurian towns, the name it was given after World War II was not a Polonised version of its former German one, but a brand new appellation honouring a local nineteenth-century Polish patriot. At the edge of the town centre is the Castle of the Teutonic Knights, one of the Order's smaller fortresses, and one with a surprisingly unassuming situation. It has been much altered down the centuries, and now serves as a museum, with displays on archaeology, local wildlife and on Wojeich Kętrzyński, the historian after whom the town is now named. Up from the castle is the church of St George, a brick-built basilica from the fourteenth century later modified into a Warmian-style hall, albeit one with a chancel. It has fine cellular vaults, though these are plastered over and thus not seen to best effect.

One of Poland's most sinister historic sites, the monumental ruins of the Wolf's Lair, the Nazi command headquarters for much of World War II, lies 5 miles (8km) east of Kętrzyn by the village of **Gierłoż**. Hitler arrived there on 24 June 1941, in preparation for the launch of Operation Barbarossa against the Soviet Union, and left on 20 November 1944, when the advancing Red Army forced his retreat westwards. He spent over 800 days in the Wolf's Lair during this period, only once making an extended sortie to the eastern front. The site was a complete fortified town inhabited by some 2,000 people, supplemented by workers who were bussed in daily. Construction work, carried out by gangs made up of prisoners-of-war and German wage labourers, began in 1940, and developments were still being carried out until shortly before the evacuation.

The Wolf's Lair was the epicentre of ten command positions, all but one of them custom-built, located throughout East Prussia, and its secluded location among woods, lakes and rivers was chosen to provide maximum security. Although well away from main roads, it lay on a railway line, and also had its own airfield 3 miles (5km) distant, with an emergency strip right beside the camp. It was equipped with its own telecommunications network, its own water supply, and its own electric power, with a diesel generator as back-up. The site was surrounded by barbed wire, the area around was strewn with mines, and camouflage netting was placed over all the roads and paths. Many of the buildings were simple wooden barracks, but huge concrete bunkers were constructed as private living quarters cum air raid shelters for Hitler and his henchmen such as Göring, Keitl and Jodl. These had walls and ceilings up to 26ft (8m) thick, and had artificial trees placed on top to ensure they were well disguised from aerial surveillance.

Hitler felt totally secure in the Wolf's Lair, though it was the setting for the Bomb Plot of 20 July 1944, the only one of some forty-odd attempts on his life which came close to success. This was a conspiracy of senior army officers who correctly diagnosed that the war was by then irretrievably lost and that its prolongation would lead to unnecessary casualties and national humiliation. Having killed Hitler, they intended to instal a democratic government and sue for peace on favourable terms. The pivotal figure in the plot was Count Claus Schenk von Stauffenberg, the Chief of Staff of the Reserve Army, who was a regular and trusted visitor to the Wolf's Lair. During a meeting in the Conference Bunker, he left his briefcase containing a primed bomb under the table close to Hitler, left the room under a pretext, then took a pre-arranged flight back to Berlin. However, in the few minutes before the bomb went off, the briefcase was moved by another officer, who was one of those killed in the blast. Hitler escaped with superficial injuries, and was able to have a summit with Mussolini later the same day. Some 5,000 people were eventually executed for their real or imagined role in the incident, a savage act of revenge which goes a long way towards explaining why there was never again a similar attempt on the Fuhrer's life.

After it was abandoned by Hitler, the Wolf's Lair was taken over for a time by the Fourth Army, then blown up in January 1945 before it could be captured by the Soviets. Such was the size of the bunkers, however, that they did not disintegrate, but merely cracked. In the decade after the war, 54,000 mines were cleared from the site, which was then opened as a public park. The red trail takes visitors round the most important ruins: these all lie north of the railway line, which was used for passenger services between Kętrzyn and Węgorzewo until 1994. Hitler's bunker (number 13), was the biggest, though Goring's (number 16) is far better preserved. A memorial plaque stands on the site of the bunker (number 3) where the July Bomb Plot took place.

The westernmost of the Masurian holiday resorts is **Mrągowo**, which is 22 miles (36km) south-west of Kętrzyn by road, on the southerly and more direct rail line between Olsztyn and Ełk. Situated on the strip of land between Lake Juno and Lake Czar, Mrągowo was the first place in the region to gain a luxury hotel. It has little in the way of sights, though there are a few nineteenth-century buildings in the centre. Among them the Town Hall, which now contains the local museum, with collections of furniture and decorative arts, and material on the churchman Krzystof Mrongoviusz, after whom the town is now named. Mrągowo's main claim to fame is the Country Picnic Festival held annually at the very end of July or beginning of August. This big country and western event, featuring all the attendant props, attracts established stars from the United States and elsewhere, as well as budding hopefuls from all over Poland.

Mikołajki, 14 miles (23km) south-east of Mrągowo, is easily the most enticing of the resorts, even though it can hardly hope to live up to its nickname of 'The Masurian Venice'. For long an obscure fishing village, it is not named after a nineteenth-century patriot, but rather after a legendary figure who finally caught the giant fish which was cutting up the nets of the local fishermen, so destroying their livelihood, by trapping it in one made of steel. Much smaller than its counterparts, and lacking any ugly high-rise development, Mikołajki stands on the shores of two lakes — Tałty to the north, and Mikołajskie to the south. These are connected by a narrow channel spanned by a road bridge and, at an oblique angle to it, an impressive pedestrian-only suspension bridge.

Overlooking Lake Tałty is the church of the Holy Trinity, a neo-Classical building with a handsome galleried interior which is one of the few historic churches in Poland retained for Lutheran worship. Alongside is the Museum of the Polish Reformation, which documents the role of Protestantism in the history of the nation. This provides a salutory reminder that, although Poland is now regarded as perhaps the most fervently Roman Catholic country in the world, until 1945 Protestants formed the overwhelming majority in many of the former German areas, and were at one time a substantial minority elsewhere.

A classy yachting marina is strung out along the eastern bank of Lake Mikołajskie. Closer to the bridge is the jetty for the cruise ships which ply the Masurian lakes. Thanks to its central location, Mikołajki is the lynchpin of the network, and the only point from which virtually every part of the system can be reached on a day trip — though for the longer voyages it may be necessary to make the return journey by bus. The shortest cruise is the round trip down Lake Mikołajskie and into the middle of Lake Śniardwy, Poland's largest lake, a vast open inland sea whose glassy waters normally look placid, yet can become treacherous when storms suddenly whip up.

Altogether very different in character is the round and shallow **Lake Łuknajno**, which is 3 miles (5km) east of Mikołajki, and linked to Lake Śniardwy by a narrow channel. The main Central European breeding ground of the wild swan, it is included on UNESCO's World Biosphere List, and is the focal point of the planned Masurian Lakes National Park. In the past, up to 2,000 swans have lived there, though the normal population nowadays is only about half that number. The lake's surroundings are marshy, and the footpath along the eastern side, which passes a research outstation of the University of Warsaw, is well away from the shore, and offers only occasional glimpses of the water. A much better view can be had from the wooden observation tower on the southern bank, though this is hard to find: the only access is on foot from the road from Mikołajki, about 1,640ft (500m) before the channel and the abandoned hamlet of Łuknajno. Whether or not the swan colony is close to the nearby shore is dependent on the prevailing wind conditions.

Another important scientific research institute is at **Popielno** on the western shore of Lake Śniardwy. One or two buses a day run from Ruciane-Nida to the south; from Mikołajki, it can be reached on car or foot by taking the road down the western side of Lake Mikolajskie, crossing via the ferry on the adjacent Lake Bełdany to Wierzba on the opposite bank, then continuing eastwards for another 1 mile (2km). Popielno is now the main breeding ground for the tarpan, the wild steppe horse that was first bred back from extinction in the Puszcza Białowieska (described in the next chapter).

Among the other animals bred at the station is the beaver, which has been re-introduced to several areas of Poland.

Popielno lies just beyond the northern tip of the **Puszcza Piska**, an unspoiled forest of some 384sq miles (1,000sq km) which still preserves some primeval characteristics. Made up of a mixture of pine and deciduous woods, it is rich in wild mushrooms and berries. Among its abundant birdlife, swans, herons and grebes are most in evidence; there are also a few eagles. One of the longer cruises available from Mikołajki is that going down the aforementioned Lake Bełdany, which vertically bisects the Puszcza Piska. The boats continue through the Guzianka lock, the only one on any of the Great Masurian Lakes, and along the lake of the same name to the double village of **Ruciane-Nida**, the main resort in the southern part of the region. From there, trips can be taken part of the way down Lake Nidzkie, circling round its small archipelago of wooded islets. Ruciane-Nida is also the terminus of one of Poland's two most scenic and popular canoe and kayak routes, which follows a serpentine 62 miles (100km) course from Sorkwity, 7 miles (12km) west of Mrągowo, passing through several small lakes en route. The route is named after the Krutynia, a beautiful dark river with an exceptionally gentle current, though it only accounts for about a quarter of the total length. Organised tours, lasting 10 days, are run along the route in summer. It is also easy enough to cover part or all of it independently: accommodation is available in waterside lodges (each of which bears the designation *stanica wodna*), located a leisurely day's paddle away from one another.

One village on the Krutynia worth visiting in its own right is **Wojnowo**, which is strung out along a side road, 5 miles (8km) north-west of Ruciane-Nida. The pleasantest approach, offering several glimpses of the river, is via Ukta to the north, which itself has a pretty setting, though nothing in the way of sights. Wojnowo is closely associated with the Old Believers (Starowiercy in Polish), a sect which broke away from the Russian Orthodox church in the seventeenth century. Remaining loyal to the old Slavonic rites and rejecting any form of ecclesiastical hierarchy, the Old Believers left Russia and settled initially in the Suwalszczyzna region described in the next chapter, where some of the villages they founded survive to this day. In the 1820s many migrated westwards to German-controlled Masuria, and Wojnowo became the main centre of their culture, a status it still maintains, though the sect, whose total number of members is now thought to be under 2,000, appears to be dying out.

About halfway down Wojnowo's only street is the molenna, the parish church of the Old Believers, a simple brick building from the early twentieth century. The woman who lives at house number 48 opposite has the keys and may be prepared to open it. Far more significant is the convent of the Old Believers, a substantial complex consisting of a simple white-plastered church, farm buildings and living quarters; it has a tranquil setting right beside the Krutynia, and is reached via a dirt track leading westwards from the southern end of the village. It was founded as a monastery, and functioned as such until 1884, when it was dissolved. The following year, a young nun was dispatched from Moscow to establish a new community. This soon numbered 25 members, but it declined after World War I and is now irretrievably doomed, with only two very elderly sisters still living there. Visitors are free to wander around the grounds: the cemetery by the river, with its array of nearly identical crosses, is a particularly atmospheric spot. Whenever a few people are around, the caretaker opens the church, which has an eighteenth-century chandelier and a number of old icons, though the most valuable of these have been moved for safekeeping to the castle in Lidzbark Warmiński.

In the northern part of the Great Masurian Lakes, the main town is **Giżycko**. It occupies a narrow spit of land between Lake Negocin to the south and Lake Kisajno to the north, which are linked by a canal which cuts through the heart of the town. The latter is an army of Lake Mamry, the second largest stretch of inland water in Poland, one which is made up of several separate lakes. By road, Giżycko is only 20 miles (33km) north-east of Mikołajki, and is a similar distance west of Kętrzyn. However, by far the most attractive way of making the former journey is by boat, a journey of over 3 hours by the excursion steamers. These travel via Lakes Tałty, Tałtowisko, Kotek, Szymon, Szymoneckie, Jagodne, Boczne and Niegocin, which are linked together by a series of canals built to provide a direct link between Lake Śniardwy and Lake Mamry.

In the centre of Giżycko, the only notable building is the parish church, which was built to a design by Karl Friedrich Schinkel; the town is named in honour of one of its former pastors, Gustaw Gizewiusz. Just west of the canal is the remaining section of the former Castle of the Teutonic Knights, which was modified in the Renaissance period by the addition of fancy gables. It is somewhat overshadowed by the huge Boyen Fortress further to the west, a typical example of Prussian military architecture of the mid-nineteenth century, and one which was formidable enough to play a strategic role in World War II, where it served as part of the Nazi command system centred on the Wolf's Lair. A couple of kilometres south of the fortress is the satellite resort village of **Wilkasy**, a far pleasanter base for exploring the area than Giżycko itself.

The northernmost town in the district is **Węgorzewo**, which lies 1 mile (2km) beyond the northern end of Lake Mamry, to which it is linked by canal. As usual, the best way of getting there is by boat. Steamers from Giżycko travel via Lake Kisajno, with its islet bird sanctuaries; they continue into Lake Dargin, pass under the bridge spanning the channel into the tiny Lake Kirsajty, then through another narrow gap at the other end into Lake Mamry proper. Węgorzewo itself was very badly damaged in both World Wars, but preserves a late sixteenth-century parish church, a very tardy example of the Gothic style, as well as the ruins of a Teutonic Knights' Castle. Equally accessible from Węgorzewo or Giżycko is the Puszcza Borecka to the east, an extensive and little visited forest in which wild boar, deer and wolves roam in freedom, and which also has a bison reserve.

The largest and easternmost town of the Great Masurian Lakes is **Ełk**, situated on the western shore of Lake Ełckie. It has the ruins of yet another castle, but is mainly of interest for its transport connections. The three railway lines which cross the district converge there, as do the corresponding roads, and it has excellent communications eastwards into the Podlasie region, the subject of the next chapter.

Further Information
— Warmia and Masuria —

Places to Visit

Frombork
Bishop's Palace
Cathedral Hill (Wzgórze Katedralne)
Open: Tuesday to Sunday 9am to 4.30pm.

Hospital of the Holy Ghost
ul. Stara
Open: Tuesday to Saturday 10am to 5pm.

Gierłoż
Wolf's Lair
Open: daily 8am to dusk.

Grunwald
Museum of the Battle of Grunwald
Open: May to September daily 9am to 6pm, October to April daily 10am to 4pm.

Kętrzyn
Castle of the Teutonic Knights
plac Zamkowy 1
Open: Tuesday to Sunday 10am to 4pm.

Kwidzyn
Castle of the Pomesanian Chapter
ul. Parkowa
Open: Tuesday to Sunday 9am to 3pm.

Lidzbark Warmiński
Castle of the Warmian Bishops
ul. Zamkowa 15
Open: 15 June to 15 September Tuesday to Sunday 9am to 5pm, 16 September to 14 June Tuesday to Sunday 9am to 4pm.

Mikołajki
Museum of the Polish Reformation
ul. 1-go Maja
Open: Tuesday to Sunday 10am to 4pm.

Morąg
Dohna Palace
Rynek
Open: Tuesday to Sunday 9am to 4pm.

Mrągowo
Town Hall and District Museum
plac Michała Kajki 1
Open: Tuesday to Sunday 10am to 3pm.

Olsztyn
Castle of the Warmian Chapter
ul. Zamkowa
Open: Tuesday to Sunday 10am to 4pm.

Olsztynek
Museum of Folk Architecture
ul. Sportowa
Open: June to August Tuesday to Sunday 9am to 5pm, May and 1 September to 15 October Tuesday to Sunday 9am to 4pm, 16 October to 30 April Tuesday to Sunday 9am to 3pm.

Reszel
Castle of the Warmian Bishops
Open: Tuesday to Sunday 10am to 5pm.

Tourist Office

Olsztyn
High Gate (Wysoka Brama)
☎ 27-27-3

6 • Podlasie

If most of Poland lies well off the beaten track, no other province is quite so removed from tourist routes as **Podlasie** (or Podlasia), the north-easternmost part of the country. Yet this is undoubtedly one of the nation's most fascinating and rewarding corners. Among its many outstanding areas of natural beauty, the Puszcza Białowieska and the Biebrza marshes stand out as truly unique landscapes, being the last surviving examples anywhere in Europe of the primeval forest and wetlands once found throughout the continent. The first of these is the only place in the province which sees much in the way of tourism, and even that is kept firmly in check by its isolated location.

Another enticement is that Podlasie is the sole area where significant vestiges remain of the ethnic, religious and cultural diversity that character-ised Polish society from the early Middle Ages until World War II. It has a large Belarussian minority and a somewhat smaller Lithuanian one, and even retains two villages populated by Muslim Tatars. Although the influential Jewish community was exterminated in World War II, a number of important monuments survive as a reminder of its historic presence. Under Communist rule, the Russian Orthodox church, formerly a strong rival to Catholicism in the region, languished in the doldrums, but it is now making a determined comeback. This is given visible expression in its building programme, which is adding a host of new places of worship to the stock of historic churches whose onion domes are a feature of the skyline of so many Podlasian towns and villages. At the same time, the Old Believers sect maintains a tenuous presence, but appears to be on the verge of dying out.

Podlasie is the only part of northern Poland which has never been subject to wholescale Germanisation, but it is only in the twentieth century that its association with the Polish state has become fixed. Its northern reaches were originally settled by a somewhat mysterious Baltic tribe known as the Jatzvingians, and it subsequently became a province of the Grand Duchy of Lithuania. In common with the rest of Lithuania, it was subject to ever-increasing Polonisation throughout the era of the Polish-Lithuanian Com-monwealth, when the Polish language and the Roman Catholic faith established pre-eminence. During the Partition period, a section of Podlasie was annexed directly by Russia, while the rest was allocated to the short-lived Congress Kingdom of Poland. Parts of the province were coveted by

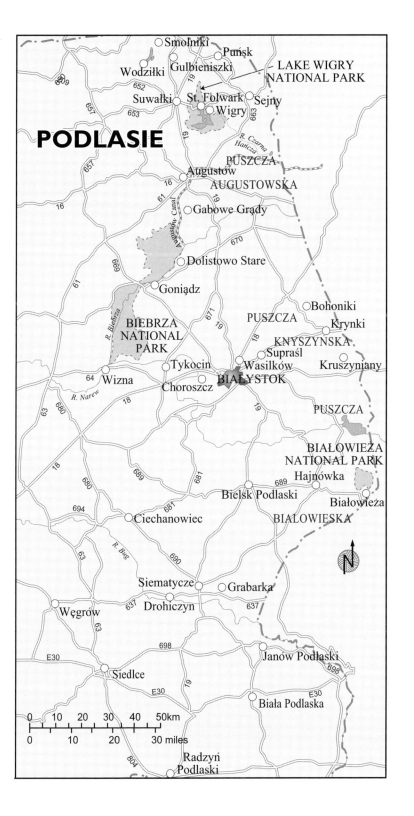

Lithuania on the resurrection of the two old nations after World War II, but Poland prevailed in this argument. When a Belarussian state was established for the first time in 1991, it saw itself as the rightful heir to at least a chunk of Podlasie, but, not surprisingly, has made no progress with its claim.

All of Podlasie's major attractions lie in the north and centre of the province. However, being fundamentally rural, even these parts can only be covered fully by means of a touring route rather than from a single base, though a fair number of places are within commuting range of Białystok, the only large city.

The Suwalszczyzna

The **Suwalszczyzna**, the extreme north-eastern corner of Poland, is often regarded as an extension of Masuria. In reality, however, the two are very different, both geographically and historically. The Suwalszczyzna's lakes are smaller and deeper, and have purer, less polluted waters; they are also sparser, though there are still some 200 in all. There are few channels linking individual lakes, so there are not the opportunities for yachting that have made the Great Masurian Lake District such a favourite destination with Polish holidaymakers. Although the slow-flowing River Czarna Hańcza, which flows almost all the way through the Suwalszczyzna, rivals the Krutynia in Masuria as Poland's most popular canoe route, the region is otherwise almost entirely undiscovered by tourism.

For centuries, perhaps for as long as a millennium, the Suwalszczyzna was inhabited by the Jatzvingians, who belonged to the Baltic group of peoples which also included the Prussians and Lithuanians. By the year 1290 the tribe, which seems to have been about 50,000-strong, suffered the same fate as its Prussian neighbours — extermination by the Teutonic Knights as a result of a stubborn refusal to convert to Christianity. However, the Knights failed to penetrate any further east, being repulsed by the Lithuanians, a warlike people who were themselves set on territorial expansion. Thus, German settlers never came to this dangerous border area, and it was not until the Polish-Lithuanian Commonwealth was at the height of its power in the sixteenth and seventeenth centuries that the first towns were founded in the Suwalszczyzna. On two subsequent occasions, the region fell under German rule, but each of these periods was short-lived and failed to leave a lasting mark.

Suwałki is the largest town in the Suwalszczyzna, but is nevertheless a provincial sort of place with little in its favour other than its easy access to the marvellous countryside around. Otherwise, the town's main asset is the presence of the Czarna Hańcza, which has an innocuous appearance as it meanders down the western side of town, but cuts an impressive wooded valley to the south of the town centre after it changes course.

The town centre, which is laid out on an irregular grid plan, has many buildings in the late neo-Classical style characteristic of the parts of Poland under Russian rule in the nineteenth century. Prominent among these are the Catholic parish church of St Alexander on plac Piłsudskiego and the

Protestant church on ul. Kościuszki, the main north-south axis. Just north of the latter, a memorial museum has been established in the birthplace of Maria Konopnicka, a nineteenth-century writer and feminist whose children's novels and patriotic songs still enjoy immense popularity in Poland. Also on this street is the Regional Museum, which contains a number of excavated artefacts of the Jatzvingian culture. Further east, beyond the bus station, is the molenna, a simple timber church which is one of three still-active places of worship in the Suwalszczynza of the Old Believers sect first mentioned in the previous chapter. It dates back to the beginning of the twentieth century, though the icons inside are far more venerable.

Overlooking the river on the western side of town is the municipal cemetery, whose divided plots provide the most telling evidence of the ethnic and religious diversity of the local populace prior to 1945. Starting from the north, there are separate Roman Catholic, Protestant, Orthodox, Jewish and Tatar cemeteries. That devoted to the Orthodox faith is particularly noteworthy: it has a picturesque funerary chapel, and a section at the rear for the Old Believers. The once extensive Jewish cemetery was desecrated by the Nazis and is now an open space, except for the modern memorial in the middle with fragments of some of the shattered tombstones.

About 4 miles (7km) north of Suwałki, near the village of **Szwajcaria**, is a Jatzvingian burial ground, one of the few tangible sites associated with the original inhabitants of the region. Located in an overgrown wood, it consists of a number of earth mounds, varying in width from 10ft to 66ft (3m to 20m), and surrounded by remnants of the layers of stones which once covered them. Outside the adjacent village of **Osinka**, a couple of kilometres farther east, and reachable from the burial ground by the trail marked with black stripes, are the excavated remains of a Jatzvingian fort.

Wodziłki, which lies about 12 miles (20km) north-east of Suwałki, is an isolated settlement at the end of a 3km-long backroad which itself lies off a minor road. Since the mid-eighteenth century, it has been home to a community of Old Believers, who have preserved the traditional rural way of life of their ancestors with no concessions to modernity. The molenna, a timber building with an octagonal tower, is older and more attractive than its Suwalki counterpart. It likewise contains an impressive array of icons; unfortunately, access to the interior is normally only possible during the Sunday morning service.

From Wodziłki, it is only a short distance as the crow flies to **Lake Hańcza**, the deepest lake in Poland, with a maximum depth of 356ft (108m). The easiest point of access is Błaskowizna on the southern shore of the lake: this is serviced by occasional buses from Suwałki, which also stop at the turn-off to Wodziłki. An alternative approach to the lake is the hour-long journey on foot along the path from **Smolniki**, 12 miles (20km) from Suwałki on the main road north. This village also has a number of fine vantage points over the hills and lakes of the surrounding countryside, the best of which is near its southern boundary. Between Smolniki and Suwałki is **Gulbieniszki**, which lies below Cisowa Góra, a hill that was for centuries the setting for pagan religious rites. Its conical shape is reminiscent of that of a volcano, but its height of just 846ft (258m) makes its nickname of 'The Polish Fujiyama' seem very fanciful, even if it offers a fine view nonetheless.

Puńsk, which lies 19 miles (30km) north-east of Suwałki, has a certain curiosity value: although ethnic Lithuanians live in many of the villages along the border, this is the only place where they constitute the overwhelming majority of the population. A lively folklore tradition is maintained, most evident during major religious festivals, which are centred on the neo-Gothic parish church, where services in both Lithuanian and Polish are held. There is also a small informal museum of Lithuanian customs, located on ul. Szkolna. Prior to the war, Puńsk had a sizeable Jewish community, but the synagogue has undergone conversion, leaving the cemetery in the north of the village as the only obvious reminder of this aspect of local history.

From Puńsk, there are regular buses to the Lithuanian capital **Vilnius** (or Wilno, as it is known to Poles), a journey for which nothing more than a passport is now needed. A beautiful city with an unusually large and well-preserved Old Town featuring many buildings in the highly distinctive local Baroque style, it was one of the great cultural centres of the Polish-Lithuanian Commonwealth, and throughout the twentieth century has been a bone of contention between the two countries. Alternative (Polish-run) bus services travel from Białystok via Suwałki, and either of these offers obvious advantages over making the journey by train (which necessitates a circuitous route through Belarus) or by car (which generally involves long delays at the frontier).

Sejny, 15$^{1}/_{2}$ miles (25km) south-east of Puńsk and 19 miles (30km) east of Suwałki, is the last Polish town before the only official road crossing-point into Lithuania at Ogrodniki, a further 6 miles (10km) east. Its skyline is dominated from the north by a huge hilltop Dominican monastery, a late Renaissance complex built in the early 1600s, to which a façade in the Vilnius Baroque style was appended 150 years later. At the opposite end of the centre is the mid-nineteenth-century synagogue, now the headquarters of an organization dedicated to promoting and preserving the varied history, art, music and customs of the border areas. A festival is held each April, with changing exhibitions throughout the rest of the year.

The main road between Suwałki and Sejny offers the easiest access to **Lake Wigry National Park** (Wigierski Park Narodowy), which was established to protect the eponymous lake and the countryside surrounding it. Within this area live nearly 200 species of birds; 45 different mammals (including wolves, lynxes, elk, deer, wild boar, badgers, otters and the park's symbol, the beaver); 17 reptiles (notably the European pond tortoise); and 25 sorts of fish. The landscape includes spruce and pine woods, wet forests, swamps, peatbogs and the River Czarna Hańcza, which flows all the way through the park, passing across the middle of the lake itself. Lake Wigry has wonderfully clear waters, and reaches a depth of up to 239ft (73m). It has numerous little wooded islets, while its shoreline is heavily indented, with many creeks and marshes. A marked footpath, whose total length is almost

A gypsy caravan in the Museum of Folk Architecture, Olsztynek (Chapter 5)

The yachting marina at Mikołajki in the Great Masurian Lake District (Chapter 5)

The Branicki Palace in Choroszcz seen from its park (Chapter 6)

The garden front of the Branicki Palace in Białystok (Chapter 6)

31 miles (50km), runs all the way round its perimeter, though it often meanders a long way from the shore.

There are also a number of agricultural hamlets, among them **Wigry**, which occupies a peninsula at the north-eastern side of the lake, a couple of kilometres from the little resort of Stary Folwark, which is 7 miles (11km) east of Suwałki on the main road to Sejny. Towering above the lakeside farms is the park's setpiece attraction, the former Camaldolese monastery; it has a marvellously photogenic setting, which can be glimpsed from many different vantage points along the shore. Wigry was one of a number of Polish foundations of this order, an eccentric offshoot of the Benedictines which aimed at a compromise solution between the solitary eremitical way of life and the communal monastic tradition. The first monks arrived in 1667 at the invitation of two successive kings of Poland's ruling Waza dynasty. However, work on erecting the monastery did not begin until a generation later, under the direction of an Italian architect, Pietro Putini. Built in a sober Baroque style, it adopts the classic Camaldolese plan, with the belfry and the twin-towered church at opposite ends, and the hermitages, where each monk spent the vast majority of his time alone, arranged in neat terraced rows in between. Monastic life at Wigry was suppressed when the Suwalszczyzna fell to Prussia in 1795. It has never been revived, but the buildings are now put to good use during the summer as a hotel.

Lake Wigry stands at the northern end of the vast expanse of the **Puszcza Augustowska**, one of the two largest stretches of uninterrupted forest in Poland, which reaches southwards to the Biebrza marshes (described in a later section of this chapter) and eastwards into Lithuania and Belarus. A mixed woodland with both coniferous and deciduous trees, it is seen at its best — as is so often the case in Poland — during the autumn. There are more than fifty lakes, sometimes grouped in chains, within the northern and central parts of the forest, and there is a sufficient number of roads for these parts to be suitable for exploration by any form of wheeled transport. In the southern reaches, on the other hand, the terrain is often impenetrable, even on foot.

The most enticing way of getting around, however, is to take to the water: either the Czarna Hańcza, which flows diagonally through the forest en route to its confluence with the River Niemen in Belarus, or the **Augustów Canal**, which begins at the confluence of the Biebrza and the Netta, continuing northwards for about 19 miles (30km) before veering eastwards to the Belarussian frontier, a further 31 miles (50km) away. This canal, the brainchild of the military engineer Ignacy Prądzyński, was begun in 1824 as the great prestige project of the ill-fated Congress Kingdom of Poland, founded nine years previously as a quasi-autonomous part of the Russian Empire. By linking up a host of lakes and rivers, it was intended to provide the country with direct access to the Baltic which would be cheaper and more secure than the traditional route along the Vistula, whose lower basin had fallen under Prussian control. Most of the Polish section of the canal, including some 40km of man-made waterway and 18 locks, had been completed by the time the Congress Kingdom was incorporated directly into Russia in 1830, but the Russians never built the final stage to the sea. Although it therefore never fulfilled its intended purpose, it has gained a new lease of life as a tourist attraction, used by both canoeists and pleasure steamers.

Cruises along the eastern section of the canal are run between mid-June and mid-September from **Augustów**, the second largest town in the Suwalszczyzna, set on the shores of Lake Necko, 19 miles (30km) south of Suwałki. Founded in the mid-sixteenth century by King Zygmunt August (hence its name), it remained a small village until the construction of the canal. It is now by far the most important resort in the region, and has spread itself out over a wide area. Other than the boat trips on the canal and the nearby lakes, it has few attractions. The one building of note is the PTTK hostel by the lakeside in the north of town, built just before the outbreak of World War II to plans by Maciej Nowicki, later one of the international team of architects responsible for the United Nations headquarters in New York. There is also a two-part Regional Museum: that on ul. 3 Maja in the chessboard-plan town centre south of the lake focuses on ethnography, while its branch directly opposite the wharf details the history of the Augustów Canal.

Gabowe Grądy, located 9 miles (14km) south of Augustów, just beyond the northern edge of the Biebrza marshes, is another village closely associated with the Old Believers. In common with its counterparts, the wooden molenna is best visited on a Sunday morning, when the services are enlivened by the participation of the female-only choir, who play an important role in preserving the sect's powerful and distinctive musical tradition as a living art form.

Białystok

Białystok, which lies 56 miles (90km) south of Augustów and 117 miles (180km) north-east of Warsaw, is the only city in Podlasie, with a population several times that of any other town in the region. It was no more than a village until the mid-eighteenth century, when the local magnate, Jan Klemens Branicki, having abandoned his ambition to gain election to the Polish crown, moved back from the capital to his estates, and made Białystok the main seat of his court. The following century, it underwent a mushroom growth as it became an important textile-producing centre of the Russian-controlled Congress Kingdom of Poland, rivalling Łódź, another late developer, at the opposite end of the country. Jews played a prominent role in the city's economic life, but nearly all of them perished at the hands of the Nazis, who massacred half the city's total population.

Given its history, it is not surprising that much of Białystok is a featureless sprawl. However, it makes a good excursion base for some fascinating destinations in the surrounding countryside, where there is a dearth of accommodation. Moreover, it has a certain curiosity value as the only Polish city to retain any vestiges of the ethnic and cultural mix that was so endemic to all the country's main urban centres prior to World War II, with the Belarussian language and the Russian Orthodox faith both retaining substantial holds. On gaining its independence for the first time in its history on the break-up of the Soviet Union, the state of Belarus went as far as to stake an official claim to Białystok and its hinterland.

Most of the historic monuments are located on or close to ul. Lipowa, which bisects the Old Town on an east-west axis. Despite its central position, it is nowadays a thoroughfare of secondary importance, overshadowed by the broad boulevards separating the Old Town from the commercial quarters. Some of the residential streets to the north and south of ul. Lipowa are still lined with the painted wooden houses once characteristic of the city, and particularly favoured by the Jewish community.

Set in expansive parkland beyond the eastern end of ul. Lipowa is the Branicki Palace, the main entrance being via a walled enclosure with a gateway in the form of a triumphal arch. The palace itself gradually evolved from a fifteenth-century castle, gaining a Baroque appearance in the late seventeenth century when the main block was remodelled by the great Dutch-born architect from Warsaw, Tylman van Gameren. At the behest of Jan Klemens Branicki, it was greatly expanded by Johann Deibel, who added side wings and an extra storey. Aesthetically, the result can be regarded as no more than a partial success, but the grand scale earned it the nickname of 'The Podlasian Versailles'. During the Polish-Soviet War in 1920, Feliks Dzierżyński, founder of the Cheka (the secret police force that was the forerunner of the KGB), proclaimed the establishment of the Polish Soviet Republic from the balcony facing the courtyard. This event was much celebrated in the Communist period but is scorned nowadays as an act of high treason.

The palace is occupied by a medical academy and is thus not a regular tourist sight, though no-one is likely to object to visitors having a quick look inside. Unfortunately, the interiors, with the exception of the stairway and the festive hall on the first floor, have all been modernised. Of more obvious appeal is the Palace Park, which has a formal French garden laid out according to a geometric design with waterways and clipped hedges, plus a more extensive section in the 'natural' English style.

Just to the west, back on ul. Lipowa itself, is a curious double church. The original part, known as the parish church, is Baroque and dates back to the early seventeenth century. Although its dimensions are no more than those of a chapel, it was, until the beginning of the twentieth century, the only place of worship in Białystok for the city's Roman Catholic majority. Throughout the nineteenth century, as the city expanded, the Tsarist authorities proscribed the building of new churches for rival denominations to their own Orthodox faith. Eventually, the Catholics overcome this by applying for the right to expand the size of their church, and duly built on a huge twin-towered structure in the neo-Gothic style which dwarfs the original building, resulting in a twenty-fold increase in its capacity. Nowadays, the 'extension' is designated both as the cathedral and as a basilica, with the parish church functioning as one of its side chapels. Regrettably, the latter is normally shut off except for masses on Sundays and very early on weekday mornings. However, it is well worth trying to see the richly varied Baroque, Rococo and neo-Classical decorations of its interior. These include the tombs of the Branicki family and an altarpiece of *The Assumption* by Jan Klemens Branicki's court painter Silvestre de Mirys, an artist born in France to an exiled Scottish Jacobite family.

Further west is the triangular-shaped market square, known as Rynek Kościuszki, dominated by the mid-eighteenth-century Town Hall, now the Regional Museum. On the ground floor is a collection of Polish painting from the last two centuries, with many of the country's leading artists, such as Wojciech Gerson, Jacek Malczewski and Stanisław Ignacy Witkiewicz, represented. The basement is devoted to archaeology, and includes material relating to the Jatzvingian tribe.

Just to the north of the Rynek is ul. Zamenhofa, named in honour of Białystok's most famous son, Ludwik Zamenhof, an eye specialist who adopted the pseudonym of Dr Esperanto (meaning 'one who hopes') and developed his own artificial language, based on a variety of common European roots, which he first published in 1887. The impetus behind this was the idealistic one of fostering better communications between different peoples, a matter of pressing concern in what was then a linguistically diverse city. Zamenhof used his own creation with great skill, making translations of several masterpieces of world literature. Although his dream of it becoming a second language for all mankind never remotely came to fruition, Esperanto retains an international following to this day, and has been far more successful than any other synthetic language. He is commemorated by a plaque on his birthplace at number 26 on the street, and by a monument in the park a block to the west.

Set in its own courtyard, back on ul. Lipowa, is the domed Orthodox church of St Nicholas. Its exterior is a stern example of the late neo-Classical style of the mid-nineteenth century, but the interior is brightly painted with frescos copied from those in the cathedral of St Sophia in the Ukrainian capital, Kiev. In what might be regarded as a neatly symmetrical piece of history, the church has become inadequate to accommodate the growth in worshippers that has occurred since the fall of Communism, and even on weekdays the congregation normally spills out into the courtyard.

Dominating the skyline of central Białystok from its position atop a hillock at the western end of ul. Lipowa is the church of St Roch, which likewise shelters under a dome, albeit this time one made of glass. It is among the most accomplished of a number of highly original Polish churches of the inter-war period which reflect a desire to forge a distinctive national architecture for a country which had only recently freed itself from a long era of foreign occupation. The architect Otakar Sosnowski's design has been described as 'jazz-modern', which seems an apt characterisation of its spiky silhouette, its compositional freedom, and its organic shape.

Białystok has recently gained another very prominent landmark as a result of the construction of the huge new Orthodox church of the Holy

Ghost a couple of kilometres to the north-west of St Roch. Although work is likely to continue for some years yet, the exterior, which re-interprets the traditional language of Orthodox architecture in an angular modern idiom, is already complete. The onion-shaped central dome is topped with a statue of the Cross, representing Christ, while the four subsidiary domes and the eight gables each have a smaller Cross, representing the Apostles.

One of the few tangible reminders of the city's Judaic heritage is the sole surviving Jewish cemetery, located on ul. Wschodnia in the north of the city, immediately east of the junction of the main roads to Sokółka and Supraśl. To its rear lies a much larger Catholic cemetery, while just to the west, on ul. Wysockiego, is an Orthodox cemetery with a picturesque funerary chapel.

Excursions from Białystok

Within easy reach of Białystok are several remarkable old villages which bear witness to the ethnic, religious and cultural diversity that was so characteristic of Poland for most of its history. As these can all be seen quite quickly, are separated by relatively large distances, and have almost nothing in the way of overnight accommodation, it is a big advantage to have a car. However, all but one of the places mentioned in this section has a direct and fairly regular bus link with Białystok. Thus it is normally possible, using the city as a base, to cover two or even three of these destinations in the course of a single day.

There are certainly no problems in reaching **Wasilków**; lying just north of the end of the built-up part of Bialystok, a few kilometres from the group of cemeteries mentioned at the end of the description of the city, it is within the municipal bus network. The Orthodox church, in the very heart of the village, completely overshadows its Roman Catholic neighbour. Built in the mid-nineteenth century in a mixed neo-Classical and neo-Byzantine style, it is arguably the most impressive of its era in Podlasie. Curiously enough, the most imposing feature is the not the church itself, but the monumental entrance gateway to the walled enclosure, which doubles as the belfry — a combination claimed as unique. As is standard practice, the church is normally only open for services, but the priest, who lives at number 17 on ul. Mickiewicza a few minutes' walk to the north-west, can usually be persuaded to open it.

The decayed town of **Supraśl**, successively important as a religious and then as a textile manufacturing centre, is 9 miles (15km) north-east of central Białystok, and is likewise serviced by city buses. It lies at the fringe of the Puszcza Knyszyńska, a large and relatively unspoilt forest stretching almost to the Belarussian frontier which is a popular weekend destination for local ramblers. At the edge of the village is a walled complex founded at the very beginning of the sixteenth century as an Orthodox Basilian monastery. However, by the Union of Brest of 1596 the westernmost outposts of Eastern Orthodoxy agreed to acknowledge the authority of the pope while preserving their own liturgy and traditions. Supraśl became a bishopric of this new denomination, usually known as the Uniate Church, though in Poland it is often styled 'Greek Catholic'. As a result, a huge Bishop's palace was raised, with the original monastic church retained as the centrepiece of its court-yard. The latter, a highly original structure which married Gothic and Byzantine architectural elements, was regarded as one of Poland's greatest buildings. Tragically, it was razed to its foundations by the Nazis, but it is currently being reconstructed — though the question as to which denomi-nation will take possession once it has been completed has caused consid-erable controversy. In the meantime, some of the haunting frescos of angels and church fathers which adorned the interior are on display on racks in the museum set up in the high and narrow Rococo chapel of the Bishop's Palace, the rest of which is now occupied by a college.

Right by the Belarussian frontier, 28 miles (45km) east of Supraśl, is **Krynki**, which has retained its original plan almost intact, the main feature of this being no fewer than twelve streets radiating out from the central Rynek. There are also some sights of note, including an eighteenth-century parish church, a nineteenth-century Orthodox church, the ruins of the neo-Classical Synagogue and a large Jewish cemetery.

Krynki is best-known as being a staging-post for visiting Poland's two remaining Tatar villages, one of which lies just to the south, the other to the north. The Tatars have played a small but notable role throughout Poland's history, first appearing among the Mongol hordes which overran the country in the thirteenth century. In 1410, a detachment of Tatar horsemen is documented among the Polish-Lithuanian army which defeated the Teu-tonic Knights at the Battle of Grunwald, and their military contribution to the national army thereafter increased, reaching a climax in the seventeenth-century wars against the Turks. Following victory at the Battle of Vienna in 1683, King Jan Sobieski made grants of land in eastern Poland to the Tatars. Direct descendants of these settlers still live in each of the two villages, though they now constitute a minority of the population. Nonetheless, the several thousand Tatars who still live in Poland — mostly in major cities such as Białystok, Warsaw and Gdańsk — make regular pilgrimages to one or the other on Moslem feast days, and many choose to be buried there. It thus seems certain that the Tatars will manage to retain a living presence in the villages, in spite of predictions that they are doomed because of the increasing reluctance of younger members of the communities to tolerate the harsh lifestyle this entails.

The larger and more attractive of the two, **Kruszyniany**, lies down a side road 7 miles (11km) south of Krynki. Its houses, mostly traditional wooden constructions with small farmsteads attached, are strung out over a distance of 1 mile (2km). Roughly in the middle of the village, concealed among trees and entered via a gate bearing the Islamic crescent-shaped moon, is the eighteenth-century mosque. Made entirely of pine and painted in green and white, it closely resembles the wooden churches so typical of rural Poland. However, its twin towers are capped by weathervanes in the inevitable crescent shape, while the usual church design is modified by the addition of a graceful little minaret and by a mihrab, the prayer niche facing Mecca. The Tatar family living in the house immediately south of the church (number 57) have the keys and are normally prepared to open it for interested visitors in return for a donation, though it is essential to be respectably dressed, and to remove shoes before entering. Inside are two rooms, the smaller being for the women, who are not allowed into the main prayer hall during acts of worship. The latter's floor is covered with oriental carpets; its walls have framed painted texts from the Koran, while the main furnishing is the mimber, from where prayers are led.

A track running east of the mosque leads up to a wood commanding a fine view over the village. This is also the site of the Mizmar, the Moslem cemetery. Grouped near the entrance are well-tended modern graves inscribed in Polish and Arabic; the inscriptions show the Tatar penchant for adding characteristic Polish endings to traditional Islamic names. Older tombstones, some with Cyrillic lettering, can be seen in the undergrowth a bit further into the wood. Also worth a look are the Orthodox church and cemetery of the local Belarussian community, located in the northern part of the village. The former is a recent concrete replacement for its wooden predecessor, which was destroyed by fire.

Bohoniki, the second Tatar village, is much smaller than Kruszyniany, and is even more remote. It lies on a very minor road, serviced by only occasional buses, 4 miles (7km) south-east of the town of Sokółka, which is on the main railway line between Białystok and Vilnius. However, buses between Krynki and Sókołka stop near Drahle, the next village to the west, meaning that, with a little bit of walking, it is possible to visit the two Tatar villages on the same day even without a car. The mosque is correspondingly smaller than its counterpart, and lacks towers, but has a character of its own, with an entrance porch curiously reminiscent of American colonial architecture of the same period. However, plans (which are displayed inside) have been drawn up for its expansion, and the foundations have been laid, though there has been a delay in starting the actual building work. The family with the keys, who live in the house immediately west of the church (number 24), are usually prepared to open it under the same conditions as in Kruszyniany. To reach the Mizmar, take the northbound track from the eastern end of the village; again, it is located on a wooded slope, and has well-tended graves from recent decades encircling the unkempt section with the older tombstones.

West of Białystok, the first destination of note is **Choroszcz**, 6 miles (10km) away on the route of urban buses, and lying back from both the main Warsaw road and the River Narew. Through the hospital grounds at the extreme western end of the village is the late Baroque palace, a country house built in the 1720s for Jan Klemens Branicki, before he commissioned the more ambitious remodelling of his residence in Białystok. The palace stands on a small artificial island at the beginning of a canal which cuts a dead straight line through its English-style park; to the side are the estate buildings, which still serve as a working farm. Most of the palace's original furnishings were lost when it was gutted by fire in 1915, but it has been restored to house the Museum of Palace Interiors, which has eighteenth- and nineteenth-century objets d'art and examples of interior design from all over Europe.

Choroszcz lies just beyond the edge of the **Narew Landscape Park** (Narwiański Park Krajobrazowy), a protected area of countryside stretching southwards along the river for some 19 miles (30km). The marshland is similar to, if ultimately less spectacular than, that of the Narew's tributary, the Biebrza, which is the subject of the following section. However, it was the village of Waniewo on the left bank of the Narew which served as the camp base for the 1992 expedition of 32 wildlife artists from 15 countries which was primarily responsible for bringing the uniqueness of the Podlasian marshes to the attention of an international audience. The artists produced a total of 2,000 paintings, sculptures and drawings of the landscape and wildlife of the two marshes, and these were subsequently exhibited around the world. Many different species of bird (183 in all) inhabit this part of the Narew basin, and all but 40 of them are known to breed there.

Down the Narew from Choroszcz, 9 miles (14km) away by the direct minor road, is **Tykocin**, whose decline has been even more calamitous than that of Supraśl. An important trading town which for centuries overshadowed Białystok, it even served as a second-string royal residence for over a century following its acquisition by King Zygmunt August in 1548. Jews traditionally accounted for half or more of Tykocin's population, and the loss of this entire community during World War II was a blow from which it has not recovered. The town charter was revoked in 1950, reducing it to the status of a village, and the total number of inhabitants has remained well below the pre-war level.

As is still evident from the very different character of the houses, Tykocin was divided down the middle into Christian and Jewish districts. The former, the eastern half, has a Rynek of highly exaggerated dimensions, lined with capacious single-storey wooden houses. Jan Klemens Branicki commissioned a monument to his grandfather Stefan Czarniecki, a hero of the seventeenth-century wars against the Swedes, to adorn the square. He also founded the Missionary college at the far end, whose church of the Holy Trinity now serves as the local parish. It has an extraordinary façade, reminiscent more of a palace than a church, with curvaceous wings forming a link to the twin corner towers. Inside are some fine Baroque furnishings, including a polychrome ceiling, ornate side chapels and an organ flanked by full-length portraits by Silvestre de Mirys of Branicki and his wife Izabella Poniatowska. To the north of the church is the Alumnat, a hospice for war veterans established in 1633. Across the bridge, on the opposite side of the marshy banks of the Narew, are the scanty remains of King Zygmunt August's once-splendid castle, which contained a valuable library and one of Poland's main arsenals. It was wrecked by the Swedes in the 1650s, and dismantled virtually to its foundations a century later.

The former Jewish district, characterised by its proud whitewashed dwellings, clusters round the Baroque synagogue, one of the finest in Poland. It was built in the 1640s, in the immediate aftermath of the lifting of the controls which formerly regulated the size of Jewish temples: thereafter, they could be as large and as prominent as was desired. The exterior impresses by its sense of mass, but it is the interior decoration which is the chief joy. This includes an impressive columned bimah in the centre of the building, and the ornate ark for storing the Torah scrolls on the east wall. A number of brightly painted Hebrew inscriptions have also survived. Now designated as the Jewish Museum, the synagogue contains a collection of liturgical objects, sacred books, and photographs of the region's lost Jewish heritage. Immediately to the west is the Talmudic House, which houses a museum of Tykocin's history, including a complete apothecary.

The Biebrza National Park

The **Biebrza National Park** (Biebrzański Park Narodowy) at the western end of the Podlasie region is the only lowland wilderness to be found anywhere in Europe, being the last example of the natural wetlands which were once commonplace to have survived relatively intact. With a total area of nearly 230 sq miles (600sq km), it is by far the largest national park in Poland, and is one which currently attracts more interest among the international scientific community than any other: it is seen as a possible model for the restoration of comparable ecosystems, which would help counteract the problems of global warming. Yet, astonishing as it seems, this marshland was virtually unknown until a few years ago. It only became a national park in 1993, having gained a limited protection status 6 years previously, and foreign visitors were completely unheard of until after the fall of Communism.

That this wondrously beautiful landscape, which is also one of the most important ornithological breeding grounds in the world, has managed to survive is due to a happy conjunction of circumstances. Down the course of history, it often formed part of the borderlands between hostile states, a factor which mitigated against permanent settlements, the first of which were not established until the end of the Middle Ages. The local peasant farmers have maintained a subsistence economy right down to the present day, never having been able to afford the drainage systems which would have made their life easier yet ruined the uniqueness of their surroundings. Nor has any government been prepared to fund the regional development programme which would have transformed the area, the Communists having lacked the ideological impetus for doing so, as the farms were smallholdings, rather than the property of landed magnates.

Traditional farming with horses and carts is still the norm in many parts of Poland, but in the Biebrza valley it is an abiding necessity, as most of the ground is far too moist to be able to support tractors. The presence of agriculture may mean that the area is not a true virgin territory, but it has had the paradoxical effect of preserving and improving the environment, by limiting the unchecked growth of vegetation that would otherwise have occurred. Indeed, a key element in the plans for the future preservation of the delicate ecological balance of the region is to encourage the continuation of the age-old farming methods.

The park consists of the middle and lower basins of the 99 mile (160km) long River Biebrza, a tributary of the Narew. Of these, the former is crossed by several artificial waterways, among them the Augustów Canal, which have altered the original ecosystem, which survives almost intact in the lower basin. The river's course is a truly amazing sight: it constantly twists and turns and frequently loops back on itself, weaving a patchwork of wet meadows and tiny islets. Each spring, the effect of this is further enhanced by the floods which inevitably follow the melting of the winter downfall. This creates a marshy landscape stretching far away from the river, though the extent of this varies considerably from year to year. It is positively crystalline in appearance, both the ground and river water being virtually free of pollution. In all, 35 different varieties of fish live there.

The Biebrza valley varies in width from 1 mile to 9 miles (2km to 15km), and the river is by no means its only important physical feature. There are also extensive tracts of still developing peat bog, which have a covering of sedge and moss; these were formed during the last Ice Age, when a retreating glacier transformed what was hitherto a shallow lake into a vast swamp. The most important of these, and one of the highlights of the national park, is the Red Marsh (Czerwone Bagno) in the north of the middle basin. This is very different in character from the riverside marshes, having a dense covering of wet coniferous forest. During the spring, it becomes an impassable quagmire. Both wet and dry woodland are found in the adjacent Grzędy Reserve, whose grass-covered sandy hills interrupt what is otherwise a very flat landscape.

In the furthest reaches of the marshes is one of the last remaining natural habitats in Europe of the wolf. Other characteristic mammals of the park are raccoon dogs, elks, red deer, roe deer, wild boar, badgers, otters and beavers. There are also large numbers of rodents, notably water and pygmy shrews, root voles, dormice and birch mice.

However, the Biebrza marshes are best known for their teeming bird life, and this is particularly visible, and audible, in spring. A total of 235 different species have been identified, of which at least 157 breed there. The population of several of these — the bittern, little bittern, shoveler, black grouse, crane, water rail, spotted crake, corncrake, ruff, great snipe, black tern, grey-headed woodpecker, redwing and the scarlet grosbeak — is probably the largest anywhere in Central Europe. In the case of the aquatic warbler, it is the highest in the world.

Although the exact habitats of the birds can vary from year to year according to the effects of the flooding, they tend to gravitate to particular geographical features. Thus on the river itself ducks, geese and grebes predominate. Though their number has declined dramatically in recent years, ruffs inhabit the soggy meadows and islets formed by the river; cranes, bittern and warblers live among the reeds. Birds of prey such as eagles, falcons and eagle owls inhabit the forest marshes. While not especially numerous, black storks are among the most visible of all the birds, thanks to their preference for the woodland adjacent to the flood plain.

As the entire Biebrza valley is so captivating, the main problem is in deciding which parts to visit, and there are a number of logistical constraints to consider. The low human population density means that public transport is very sparse. Having a car is therefore an obvious advantage, though during the annual thaw and at times of heavy rain some of the roads can be rendered impassible for all except four-wheel-drive vehicles. However, none of this need matter very much, as many places which are easy of access offer a more than adequate taste of the stunning beauty of the marshes.

For example, the extreme south-western corner of the park can be entered from near the village of **Wizna**, 9 miles (15km) west of Tykocin on the main road from Białystok to Łomża, which is served by regular buses. Just before the turn-off is a long bridge over the Narew, offering a fine panorama over the river just after it has merged with the Biebrza. The sandy path along its left bank makes for an attractive walk, leading past a wide variety of scenery, including the spectacularly wide confluence of the two rivers, en route to the hamlet of Wierciszewo, a walk of about 2 miles (3km). A bit further north, and accessible by occasional buses from Wizna, are several other tiny farming communities — Rutkowskie, Burzyn and Szostaki — which are each set well above the river and command views across to the wide expanse of the Łaski marsh to the east.

The so-called Tsar's Road runs along the eastern side of the Łaski marsh, linking Strękowa Góra on the Narew with **Goniądz**. Located at the point where the Biebrza passes from its middle to its lower basin, the latter is the only place in the immediate vicinity of the Biebrza National Park large enough to be considered a town. It lies on the main rail line between Białystok and Ełk, but the station is inconveniently located 3 miles (5km) away from the town, which is built on an escarpment high above the river. There are several fine vantage points, and the views are particularly beautiful at sunset.

Dolistowo Stare, 7 miles (12km) upstream from Goniądz, is another possible jumping-off point. It is linked with Białystok by several buses per day, and has a wide variety of scenery in its immediate vicinity. Over the bridge at the eastern end of the village, a rough road (which is often flooded in spring) closely follows the course of the river for the 6 miles (10km) to Dębowo, which marks the upper limit of the true marshland, then continues via Gabowe Grądy to Białobrzegi and thence to Augustów. At certain times of the year, the Red Marsh is accessible on foot from the road between Dolistowo and Dębowo. A more reliable approach is from the north, via the villages of Kuligi or Ciszewo, which lie on the loop side road off the main road between the towns of Grajewo and Rajgród.

The Puszcza Białowieska

The **Puszcza Białowieska** to the south-east of Białystok is another truly great natural wonder, the last of the vast primeval forests which once covered much of Europe to preserve many of its original characteristics. It occupies a total area of 480sq miles (1,250sq km). Although its ecosystem has inevitably been subject to considerable alteration down the centuries, particularly by the intrusion of agriculture, the forest was saved from the devastation suffered by all its counterparts because of its status as a favourite hunting ground of the Kings of Poland and Grand Dukes of Lithuania, then latterly of the Tsars of Russia. When Poland gained its independence after World War I, the forest was recognised as a national treasure, and has been subject to rigorous conservation measures ever since.

A total of 990 vascular plants have been identified in the Puszcza Białowieska, plus over 500 different mosses and lichens and over 1,000 fungi. These figures include many species rarely encountered elsewhere. The forest is mixed in character, and features 26 varieties of trees, some so imposing that individual examples have been given official designations as 'monuments of nature'. Of these, the tallest and most ubiquitous are the spruces, which often attain the towering height of 164ft (50m). Lime trees, ashes and oaks also feature among the upper levels of the treeline; some of the oaks are hundreds of years old, and have a diameter of up to 7ft (2m). Growing among these, but at a lower level, are elms, maples and hornbeams. Ashes and alders are found along the banks of the streams which cut through the forest. Spruces also occur on peat bogs, and on the poorer sandy soils, where pines, birches and aspens are also found.

Over 150 breeding birds, two-thirds of the Polish total, live in the forest. These include many woodland species which have been able to adhere to the original behavioural patterns of their natural habitat, which elsewhere they have had to adapt or abandon. The largest colonies are of flycatchers, river warblers, hazel grouse, rosefinches, nutcrackers, swifts, woodcocks, sandpipers, woodpeckers (nine different species) and owls (eight different species).

Among the mammals roaming the forest are 2,000 roe deer, 1,500 red deer, 1,300 wild boar, plus elks, lynxes and wolves. However, the Puszcza Białowieska is renowned above all for two species — the tarpan and the European bison. The former, a wild horse of the steppe type, is mouse-grey in colour and has a dark stripe all along the back. In the 1780s, the last original survivors were transported to the private zoo of the Zamoyski family near Zamość. They were later given away to local peasants, who cross-bred them with domestic species. In the 1930s, specimens showing tarpan traits were identified and brought back for selective breeding. Gradually, creatures which closely resemble the otherwise extinct original tarpan have evolved, and some of these have been released back into the wild.

Bison were traditionally the prize prey of the royal hunts; these huge, lumbering creatures lived freely in the forest until 1919, when they were killed off by a starving local populace. Ten years after this, and 2 years after the extermination of the European bison in the Caucasus, its last remaining natural habitat, a number of creatures were brought back from zoos and a breeding programme commenced. In 1952, the first bison were sent back into the forest, and around 250 now live there in freedom. For most of the year, the females and their young roam in groups of around a dozen head. The males lead a solitary existence, except during the mating season in August and September, while the females leave their herds in May and June, when the calves are born.

Visitors almost invariably enter the Puszcza Białowieska via **Hajnówka**, a town founded on the timber trade, situated just beyond the western fringe of the forest, 40 miles (65km) south-east of Białystok. In its northern outskirts is the Orthodox church, a striking modern design built in the 1970s and 80s by a team of Polish, Bulgarian and Greek artisans. Each May, it forms the setting for a festival of Orthodox music. Hajnówka is not otherwise attractive, but serves as the transport hub for the region. Unfortunately, the cuts in train services which followed the downfall of Communism have taken a heavy toll on the forest railways (which included a whole network of narrow gauge lines for the transport of timber). The only one still used for scheduled passenger services is that going north-east to Cisówka. Tiny diesels run along this route, which crosses directly over Lake Siemianówka, the largest stretch of water in the region. Additionally, the $7^1/_2$ mile (12km) narrow guage line south from Hajnówka to Osada Topito is open for excursion services in summer.

Białowieża, hard by the Belarussian frontier, 12 miles (19km) east of Hajnówka, is a sleepy rural backwater which nevertheless serves as the one and only tourist base for exploring the forest. Facilities are rudimentary, though not everyone regards this as a drawback; development has been kept firmly in check by the fact that isolation from the main urban and tourist centres means that, for most of the year, the volume of visitors is far less than might be expected for a place of such outstanding natural interest. The spectacular rail link with Hajnówka has been suspended, probably permanently, but the journey by bus or car, whether along the main road or the backwoods route via several agricultural hamlets, gives a good taste of the scenery.

At the western end of Białowieża's main street is the Orthodox church, a typical example of the Russian-sponsored brick architecture of the nineteenth century. It has a highly unusual ceramic inconostasis inside. Beyond the church is the Palace Park, a small landscaped area bounded by the River Narewka. The palace itself, built for the Russian royal family at the end of the nineteenth century, was destroyed by the Nazis, and subsequently razed. Its stables have been converted into a tourist lodge, while a modern glass and concrete structure occupies the site of the palace itself. Part of this is now a slightly more upmarket hotel; the rest contains the Natural History Museum. The exhibits include a range of stuffed animals and birds, displays on the history of the forest, local archaeology and plant protection, and a section on bee-keeping and wood distillation.

An open meadow separates the Palace Park from the gates of the **Białowieża National Park** (Białowieski Park Narodowy) to the north. Founded in 1947, this inaugurated the Polish national park system, a highly successful scheme that is still being expanded. Subsequently, it was included on the UNESCO list of World Biosphere Reserves, later gaining the even more prestigious designation as a World Heritage Site, one of very few natural wonders so honoured. The park places the best-preserved section of the Puszcza Białowieska — about a tenth of its total area — under permanent protection, with almost all of it declared a strict nature reserve.

In contrast to the country's other national parks, access is controlled, and before gaining admittance it is necessary to hire a qualified guide (English-speakers are available) from the PTTK tourist office just outside the southern gates of the Palace Park. There is a choice of going on foot (whether individually or in small groups) or by a horse-drawn cart, which can carry up to four people. If prices are relatively high by Polish standards, they are extremely reasonable for anyone with Western money, particularly if the opportunity to share costs arises. Even although the tours tend to concentrate on a small area close to the entrance, an astonishing variety of landscapes can be seen, with the gargantuan trees and dense undergrowth combining to produce a dank, eerie atmosphere far more atmospheric than the normal run of forests. Among the most memorable sights are the trees which have crashed to the ground, where they lie horizontally, slowly rotting away over the course of several decades. Sadly, there is only a slim chance of encountering bison, or any of the other wild animals, as these tend to stick to the farther reaches of the reserve, to which only the park's own scientists and visiting specialists are allowed access.

Because of the regimented nature of the trips in the park, many visitors prefer those parts of the forest which lie outside its boundaries. These can be explored with considerably more freedom, though cars are allowed only on the designated roads, and walkers must stick to the marked trails. There are also a couple of important setpiece attractions, at least one of which is included at no extra charge as a supplement to the guided tour of the national park.

One of these is the Bison Reserve (Rezerwat Żubrów), some 4 miles (6km) west of Białowieża; the entrance is about ½ mile (1km) down a dirt track leading north from the main road to Hajnówka. Laid out in the manner of a zoo, the reservation pioneered the breeding of bisons and tarpans, though the main centre for the latter is now Popielno in Masuria. The success of these projects has meant that both of these animals have been re-introduced not only into the local forest, but also returned to several other wilderness areas in Poland. Given the unlikelihood of encountering either in the wild, the reservation offers the consolation of seeing them against the backdrop of their natural environment. Also on view is the żubroń, a hybrid creature formed by breeding bison with domestic cattle.

About 2 miles (3km) north of the Bison Reserve by footpath, or 4 miles (6km) north-west of Białowieża by the back roads, is the Royal Oaks Way (Szlak Dębów Królewskich). Arguably the most impressive sight in the whole of the Puszcza Białowieska, this is an avenue of stately oak trees, each of which is several hundred years old and named after a Polish or Lithuanian ruler. Nearby, the gentle Łatownia, one of several dark forest streams, makes for an effective backdrop. En route, about ¹/₂ mile (1km) out of Białowieża, it is worth stopping off at the small *skansen* of old rural buildings which is currently being set up, though as yet it is not officially open.

Southern Podlasie

The southern part of Podlasie is even further off the beaten track than the rest of the province, but its obscurity is largely justified, as it has only a few outstanding sights. Nonetheless, it does contain a fair number of places which are worth a stopover on the way to or from somewhere else. It would be easy enough, for example, to devise a backwoods route from Białystok to Lublin or Zamość from the places described in this section, as an alternative to going the long way round via Warsaw.

Bielsk Podlaski, 31 miles (50km) south of Białystok, is centred on a Rynek with a range of historic buildings: the Town Hall, now the Regional Museum, and the Carmelite monastery are both Baroque, whereas the parish church is a neo-Classical design commissioned by Izabella Branicki. The town is an active centre of the Belarussian and Orthodox culture, with the only icon painting school in Poland. There are three wooden Orthodox churches, the most imposing being the seventeenth-century building dedicated to St Michael the Archangel on ul. Mickiewicza south of the Rynek.

Ciechanowiec, 28 miles (45km) south-west of Bielsk Podlaski, is a large village notable only for its Museum of Agriculture, set up in the estate of a nineteenth-century palace. This features a *skansen* of rural buildings brought from both Podlasie and Mazovia, including peasants' cottages, a manor house, granaries, a water mill, a windmill, and a number of beehives. There are also displays of historic farming equipment.

Siemiatycze, which lies 31 miles (50km) south of Bielsk and 24 miles (38km) south-east of Ciechanowiec, has a few historic buildings, including a part Renaissance, part Baroque missionary church, a neo-Classical synagogue and a nineteenth-century Orthodox church. However, it is best-known as the nearest town to **Grabarka**, Poland's main place of pilgrimage for those of Orthodox faith, which lies down a side road 5 miles (8km) to the east. Unlike Siemiatycze, it can also be reached by train, as the station of Szyce, 31 miles (60km) south-west of Hajnówka on the line to Warsaw, is only ¹/₂ mile (1km) away. Grabarka's pilgrimage church and convent, which is inhabited by a dozen nuns, stand atop a hill. The original wooden church was set alight by vandals in 1990, and has been replaced by a brick structure which closely mirrors its architecture. Below is an amazing forest of wooden crosses of disparate sizes, said to number some 20,000 in all. These have gradually accumulated since 1710, when the hill first became associated with a miracle. The main annual event is the Spas, or the Feast of the Transfiguration of the Saviour, an all-night vigil which begins at 6pm on 18 August and continues unabated until its culmination with the Great Liturgy at 10am the following morning.

Although nowadays no more than a village, **Drohiczyn**, which occupies a commanding situation above the River Bug 12 miles (19km) south-west of Siemiatycze, has existed since the eleventh century, and was for long the chief town of Podlasie. In addition to a large number of wooden houses and an old-fashioned chain bridge, there are three fine religious institutions from the Baroque period — the Franciscan monastery, whose tall tower dominates the Rynek; the Benedictine convent, which has an outstanding Rococo façade, and the Jesuit college, which was taken over and expanded by the Piarists in the eighteenth century. The Góra Zamkowa, the hill where the castle formerly stood, commands a fine panorama over the valley.

A further 28 miles (45km) west, close to the historic border with Mazovia, is **Węgrów**, which is associated with the Krasiński family, one of the handful of great dynasties which for centuries owned much of eastern Poland. They employed Tylman van Gameren, the leading architect of Baroque Warsaw, to provide two churches for the town. Of these, the parish church is a hybrid, preserving part of its fire-ravaged Gothic predecessor. Tylman transformed the original hall design into a spacious basilica, which was adorned with illusionistic frescos by an Italian, Michelangelo Palloni. The same artist also decorated the Reformed Franciscan monastery just to the east, which Tylman designed from scratch.

Siedlce, 17 miles (27km) south-east of Węgrów, lies on the main road and rail lines between Warsaw and Moscow, 74 miles (120km) from the former. Nowadays the largest town in Podlasie after Białystok, it was formerly associated with another prominent aristocratic dynasty, the Czartoryskis, and flourished in the late eighteenth century under the artistic patronage of Aleksandra Czartoryska, who married into another leading local family, the Ogińskis. She commissioned a Romantic landscaped garden at the eastern end of the town centre; once considered among the most beautiful in Poland, it now serves as the municipal park and is rather a shadow of its former self. In its grounds stands the neo-Classical Ogiński Palace, now used as local government offices, while just to the south is the domed Ogiński Mausoleum, which was designed by a painter, Zygmunt Vogel. Diagonally opposite the south-west corner of the park is the Post Office, a fine neo-Classical building by the Italian architect Antonio Corazzi, while a little further south are two Baroque setpieces, the church of St Stanisław and the Town Hall.

Another 40 miles (65km) in the direction of Moscow is **Biała Podlaska**, which was for long the property of yet another magnate family, the Radziwiłłs, who were of Lithuanian origin. Their palace at the south-western end of the town centre was a splendid late Renaissance complex, but it has suffered considerable damage down the centuries, and only some original features, including a gateway, two towers and a chapel still survive. Just to the east is the church of St Anne, which is of similar vintage and contains the Radziwiłł mausoleum. Some 12 miles (20km) north of town, close to the Belarussian border, is **Janów Podlaski**, home of Poland's leading stud farm, established in 1817 by Tsar Alexander I of Russia. It has gained an international reputation for its breeding of pedigree Arabian horses.

Some 31 miles (50km) south-west of Biała Podlaska is **Radzyń Podlaski**. The Potocki Palace on the south side of the town centre is named after the dynasty who formerly ruled the town. Among its many distinguished members was Jan Potocki, a colourful figure from the turn of the nineteenth century who was a world traveller, a pioneering hot air balloonist, and the author of a huge and extraordinary fantasy novel, *The Manuscript found at Saragossa*. Such was the splendour of the whole complex that, in common with its counterpart in Białystok, it gained the nickname of 'The Podlasian Versaillers'. It owes its present appearance to a Rococo re-building carried out in the 1750s by the Italian architect Jacopo Fontana. The side wings are unusually splendid, each featuring a gateway and a tower. This was necessitated by the fact that the main block faces away from the town, allowing no opportunity for linking the two in the normal axial relationship. The building retains much of its rich sculptural decoration, but almost all the interiors have been lost; the formal gardens have similarly fallen into neglect, but retain some original features, along with a handsome orangery, which is also the work of Fontana. Immediately to the north is the parish church, a fine Mannerist structure containing the mausoleum of the Mniszchów family, the previous owners of the town.

Further Information
— Podlasie —

Places to Visit
Białowieża
Natural History Museum
Palace Park
Open: Tuesday to Sunday 9am to 4pm.

Białystok
Town Hall (Regional Museum)
Rynek Kościuszki
Open: Tuesday to Sunday 10am to 5pm.

Bielsk Podlaski
Town Hall (Regional Museum)
Rynek
Open: Tuesday to Sunday 10am to 5pm.

Choroszcz
Museum of Palace Interiors
Open Tuesday to Sunday 10am to 3pm.

Supraśl
Bishop's Palace
Open: Tuesday to Sunday 9am to 3pm.

Suwałki
Maria Konopnicka Museum
ul. Kościuszki 31
Open: Tuesday to Friday 9am to 4pm, Saturday and Sunday 10am to 5pm.

Regional Museum
ul. Kościuszki 81
Open: Tuesday to Friday 9am to 4pm, Saturday and Sunday 10am to 5pm.

Tykocin
Synagogue (Jewish Museum)
Open: Tuesday to Sunday 10am to 5pm.

Talmudic House (Local Museum)
Open: Tuesday to Sunday 10am to 4pm.

Tourist Offices
Białowieża
ul. Kolejowa 17
☎ 12-295

Białystok
ul. Skłodowskiej-Curie 13
☎ 41-76-2

7 • Red Ruthenia

The area which currently forms the south-easternmost part of Poland lay outside the boundaries of the nation that emerged at the end of the Dark Ages, though it was incorporated into the early Polish state established by Mieszko I and his son Boleslaw the Brave in the late tenth century. However, this arrangement did not long survive the latter's death: the territory was taken over by the neighbouring Ruthenians (ancestors of the present-day Ukrainians), and became part of a large province known as **Red Ruthenia (Ruś Czerwona)**.

The whole of Red Ruthenia was conquered by King Kazimierz the Great in the latter half of the fourteenth century, and thereafter served as Poland's eastern bulwark until the Partition era, when all but a small northern section was taken over by the Austrians, forming the main component of a new province named Galicia. Following the Austrian Empire's collapse in World War I, ownership of Red Ruthenia was disputed between the resurrected Polish state and the Soviet Union. The matter was initially resolved in Poland's favour as a result of its stunningly conclusive victory in the Polish-Soviet War of 1919-20 — the only defeat the Red Army ever suffered in the field. However, the Soviets turned the tables in 1945, when Stalin gained international backing for his plan to force Poland to cede most of Red Ruthenia to the Soviet Republic of the Ukraine, in return for compensatory territorial acquisitions elsewhere at Germany's expense. The Poles were left with a rump, approximately equivalent to the portion they had held a thousand years before.

Despite its truncated size, the part of Red Ruthenia still belonging to Poland ranks among the country's most fascinating and diverse regions, one that makes a very satisfying basis for a touring trip of a week or more. The southernmost part, in and around the mountain ranges of the Bieszczady and Beskid Niski, is an unspoiled rural area, much of it wilderness, which is ideal for long yet not unduly demanding walks. For several centuries, two ethnic minority groups, the Lemks and the Boyks, had their homelands there. Most were forcibly expelled in 1947, but their wooden churches, originally built for either the Orthodox or Uniate rite, survive as a reminder of their former presence.

Timber churches, this time built by ethnic Poles, usually for Roman Catholic worship, are also characteristic of the lower-lying areas further

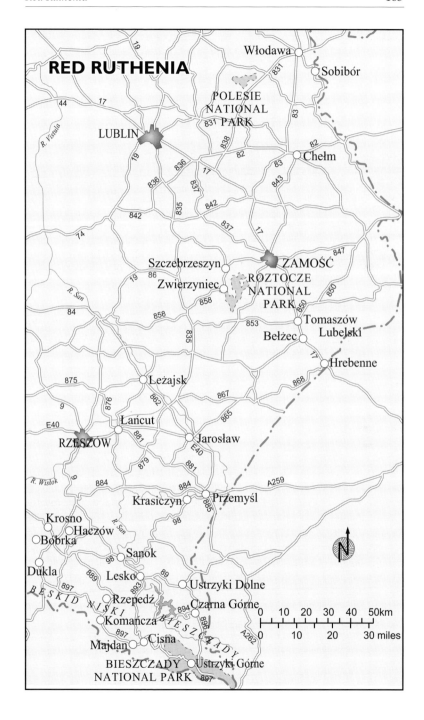

north. One of the great benefits in touring Red Ruthenia by car is in the freedom this affords to stop off and admire these wonderful buildings, whose sheer invention and artistry entitles them to be considered among the finest expressions of folk architecture to be found anywhere in Europe. Note that, while the finest and most easily accessible are detailed in this chapter, others can be found in literally dozens of villages not described here.

In the northern part of Red Ruthenia, there are more obvious setpiece attractions, including several magnificent castles and palaces built by the great landed magnates. Of these families, the Zamoyskis went a stage further than their rivals in establishing the planned town of Zamość, a treasure of Italian Renaissance architecture which is unquestionably among the most rewarding tourist destinations in Poland. In and around Zamość can also be found some of the best-preserved monuments of Poland's Jewish community, which traditionally had a strong presence in these parts. For several centuries, it was the largest in the world, but was all but wiped out by the Nazis in a systematic programme of genocide whose early stages were enacted in two of the extermination camps they established in the region.

The Chełm District

The northernmost part of Red Ruthenia — which borders Podlasie to the north and Little Poland to the west, with the River Bug forming a natural border with the Ukraine to the east — is known as the district of Chełm after its only major town. An independent duchy in early medieval times, the area retains its place on the modern map of Poland as an administrative division. The population density of this rather backward agricultural area is the lowest in the country, and it would be difficult to find anywhere further from the beaten tourist track.

Włodawa, at its extreme north-east corner, is a small historic town, still preserving a large number of traditional wooden houses, lying directly on the River Bug, 48 miles (77km) south-east of Biała Podlaska. The parish church is one of a number of outstanding late Baroque churches erected in eastern Poland by the Italian architect Paolo Antonio Fontana, and features two of the distinctive hallmarks of his style — a dramatically articulated façade, and an elliptical nave. Facing it from the other side of the Rynek, in a juxtaposition typical of a region which historically had a diverse religious mix, is the neo-Classical Orthodox church.

Prior to 1945, some 60 per cent of Włodawa's inhabitants were Jews, and the town was a notable centre of Jewish cultural life. Although the community itself was a casualty of the Nazi 'Final Solution', three of its public buildings still survive, making up one of the most important Jewish monumental ensembles to be seen outside Cracow. The main synagogue is a palatial Baroque temple erected in the 1760s with financial help from the Czartoryskis, one of Poland's leading aristocratic families. It consists of a high prayer hall set under a mansard roof, with smaller halls for the women to the north and south. Of the original decorative scheme, the vault medallions still survive. Their symbolic carvings are mirrored in the painted decoration of the Holy Ark, which had to be replaced in 1934, after its predecessor was destroyed in a fire. The building now houses the District Museum, which is devoted to ethnographic material and temporary exhibitions. It is due to expand into the two adjacent Jewish buildings — the mid-nineteenth-century Little Synagogue and the 1920s Teaching House.

Most of Włodawa's Jewish inhabitants were massacred at **Sobibór**, 7 miles (12km) to the south, the third oldest of the concentration camps earmarked by the Nazis for the specific purpose of extermination, rather than slave labour. Up to a quarter of a million people from all over Europe, mainly Jews, met their deaths there. As German defeat became inevitable, the camp was torched by the SS in an attempt to cover up their crimes. Thus, unlike similar camps further west, which remained operational for longer, nothing substantive remains. Instead, there is only a post-war memorial to the victims, together with a mound made from their ashes.

South-west of Włodawa lies an extensive and totally undeveloped lakeland which is even more sparsely populated than the rest of the district, being punctuated only by a few straggling farming communities. In 1990, the part of this of greatest natural interest, one of the last intact peat swamps anywhere in Europe, was designated as the **Polesie National Park** (Poleski Park Narodowy). This has a miniature form of both tundra and forest tundra ecosystems. The landscapes include mixed forest swamps, alder swamps, willow-alder thickets, wet and dry meadows, peatbogs and lakes. A large variety of reptiles and amphibians, notably the European pond tortoise and the natterjack, inhabit there areas, as do forty different species of fish. Otter, elk and wolves are among the mammals which live in the park, while there are at least 150 species of breeding birds, including about a dozen which are under threat of extinction.

Even among Poles, the Polesie National Park is little-known, and the nature of the terrain means that, despite its compact area, it is one of the most difficult to explore. With a car, the easiest way of seeing a cross-section of the scenery is to approach from the western side: from Stare Orchezów a side road leads 3 miles (5km) east to Zienki, just beyond which is another road cutting right through the heart of the park. Unfortunately, this stutters to a dead end, and it is necessary to continue on foot for the short distance to the village of Wólka Wytycka at park's eastern edge. An alternative approach is via the main road between Włodawa and Lublin, which is serviced by occasional buses. One possible jumping-off point is Wytyczna, 15^1/$_2$ miles (25km) south-east of Włodawa and 1 mile (2km) east of Wólka Wytycka, which lies on the shore of Lake Wytyckie, the largest lake in the area. An alternative is Urszulin, a further 4 miles (6km) towards Lublin. From there, a side road leads 3 miles (5km) west to Stare Zalucze; it is then only a short distance by the marked footpath to Lake Łukie, one of the park's principal beauty spots.

The city of **Chełm**, 29 miles (47km) south of Włodawa and 18 miles (29km) west of the Ukrainian border, was founded by the Ruthenians in the tenth century, and thus was already 400 years old at the time it became

Polish. It was repeatedly ravaged in the seventeenth-century wars against the Swedes and the Cossacks, and its principal monuments date from the following century, when it enjoyed a major revival. Chełm's setting, on and around a 725ft (221m) high chalk hill, the Chełmska Góra, gives it an enormous sense of grandeur which is all the more pronounced by the lack of any other sizeable towns in the entire region.

A complete episcopal quarter occupies the summit of the Chełmska Góra. The church of St Mary was begun in 1735, probably to plans by Fontana, as the cathedral of a Uniate bishopric, but since 1864 has been used for Roman Catholic services. Alongside are several other buildings associated with the Uniate episcopacy — the Bishop's Palace, the monastery of the Basilian Friars and the Uściłuska Gate. From the Middle Ages onwards, the hill and its surroundings were extensively exploited for their mineral wealth, and there is a labyrinthine network of passageways on several levels stretching for a total of 25 miles (40km). A small part of this can be visited: the entry is at number 29 on ul. Lubelska, which sweeps down from the eastern side of the hill into the heart of the town centre.

Towards the southern end of the same street is the parish church, built by Fontana in the 1750s as a Piarist monastery. Its bravura façade has concave-sided towers with diagonal settings which are strikingly reminiscent of the Viennese Baroque style. Inside, the nave, in the shape of an elliptical octagon, is frescoed with scenes from the Life of the Virgin; the Acts of the Apostles are depicted in the chancel, while the side chapels illustrate the career of St John Calasanza, the founder of the Piarist order. The monastic quarters now contain the Regional Museum, with displays on local archaeology, history, ethnography and crafts. A block to the south is another Baroque complex, the monastery of the Reformed Franciscans, while at the northern end of the town centre is the mid-nineteenth-century Orthodox church.

Chełm traditionally had a large Jewish population — around half the total on the eve of World War II, having once been as high as 70 per cent — but there are only a few reminders left of their culture, most notably the Little Synagogue, the smaller of the two which once graced the centre. Now in secular use, it was built in 1914 at the junction of ul. Kopernika and ul. Krzywa, just to the north-west of the parish church. The Jewish cemetery lies below the north side of Chełmska Góra at the corner of ul. Kolejowa and ul. Starościńska. It was founded in the sixteenth century, but preserves only a few historic tombstones, most of which were uprooted by the Nazis and re-used as paving stone.

Zamość

Zamość, 40 miles (65km) south of Chełm and 53 miles (85km) south-east of Lublin, ranks among the brightest jewels of Polish culture. Not only is it the supreme achievement of the nation's long and fruitful association with Italy, it is one of the world's most successful-ever examples of urban planning on the grand scale. It was founded in 1580 by Jan Zamoyski, Chancellor and Grand Hetman of Poland and, alongside Copernicus, the country's most complete personification of Renaissance Man, with a towering reputation as a politician, soldier, scholar and artistic patron. Desirous of providing his estates — which stretched over an area of 1,461 sq miles (3,800 sq km), and included 149 villages and 6 towns — with a fitting capital, he decided to found a brand new town on the site of his birthplace.

Zamoyski had studied at the famous old university in Padua, and it was to a native Paduan, the architect and town planner Bernardo Morando, that he turned for the fulfilment of his dream, the realization of the Italian Renaissance vision of an ideal city. There had been many earlier attempts at this in Italy itself: some got no further than artists' impressions, while others were abandoned half-built, as the gap between funds and costs became unbridgeable. Much of Zamość, however, was constructed within the lifetime of Zamoyski, who died in 1605, having outlived Morando by 5 years. The rest was finished in the next few decades and, despite various later alterations, survives essentially intact to this day as the unspoiled centre of a city whose present-day population is more than twenty times higher than the 3,000 Zamoyski originally budgeted for.

Although Morando adopted the old medieval chessboard layout, he modified it according to Renaissance tenets by placing the key public buildings in axial relationships to one another. Most of these he designed and built himself in the late Renaissance style known as Mannerism. Morando was also responsible for the fortification system enclosing the town, which incorporated all the most up-to-date principles of military architecture and included seven bastions, three gates, a moat and artificial lakes. This proved its worth in the seventeenth-century wars against the Cossacks and Swedes, being one of only two places in the country to withstand the latter. It was greatly strengthened after Zamość came under Russian control in the early nineteenth century, only to be partially dismantled and turned into a promenade in 1866 in order that the town, which was no longer strategically important, could expand.

The secret behind the success of Zamość was the way the theory of the ideal city was given a hard practical application. If the fortification system was one manifestation of this, another example lay in the economic sphere. Lying at the junction of two major trade routes — Lublin to Lwów and Cracow to Kiev — Zamość was an excellent place for a merchant to have his main base. Thus Jewish, Italian, Armenian, Greek, Hungarian and Scottish entrepreneurs settled in the town soon after its foundation. In accordance with the uniquely tolerant atmosphere then characteristic of Poland, those who did not subscribe to the Catholic faith were allowed to erect their own places of worship — even although the academic tradition that was a key component of the town's life from its inception was based on the propagation of Counter-Reformation doctrines.

At the heart of Zamość's chessboard plan is a large square, the Rynek Wielki, which measures 328ft by 328ft (100m by 100m) and is lined by rows of richly decorated mansions whose arcaded street fronts impart a distinctly Mediterranean touch. This in itself is not as incongruous as it might appear: Zamość has the sunniest climate in Poland, one quite markedly warmer and drier than that of the Roztocze region immediately to the south. Not only does the Rynek Wielki surpass all its Polish counterparts in its sense of grandeur, it differs from them in being entirely a monumental showpiece: it is not and never has been an open-air market, this function being devolved on the smaller and less imposing squares to the north and south.

Also untypical is the position of the Town Hall, which is placed on the northern side, rather than, as is normal in Poland, in an isolated setting in the middle of the square. The dignified main elevation of Morando's original building survives largely intact, though it was subject to a number of Baroque modifications, notably the heightening of the tower and the addition of a showy entrance stairway which is often used as an open-air theatre in summer. These bravura Baroque touches could easily have ruined the Town Hall's architectural integrity, but instead help to endow it with a wonderful sense of fantasy. There are no historic interiors to see, but there is a memorial room devoted to the town's most famous daughter, Róża Luksemburg, who was born just off the square at number 37 on ul. Staszica. She began her career as a Jewish progressive before moving to Germany where, under the name of Rosa Luxemburg, she became joint leader of the abortive 1918 Revolution. Her subsequent murder made her a heroine of the international left, but her reputation has been the subject of much dispute since the fall of Communism, leaving a question mark over the continued existence of such memorials.

Immediately to the right of the Town Hall is a block containing the five most magnificent mansions in the town, each painted a different colour. These are the only houses which still have the highly elaborate attic gables that were once a feature of all the houses on the square. Traditionally, they were inhabited by the Armenian merchants who formed Zamość's commercial elite, though the green house (number 30) nearest the Town Hall was built by Morando for a professor at the Academy. A century later, it was partially remodelled, with the addition of statues of Christ, the Virgin Mary, St John the Baptist, St John the Evangelist and St Thomas. Its yellow neighbour (number 28) is somewhat plainer, but the red house (number 26), which dates back to the 1630s, preserves its original decoration. At the first-floor level is a statue of St George, while between the windows of the second storey are symbolic carvings of lions guarding the house against evil, represented in the guise of a dragon.

Much of the fabric of the interior, including tiebeam wooden ceilings and window and door frames, also survives, and can be seen in the course of a visit to the Regional Museum, which features archaeological finds, documentary material on the Zamoyskis, and products of the town's celebrated printing workshop. It spills over into the adjoining blue house (number 24), which has likewise preserved its original façade. This is the most obviously oriental in appearance of the group, with stylized floral and geometric friezes and a grotesque carving of a married couple. The pink house (number 22), with a Baroque group of the Virgin trampling a dragon, marks the extreme north-east corner of the square, though the block continues without interruption along ul. Ormiańska to the east.

On the three other sides of the square, the houses are plainer, having been stripped in the nineteenth century of their attics, and often their decoration as well. They remain attractive nonetheless and, while none is a regular tourist sight, many serve as shops, cafés or public offices and can thus be visited. Those on the south side are the oldest: number 19 is a particularly good example of the Mannerist style, while number 23 was the home of Zamoyski's heirs, and number 25 was built by Morando as his own residence. The east side was inhabited by a mixture of merchants and scholars, though number 2 has been a pharmacy since its inception, and retains a complete set of nineteenth-century apothecary equipment. On the west side of the square, number 5 is particularly notable. In the late seventeenth century, it belonged to Jan Link, military engineer to the Zamoyskis, who added to the façade busts of Minerva and Hercules and palm leaves and arms symbolizing victory. Number 7, which has a frieze of monkeys on its side elevation, and typical Mannerist decoration on the main façade, is an original Morando design, and was once the property of the architect himself, though he later sold it.

To the south-west of the Rynek stands the collegiate church, which was begun by Morando and finally completed in 1630 by his successor as architect to the Zamoyskis, Jan Jaroszewicz. The exterior was mutilated in the nineteenth century, but the interior is a beautiful Italianate basilica, featuring graceful arcades, an elaborate coffered vault and an imposing organ gallery. In the presbytery are a silver Rococo tabernacle and a cycle of seventeeth-century paintings, attributed to Domenico Tintoretto, illustrating the life of St Thomas, one of the church's patrons. Immediately to the south is the Baroque family chapel and vault of the Zamoyskis, with a simple marble slab on the floor commemorating the founder of the town.

The church's detached belfry was added in the middle of the eighteenth-century, though its main bell, one of the largest in Poland, is a hundred years older. In summer, it is possible to ascend for a view over the town which embraces part of the Rynek Wielki. On the opposite side of the church is the dean's house, known as the Infułatka, entered via a graceful Doric portal designed by Morando. It now houses the Diocesan Museum, which includes a bronze font, reliquaries and other sacral objects, and historic liturgical vestments.

Just to the west is the Szczebrzeszyn Gate, one of the three gateways of the original fortification system. Across the road is the Arsenal, which was built by Morando but successively remodelled, notably in the early nineteenth century, when the neo-Classical portico was added. This fulfilled its original function right up until Zamość's demise as a fortress. Nowadays, it contains a small museum, principally devoted to historic weapons, but also with two scale models, one showing Zamość as it was in the seventeenth century, the other as it is today. Immediately to the north is the vast bulk of the Zamoyski Palace, which is built round all four sides of an open courtyard, and also has two protruding wings. Little remains of Morando's original design, the oldest building in Zamość, as it was reconstructed in the Baroque and neo-Classical periods, then stripped of all its decoration when converted to serve as a military hospital a decade after the Zamoyskis' ownership of the town ended in 1821. Nowadays, it houses the local law courts.

A little further to the north is the most celebrated part of the fortifications, the Old Lublin Gate. In 1588, while it was still under construction, the captured Archduke Maximilian of Austria, a contender for the Polish throne, was marched through it following his defeat by Zamoyski at the Battle of Byczyna. To commemorate the event, it was walled up, and hence never served its intended function. Directly across ul. Akademika is the Academy, an institution founded in 1594 as the third seat of higher education in the Polish-Lithuanian Commonwealth. The building itself, constructed round a central courtyard and containing living quarters for the staff and students as well as lecture rooms and a library, was not constructed until the 1630s, and is consequently early Baroque rather than Mannerist in style.

Another block further east, immediately to the rear of the Town Hall, is the old salt market, the Rynek Solny, whose arcaded houses were inhabited mainly by Jewish merchants. The Old Synagogue on ul. Bazylańska, the next street to the east, is a Mannerist building erected in the second decade of the seventeenth century. Arguably the most beautiful Jewish temple ever built in Poland, it consists of the usual format of a main prayer hall with women's halls to the north and south. It survives in reasonable shape and is now used as the municipal library. Outside, the polychromy has been renewed; inside, some of the decoration remains, including the Holy Ark, Hebrew inscriptions, stylized symbolic paintings, stuccowork and candelabra. The building adjoining the Synagogue to the west was originally the home of a Hebrew scholar, and was later a Jewish elementary school. Two further Jewish legacies are on ul. Zamenhofa to the north: number 3, currently a jazz club, was the ritual bathhouse, while number 11, now a tourist lodge, was the elders' assembly hall.

Set in its own peaceful grounds at the extreme south-eastern edge of the Old Town is the domed church of St Nicholas, built by Jan Jaroszewicz for the Greek merchants of Orthodox faith, with a tower which served as part of the defensive system. It was later assigned to the Basilian monks of the Uniate rite, but is now used for Roman Catholic worship. Architecturally, it shows Mannerism passing into the Baroque, and the latter is recognisably the style of Jaroszewicz's next church, the Franciscan monastery on plac Wolności immediately to the north. This has also had a chequered career, and now looks rather too squat, having been stripped of its belfry. For most of the nineteenth century, it was used alternately as a gunpowder magazine and barracks, and after World War I became a cinema. It remained as such until 1993, when it was re-consecrated as a parish church. Opposite are the neo-Classical New Lwów Gate and Morando's Old Lwów Gate. Adjoining the latter is an intact nineteenth-century bastion, whose passageways and open-air promenade have recently been taken over by market traders.

Another well-preserved part of the Russian-built part of the defences is the Rotunda, which lies about $^1/_2$ mile (1km) south of the collegiate church.

It is now a Museum of Martyrology in honour of the victims of the Nazis, who used it as a transit camp and execution ground, killing some 8,000 people in all. Zamość itself was a target of the Nazi's brutal racial policies: they named it 'Himmlerstadt' in honour of the SS chief, and intended clearing it, along with hundreds of outlying villages, of the indigenous Polish population, replacing them with German settlers.

The Roztocze

Zamość lies just outside the **Roztocze**, an upland area of some 68 miles by 12 miles (110km by 20km), which stretches in a south-easterly direction deep into what is now the Ukraine. The hills, which are cut by numerous valleys, are composed of a mixture of chalk and calcareous rocks covered with an upper layer of sand and loess; most are between 980ft and 1,300ft (300m and 400m) in height. Both the slopes, which rise quite abruptly, and the summits, which are invariably flattened, are densely forested.

Szczebrzeszyn, 13 miles (21km) west of Zamość, lies near the extreme north-west end of the Roztocze. Although not much more than a village by present-day standards, it preserves a handful of monuments contemporary with those in its celebrated neighbour, including no fewer than three churches — the parish church, the former Uniate church and the Franciscan monastery of St Catherine. From the same period is the synagogue on ul. Sądowa east of the Rynek, which conforms to the standard pattern of a main prayer hall under a mansard roof with smaller halls for the women to the north and south. It has been well restored following extensive damage at the hands of the Nazis, and is now the local cultural centre. Further east, on ul. Cmentarna, is the Jewish cemetery, which preserves some 400 historic tombstones.

Another 7 miles (11km) south is **Zwierzyniec**, which can also be reached directly from Zamość by a minor road. This little town stands on the banks of the pretty River Wieprz, which cuts a mazy course through the heart of the western part of the Roztocze. The whitewashed Baroque parish church has a picturesque setting on an island, linked to the shore by a causeway, in the middle of the town centre lake. Nearby are the historic premises of the oldest still-functioning brewery in Poland, founded back in 1806. A bit further south is another prominent nineteenth-century building, the former administration office of the Zamoyski family estates.

The latter is now used by the management of the **Roztocze National Park** (Roztoczański Park Narodowy), which was set up to preserve the most scientifically significant part of the region. Over the centuries, this had been spared from commercial exploitation by having served as the hunting grounds and private zoo of the Zamoyskis. Most of the park is forested, with pines accounting for over half the total number of trees. Next most common are firs and beeches, which are unusually large, often growing up to 164ft (50m) in height and 5ft (1.5m) in diameter. Ancient oaks can also be seen, along with hornbeams, elms, ashes, spruces, larches, maples, sycamores, lindens and rowans. A curiosity of the plant life is that it includes specimens typical of both mountain and lowland terrains. Among several orchids, lady's slippers are prominent. Coralwort, snowdrops, anemones, foxgloves, gentia and sundews are among the other characteristic examples of the local flora.

The Roztocze was the last natural habitat of the Polish wild horse known as the tarpan. In its pure form, this creature died out in the nineteenth century as a result of being cross-bred with domestic horses, but scientists have been able to breed it back, and since 1982 tarpans have once roamed the area in freedom. Wild boar, red and roe deer, foxes, wolves, martens, beavers, shrews and bats are among the other animals living within the park. There are also many birds of prey, including eagles, buzzards, kestrels, ospreys, sparrow-hawks and goshawks, among the 160 different varieties of birdlife.

Unlike most of Poland's national parks, the Roztocze is quite suitable for exploration by car: it has only a few footpaths, and these are often poorly marked. Fortunately, two of the park's main beauty spots are very close to Zwierzyniec. From just beyond the administration building, a trail leads up to Bukowa Góra, one of the five strict nature reserves, notable for its impressive cluster of tall trees. From there, it is possible to return to Zwierzyniec by descending via the other side of the hill, then following the road back round. This passes Lake Echo, whose peaceful dark waters are the breeding ground for numerous waterfowl, including black storks, grebes, coots, flycatchers, doves, water hens and wild ducks.

Tomaszów Lubelski, 26 miles (42km) south-east of Zamość, was named after Jan Zamoyski's son Tomasz. Its church of the Annunciation, originally Uniate but now Roman Catholic, is one of Poland's most beautiful wooden buildings. Dating from the 1720s, it eschews the essentially Gothic influence of so many churches in this material, taking instead stone Baroque architecture as its model, above all in the twin façade towers with their bulbous domes.

Bełżec, which is 5 miles (8km) south, was the most horrific of the early Nazi death camps, one which set the trend for the even more ghastly crimes later enacted at Auschwitz, with a death toll estimated at up to 600,000. Having outlived its usefulness, it was completely razed by the Nazis themselves, and the post-war memorial is now the only reminder left of the site. A further 9 miles (15km) south-east is **Hrebenne**, a road crossing-point into the Ukraine with another outstanding wooden church originally built for the Uniate rite. This dates from the very end of the eighteenth century and again has a pronounced Baroque aspect, not least in its octagonal domes.

The Middle San Basin

Between its source in the Bieszczady and its confluence with the Vistula, the River San waters a broad fertile basin, where it is fed by several tributaries. Several historic towns lie within this area, particularly in the valleys of the Wisłok and the San itself.

The most northerly of these is **Leżajsk**, which is set back from the left bank of the San, about 62 miles (100km) south-west of Zamość. Its name is well-known all over Poland thanks to its beer, which is one of the three most commonly encountered on restaurant menus. However, the town also has a major historic monument in the Bernardine monastery, a fortified Baroque complex located about 1 mile (2km) north of the centre. The pride of the church is the organ, made at the end of the seventeenth century by Jan Głowiński of Cracow: one of the largest and finest instruments in the country, it has its own festival in May each year. Not only does it have a marvellous tone, its case and gallery are masterpieces of decorative art, with a rich figural programme that includes a depiction of King Jan Sobieski's victory over the Turks. Also in the church are a splendid set of Rococo choir stalls, numerous large altars, and a much venerated painting of the Madonna, which draws crowds of pilgrims for all the Marian celebrations, especially the Feast of the Assumption on 15 August. In the centre of Leżajsk, the attractions are more low-key, but include a late Renaissance parish church, a Baroque Town Hall, and a number of eighteenth- and nineteenth-century houses.

Rzeszów, 26 miles (42km) south-west of Leżajsk, was founded by the Ruthenians, and later passed through the hands of various aristocratic Polish dynasties. It became increasingly important during the Austrian rule of the Partition period, towards the end of which is gained several imposing buildings in the Viennese Secessionist style. After World War II, it was made the focal point of the industrial re-generation of south-eastern Poland, and it is now easily the largest city in the region.

This development means that Rzeszów is now an ugly sprawl of tower blocks and factories, though the Old Town does survive as its core. On the central Rynek are the Town Hall, originally sixteenth-century but remodelled in a heavy neo-Gothic style, a statue to Tadeusz Kościuszko, hero of the American Wars of Independence and the Polish struggles against the Partitioning powers, and a number of historic houses. One of these contains the Ethnographic Museum, featuring a collection of folk art and costumes. On ul. Bożnicza, just off the north-eastern end of the square, are two former Jewish temples. The first of these, the Old Synagogue, is mostly seventeenth-century in date, and now contains the city archive. Immediately to the north is the New Synagogue, built by an Italian architect, Giovanni Belotti, in the early eighteenth century; this now functions as a commercial art gallery and cafe.

On plac Farny, the next square to the west of the Rynek, is the parish church. Originally Gothic, it was remodelled in the Baroque period, and is primarily of interest for the Renaissance tombs of the Rzeszowski family, the first Polish owners of the town. To the west is the Bernardine monastery, built in the 1620s at the behest of Mikołaj Ligęza, the most prominent member of the next local dynasty. It is a very early example of the Baroque style, with a groundplan and a high altar which are both still clearly Renaissance. Presiding over the chancel in a highly theatrical arrangement are eight alabaster busts of members of the Ligęza family. To the side of this is an elaborate Baroque chapel containing a supposedly miraculous sixteenth-century statue of the Virgin. The walls are frescoed with scenes illustrating how 100 different people were cured as a result of her intercession. Outside the monastery is the Monument to the Revolutionary Movement, a typically bombastic example of the Socialist Realist memorials once common throughout Eastern Europe, but which elsewhere have usually been removed.

South of the parish church is ul. 3 Maja, about halfway down which is the Piarist monastery, which was likewise founded by Mikołaj Ligęza. The church's façade, which was not added until later, was designed by Tylman van Gameren, the Dutch-born architect who built so much of Warsaw. Nowadays, the monastic quarters are occupied by the Regional Museum. This is mostly devoted to changing exhibitions on historical themes, though it is worth visiting for the sake of seeing the interiors, and in particular the frescoed vaults. At the end of the same street is the Savings Bank, a whimsical fantasy castle that is by far the most eye-catching of the city's Secessionist buildings.

A little way down ul. Zamkowa is the Lubomirski Palace, the summer residence of the third and last of the Rzeszów dynasties. Built in the early eighteenth century by Tylman van Gameren, it now serves as a music college. Occupying a commanding position in splendid isolation at the extreme southern end of the Old Town is the castle, a huge fortified block built in the late sixteenth centuries for the Ligęzas. It was re-modelled on several subsequent occasions, but still retains its ramparts and bell tower. For long used as a prison, it is currently the seat of the law courts.

Łańcut, 11 miles (17km) east of Rzeszów and 17 miles (28km) southwest of Leżajsk, is totally dominated by its palace, which is set in a spacious landscaped park at the edge of the town centre. Other than former royal residences, it is the most famous stately home in Poland, one associated with several of the country's leading aristocratic clans. It ceased to be a private residence in 1944 when the last owner, Alfred Potocki, who was believed to be Poland's wealthiest man, went into exile, taking many of the most valuable contents with him. He left the building itself at the mercy of the Red Army, leaving a sign labelled 'Polish National Museum' in Polish and Russian. This ruse saved it from destruction, and soon afterwards the designation became official.

The present palace was begun in the 1620s for Stanisław Lubomirski to plans by an Italian architect, Matteo Trapola. It was essentially a fortified structure, set behind a pentagonal bastion which was built according to the most advanced defence principles of the day. From the late eighteenth century, it was progressively remodelled in Baroque and neo-Classical styles for Izabela Lubomirska, a member of the Czartoryski family. Although parts of the bastion were retained, they were reduced to serving a picturesque function only. Remodelling continued under the Potockis, who inherited the palace by marriage. At the turn of the twentieth century, the exterior was given a neo-Baroque appearance, and the building was equipped with all the mod cons of the day, such as electricity, central heating and telephones.

The tourist circuit takes in around fifty different rooms, which together illustrate the changing tastes in interior design. Of the original palace, the only surviving chamber is the Zodiac Room under one of the towers, which preserves some excellent seventeenth-century stuccowork by Giovanni Battista Falconi. There are examples of Rococo frippery and of Chinoisserie, as well as several distinguished neo-Classicism chambers. These include the Ballroom, the setting for the Old Music Festival in May each year; the Dining Room, with a table capable of seating eighty people; and the Sculpture Court, with its trompe l'œil paintings of a vine-covered trellis and a valuable collection of statues, including *Henryk Lubomirski as Eros* by the great Venetian sculptor Antonio Canova. The most highly prized interior of all is the intimate theatre, which preserves its old stage sets and cranking machinery.

Built on to the south-west corner of the palace is the Orangery, a handsome neo-Classical structure by Christian Piotr Aigner, who was also responsible for many of the finest interiors of the main building. The same architect built the various whimsical buildings dotted throughout the park — the Glorietta, the mock temple placed in front of the palace; the Little Castle, a Romantic fantasy at the north-eastern end of the grounds; and the Riding Hall, which occupies a similar position to the south-east.

Across ul. 1 Maja from the last-named are the former stables. These now house the Icon Museum, though only part of the total collection of 1,000 examples from the fifteenth century onwards is on view at any one time. Opposite is the Coach House, which contains over fifty historic coaches, carriages and sleighs — one of the largest displays of its kind in Europe. A few of these can be hired for a horse-driven trip around the grounds.

Just west of the palace park is the only interesting building in the town centre, the former synagogue, now the Jewish Museum. Built in the 1760s, it was closely associated with the revivalist Hassidic sect. Inside, the central bimah survives intact, along with its colourful paintings and stucco from the early twentieth century. The older decoration on the main walls has also been preserved: this includes painted Hebrew prayers, the signs of the Zodiac, symbolic animals and plants, and depictions of the main Jewish feasts.

Back on the River San, 22 miles (35km) upstream from Leżajsk and a similar distance east of Łańcut, is **Jarosław**. For several hundred years the town, which takes its name from the Ruthenian prince who founded it in the eleventh century, was one of Central Europe's most important trade fair centres, and was inhabited by merchants of many different nationalities. The main monumental legacy of this is the Orsetti Mansion on the southern side of the Rynek, built in the late sixteenth century for the Italian family after whom it is named. It possesses a graceful loggia and a richly decorated attic, while the interior, now housing the District Museum, retains its original polychromed woodbeam ceilings. From another mansion on the south side of the Rynek, guided tours are run round the extensive network of under-ground town cellars, which were used not only for storage purposes, but also for shelter in time of war. Another key building on the square is the Town

Hall, which was originally Gothic but several times remodelled. Jarosław has several notable churches. North of the Rynek are the Renaissance parish church and, on the hill beyond, a fortified Benedictine convent, while to the east is the mid-eighteenth-century Uniate church. The western part of town is dominated by the twin-towered Dominican monastery; this was originally built by the Jesuits in the seventeenth century, is likewise fortified and contains a Gothic carving of the Pietà.

Przemyśl lies down the curvaceous course of the San from Jarosław, 21 miles (34km) away by road. Another Ruthenian foundation, it became a major episcopal centre under Polish rule, and the towers of the monastic houses dominate the cityscape to this day. In the second half of the nineteenth century, the Austrian occupiers made Przemyśl into one of Europe's strongest fortresses, defended by a 9 mile (15km) long inner circle of walls and a 28 miles (45km) long outer ring. Much of this was destroyed in World War I, when the garrison was starved into submission by the Russians, though surviving sections can be seen all over the city. As a result of the boundary changes formalised in 1945, Przemyśl now lies hard by the Ukrainian frontier, and swarms with cross-border traders. The nearest crossing-point is 9 miles (14km) to the west, on the main road to Lwów (now L'viv), which was for centuries one of Poland's largest and most culturally vibrant cities.

Przemyśl's Old Town clings to the hillside on the southern bank of the San. The central Rynek preserves a number of eighteenth- and nineteenth-century houses, while just to the side is the Baroque Franciscan church. This has a resplendent columned façade with a double stairway, while the interior is crammed with Rococo adornments, which include illusionist frescos, numerous altars, the pulpit and the organ. A block to the rear is the former Jesuit church, whose college buildings are now occupied by the Diocesan Museum. Further uphill is the Carmelite church, a seat of a Uniate bishop prior to 1945. It subsequently became a Roman Catholic parish church, but was recently returned, after a prolonged and heated dispute, to the Uniates. Alongside, the former Uniate Bishop's Palace now contains the Regional Museum. In addition to the usual archaeological and ethnographical displays, this features a valuable collection of Ruthenian icons brought from Uniate churches throughout the region.

West along ul. Katedralna from the Jesuit church is the cathedral. As so often in Poland, the original Gothic building was completely transformed in the Baroque era but, most unusually, the chancel was later returned to its former appearance. Below this, the foundations of the previous Romanesque rotunda have been uncovered. Among the Baroque additions are the detached belfry, the elliptical chapel of the Fredo family and the octagonal chapel of the Drohojowski family. At the highest point of the Old Town, and commanding a fine view is the castle, now rather ruinous but including a Renaissance section by an inspired Italian architect, Galeazzo Appiani.

At **Krasiczyn**, an otherwise insignificant village 6 miles (10km) west of Przemyśl, Appiani built a Renaissance palace for the local magnate Marcin Krasicki. Constructed in a single burst of activity between 1592 and 1610,

he Tatar mosque, Kruszyniany (Chapter 6)

The Tatar mosque, Bohoniki (Chapter 6)

he Orthodox church, Białowieża (Chapter 6)

The gateway-cum-belfry of the Orthodox church, Wasilków (Chapter 6)

The River Biebrza near Dolistowo Stare after the spring floods (Chapter 6)

Stork in flight over the Biebrza marshes (Chapter 6)

this shows total unity of design and undoubtedly ranks among the finest and most distinctive buildings in the whole of Poland. It is further enhanced by its setting in a lovely landscaped park planted in the nineteenth century with a host of rare and exotic trees and shrubs. The palace itself has four corner towers of markedly different shape, each of which has a name. Starting from the south-west and proceeding clockwise, they are called God, the Pope, the King and the Nobility. The God tower is domed, and built over a chapel, while the King tower, with its six little turrets, is uncannily anticipatory of the Romantic architecture of the nineteenth century. There is also a fifth tower, six storeys high and built to a square groundplan, guarding the entrance to the courtyard, and approached via long bridge over the now dried-up moat. In addition to attics and balustrades, the ornamental decoration of the palace includes *sgraffito* friezes: hunting scenes on the garden side, Classical and Biblical stories and portraits of kings in the courtyard. These have been renewed during recent restoration works, which are set to continue for many years yet, with the result that the interior is unlikely to be accessible for the foreseeable future.

The Bieszczady Region

The extreme south-eastern corner of Poland is composed of the Bieszczady mountains and their foothills, the Góry Słonne. In the Middle Ages, a few towns with a mixed Ruthenian and Polish population were established at the northern fringe of this region, on the main trade route between Cracow and Russia. Everything else remained an uninhabited wilderness until the fifteenth and sixteenth centuries, when it was settled by Ruthenian farmers and Wallachian nomads, descendants of the ancient Thracians who had gradually been forced northwards. In time, two distinct ethnic groups emerged from the intermarriage of these peoples — the Boyks (Boykowie) and the Lemks (Łemkowie) or Rusnaki.

The former inhabited the highest parts of the Bieszczady and in the area (now part of the Ukraine) directly to the east, while the latter lived on the lower western fringe and in the Beskid Niski and Beskid Sądecki beyond. Both groups were farmers, breeding cattle, sheep and goats. Each spoke their own dialect, a form of Ukrainian. Both practised a vigorous form of folk art, particularly manifest in the extraordinarily inventive and picturesque wooden churches found in almost every village, whose style of construction remained essentially unchanged down the centuries. Most of these followed the Uniate rite, though others remained loyal to Eastern Orthodoxy. Generally speaking, the Boyks were poorer and more conservative than the Lemks, and less prone to outside influences than their neighbours, who lived in close proximity to Poles and Hungarians. This distinction is reflected in their architecture. Boyk churches show lingering Byzantine influence, and generally have a large central dome over the nave, with two smaller domes of equal size over the narthex and sanctuary. Lemk churches, on the other hand, often feature a west tower, and adopt the principle of domes descending in size towards the east end.

This ethnic patchwork was tragically broken up in the aftermath of World War II. A para-military group known as the Ukrainian Partisan Army (UPA) took refuge in the wide spaces of the Bieszczady, and continued fighting for the independence of its perpetually subdued country for 2 years after the cessation of hostilities elsewhere in Europe. It remains a matter of dispute as to what extent they were actively supported by the Boyks and the Lemks, but Poland's Communist government decided on a drastic course of action when the deputy defence minister and erstwhile commander of the International Brigade in the Spanish Civil War, General Karol Świerczewski, was assassinated by the UPA in March 1947.

The following month, in an exercise codenamed Operation Vistula, virtually the entire Boyk and Lemk population, upwards of 200,000 in all, was forcibly evacuated and re-settled in areas recently gained from Germany. Their villages were either razed to the ground, or else re-populated with Poles, albeit at only a fraction of their previous density. The churches were either abandoned, or else handed over to the Roman Catholics. Much of the Bieszczady returned to being a wilderness, and several parts were subsequently designated as protected landscapes. Despite a modest migration back to the region since the fall of Communism, particularly by Lemks, the situation remains little changed to this day.

Sanok, located on a bluff high above the River San, 38 miles (62km) south-west of Przemyśl, is the main gateway to the Bieszczady region. The town is a major industrial centre, best-known for the production of the Autosan buses that are a familiar sight all over Poland. Although not particularly attractive in itself, it is an excellent touring base, and also boasts two really outstanding museums.

The first of these is the Historical Museum housed in the castle, a much-remodelled sixteenth-century building located directly above the river, and just beyond the north-east corner of the Rynek. Supplementing the standard displays of archaeology, local history and paintings is the largest collection of Ruthenian icons to be found anywhere in the world outside Moscow. These range in date from the fourteenth to the eighteenth centuries, and were brought from the former Uniate churches throughout the region. They show an evolution in style from the rigid Byzantine hierarchy of the early works to a clear Roman Catholic influence in those painted after the foundation of the Uniate church in 1596.

Facing the castle from the south is a branch museum, the Beksiński Gallery, devoted to the paintings of one of Poland's leading contemporary artists, Zdzisław Beksiński, a native of Sanok. Influenced by both Expressionism and Surrealism, his compositions are notable for their hallucinatory, dream-like sense of fantasy. On the other side of the castle is a late eighteenth-century Orthodox church.

About 1 mile (2km) north of the town centre, on the opposite bank of the San, is the Museum of Folk Architecture, which is generally agreed to be Poland's premier *skansen*. The buildings are arranged into five sections, each representing a different ethnic group from south-east Poland — the

Boyks, the Lemks, the Dolinianie (the dalesmen of the region around Sanok), and the eastern and western Pogórzanie (the inhabitants of the foothill areas further west). In addition to numerous farmsteads, the exhibits include a watermill, sawmill, a windmill, a fire station, a school, an inn and a cluster of beehives. There are also three intact churches. That near the entrance is the oldest: it dates back to the 1670s and comes from the village of Bączal Dolny. It was used for Roman Catholic services and has a complete set of late Baroque furnishings inside.

Both of the other churches were formerly Uniate, and are to be found in the section devoted to the Boyks, which is beautifully landscaped on the hillside. The larger of these dates from the 1730s and formerly stood in the village of Grąziowa. It is a classic Boyk design, with hipped mansard roofs, an arcade running all the way round the building, and a two-storey porch from whose upper level women could observe the service. Inside is a nineteenth-century iconostasis, while the detached belfry alongside, which is older than the church, was brought from another site. At the foot of the hill is an intact mid-eighteenth-century ensemble from the village of Rosolin, consisting of church, belfry and mortuary. The perfectly proportioned church is a little masterpiece, though it is untypical of Boyk architecture, showing clear Roman Catholic influence. It may have been designed by a Pole named Antoni, who signed the folksy paintings inside which take the place of the traditional iconostasis.

Within easy reach of Sanok two outstanding wooden churches, both originally built for the Orthodox rite, can still be seen in situ. That at **Czerteż**, 3 miles (5km) along the main road to the west, dates back to the 1730s and preserves its original iconostasis, though it is now used for Catholic worship. The oldest surviving wooden Orthodox church in Poland is at **Ulucz**, which is on a minor road 9 miles (15km) down the San from Sanok; it is no longer used for services and is now an outstation of the *skansen*. Begun around 1510, it gained its present form the following century. Its central dome has been moulded into the shape of an octagon, while the western section has an amazing roof with spreading eaves which covers both the narthex and the exterior gallery. Inside is a dignified seventeenth-century iconostasis.

Lesko, 9 miles (15km) south-west of Sanok, is built on a clifftop high above the San. It marks the starting-point of the main loop road which goes all the way round the Bieszczady mountains, as well as its smaller counterpart which travels round Lake Solińskie, the hydroelectric and watersports centre just to the south. The town itself is best-known for its Jewish heritage, having been settled by Sephardi Jews expelled from Spain. A certain Spanish influence is manifest in the architecture of the fortified Renaissance synagogue, nowadays a commercial art gallery, which is located just off the Rynek. Downhill and to the right is an extensive Jewish cemetery with over 1,000 historic tombstones, many with beautiful carvings. At the entrance to town from the Sanok road is the castle, which was completely rebuilt as a neo-Classical palace, and is now a holiday home and hotel.

Ustrzyki Dolne, 15¹/₂ miles (25km) south-east of Lesko, is the last town before the mountains. During the summer, it has a rail link with Przemyśl, which international boundary changes have elevated into an attraction in its own right: the train travels via the Ukraine, passing through, but not stopping at, a couple of Ukrainian villages en route. Currently, this is the only way of seeing anything of the Ukraine without having to buy a visa. Other than this, Ustrzyki Dolne has only a few low-key attractions to offer: the former synagogue on the Rynek, which is now a library; a nineteenth-century Uniate church on nearby ul. Kopernika; and the Bieszczady National Park Museum on ul. Belzka.

Several fine wooden churches of the Boyks can be seen in the villages near Ustrzyki Dolne. **Krościenko**, on the rail line to Przemyśl, 7 miles (11km) to the north-east, has one dating from the end of the eighteenth century which is still used for Orthodox services. The village was settled by Greek refugees after World War II, and some still live there. Another notable church, dating from a few decades later, is in **Liskowate**, the next village to the north.

Even closer to Ustrzyki Dolne is **Równia**, which lies down a side road to the south-west, and is also accessible in less than an hour via the more direct route of the footpath marked with blue stripes. Built in the latter part of the eighteenth century, the church has three domes, the central one of which rises in tiers, while the outer ones are shaped liked bells. Further down the same side road, or 5 miles (8km) south of Ustrzyki Dolne by the main road into the mountains, is **Hoszów**. Hidden among the trees at the far end of the village is a late nineteenth-century church in the architectural style of the Husuls, an ethnic minority whose traditional homeland now lies entirely within the Ukraine. They were even more loyal to Byzantine models than the Boyks, favouring a cruciform plan based around a single central dome.

Several more wooden churches lie further south. On the main road, those in **Żłobek** and **Czarna Górne** both date from the 1830s; the former has lost its interior decoration, but the latter still preserves its original iconostasis. **Polana**, 6 miles (10km) west of Czarna Gorne on the road to Lake Solińskie, has a church in the style of those in the Trans-Carpathian region of the Ukraine. The village, which stands at the northern edge of one of the Bieszczady's protected areas, the San Valley Landscape Park (Park Krajobrazowy Doliny Sanu), is a small holiday centre with private rooms available for rent. It is particularly popular with riding enthusiasts: local hucule horses (which were originally wild, but are now domesticated) can be hired there for exploring the countryside.

East of Czarna Górne, a side road leads to **Bystre**, whose early twentieth-century church, regrettably now disused, remains loyal to the traditional forms but is built on a noticeably larger scale. Its nineteenth-century counterpart in neighbouring **Michniowiec** has had its interior redecorated in line with its changed needs of Catholic worship. Back on the main road, the mid-eighteenth-century church at **Smolnik**, the last village before entering the mountains proper, lies on a hillock at the crossroads south of the village. The church at **Chmiel**, 4 miles (7km) along the westbound road which closely follows the course of the River San, was built in the first decade of the twentieth century in traditional Ukrainian style. Returning to Smolnik, it is a further 11 miles (18km) down the main road to **Ustrzyki Górne**. A straggling community spread out along the valley of the Wołosaty, a tributary of the San, it offers breathtaking views in all directions.

Ustrzyki Górne is the main hiking base for the **Bieszczady National Park** (Bieszczadzki Park Narodowy), in whose heart it lies. This otherwise virtually uninhabited area protects the highest part of the mountain range. Together with adjacent areas in Slovakia and the Ukraine, it forms the UNESCO-listed Eastern Carpathians World Biosphere Reserve. Up to a level of 3,772ft (1,150m), the mountains are covered with a typical Carpathian beech forest, seen at its glorious best when cloaked with autumnal colouring. Beeches account for about 85 per cent of the total number of trees. Firs, sycamores and maples are also indigenous, as are the alders which grow along the banks of the streams. Additionally, there are recent plantations of pine, spruce and larch. Between 3,772 and 3,936ft (1,150 and 1,200m) dwarf beeches are found. Higher up there are only the *połoniny*, bare windswept meadows which are unique in Poland and are primarily responsible for imbuing the Bieszczady with an instantly recognizable character. Whortleberries and cowberries grown among the high tufted hairgrass, which for centuries was used for grazing purposes by Boyk farmers.

The lynx is the emblem of the park; other mammals living there include wild cats, wild boar, red and roe deer, brown bears, elks, wolves and European bison, which were re-introduced in the 1960s. Among more than 100 bird species are predators such as eagles, eagle owls, buzzards, vultures and ravens.

A certain amount of the park can be seen by car. From Ustrzyki Górne, the Bieszczady loop road continues through the middle of the park, then on into the lower western part of the range traditionally inhabited by the Lemks. Another well surfaced road leads east to the Rozsypaniec pass on the border with the Ukraine. However, the best of the scenery can only be experienced on foot, via the excellent network of marked trails. These are not especially strenuous and present no obvious difficulties, though it is essential to be well prepared for the sudden and sharp changes in weather which are liable to occur on the *połoniny*. Most walkers base themselves in Ustrzyki Górne and make day trips into the mountains. For those wishing to explore the remoter corners, there are several mountain refuges offering overnight accommodation. Additionally, there are more basic shelters and bivouac sites for those with their own tent.

The highest peaks, which together make up the so-called Bieszczady Crown, lie east of Ustrzyki Górne. These comprise Szerocki Wierch (4,159ft/ 1,268m), Tarnica (4,415ft/ 1,346m), Krzemień (4,379ft/ 1,335m), Kopa Bukowska (4,303ft/ 1,312m), Halicz (4,372ft/ 1,333m) and Rozsypaniec (4,175ft/ 1,273m). It is possible to combine several of these in one day, following the red path from Ustrzyki Górne; the initial approach can be speeded up by driving straight to the Rozsypaniec pass and ascending directly from there. North of the peaks is the wildest and loneliest part of the park, where the traces of several razed villages can be seen; this area can also be approached by car via the side road from Stuposiany, which lies between Smolnik and Ustrzyki Górne. The young River San, at this point no more than a stream, forms the continuous frontier with the Ukraine, and should on no account be crossed.

West of Ustrzyki Górne, the blue trail leads to the summit of Wielka Rawka (4,271ft/1,302m) on the border with Slovakia; the return walk can be done comfortably in less than a day. However, the most rewarding scenery in the park lies on the western section of the red trail. This ascends through the woods to the Połonina Caryńska, a long ridge whose highest point is (4,254ft/1,297m), with spectacular views over virtually the whole range. The path traverses this, then descends to the crossroads and bus stop of Brzegi Górne. It then continues up to the Połinina Wetlińska, where there is a full-equipped mountain refuge. At the far end of this ridge, whose maximum height is (4,110ft/1,253m), there is a choice between descending to Wetlina, the tiny alternative resort to Ustrzyki Górne, or continuing on to the summit of Smerek (4,008ft/1,222m), from where the path descends to the hamlet of the same name, which lies just outside the park boundaries.

The main resort for the western part of the Bieszczady is **Cisna**, 22 miles (35km) north-west of Ustrzyki Górne, and 22 miles (36km) south of Lesko. Its main attraction is the narrow-gauge forest railway which starts from the hamlet of **Majdan**, 1 mile (2km) to the west and runs for 15$^{1}/_{2}$ miles (25km) along the valleys of the Osława and Osławica. Built by the Austrians in the nineteenth century for military purposes, it is still used by the local logging industry. Between June and September, a special tourist train makes a daily return journey along the entire route, giving the opportunity of seeing some otherwise virtually inaccessible scenery, including several sparkling little forest lakes. Because of the steep gradient, it travels at little faster than walking pace on the outbound journey.

The northern terminus of the narrow-gauge railway is **Rzepedż**, which has both a road and a standard gauge rail link with the small industrial town of Zagórz, midway between Sanok and Lesko. On the west side of the village is a typical Lemk wooden church built in the 1820s. It is used for Uniate worship, and has both an iconostasis and Catholic-style devotional paintings. The church in **Turzańsk**, just over $^{1}/_{2}$ mile (1km) east of Rzepedż, is a decade younger and altogether more sophisticated in design, featuring no fewer than six steeples, each crowned with a graceful onion dome. It follows the Orthodox rite, and still preserves its original interior decoration. Another wooden Orthodox church of the same period is in **Szczawne**, 3 miles (5km) north of Rzepedż.

Komańcza, 3 miles (5km) south-west of Rzepedż, offers a tantalising reminder of the religious diversity once characteristic of the whole Bieszczady region. Despite being no more than a small village, it has four different places of worship, including three parish churches. The large modern building in the centre was constructed in the 1980s by the local Uniate majority, who had previously made an unsuccessful petition for the early nineteenth-century wooden church at the western end of the village, which is currently used by the Orthodox community. At the opposite end of the village is another wooden church, built in the 1950s by the Roman Catholic newcomers. About ¹/₂ mile (1km) further north is the convent of the Nazarene Sisters, where Poland's redoubtable post-war Primate, Cardinal Stefan Wyszyński, lived under house arrest from 1955-6, the latter part of the 3-year internment imposed by the Communist authorities for his opposition to the regime. The church is now something of a shrine to his memory, attracting large numbers of Polish pilgrims.

The Eastern Beskid Niski and Pogórze

Immediately west of Rzepedż and Komańcza, the Bieszczady gives way to another mountain range, the **Beskid Niski** (literally, the Low Beskids). This is divided into western and eastern sections, marking both the geographical division of the East and West Carpathians, and the historical boundary between Red Ruthenia and Little Poland, which also cut through the **Pogórze**, the foothills immediately to the north. The eastern sections of the Beskid Niski and the Pogórze see very little foreign tourism. Scenically, they are totally eclipsed by the Bieszczady and by the mountains further to the west, though there are a few notable historic towns.

The lowest crossing-point anywhere in the Carpathians is the Dukla Pass, a frontier post between Poland and Slovakia which was the scene of bloody battles in both World Wars, the latter of which was responsible for over 100,000 casualties. A further 11 miles (17km) north is **Dukla** itself, which is 28 miles (46km) from Komańcza, and linked to it both by main road and by a hiking trail marked with red stripes which traverses virtually the whole of the eastern part of the Beskid Niski. Despite its strategic importance, Dukla has never been much more than a village, and it only has a couple of historic sights. Of these, the parish church is notable for its unusually complete late eighteenth-century decoration, including two chapels founded by the local grandees, the Mniszech family. The former Mniszech Palace is now the Regional Museum, whose historical displays predictably focus on the battles fought at the nearby pass.

Bóbrka, located down a side road some 7 miles (12km) north of Dukla, is an improbable claimant to the title of cradle of the international petroleum industry. In 1854, a local engineer, Ignacy Łukasiewicz, inventor of the kerosene lamp and of a method for refining oil, sank what may have been the world's first oil well at a site south of the village. Others soon followed and some of these remain in operation to this day, despite their rudimentary technology. The original well and its derrick form the centrepiece of the Museum of the Oil Industry, an interesting variant on the familiar *skansen* format.

Krosno, 6 miles (10km) north of Bóbrka, and 25 miles (40km) west of Sanok, is nowadays the main petroleum centre in Poland, though it only produces a fraction of the country's requirements. The town is also a leading glass manufacturer. Within the inevitable industrial sprawl, the small historic core provides a reminder of the town's early days as a staging post on the trading routes between Cracow and Russia. On the Rynek are the old municipal pillory and a number of arcaded houses. The Wójtowska Mansion at number 12 preserves its original Renaissance appearance, but most of the others were rebuilt in the eighteenth or nineteenth centuries. Just off the south-east corner of the square is the Franciscan church, which boasts a number of fine tombs of local notables, including that of Jan Kamieniecki, which was carved by the Italian Renaissance master Giovanni Maria Mosca, sculptor at the royal court in Cracow. The rich stucco of the Oświęcim family chapel is by another prominent Italian-born craftsman, Giovanni Battista Falconi, best-known for his work at Łańcut. On ul. Piłsudskiego is the parish church, originally Gothic, but with a Baroque overlay. At the top end of the same street, the former Bishop's Palace houses the Regional Museum, which is mainly devoted to the two main local industries, the highpoint being an impressive collection of historic kerosene lamps.

Haczów, on a side road 6 miles (10km) east, boasts the oldest and largest timber church in Poland. Although the belfry and the exterior gallery were not added until the 1620s, the nave and chancel date from around 1450. The exceptional width of the former necessitated the construction of aisles, which are rarely encountered in wooden architecture. Outside are carved corbels in the shape of human masks, while inside are murals of the Passion of Christ and the Life of the Virgin.

Several other notable old wooden churches can be seen in the villages just to the east on the main Sanok to Rzeszów road. That at **Humniska**, 9 miles (15km) from Haczow, is sixteenth-century, as is its counterpart in **Blizne** 4 miles (7km) to the north, which retains its original painted interior. From the latter, a side road leads 2 miles (3km) west to **Jasienica Rosielna**, whose eighteenth-century church has Rococo decoration. Back on the main road, another sixteenth-century church can be seen at **Domaradz**, a road junction 4 miles (7km) north of Blizne; this village also has an eighteenth-century inn.

Further Information
— Red Ruthenia —

Places to Visit

Bóbrka
Museum of the Oil Industry
Open: May to September Tuesday to Sunday 9am to 5pm, October to April Tuesday to Sunday 9am to 3pm.

Chełm
Regional Museum
ul. Lubelska
Open: Tuesday to Sunday 10am to 3pm.

Dukla
Mniszech Palace (Regional Museum)
Open: May to September Tuesday to Sunday 9am to 5pm, October to April Tuesday to Sunday 9am to 3pm.

Jarosław
Orsetti Mansion (Regional Museum)
Rynek
Open: Tuesday to Thursday, Saturday and Sunday 10am to 2pm, Friday 10am to 6pm.

Krosno
Regional Museum
ul. Piłsudskiego 16
Open: Tuesday to Sunday 10am to 3pm.

Łańcut
Palace, Icon Museum and Coach
Museum
Open: 16 April to 14 October Tuesday
to Saturday 9am to 2.30pm, Sunday
9am to 4pm, 16 January to 15 April
and 15 October to 30 November
Tuesday to Sunday 10am to 2.30pm.

Synagogue and Jewish Museum
ul. Zamkowa
Open: May to September Tuesday to
Sunday 10am to 4pm.

Przemyśl
Diocesan Museum
ul. Katedralna
Open: Tuesday to Sunday 10am to 3pm.

Regional Museum
ul. Katedralna
Open: Tuesday, Wednesday, Saturday
and Sunday 10am to 2pm, Thursday
10am to 5pm, Friday 10am to 6pm.

Rzeszów
Ethnographic Museum
Rynek 6
Open: Tuesday to Thursday 9am to
2pm, Friday 9am to 5pm.

Regional Museum
ul. 3 Maja 19
Open: Tuesday and Friday 10am to
5pm, Wednesday and Thursday 10am
to 3pm, Saturday and Sunday 9am to
2pm.

Sanok
Castle (Historical Museum)
ul. Zamkowa
Open: 15 April to 15 October Tuesday
9am to 3pm, Wednesday to Sunday
9am to 5pm.

Museum of Folk Architecture
Biała Góra
Open: 15 April to 15 October Tuesday
to Sunday 8am to 5pm, 16 October to
14 April Tuesday to Sunday 9am to
2pm.

Ustrzyki Dolne
Bieszczady National Park Museum
ul. Belzka 7
Open: Tuesday to Saturday 9am to 2pm.

Włodawa
Synagogue (District Museum)
ul. Korolewska
Open: Tuesday to Friday 10am to 3pm,
Saturday and Sunday 10am to 2pm.

Zamość
Arsenal
ul. Zamkowa
Open: Tuesday to Sunday 10am to 4pm.

Diocesan Museum
ul. Przybyszewskiego
Open: Tuesday to Sunday 10am to 2pm.

Regional Museum
Rynek Wielki 26
Open: Tuesday to Sunday 10am to 4pm.

Rotunda (Museum of Martyrology)
Open: 15 April to 30 September
Tuesday to Sunday 9am to 6pm,
1 October to 14 April Tuesday to
Sunday 10am to 5pm.

Tourist Offices

Przemyśl
ul. Ratuszowa 8
☎ 473-09

Zamość
Rynek Wielki 13
☎ 22-9

8 • Little Poland:
Sandomierska

Little Poland or **Małopolska**, which forms the subject of the next three chapters, was the home in the Dark Ages of the Vistulanians, who merged with their northern tribal neighbours, the Polonians of Great Poland, to form the Polish nation. The name of the territory is a real misnomer, having little to do with actual size, being instead a reflection of the dominance of the Polonians in the nation's early life. However, Little Poland had gained precedence over its neighbour by the mid-eleventh century, and has retained its dominance ever since.

With the inevitable exception of the Partition period, Little Poland has always been a component part of the Polish state, and it is in this province that the sense of a separate and distinctive nation and culture is most acute. Paradoxically, the influence of outsiders is nonetheless very marked. A quite astonishing proportion of the finest buildings — from the Romanesque monasteries of the twelfth and thirteenth centuries, via the Renaissance and Mannerist town halls and the ubiquitous Baroque churches and stately homes to the grand neo-Classical public structures of the nineteenth century — were built by Italians. This is, in large part, a quirk of the social system which developed in Poland, whereby there was an unusually large and wealthy aristocracy with the means to attract the best skilled craftsmen from abroad, and a correspondingly small native artisan class. For centuries, most towns in the region also had a large Jewish population — occasionally even amounting to a majority. This community was all but wiped out in the Nazi extermination camps of World War II, though its distinctive mark is still evident in many townscapes.

Historically, Little Poland was divided into two counties. **Sandomierska**, which is described in this chapter, was always the poorer relation of Krakowska, its western neighbour. It takes its name from Sandomierz, originally its principal city and one of Poland's leading mercantile centres but now a picturesque country town well away from today's main commercial, and tourist, routes. Together with the even more time-warped town of Kazimierz Dolny further down the River Vistula, it ranks among Poland's most attractive urban destinations. The larger towns in the region are in general far less enticing though both Lublin — which has long been the region's dominant city — and Tarnów have well-preserved historic cores.

With its liberal sprinkling of historic villages and distinctive patches of scenery, Sandomierska is best explored as a continuous touring route. The

various sections in the chapter together form a more-or-less circular itinerary. Alternatively, individual sections can easily be combined with adjacent routes described in Chapters 7, 9 and 10.

Lublin

Having tripled its population since World War II, **Lublin** has become the main metropolis of eastern Poland. Considering that it has never been more than a regional capital, the city has been the setting for some momentous events in Poland's history — most notably the Union of Lublin of 1569 which transformed the longstanding dynastic relationship between Poland and Lithuania into a unitary state known as the Polish-Lithuanian Commonwealth, which stretched all the way from the Baltic to the Black Sea, and was thus the largest country in Europe. In 1944, Lublin became the first major Polish city to be liberated from the Nazis, and was for several months the seat of the provisional Communist-led government established with Soviet backing. More recently, it has come to be regarded as a cradle of the popular uprisings which eventually led to the demise of Communism, a strike in 1980 presaging the more famous events in Gdańsk shortly afterwards which led to the birth of the Solidarity trade union.

Lublin now spreads over a wide geographical area, though most of the main sights are in the well-preserved if rundown Old Town, which stands on a high spur, and the commercial quarter on its western side. The skyline is dominated by the so-called castle, a large but bizarre-looking pile which stands in splendid isolation at the north-eastern end of the Old Town. In fact, this building, which has appropriately been compared to a film set, is not what it appears to be at all. Of the medieval fortress, little more than a tower survives. The rest, which had long been in disrepair, was pulled down in the early nineteenth century and replaced by the present structure, which was intended from the outset to be a prison, and indeed served as such until after World War II. It now contains the Regional Museum, an extensive and diverse collection which includes sections on archaeology, folk art and costumes, arms and armour, and Polish painting. The last of these is notable for two historical canvases by Jan Matejko, of which *The Union of Lublin* is a typical example of his blockbuster style, while *The Admission of the Jews into Poland* is in a surprisingly small-scale and reflective vein.

Within the castle courtyard is the church of the Holy Trinity, which was commissioned in 1395 by King Władysław Jagiełło, the first joint ruler of Poland and Lithuania. Unfortunately, it is under a seemingly interminable restoration programme, with access normally allowed only on the last Sunday of each month. The graceful vault of its square nave rests on a single central pillar, while the whole interior is covered with early fifteenth-century frescos of the Glorification of the Trinity, Old and New Testament scenes, and portraits of saints. These are the best of four surviving cycles (the others are in Sandomierz and Wiślica, both described in this chapter, and in the Wawel Cathedral in Cracow) executed by a team of Ruthenian artists in a Byzantine-influenced style. Most unusually for the period, they bear the signature of the head of the workshop, a man by name of Andrei.

From the castle, ul. Zamkowa leads uphill through the Castle Gate, a plain neo-Classical structure by the leading Warsaw architect of the day, Domenico Merlini. Ul. Grodzka, which is lined with crumbling tenements, continues up to the Rynek, in the middle of which is the outsized Town Hall, whose present exterior appearance is likewise due to Merlini. In a previous incarnation, the building was the supreme law court for Little Poland, a tradition celebrated in the Museum of the Crown Tribunal housed in the cellars, one of the few parts of the labyrinth below the Rynek readily accessible to the general public.

Elsewhere on the square are a number of historic mansions. Most have been remodelled repeatedly, but the Konopnica House (number 12) at the south-eastern end retains its late Renaissance façade, complete with lively carvings of masks and fantastic beasts. Also of particular note, though rebuilt in the eighteenth century, are the Lubomelski House (number 8) on the north side, which is now a wine bar and nightclub, and the Klonowic House (number 2) on the west side. The latter is named in honour of the Renaissance-era poet and mayor Sebastian Fabian Klonowic, who is depicted together with other literary luminaries of the city in the *sgraffito* decoration on the façade.

From the Lubomelski House, ul. Złota leads to the Dominican monastery, the setting for the signing of the Union of Lublin. Originally Gothic, the church was rebuilt in the late Renaissance period, when the perfectly proportioned chapel of the Firlej family was added to the south side of the nave. Slightly later in date is the Baroque Holy Cross chapel off the sanctuary, which has stuccowork attributed to Giovanni Battista Falconi. Just inside the doorway to the church is a curious eighteenth-century painting showing the great city fire of 1719. Opposite the monastic buildings is the neo-Classical Old Theatre; it dates back to 1821 and is thus one of the oldest still-functioning stages in the country.

A few paces to the south-west of the Rynek is the Cracow Gate, the only significant survivor of the medieval city walls. It was built in the mid-fourteenth century, given a Renaissance upper storey in the sixteenth century, and a Baroque helmet in the eighteenth century. The Historical Museum located inside presents documentary material on the city's history, though the main attraction is the view from the top, which embraces both the Old Town and the commercial quarter. A marginally better vista can be had from the neo-Gothic Trinitarian Tower down ul. Jezuicka to the east, which is also the home of the small Diocesan Museum.

Immediately to the rear of the latter is the cathedral, originally a Jesuit church, built at the very end of the sixteenth century to plans by Gianmaria Bernardini. The sternly neo-Classical columned façade was added in the early nineteenth century by Antonio Corazzi. Inside, the church has a spacious Baroque feel, an effect enlivened by the trompe l'oeil frescos by the eighteenth-century Moravian artist Józef Majer which cover most of the available wall space. At the rear of the complex is so-called Acoustic Chapel, the former sacristy; it gets its nickname from the fact that two people facing away from each other at opposite corners can hold a conversation in whispers. The frescos, again by Majer, are reproductions of those destroyed in World War II, though those in the adjoining domed treasury are originals.

Several other historic monuments lie beyond the confines of the medieval boundaries of the Old Town. On the southern side of plac Wolności, which lies a block south of Krakowskie Przedmieście, the main thoroughfare running west from the Cracow Gate, is the early seventeenth-century Bernardine monastery, which is notable for being the earliest example of the Lublin Renaissance style. This original if unsophisticated architectural idiom, found throughout the province, is characterised by its rich decorative effects, both inside and out, which adapt the florid shapes of late Gothic to a Renaissance format. On ul. Narutowicza, south-west of plac Wolności, is the church of St Mary the Victorious, founded by King Władysław Jagiełło in celebration of his defeat of the Teutonic Knights at the Battle of Grunwald in 1410.

Plac Litewski, which lies further west along Krakowskie Przedmieście, is a large square with a trio of grandiose palaces along its northern side. In the small park in front is a cast iron monument erected in the 1820s in commemoration of the Union of Lublin. Another block to the west is the Protestant church, a severe neo-Classical design of the 1780s.

On ul. Świętoduska, which runs north from the eastern end of Krakowskie Przedmiescie, is the Carmelite church of St Joseph, whose façade ranks as one of the finest achievements of the Lublin Renaissance style. The church of the Transfiguration, located beside the main bus station, immediately north of the castle, belongs to the same period, but is much plainer. It was built for the then new Uniate rite, but is now used for Orthodox worship. A short distance further east is the main Jewish cemetery, one of the few tangible reminders of a community which, until the last war, made up over a third of Lublin's population.

Most of the local Jewry perished at the concentration camp in Majdanek, which lies 2 miles (4km) south-east of the centre, within the present-day municipal boundaries. This was the largest Nazi camp after Auschwitz-Birkenau, and was used both for slave labour and extermination purposes. An estimated 350,000 people — three times the population of Lublin itself at the time — perished there, the largest number being Jews brought from all over Europe. A significant part of the camp has survived — including the whole of one of the five fields of prison barracks, plus the gas chambers, the crematorium, several watchtowers and the formerly electrified barbed wire fence. To celebrate the twenty-fifth anniversary of the camp's liberation, a monument to the dead was placed near the entrance, while a mausoleum containing their ashes was erected at the far end.

Off the Warsaw road, 3 miles (5km) west of the city centre, is the Lublin Village Museum (Museum Wsi Lubelskiej), a small but growing *skansen* set among orchards and gardens. It currently displays several complete farmsteads, a windmill, an oil mill, a kiln and a smithy.

The Lubelszczyzna

With the obvious exception of the city itself, the **Lubelszczyzna**, the province of Lublin, is essentially rural in character. Its attractions are well spread out, though those of the greatest tourist appeal are concentrated in a small area on and around the River Vistula. These merit at least a couple of days' exploration in their own right, though any of the destinations mentioned in this section can comfortably be made the goal of a day excursion from Lublin.

North of the city are two places which can easily be combined in the same trip. **Lubartów**, 19 miles (30km) away, was founded in the sixteenth century as a privately-owned town of the Firlej family. The palace, now used as local government offices, dates from the early years of the town, but was later significantly remodelled — firstly in the 1690s by the Dutchman Tylman van Gameren, then again 50 years later by the Italian Paolo Antonio Fontana. Before undertaking this, Fontana had been commissioned by the Sanguszkos, who had succeeded the Firlejs as owners of the town, to build the parish church. His design shows a clear debt to the Austrian Baroque style. Its principal features, a striking twin-towered façade crowned with a gable and a long elliptical nave surrounded by a ring of chapels, were repeated in his later churches in Włodawa and Chełm described in the previous chapter.

The hamlet of **Kozłówka**, 7 miles (11km) to the west of Lubrartów, clusters round a huge palace originally built in the 1740s for the Bielinski family. By the end of the same century, it had been acquired by a far more famous and powerful clan, the Zamoyskis. However, it was not until the last quarter of the nineteenth century that major changes to the original Baroque fabric were made to create something more in line with the grand eclectic aristocratic tastes of the period. Thus the exterior was re-faced, and various additions were made, including the impressive iron gates, a chapel modelled on that in the Royal Palace in Versailles, and various outbuildings. The interior is positively crammed with works of art, with paintings — many of which are copies of old masters and hence of little monetary value — hung tightly together right up to ceiling level. In the former theatre is an entertaining permanent exhibition of Socialist Realist art which offers a rare chance to see the sort of officially-sponsored paintings and sculptures which formerly dominated museums and public places throughout the Communist world. These fall into two main categories: bloated icons of Marx, Lenin, Stalin, Mao, Ho-Chi-Minh and other leaders, and heroic narratives of the everyday lives of workers and peasants.

Nałęczów, 16 miles (26km) west of Lublin, is another place which conjures up a vanished era and culture, in this case the society of artists and intellectuals who strove to keep a sense of Polishness alive throughout the traumatic 123-year-long Partition period. They made Nałęczów the most popular resort in the Russian-ruled part of the country, a worthy rival to Zakopane in the Austrian sector. The recuperative spa waters and the favourable micro-climate, with its unusually pure air, ensure that plenty of visitors, particularly those recovering from heart ailments, still choose Nałęczów for a restful vacation.

Predictably, the main focus of the town is the Spa Park, which is beautifully landscaped with a wide variety of trees. At its southern end is Nałęczów's oldest building, the Małachowski Palace, which dates from the 1770s. Its Ballroom, whose decoration is a fricassee of Baroque, Rococo and neo-Classical, is the setting for conferences and concerts. Part of the Palace is given over to a museum dedicated to Bolesław Prus, one of the leading figures of nineteenth-century Polish literature, best-known for *The Doll*, a huge social novel set in Warsaw, and *The Pharaoh*, an allegorical epic about ancient Egypt; both are available in English translations. In the middle of the park are the other main spa buildings — the Old Baths, the Sanatorium, and the so-called English Villa, a neo-Gothic mansion housing the administration headquarters. Further north, on the hill called Armatnia Góra, is the Zakopane-style house, now a museum, that was specially built for Stefan Żeromski, a younger contemporary of Prus. He was particularly accomplished at writing short stories, some of which have been translated into English.

Kazimierz Dolny, which lies 12 miles (19km) west of Nałęczów, is undoubtedly the best-loved small town in Poland. It has probably been captured more often on canvas than anywhere else in the country, and with just cause: not only does it have a wonderfully picturesque setting, rising in terraces above the River Vistula, it is the setting for quite magical and constantly changing contrasts of colour and light, with the gleamingly white stone buildings, nestling under red and grey tiled roofs, offset against the blue of the river, the yellow of its sandbanks, and the green of the wooded surroundings. A quiet rural community on weekdays, Kazimierz changes character completely at weekends, when it is inundated with visitors, particularly from Warsaw. This duality is seen at its starkest on Fridays: farmers descend on the town in horses and carts for the morning market, and have not long packed up and gone home when the first of the bohemian set arrive for the weekend.

Kazimierz is named after King Kazimierz the Just, who in the 1170s bestowed the existing settlement on monks of the Premonstratensian order. Two centuries later, King Kazimierz the Great endowed it with full municipal rights; the suffix 'Dolny', meaning Lower, distinguishes it from the town, nowadays a suburb of Cracow, he founded further up the Vistula. In the sixteenth and early seventeenth centuries, it became one of the richest towns in Poland, thanks to the immensely profitable trade down the Vistula, notably in grain, but also in salt, beer and wine. It went into economic decline as a result of the seventeenth-century wars against the Swedes, and never recovered. After World War I, it was 'discovered' by painters who were enchanted not only by the light, but also by its faded grandeur and by the exotic flavour that stemmed from having a predominantly Jewish population, as it had had for over a century. Although it sustained some damage in World War II, Kazimierz is nonetheless the least changed historic town in Poland, with a population of fewer than 5,000.

The spacious Rynek is the hub of town life: it has a wooden well in the middle and is lined with a picturesque jumble of houses, many of them arcaded. Of these, the oldest and most spectacular are the paired mansions of the Przybyło brothers at the south-eastern corner, which were built in the early seventeenth century in Lublin Renaissance style. Their façades are festooned with vigorous if unrefined carvings. The focal point of each is a relief of the respective brother's patron saint — St Nicholas for Mikołaj, St Christopher for Krzysztof, the latter being a particularly arresting composition, showing the outsized giant carrying a tree trunk instead of the normal staff, with a crayfish symbolising the water below. There are also carvings of Biblical scenes, warring animals, plants and medallion heads, as well as inscriptions and decorative features such as strapwork and scrollwork. The Gdańsk House at number 32 on the square is a fine example of a Baroque mansion of the late eighteenth century; the other buildings are later in date, and some are modern.

Just off the north-western edge of the Rynek is the Museum of Silverware. This hosts temporary exhibitions, usually of graphic art, on the ground

Tarpans in the Bison Reserve in the Puszcza Białowieska (Chapter 6)

An owl perched on an ancient oak tree in the Royal Oaks Way in the Puszcza Białowieska (Chapter 6)

Zamość's main square, the Rynek Wielki, with the Armenian merchants' houses (Chapter 7)

Historic carriage outside the palace stables in Łańcut (Chapter 7)

floor, while the permanent collection occupies the historic cellars below. Most of the exhibits, which are drawn from all over Poland, are from the seventeenth to the nineteenth centuries, though there are a few older items as well. Liturgical pieces from both Christian and Jewish traditions are on display, as well as plenty of secular objects.

Several fine Renaissance houses can be seen on ul. Senatorska, a block to the rear of the Rynek. The most imposing of these is the Celej Mansion at number 17, which was owned by a merchant family of Italian origin. Its attic, which is half the total height of the building, is profusely decorated with stylized shell-shapes and carvings of Biblical figures and fantastic animals. Inside, the Kazimierz Museum has a section on the history of the town on the ground floor, and displays of the work of the local school of painters upstairs. Set on a terrace above, commanding a fine view over the town centre, is the Reformed Franciscan monastery. Its present appearance is the result of a remodelling carried out on the original seventeenth-century structure in the mid-eighteenth century. Inside are Rococo altars and Renaissance funerary plaques to prominent local citizens, among them the Przybyło brothers.

Immediately east of the Rynek is the former Jewish quarter, The eighteenth-century synagogue, the fourth on the site, was destroyed by the Nazis, but was rebuilt after the war and now serves as a cinema. Although its overall appearance was simplified, the octagonal wooden dome over the main prayer hall was faithfully reconstructed. On the Mały Rynek, the small market square to its rear, are a series of nineteenth-century wooden stalls formerly used by Jewish butchers, while the house at number 8 on ul. Lubelska is a recognisably Jewish dwelling.

Overlooking the Rynek from the hillside to the north is the parish church of St John the Baptist and St Bartholomew. An excellent example of the Lublin Renaissance style, it was built in the late sixteenth and early seventeenth centuries, incorporating some of the masonry of its predecessor, which had been left as a ruin following the great fire of 1561 which destroyed much of the town. A curiosity of the gabled exterior is that the belfry is lower than the height of the nave. Inside, the vaults are covered with fine stuccowork, while the furnishings include a candelabrum made from deer antlers and the oldest still-functioning organ in Poland, which is contemporary with the church and housed in a splendidly carved case. There are several sumptuous chapels, notably that of the Górski family on the south side of the nave.

Higher up is the castle of Kazimierz the Great, now very ruinous, but commanding a fine view over the town and the Vistula. An even better view can be had from the top of the watchtower beyond, which is the oldest surviving building in town, perhaps dating back to the thirteenth century. A third good vantage point is from the top of the Three Crosses Hill, reached in just a few minutes by a footpath from the east side of the parish church. The crosses themselves were raised in 1707 following a plague which decimated Kazimierz's population.

Along the banks of the Vistula are a few survivors of the dozens of granaries which once dotted the townscape as a consequence of the importance of the grain trade. With its first-floor loggia and tapering three-storey gable, the late sixteenth-century Ulanowski Granary at number 40 on ul. Puławska is as impressive in its own way as the town's finest mansions. Its tie-beamed halls now house the Museum of Natural History, which has sections on geology, mineralogy, flora and fauna. There are also plans to locate a museum in the slightly later Faierstein Granary alongside. Another granary to the north houses the local youth hostel, while its counterpart at the southernmost end of the town waterfront is now a tourist lodge.

About $^1/_2$ mile (1km) south of the town centre, on the left-hand side of the road to Opole Lubelski, an imposing monument to the Jews of Kazimierz was erected in 1985. It consists of a 'broken' wall bearing several hundred fragments of tombstones brought from the local cemeteries, which were both desecrated by the Nazis. A few intact tombstones have been placed alongside.

The whole area around the town, including a stretch on the opposite side of the Vistula, has been designated the **Kazimierz Landscape Park** (Kazimierski Park Krajobrazowy). This differs from most other such parks in Poland, firstly by including a fair number of historic as well as natural sights, and secondly in incorporating a high percentage of farmland. Nonetheless, there is an amazing range of scenery in this relatively small area. Not the least of the attractions is the Vistula itself, which is remarkably untamed for such a major river, and regularly changes appearance, with islets and sandbanks being liable to appear and disappear. Although much of the forest has been reclaimed for agriculture, many patches of woods remain: oaks, lindens and hornbeams are the most common trees, while poplars, alders, ashes, aspens, birches and maples are also found. However, the most remarkable feature of the landscape is the prevalence of small wooded gorges, particularly along the Nałęczów Plateau in the north of the park, formed by water erosion on the thick upper layer of loess. This process is still continuing, and can lead to marked physical changes in a short space of time. The western part of the plateau has the densest network of gullies in the whole of Europe. No fewer than seventeen different species of bat are known to live in the park, which is also inhabited by many small mammals and both nesting and migratory birds.

Among the setpiece attractions is the castle above the village of **Bochotnica**, midway between Kazimierz and Puławy; it can be reached directly on foot from the former in well under an hour via the blue trail. According to legend, it was constructed by order of King Kazimierz the Great as a secret hideaway for himself and his beautiful Jewish mistress Esterka, and was linked by underground passageway to the castle in Kazimierz. In the fifteenth century, it was the seat of a notorious robber baroness named Katarzyna Oleśnicka, who stole with seemingly equal relish from peasants, merchants and fellow-landowners. The building is documented as ruined in the sixteenth century, and it has been surmised that this may well have been an act of revenge by one or more of her victims. From Bochotnica, the path continues northwards via an area honeycombed with gorges.

Another section of the same trail goes south from Kazimierz along the bank of the Vistula to **Męcimerz**, just under 2 miles (3km) away. The hamlet consists entirely of wooden farm buildings, including a windmill. Some of these have been brought from other locations, making it a fully working version of a *skansen* museum. There is a fine outlook point right by the river, and another on the nearby Góra Albrechtówka; both offer a glorious view across the water to Janowiec castle.

Continuing southwards, the blue trail passes the islet of Kępa Zastowska, a bird sanctuary which is the only Polish nesting ground south of the Baltic of the oystercatcher. Gulls, terns, coots, wild ducks and moorhens are among the other species which breed there. The path continues on to Podgórz, at the edge of a ridge running 3 miles (5km) inland to **Rogów**, which lies immediately south of a labyrinthine network of ravines nicknamed 'The Octopus'. About halfway along the ridge, near the village of Dobre, is a viewpoint offering a panorama which on clear days stretches as far as the Holy Cross Mountains.

Janowiec is sited within the small section of the park which lies on the west bank of the Vistula. Occasional excursion boats run from Kazimierz in summer, but to get there by road involves a detour via Puławy. The castle is no more than a shell but is an awesome sight nonetheless, not least because of its commanding situation high above yet well back from the river. It was originally the property of the Firlej family, but later passed to the Lubomirskis, who expanded it into one of the largest residences in Poland, with over 100 rooms in all. In 1783, it was gambled away in a card game, and later fell into disrepair. Between 1945 and 1975, when it was acquired by the state, it was the only castle in Poland to be privately owned. Some remedial restoration is being carried out on the ruins, which, according to legend, are haunted by the ghost of a maiden who was locked up in the tower by her aristocratic father for having had the temerity to fall in love with a fisherman. The parish church in the centre of the village is also worth a visit: it was built in Renaissance style in the sixteenth century, re-utilising the walls of its fourteenth-century predecessor. In the chancel is the double tomb of Andrej and Barbara Firlej, carved in the workshop of Santi Gucci, one of the outstanding group of Italian sculptors based at the royal court in Cracow.

Puławy, which is 7 miles (11km) north of Kazimierz and 30 miles (48km) north-west of Lublin, is nowadays a medium-sized industrial town, albeit one which preserves reminders of its period as one of Poland's leading cultural centres. Its period of glory began in the 1730s, when it came into the possession of the Czartoryski dynasty, and peaked during the early years of Partition, when the family played the vanguard role in the struggle to keep Poland's sense of national identity alive, establishing the country's first-ever museum with that specific purpose in mind. This heady era came to an abrupt end with the failure of the 1830 insurrection against Russia, in which the Czartoryskis were heavily involved. They were forced into exile, and took their treasures with them to Paris. These returned to Poland later in the century, but to Austrian-ruled Cracow, where they can still be seen.

The palace, set in extensive landscaped grounds not far from the Vistula, pre-dates the Czartoryskis, the original block having been built in the 1670s by Tylman van Gameren for the previous owners, the Lubomirskis. Another fine architect, Christian Piotr Aigner, embellished this with side wings for the Czartoryskis, but the building was unfortunately re-modelled on two subsequent occasions, losing much of its character in the process. It is now an agricultural college and thus not a regular tourist site, though it is possible to make an informal visit of the interior. Tylman's entrance hall has still been preserved; there are also two nicely contrasting nineteenth-century interiors in the Music Room and the Gothic Room.

The Palace Park was laid out in the late eighteenth and early nineteenth centuries by order of Iszbella Czartoryska. It was planted with 260 different varieties of trees, about half of them foreign, among which are dotted a series of whimsical garden buildings designed by Aigner. An avenue of lindens leads from the palace to the Temple of the Sibyl, the original home of the Czartoryski museum, and still the setting for temporary exhibitions. It is modelled on the Temple of the Vesta in Tivoli near Rome, even echoing its dramatic setting by being placed overlooking a steep bluff. Opposite is the Gothic House, a mock-medieval fantasy which was built to hold the non-Polish part of the collections. An avenue leads north to the Roman Gate, a folly deliberately built to look like a ruin. From there, a humpbacked bridge crosses over the busy ul. Głęboka, leading to the Greek House, a porticoed orangery which is now a public library.

From the Temple of the Sibyl, a path leads down towards the overgrown lake, passing a marble sarcophagus to the Czartoryskis which is modelled on the Mausoleum of Scipio in Rome. At the far eastern end of the grounds is the Marynka Palace, a dignified, classically-inspired example of the late Baroque style built as a private residence for Izabella's daughter. Beyond the western end of the lake, immediately below the main Palace, are a sculptural group of Tancred and Clorinda, the Chinese House, and a cave hammered out of the rock to serve as the home of a 'real' hermit. Further along, outside the present boundaries of the park, is the Rotunda, the former palace chapel, now a parish church. A free copy of the Pantheon in Rome, it has a particularly dapper interior: the cupola's balcony rests on twelve Ionian marble columns and there is an integrated set of neo-Classical furnishings, consisting of pulpit, pews, confessionals and altar.

The Sandomierz Basin

Sandomierz, which lies about 62 miles (100km) down the Vistula from Puławy, just south of the confluence with the San, is one of the most venerable towns in Poland, as well as one of the most attractive and picturesque. Both Neolithic and Roman settlements preceded the town founded in the seventh or eighth centuries by a local chieftain named

Sudomir. This duly became one of the principal towns of the early Polish state, but it was destroyed in the Tatar invasions of the thirteenth century, whereupon it was re-founded a short distance away on an elongated, sharply sloping spur high above the river. For several centuries Sandomierz flourished as an immensely prosperous trading, academic and cultural centre. This golden era came to an abrupt end with the Swedish 'Deluge' of the 1650s, from which it has never really recovered. Thanks to the intervention of a Russian colonel who moved the front away from the town, it came through World War II unscathed and stands today as a remarkable period piece of a prosperous medieval city — one that has neither grown very big, nor been sanitised into a museum-piece.

There are any number of vantage points offering dramatic vistas of Sandomierz's skyline. One of the best of these, and a good place to begin a tour, is from the bridge over the Vistula which serves as one of the main approaches to the town. Round to the left, overlooking a channel of the river, is the last surviving example of the once-numerous granaries. From there, a narrow road curls steeply uphill to the Old Town, providing an alternative approach to the several stairways which link the upper level with the valley floor. On the left, the castle formed the first line of defence. The original fourteenth-century fortress was gradually modified into a four-sided Renaissance palace, but this was blown up by the Swedes, leaving only one wing intact. It now contains the Regional Museum, with collections of paintings, folklore and local history, and a café.

A little further uphill is the cathedral, which likewise dates back to the fourteenth century. It was originally a collegiate foundation, and has only been the seat of a bishop since 1818. The Baroque façade and towers are unfortunate additions to what is otherwise the finest authentically Polish example of the Gothic hall church design, an architectural form usually associated with Germany. Inside, the capitals have carvings of animals and foliage, while the furnishings include Renaissance stalls and candlesticks. An exotic touch is provided by the Byzantine frescos in the chancel. These were painted in the 1420s by a team of Ruthenian artists, and depict scenes from the lives of Christ and the Virgin, as well as portraits of saints. Equally curious are the large, highly detailed canvases in the nave, the work of an eighteenth-century painter, Karol de Prevot. Those on the side walls illustrate the martyrdoms suffered by the early saints in ancient Rome. Their counterparts on the west wall, below the Baroque organ, form a pictorial history of Sandomierz, including its sackings at the hands of the Tatars and Swedes.

Directly opposite the cathedral are a detached Baroque belfry and two eighteenth-century mansions. To the rear of the second of these is the fifteenth-century Długosz House, the home of the historian Jan Długosz, one of the first important writers in the Polish language, author of a monumental twelve-volume history of the nation from its origins right up to his own day. It now contains the Diocesan Museum, which features some outstanding medieval paintings and sculptures, as well as vestments, furniture, ceramics and painted glass. Immediately to the north of the Długosz House is a building topped with pretty Renaissance gables. This is the single surviving wing of the Collegium Gostomianum, an early seventeenth-century Jesuit foundation which was the first grammar school in Poland.

From the cathedral, ul. Mariacki goes uphill past several more ecclesiastical residences to the Rynek, where open-air markets are held on Tuesdays. Standing in a slightly off-centre position in the open part of the square is the Town Hall, a typically Polish confection of various epochs. The main body of the building is in the brick Gothic style of the fourteenth century; the Renaissance attics were added in the sixteenth century, the tower and clock in the early seventeenth century, the helmet not until another 200 years later. Inside, there is a small museum on the history of the town.

The most imposing mansion on the Rynek is the Oleśnicki House at number 10, which preserves its arcaded front. It is believed to have been the setting for the signing of the Sandomierz Concordat of 1570, an agreement which marked the beginning of religious tolerance in Poland at a time when bitter conflicts between different denominations were the norm throughout the rest of Europe. Other notable houses on the square are number 27, which was built for a Hungarian merchant and likewise retains its arcades; number 23, originally the residence of a Greek merchant; number 14, the home of the sixteenth-century Polish composer Mikołaj Gomułka; number 5, which belonged to the Jesuits; and number 4, which has a fine Renaissance portal.

On ul. Oleśnickiego, to the rear of the Oleśnicki House, is the entrance to the Underground Tourist Route. This passes through a maze of storage cellars and tunnels which were built under Sandomierz during its heydays of commercial prosperity, eventually re-surfacing outside the Town Hall. Because it was never properly re-inforced, this subterranean labyrinth was very nearly the cause of Sandomierz's undoing. The first subsidence occurred in the mid-nineteenth century, and in the 1960s there were fears that the whole town would gradually slide into the Vistula. However, the necessary remedial measures were taken, and the network was opened to the public, quickly becoming a major tourist attraction.

On ul. Żydowska, just round the corner from the entrance, is the former synagogue, which was built in the seventeenth century and subsequently extended. It still preserves its interior decoration, but now houses the municipal archives and cannot normally be visited. On either side are surviving sections of the fourteenth-century town walls. The stretch protecting the narrow northern side of the Old Town has also been preserved. This includes the monumental Opatów Gate, which in summer can be ascended for a view stretching over the rooftops to the Vistula and the whole Sandomierz Basin.

Immediately south of the gateway is the Hospital of the Holy Spirit, founded in 1292 and thus one of the oldest in Poland. The present church is a fifteenth-century Gothic structure remodelled in Baroque style and later given a neo-Classical façade. On the opposite side of the Opatów Gate, just outside the boundary of the Old Town, is a large Baroque complex which was originally a convent but is now a theological college. Its church, dedicated to St Michael, boasts a canopied wooden pulpit arranged as a genealogical tree of the Benedictine order.

Sandomierz was originally located below the spur and much closer to the Vistula. The only building to have survived from the period prior to the Tatar invasions is the church of St James, which lies just a few minutes' walk west of the castle. It was built in the 1220s as part of a Dominican monastery, and is thought to have been the first brick basilica in Poland. From the outside, it looks like a pure example of Romanesque architecture, but the interior arcades adopt the pointed arch of the emergent Gothic style. The northern portal is particularly beautiful, while the detached belfry contains two of the country's oldest bells, dated 1314 and 1389 respectively.

A little further to the west is the Gothic church of St Paul, beside which is the entrance to the Queen Jadwiga Gorge, the prettiest of the many loess ravines around Sandomierz, with a length of 1,640ft (500m) and a depth of 33ft (10m). Just beyond the church is a cemetery which offers a really wonderful panorama through the orchards, embracing the whole of the western side of the Old Town's spur.

The shortest excursion from Sandomierz is to the so-called **Pepper Mountains** (Góry Pieprzowe), a mere 1 mile (2km) to the east. One of the oldest geological features of Poland, this consists of a 500 million-year-old outcrop of Cambrian rocks, above which are various quaternary formations and a thick layer of loess. It takes its name from the colour and texture of the rocks, and in particular for their propensity to crumble like crushed pepper. The outcrop has been designated a strict nature reserve because of its rich flora, which includes yarrow, esparto grass, dwarf cherries, wild pear trees, juniper, hawthorn and blackthorn. It also has what is claimed as Europe's largest natural rose garden, featuring fifteen different types of briar roses.

On the opposite side of the Vistula from Sandomierz, 18 miles (29km) away by the direct road via the heavily polluted town of Tarnobrzeg, hub of the Polish sulphur industry, is **Baranów Sandomierski**, which boasts one of the country's most imposing and best preserved stately homes, the Leszczyński Palace. This splendid example of Renaissance architecture was built between 1591 and 1606 for the eponymous aristocratic dynasty, which also held extensive estates in Great Poland; the architect is not recorded, though the building is generally attributed to Santi Gucci. The palace is cunningly designed in order to make it appear grander than it actually is. Thus the resplendent main front is a façade in both senses of the term, as there are no rooms behind it. For similar reasons of economy, the two-storey courtyard is built up on only three of the four wings. This majestic composition is undoubtedly the finest feature of the palace: it includes an idiosyncratic double stairway and much excellent detail, notably a truly inspired set of grotesque carved heads on the ground floor plinths. In the 1680s, some of the interiors were transformed in Baroque style by Tylman von Gameren. A few of these can be visited in the course of the tourist circuit round the palace; the rest of the building is now a plush conference centre and hotel.

There is also a more roundabout route to Baranów, one offering the advantage of by-passing Tarnobrzeg. This goes via **Koprzywnica**, 10 miles (16km) south-west of Sandomierz, a village which grew up around a Cistercian monastery built in the first half of the thirteenth century by Italian masons. Apart from the façade and towers, added in the Baroque period, it is a plain but fairly typical example of the order's characteristic architectural style, incorporating Gothic elements into a Romanesque framework. Inside, there are fragments of medieval frescos and a high altar of *The Assumption* by the leading Polish-basel artist of the seventeenth century, Bartholomäus Strobel.

Klimontów, 7 miles (12km) north-west of Koprzywnica, has a varied assemblage of monuments. On the west side of the Rynek is the parish church, an early Baroque design by the Swiss architect Lorenzo Muretto, who is known in Poland as Wawrzyniec Senes after his birthplace, Sent in the Grisons. Inside, some fine stuccowork by Giovanni Battista Falconi has survived, though Muretto's design was modified to its detriment in the late eighteenth century, when the cupola, façade and tower were added. East of the Rynek are a neo-Classical synagogue and a Jewish cemetery preserving many historic tombstones. In the village outskirts is a Dominican monastery, a late Renaissance complex from the early seventeenth century which shelters a Byzantine icon of *The Madonna and Child*.

Down a side road 8 miles (13km) north-west of Klimontów is **Ujazd**, an insignificant community standing in the lee of the Krzyżtopór Palace, the most spectacular ruin in Poland. No other building provides quite such telling evidence of the stupendous wealth enjoyed by Poland's landed magnates in the heyday of the Polish-Lithuanian Commonwealth, for at the time of its completion in 1644 it ranked as the largest residence in Europe, surpassing all the continent's royal palaces in size. It retained this status until the construction of Versailles, although the Swedes had reduced it to a semi-ruinous state only eleven years after construction work had ended.

The Krzyżtopór was commissioned by Chancellor Jerzy Ossoliński, and was built in little more than a decade by Lorenzo Muretto in a broadly Mannerist style, rather than the Baroque idiom he used for the church in Klimontów he built immediately afterwards. Muretto chose an extremely complicated ground plan, featuring a pentagonal fortification system enclosing the residential quarters, which have two courtyards, the larger being trapezoid in shape, while the smaller is oval. According to legend, the design of the palace incorporated a number of symbolical references to the calendar, having the same number of towers as the seasons, the same number of halls as the months in the year, the same number of rooms as the weeks in the year, and the same number of windows as the days in the year — including one specially for leap years which was otherwise walled up. Surviving evidence suggests that the palace was actually rather spartan, relying solely on size, rather than on decoration, for its effect. However, by the entrance are two well-preserved reliefs which explain the castle's name: a cross (*krzyż*), symbol of the Counter-Reformation championed by the Ossolińskis, and an axe (*topór*), the emblem of the dynasty.

Opatów, 10 miles (16km) north-east of Ujazd and 20 miles (32km) north-east of Sandomierz, still preserves portions of its sixteenth-century walls, including the Warsaw Gate. The town's main monument, however, is the church of St Martin, a twelfth-century collegiate foundation while retains much of its original Romanesque appearance, though it was modified in the Gothic period. It houses a number of splendid Renaissance tombs of the Szydłowiecki dynasty. Particularly outstanding is that of Chancellor Krzysztof Szydłowiecki, which incorporates a bronze bas-relief cast by Giovanni Cini showing the whole town mourning his death. On the opposite side of the River Opatówka from the town centre is the Bernardine monastery, an eighteenth-century complex whose church has a rich Rococo interior.

The Tarnów Region

Tarnów, which lies midway along the main road and rail lines between Cracow and Rzeszów, about 71 miles (115km) south-west of Sandomierz, is a bustling regional centre. It was founded in the Middle Ages as a staging post on various trade routes, notably that from Cracow to Hungary, and was for long the private property of the Tarnowski family. Together with its surrounding region, it formed part of the Austrian province of Galicia during the Partition period, whereas the rest of Sandomierska fell under Russian rule. Although now rather sprawling, Tarnów has what is by Polish standards an exceptionally well-preserved Old Town. This occupies a hilly site above the modern quarters, and has several stairways bridging the gap between the upper and lower levels.

The most prominent landmark is the cathedral, which stands in the middle of its own square, plac Katedralny, at the western end of the Old Town. Although built around the turn of the fifteenth century, its exterior has a predominantly neo-Gothic appearance as a result of a drastic re-facing carried out at the end of the nineteenth century. Inside, there is a spectacular array of funerary monuments, including several designed by the Italian Renaissance sculptors who worked at the royal court in Cracow. In the nave, pride of place goes to the tomb of Barbara Tarnowska: the graceful figure is attributed to Bartolommeo Berrecci, while the frame is by Giovanni Maria Mosca. The latter was also responsible for the huge monument in the chancel to General Jan Tarnowski, which features friezes depicting his military victories. Also in the chancel is the even larger monument to the Tarnowskis' in-laws, the Ostrogskis, a Mannerist composition from the 1620s carved by Willem van den Block and Johann Pfister.

Until it was raised to the seat of a bishop in 1785, the cathedral was a collegiate church, and the former college buildings can be seen on the western side of the square. They now house the Diocesan Museum, the oldest of its type in the country. This has an excellent collection of Gothic devotional paintings and sculptures, most of which are the products of the artistic schools of Cracow and Nowy Sącz. Another highlight is the treasury of the Benedictine abbey of Tyniec, which was brought to Tarnów following the Napoleonic suppression. It features valuable examples of Gothic, Renaissance and Baroque goldware and silverware, along with historic ecclesiastical vestments and manuscripts.

The adjoining Rynek forms a pair with plac Katedralny, in a deliberate juxtaposition of the sacred and secular. Occupying the customary position in the centre of the square is the Town Hall. Its tower and lower storeys are in the same brick Gothic style as the original parts of the cathedral, while the Renaissance attic and its carved mascarons are clearly modelled on the great Cloth Hall in Cracow. Now designated as the Regional Museum, it preserves some fine original interiors, notably the Great Hall on the first floor, which is hung with a large collection of typically Polish aristocratic portraits. Elsewhere, there are displays of ceramics, glass and weapons from Poland and abroad. There is also a well-documented section on the life of the local hero Józef Bem, who played a leading role in the 1830-1 insurrection against the Russians, before moving to Hungary where he was similarly prominent in the anti-Habsburg revolution of 1848, eventually ending his career as a soldier of fortune in the service of the Turks in the Middle East. Temporary exhibitions are held in the museum's annexe in the fine row of arcaded mansions on the north side of the Rynek.

The eastern part of the Old Town is associated with the Gypsies, some of whom settled there after their roaming lifestyle was outlawed in 1964; at number 13 on ul. Żdowska is the only Gypsy restaurant in Poland. This street, and others nearby, were traditionally the hub of Tarnów's Jewish quarter, and the empty mezuza boxes outside some of the houses are ghostly reminders of the former occupants, the vast majority of whom perished at the hands of the Nazis. Of the seventeenth-century Old Synagogue, only the bimah survives, standing forlorn under a protective canopy in a small garden on the north side of ul. Żydowska.

One important Jewish public building which can still be seen is the Ritual Bath House, a mock-Moorish fantasy located just beyond the north-eastern extremity of the Old Town. This site has a special poignancy, as it was from there that a transport of 728 prisoners (including ethnic Poles as well as Jews) set out on 13 June 1940 to become the very first inmates of the new concentration camp at Auschwitz. About 10 minutes' walk to the north, straight ahead on ul. Nowodąbrowska, then right along ul. Słoneczna, is the Jewish cemetery, one of the largest in Poland, with several thousand tombstones from the seventeenth century onwards. The entrance gates are copies of the originals, which are now in the Holocaust Museum in New York.

Near the top end of ul. Krakowska, the busy shopping street which slopes downhill in a westerly direction from the Old Town to the stations, is a late eighteenth-century manor which is now home to the Gypsy Museum. In the house itself is extensive documentary material, enlived with plenty of photographs, on the history of the Gypsies in Poland. Four brightly painted if rather rundown Romany caravans are parked in a shed in the yard to the rear. During the summer, this area is turned into a mock-up of a traditional encampment, with occasional displays of music and dancing.

South of the Old Town are two beautiful wooden churches of the type associated with the Carpathian mountains. At the far end of ul. NMP, about 10 minutes' walk from the Rynek, is St Mary's, which dates from the middle of the fifteenth century and is thus one of the earliest surviving examples of its kind in the country. Inside, it is richly decorated in a folksy manner. On the opposite side of the large cemetery, a further 5 minutes' walk to the south, is the church of the Holy Trinity, which is about a century younger and has slightly more sophisticated interior decoration, including a Baroque high altar. Notwithstanding the proximity of the railway, it has an even more rustic setting than its neighbour, and seems a very long way in spirit from the bustle of the nearby city centre.

Within easy reach of Tarnów are a number of interesting villages. **Dębno**, 13 miles (21km) along the main road to Cracow, clusters round a small brick castle, the only intact late Gothic defensive structure in the whole of southern Poland. In reality no more than a fortified house, it was built in the 1470s for a local nobleman, Jakub Dębiński, and later prettified by the addition of numerous Renaissance ornamental features. The interiors, which are tastefully furnished in a variety of period styles, include the chapel, the Knights' Hall and the Concert Hall; the last of these houses a seventeenth-century organ and features occasional musical recitals.

A further 13 miles (21km) west is Bochnia, from where a side road leads 4 miles (6km) south to **Nowy Wiśnicz**, whose grandeur belies its tiny size. The castle, occupying a commanding position on a wooded hill, is an early Baroque structure built between 1615 and 1621 by the Italian Matteo Trapola for Stanisław Lubomirski — the same architect and patron who were responsible for Łańcut, Poland's most famous stately home. Like its celebrated later counterpart, it has a pentagonal defensive system protecting the main residential block. Seriously damaged by fire in 1831, it is currently the subject of an ambitious restoration programme, though a number of chambers can be visited, including the Great Hall with its fine stuccowork by Giovanni Battista Falconi. Further uphill, the monastery of the Discalced Carmelites, which Trapola built immediately after completing work on the castle, was once equally imposing, but has suffered even more: the church was blown up by the Nazis, while the conventual buildings are now used as a maximum security prison. Between the two is a nineteenth-century wooden house known as Koryznówka. The great historical painter Jan Matejko often spent his holidays there, and it is now a museum in his memory. Also worth visiting is the parish church on the Rynek, the earliest of Trapola's buildings in the village.

Zalipie, some 19 miles (30km) north of Tarnów, has ranked since the late nineteenth century as one of the most vibrant centres of folk art in Poland. Traditionally, the locals decorate their houses and barns — and even their wells and dog kennels — with brightly coloured floral motifs and many examples of these can be seen throughout what is a very scattered village. They also produce a wide range of handicrafts, such as hand-cut silhouettes, straw dolls, paper flowers, painted furniture, coloured Easter eggs, embroideries and regional costumes, though all these activities unfortunately now seem to be on the wane.

Close to the Vistula, about 9 miles (15km) east of Zalipie, is **Szczucin**, whose Museum of Road Building is one of the country's most offbeat collections. Displayed in its outdoor section are a number of historic steamrollers, locomobiles, agrimotors and other machines, while inside are scale models, uniforms of workers and officials, and documentary material on the industry.

The Little Poland Upland

The **Little Poland Upland** (Wyżyna Małopolska) is an extensive area bounded by the Rivers Vistula and Pilica which contains a large number of attractions, both historic and scenic. As nearly all of these can be seen quite quickly — there is not a single place likely to detain anyone for more than a day — and as the sights are spaced out at fairly regular intervals, it makes for an ideal touring route.

An obvious starting point is **Wiślica**; it lies about 19 miles (30km) by road from Szczucin, and is also easily accessible from Cracow. Nowadays an insignificant village with a population around the thousand mark, archaeological excavations carried out in the 1960s uncovered evidence which suggested that it may well have been both the capital of the Vistulanian tribe and the cradle of Polish Christianity.

The dominant building is the church of the Nativity of the Virgin, one of three collegiate churches founded in the mid-fourteenth century by Kazimierz the Great as expiatory offerings following the healing of his long-standing rift with the papacy. Over the south doorway is a relief showing the king dedicating the church to the Virgin and Child. The interior is a brilliantly original design, in which the nave is divided into two by a row of arcades down its central axis, from which spring spectacular vaults in the shape of palm trees bearing elaborate keystones with carvings of Biblical figures and coats-of-arms. In the chancel are Byzantine-influenced frescos from the end of the fourteenth century, and a stone statue of the Virgin and Child. Underneath, though not normally accessible, are the remains of two previous churches, including a Romanesque gypsum floor with depictions of various people — perhaps the original donor and his family — at prayer, as well as plant and animal motifs.

Under a protective pavilion to the rear of the presbytery are the remains of an even earlier church, together with a basin, presumed to be a baptismal font, which has been dated to around AD880, making it the oldest Christian artefact in the country. To the south is the Długosz House, where the great historian lived before moving to Sandomierz. The Wiślica Museum, to the side of the Rynek, contains documentary material on the town, along with a reproduction of the floor under the Collegiate church.

Pińczów, 17 miles (28km) to the north-west, is another place whose present provinciality is in stark contrast to its colourful past. In the sixteenth century, it was one of the strongest bastions of the Polish Reformation, home of a Protestant academy founded in 1551. Later the same century, it become the home of a prominent school of stonemasons, who were attracted by the proximity of several quarries yielding fine white limestone. Until well into the following century, this was Poland's leading centre for the production of door and window frames for the magnificent new stately homes then springing up all over the country; the workshops also produced church altarpieces and the grand dynastic funerary monuments that were so much in demand. The town is overlooked by its finest building, the hilltop chapel of St Anne, a beautiful cube-shaped design generally attributed to the doyen of the local masons, Santi Gucci. Unfortunately, the town centre was badly damaged in World War II and has only a few sights of note. These include St John's church on the Rynek, a fifteenth-century Gothic building with a predominantly Baroque interior, and the seventeenth-century synagogue on nearby ul. Klasztorna, an abandoned relic of the once-dominant local Jewish community.

A further 17 miles (28km) to the north-west is **Jędrzejów**, which grew up as an appendage to a Cistercian abbey established by monks from Burgundy. The monastic complex survives at the north-western end of town. Built at the turn of the thirteenth century, it is a pure Romanesque design, rather than the part-Gothic hybrid characteristic of this order, though the original architecture was subsequently much modified, particularly in the Baroque period. The town's other big attraction is the Gnomonical Museum on the Rynek, one of the three largest collections of sundials in the world, with several hundred examples from the sixteenth century onwards. Of these, the most celebrated is one which belonged to King Stanisław Leszczyński: it was attached to a cannon which fired a salute at 12noon.

Mnichów, 6 miles (10km) down the main road to the north-east, is a small village with an outstanding wooden church. Built in the mid-eighteenth century and dedicated to St Stephen, this shows the clear influence of the monumental stone Baroque architecture of the period, particularly in its imposing twin-towered façade and the central dome. Many of the furnishings — including the pulpit, confessionals, font and side altars — are further demonstrations of the skill of the local carpenters.

Tokarnia, a further 6 miles (10km) north, is itself nondescript, but has a major tourist drawn in its Ethnographic Park, the *skansen* for the entire Little Poland Upland region, which is located in a vast open field at the southern entrance to the village. This displays some thirty redundant rural buildings, though in time it is hoped to treble the number, so making it one of the largest open-air museums in the country. In addition to the expected farmsteads and cottages, the exhibits include a grand manor house, a pharmacy, a windmill, a horse-powered mill, and a collection of folk sculptures.

Not the least of the *skansen's* attractions is the view it offers of the castle in **Chęciny**, 3 miles (5km) to the north. Standing atop a narrow rocky ridge, this fortress, built at the turn of the fourteenth century and at one time in royal service, occupies a position of total dominance in the landscape. Although now a ruin, substantial parts of the masonry survive, including the outer walls, the square gate tower and the two cylindrical towers, which were both given brick tops at a later date. The town centre has a decayed appearance, but still preserves its medieval street plan and a few historic buildings. These include the parish church on the south side of the Rynek, which has an unaltered seventeenth-century organ still in full working order, and the early Baroque synagogue just east of the square, nowadays the local cultural centre.

Another 2 miles (4km) to the north, on the outskirts of the village of **Zgórsko**, is what is probably the region's most popular sight, the Paradise Cave (Jaskinia Raj). Rediscovered as recently as 1964, it was inhabited by cavemen 50,000 years ago, but has latterly been the home only of bats and insects. There are many beautiful stalactite and stalagmite formations, some of which have been given nicknames, such as 'The Debris Chamber' and 'The Columned Hall'. These can be seen in the course of the compulsory guided tours, which take in 492ft (150m) of passageway out of a total length of 787ft (240m). It is advisable to come early, as a daily quota of admissions is imposed for conservation reasons.

Only a short distance beyond are the outer suburbs of **Kielce**, one of the largest cities in central Poland. Despite its size, and its fine setting below the Holy Cross Mountains, Kielce can be seen in a short visit, as it retains absolutely nothing from its medieval past, and only a few notable monuments from its Baroque heyday. Instead, it has a predominantly nineteenth-century centre surrounded by a modern urban sprawl.

By far the most imposing building is the Bishops' Palace on plac Zamkowy at the southern end of the city centre. This was built between 1637 and 1642 as a summer residence of the bishops of Cracow, the long-time owners of the town, and was built by an Italian architect, Tommaso Poncino, perhaps using plans supplied by a colleague, Giovanni Battista Trevano. The façade of the main block, with its entrance loggia and hexagonal towers, is still Mannerist in appearance, though the overall appearance of the building, and in particular the outstretched wings, is Baroque. There are some splendid interiors, notably the Hall of Portraits, the former dining room, which is adorned with rows of likenesses of the Cracow bishops. Three of the apartments have framed ceilings with paintings by the Venetian Tommaso Dolabella: these depict episodes of contemporary history, such as the trial of the Arian sect and battles against the Russians and Swedes. The reception rooms contain sixteenth- to eighteenth-century furniture; tapestries from France, Flanders, Holland and Poland; Oriental carpets, silk hangings and embroideries; and goldware, silverware, ceramics and objets d'art from all over Europe. There is also a gallery of Polish painting, with works by leading artists such as Piotr Michałowski, Jacek Malczewski, Wojciech Gerson and Stanisław Wyspiański; a collection of European and Asian weapons; and memorabilia of Marshal Józef Piłsudkski, the father of the modern Polish state.

On a terrace above the Bishop's Palace is the cathedral. This was originally a collegiate foundation, only becoming a diocesan seat in its own right after the Cracow bishops had relinquished control of the city. The present structure, which has a detached belfry and a freestanding baptistery, is a Baroque re-build of the Romanesque original. It is crammed with period furnishings, though these are overshadowed by the red marble tomb of Eliżbieta Zebrzydowska, an Italian Renaissance masterpiece attributed to Giovanni Maria Mosca.

On the opposite side of ul. Jana Pawła II is the eighteenth-century building of the grammar school. It is now a museum of memorabilia of Stefan Żeromski, one of several eminent Polish men of letters to be educated there; among the others were Bolesław Prus and the widely-translated contemporary novelist, Gustaw Herling. On the Rynek, a few blocks to the north, several tenements have been knocked together to house the Regional Museum. In addition to temporary exhibitions, this has displays of contemporary Polish painting, the archaeology and natural history of the Holy Cross Mountains, and regional folk art, featuring costumes, embroideries, paper cut-outs, children's toys, woodcarvings and pottery.

The only other monument in Kielce worthy of mention is the Bernardine monastery, an eighteenth-century Baroque complex located on top of the 1,046ft (319m) high Góra Karczówka, a little over 1 mile (2km) west of the cathedral. One of the chapels in the church contains a much-venerated statue of St Barbara which is crafted from the local lead that has been such a cornerstone of the economy. The hill also has the bonus of a fine view over the city and the region.

Oblęgorek, 11 miles (17km) north-west of Kielce, was a totally obscure village until 1900, when the Polish Society built a home there for the great writer Henryk Sienkiewicz to celebrate the silver jubilee of his literary activity. By this time, Sienkiewicz had already produced the historical blockbusters on which his reputation as the Polish Dickens lies. These include *Quo Vadis*, an epic about the early Christians in ancient Rome which won him the Nobel Prize for Literature in 1905 and subsequently became a favourite source for movie moguls; and the vast trilogy about Poland's seventeenth-century wars with the Cossacks, Swedes and Turks Cossacks: *With Fire and Sword*, *The Deluge* and *Fire in the Steppe*. During his years at Oblęgorek, where he remained until the outbreak of World War I, Sienkiewicz began to play a direct role in Poland's struggles to regain independence. In exile in Switzerland, he helped form the Polish National Committee, which the Western allies came to recognize as a provisional government, but his death in 1916 meant that he did not live to see the re-birth of his country. The mansion, built in the Eclectic style, is now a museum and is set in a landscaped park planted with ancient oaks and a variety of other trees. On the ground floor, the rooms are still furnished as the author knew them; upstairs are exhibitions on his life and work.

The **Holy Cross Mountains** (Góry Świętokrzyskie), which stretch west to east for some 70km, are among the oldest in Poland, formed some 300 million years ago in the Palaeozic era, and consisting of a mixture of sandstone, slate and quartz. Although they only reach a maximum height of just over 1,970ft (600m), they are nonetheless are a prominent feature of the landscape, marking a sharp break from the flat countryside on either side. Formerly, they were thickly forested, but the lower slopes were long ago cleared for agriculture, and traditional farming methods are practised there to this day.

The highest and least spoiled part of the chain has been designated the **Holy Cross Mountains National Park** (Świętokrzyski Park Narodowy). This includes the whole of the Łysogóry range, whose name literally means 'Bald Mountains', though it is in fact covered with a forest, known as the Puszcza Jodłowa, which still has primeval characteristics. Fir trees are predominant, though beeches, pines, oaks, larches, birches and alders are also present. A footpath traverses the entire 11 miles (18km) length of the range: this is a straightforward walk presenting no difficulties, other than the occasional erratic marking, and can easily be accomplished in 5 hours or less. It therefore makes for a comfortable day excursion from Kielce, taking one of the regular buses to the eastern or western entrance to the park, and another back from the opposite end. For those not wishing to make this long hike, the main highlights of the park can be covered in a short excursion by car, though even here a certain amount of walking is still necessary.

The best approach to the park is via the village of **Nowa Słupia** on its eastern side, some 22 miles (35km) from Kielce. Iron smelting has been carried out in the vicinity since at least the second century, and the tradition is celebrated in the Museum of Ancient Metallurgy, on the site of one of the oldest furnaces, just below the park entrance, as well as in a festival held annually on the second weekend in September. Near the museum is an enigmatic rock statue covered by a protective canopy, popularly known as *The Pilgrim*, though it is probably a representation of St Emericus.

It is then a lovely 20 minute walk via the blue trail up through the woods to the summit of Łysa Góra (1,952ft/595m) and **Święty Krzyż**, the monastery of the Holy Cross, the building after which the mountains are named. This can also be reached by occasional direct buses from Kielce, but private cars have to be left either in Nowa Słupia or in the car park beside the Jodłowy Dwór hotel in the hamlet of Szklana Huta, 1 mile (2km) west of the monastery. Despite its isolated position — a factor which persuaded the Nazis to make it a prisoner-of-war camp — Święty Krzyż attracts hordes of pilgrims for the big religious festivals, including two local events which take place on the Sundays nearest to 1 June and 14 September.

A twelfth-century Benedictine foundation, it occupies a site that had previously been used for pagan worship for hundreds of years. Of the original Romanesque building, only a doorway survives. The church has been repeatedly rebuilt, most recently at the end of the eighteenth century. It has a monumental and very dignified late Baroque exterior, but the interior is a rather cold piece of neo-Classicism. Adjoining is a Gothic cloister of the fifteenth century. On its east side is the seventeenth-century Oleśnicki

The River Wołosaty at Ustrzyki Górne (Chapter 7)

The Połonina Caryńska, a mountain meadow in the Bieszczady National Park (Chapter 7)

A typical farmstead of the Lemk ethnic minority, now in the Museum of Folk Architecture, Sanok (Chapter 7)

The Rynek in Kazimierz Dolny, looking towards the parish church (Chapter 8)

chapel, which features the early Baroque double tomb of the founder and his wife and a cupola adorned with frothy Rococo frescos. Some of the rooms on the north side of the cloister contain a museum celebrating the missionary activities of the current incumbents, the Oblates of St Mary of the Immaculate Conception; it includes many ethnographic objects, particularly from Africa. The west wing of the monastery houses the National Park Museum, with displays on the local flora, fauna, geology and archaeology.

Close to the ugly radio and television transmitter which lies immediately west of the monastery, a path leads to a belvedere offering a grandstand view of the quartzite boulder field (*gołoborza* in Polish) on the northern slope of Łysa Góra. This is the most spectacular example of what is a distinctive geological feature of the Holy Cross Mountains. The fields, which are devoid of herbaceous plants, were formed by glaciers during the quaternary period.

Another boulder field can be seen on Łysica (2,007ft/612m), the highest peak in the Holy Cross Mountains, which lies at the western end of the Łysogóry range, immediately above **Święta Katarzyna**. This village is centred on a Benedictine convent, originally fifteenth-century Gothic but rebuilt in the nineteenth century; it also has a small wooden pilgrimage chapel dedicated to St Francis, located near the park entrance.

The northern part of the national park incorporates the easternmost section of the Klonowskie range, including a couple of summits, Psarska (1,351ft/412m) and Miejska (1,404ft/428m). These can be reached via the blue trail from Święta Katarzyna. An alternative approach is via **Bodzentyn** which lies immediately below them, 7km from Święta Katarzyna by road. The village has a mid-fifteenth-century parish church which contains two major works of art from Cracow: a painted Gothic retable of *The Assumption* and a Renaissance high altar originally made for the Wawel cathedral, carved by a team of Italian sculptors led by Giovanni Cini. Alongside the church are the ruins of a palace once owned by the Cracow bishops.

Beyond the Holy Cross Mountains, in the peaceful valley of the River Kamienna some 27 miles (43km) north-east of Kielce, is **Wąchock**, another late twelfth-century foundation by the then rapidly expanding Cistercian order. The monastery, which still dominates the village, was constructed early the following century, probably by the same Italian masons who later built Koprzywnica. Its church's distinctive Transitional-style architecture is still in evidence inside as well as out, in spite of the prevalence of Baroque furnishings. The monastic quarters were rebuilt in the seventeenth century, when they were given a palatial late Renaissance exterior. Nonetheless, the original refectory and chapter house both survive, the latter being a particularly elegant little chamber with lovely foliage carvings on the capitals and corbels.

On the main road 27 miles (44km) north of Kielce, or 15 miles (24km) north-west of Wąchock, is **Szydłowiec**, an evocative little town with plenty of reminders of its past prosperity. The castle, set on an artificial moated island to the north-west of the centre, was begun in the 1470s by the local lord, Stanisław Szydłowiecki. It was expanded by his son Mikołaj early the following century and further remodelled in late Renaissance style another hundred years later by the Radziwiłłs, the new owners of the town. Nowadays, the castle serves a variety of functions, containing the local library and cultural centre, as well as the excellent Museum of Polish Folk Musical Instruments. The only one of its kind in the country, this features an array of fiddles, drums, tambourines, hurdy gurdys, bagpipes, accordions, whistles and rattles. Recordings of many of the instruments can be heard during the course of a visit.

Set in its own close immediately south of the Rynek is the parish church, a late Gothic building of mixed stone and brick constructed, together with its rustic detached bell tower, around the turn of the sixteenth century. Inside, the nave is covered with a remarkable polychromed wooden roof. Contemporary with the building is a beautiful polyptych, painted in a Cracow workshop and featuring a central panel of *The Assumption* with devotional portraits of members of the Szzydłowiecki family. The Renaissance tomb of Mikołaj Szydłowiecki was likewise made in Cracow, in the studio of the royal sculptor Bartolomeo Berrecci. There is also a fine neo-Classical monument to Mikołaj Radziwiłł, carved by Giacomo Monaldi.

In the middle of the Rynek itself is the Town Hall, a typical example of Polish Renaissance architecture of the early seventeenth century, with graceful little turrets and a tall tower with an octagonal superstructure. Like many of its counterparts, it was modelled on the great Cloth Hall in Cracow and designed by Italian architects, in this case the brothers Caspare and Alberto Fodyga. About 10 minutes' walk away, on the eastern edge of the town, is a large Jewish cemetery with several thousand historic tombstones.

In the village of **Orońsko**, 9 miles (14km) north of Szydłowiec, the Centre for Polish Sculpture has been established in the nineteenth-century manor house and estate that was originally the property of the painter Józef Brandt. This provides a highly amenable working environment and showcase for the country's best sculptors, who have the opportunity to display their latest works in either the exhibition hall or the outdoor display area in the grounds. The manor house itself, furnished as it was a century ago, is also open to the public, and a hotel has been set up in the former granary.

Not far to the north is the large city of **Radom**, which is essentially a product of the Industrial Revolution and still ranks among the country's leading manufacturing centres. It has some grand nineteenth-century buildings, but the only real tourist attraction is the *skansen*, the Radom Village Museum (Muzeum Wsi Radomskiej) in the extreme south-western outskirts, about halfway along the 11 mile (18km) road linking Orońkso with the city centre. The collection includes around 200 beehives of all shapes and sizes along with five windmills and various farm buildings and wooden houses from the surrounding region.

Further Information
— Little Poland: Sandomierska —

Places to Visit

Baranów Sandomierski
Palace
Open: Tuesday to Saturday 9am to
2.30pm, Sunday 9am to 3pm.

Dębno
Castle
Open: Tues and Thurs 10am to 5pm,
Wed and Fri 9am to 3pm, Saturday 9am
to 1pm, Sunday 10am to 4pm.

Jędrzejów
Gnomonical Museum
Rynek 7-8
Open: 15 April to 15 October Tuesday
to Sunday 9am to 4pm, 16 October to 14
April Tuesday to Sunday 9am to 3pm.

Kazimierz Dolny
Celej Mansion (Kazimierz Museum)
ul. Senatorska 11-13
Open: May to September Tuesday to
Sunday 10am to 4pm, October to April
Tuesday to Sunday 10am to 3pm.

Museum of Natural History
ul. Puławska 54
Open: Wed to Mon 10am to 3pm.

Museum of Silverware
Rynek 19
Open: May to September Tuesday to
Sunday 10am to 4pm, October to April
Tuesday to Sunday 10am to 3pm.

Kielce
Bishop's Palace
plac Zamkowy
Open: May, June, September and October Tuesday to Sunday 9am to 4pm,
July, August and November to April
Wednesday to Sunday 9am to 4pm.

Regional Museum
Rynek 3-5
Open: Tuesday and Thursday to
Sunday 9am to 4pm.

Żeromski Museum
ul. Jana Pawła II
Open: Mon, Tues, Thurs and Fri 9am to
3pm, Wed 12noon to 6pm.

Kozłówka
Palace
Open: March to November Tuesday,
Thursday and Friday 10am to 4pm,
Wednesday 10am to 5pm, Saturday
and Sunday 9am to 5pm.

Lublin
Castle (Regional Museum)
ul. Zamkowa 9
Open: Wed to Sun 9am to 4pm.

Cracow Gate (Historical Museum)
plac Łokietka 2
Open: Wednesday to Saturday 9am to
4pm, Sunday 9am to 5pm.

Lublin Village Museum
al. Warszawska 96
Open: April to October Tuesday to
Sunday 10am to 5pm.

Majdanek Concentration Camp
ul. Droga Męczenników Majdanka 67
Open: May to September Tuesday to
Sunday 8am to 6pm, October to April
Tuesday to Sunday 8am to 3pm.

Museum of the Crown Tribunal
Rynek 1
Open: Wednesday to Saturday 9am to
4pm, Sunday 9am to 5pm.

Trinitarian Tower (Diocesan Museum)
ul. Jezuicka
Open: Tuesday to Sunday 10am to 5pm.

Nałęczów
Małachowski Palace (Prus Museum)
Spa Park (Park Zdrój)
Open: Tuesday to Sunday 10am to 3pm.

Żeromski Museum
ul. Żeromskiego 2
Open: Tuesday to Sunday 10am to 3pm.

Nowa Słupia
Museum of Ancient Metallurgy
Open: Tuesday to Sunday 9am to 4pm.

Nowy Wiśnicz
Castle
Open: Tues to Fri 9am to 2pm, Saturday 11am to 2pm, Sunday 12noon to 4pm.

Oblęgorek
Sienkiewicz Mansion
Open: May, June, Sept and Oct Tues to Sun 9am to 4pm, July, August and Nov to April Wed to Sun 9am to 4pm.

Orońsko
Centre of Polish Sculpture
Open: Wed to Sun 10am to 3pm.

Puławy
Gothic House
Palace Park
Open: Tuesday to Sunday 10am to 3pm.

Radom
Radom Village Museum
ul. Szydłowieckie 30
Open: April to October Tues to Fri 8am to 3pm, Sat and Sun 12noon to 6pm, Novr to March Tues to Fri 11am to 3pm.

Sandomierz
Castle (Regional Museum)
ul. Zamkowa
Open: Tues to Fri 9am to 4pm, Saturday 9am to 3pm, Sunday 10am to 2pm.

Długosz House (Diocesan Museum)
ul. Długosza
Open: April to October Tues to Sat 9am to 12noon and 1 to 5pm, Sun 1 to 5pm, November to March Tues to Sat 9am to 12noon and 1 to 3pm, Sun 1 to 3pm.

Szuczin
Museum of Road Building
Open: Tuesday to Friday 9am to 3pm, Saturday and Sunday 10am to 2pm.

Szydłowiec
Castle (Museum of Polish Folk Musical Instruments)
Open: Tuesday to Friday and Sunday 9am to 3pm, Saturday 10am to 5pm.

Święty Krzyż
Holy Cross Mountains National Park Museum
Open: April to October Tuesday to Sunday 10am to 4pm, November to March Tuesday to Sunday 9am to 3pm.

Tarnów
Diocesan Museum
plac Katedralna
Open: Tuesday to Saturday 10am to 3pm, Sunday 9am to 2pm.

Gypsy Museum
ul. Krakowska
Open: Tuesday to Friday 9am to 3pm, Saturday and Sunday 10am to 2pm.

Regional Museum
Rynek
Open: Tuesday to Friday 9am to 3pm, Saturday and Sunday 10am to 2pm.

Tokarnia
Ethnographic Park
Open: April to October Tuesday to Sunday 10am to 5pm, November to March Tuesday to Friday 10am to 12.30pm.

Wiślica
Wiślica Museum
Open: Tuesday to Sunday 10am to 3pm.

Zgórsko
Paradise Cave
Open: April to November Tuesday to Sunday 9am to 5pm.

Tourist Offices

Kazimierz Dolny
Rynek 27
☎ 10-046

Kielce
ul. Sienkiewicza 72-74
☎ 662-424

Lublin
Krakowskie Przedmieście 78
☎ 244-12

Sandomierz
Rynek 25-26
☎ 223-05

9 • Little Poland:
The Cracow-Częstochowa Upland

The western half of **Little Poland**, traditionally known as Krakowska, contains many of the country's greatest historic and natural attractions. It consists of two distinctive geographical areas, separated by the valley of the River Vistula — the Carpathian mountains and foothills, which are described in the next chapter, and the **Cracow-Częstochowa Upland** (Wyżyna Krakowsko-Częstochowska), the subject of the present chapter.

If this upland is not so obviously spectacular as its mountainous neighbour, it still ranks among Poland's most appealing and distinctive landscapes. The Jurassic limestone from which it is formed dates back some 150 million years, and has been subject to constant erosion. All kinds of wonderful rock formations have resulted from this, including steep cliffs, natural gateways and fantastically-shaped individual outcrops, as well as the overwhelming majority of Poland's caves, around a thousand in all, many of which have yet to be explored fully. In the fourteenth century, a chain of dramatically-site castles, often appearing to grow straight out of the living rocks, was erected along the upland to protect the frontier with Silesia, which was then under Bohemian control. Most of these were destroyed in the Swedish 'Deluge' of the 1650s, but the surviving parts rank among the most picturesque ruins in Europe, fully worthy of comparison with their more famous Spanish counterparts. They are now linked by a popular walking route and parallel road, the Eagles' Nests Trail (Szlak Orlich Gniazd).

At either end of the upland are the two large cities which give it its name. Częstochowa is one of the three leading pilgrimage centres in Europe, but is otherwise completely upstaged by Cracow, the most beautiful, historic and rewarding city in Poland, as well as the one which best encapsulates the Polish sense of nationhood. The city's early history is shrouded in myth: it was reputedly founded in the Dark Ages by a prince named Krak, who slew a fearsome dragon which terrorised the local population. Cracow was certainly among the main strongholds of the Vistulanian tribe, and became the seat of one of the Polish bishoprics established in the year 1000. In 1036 it supplanted Gniezno as the national capital, and developed as a major trading city populated by merchants of many different nationalities. Its growth and prosperity were facilitated by the granting of a charter in 1257, and in 1364 its prestige was further enhanced by foundation of a university, the country's first.

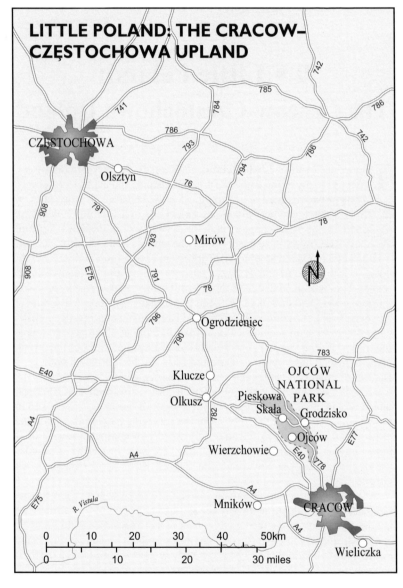

LITTLE POLAND: THE CRACOW–CZĘSTOCHOWA UPLAND

Cracow's position as the unchallenged hub of most aspects of Polish life was dealt a mortal blow by the union with Lithuania in 1569, which left it isolated in the extreme south-western corner of a vast empire. Warsaw, with its far more central location, immediately replaced it as the seat of parliament, and took over as national capital in 1596. Although Cracow then went into decline, history has subsequently treated it far more kindly than any other Polish city. During the Partitions, it was the only place in the country which enjoyed a period of freedom from foreign control, having the rank of a quasi-independent city-state, the Republic of Cracow, from 1815 to 1846. Even after it lost this status, it came under the relatively benign rule of the Austrians, and as a result was able to play the leading role in the struggles to keep the national culture alive. Cracow survived World War II without any major losses to its historic fabric, and in 1978 was one of the twelve places chosen to inaugurate UNESCO's World Heritage List, which was set up to ensure permanent protection for global civilization's most precious legacies. In the same year the city's archbishop, Cardinal Karol Wojtyła, was elected pope, the first non-Italian since the sixteenth century to hold the post.

Quite apart from its own intrinsic attractions, Cracow makes a first-class touring place. Everywhere in this chapter, with the arguable exception of Częstochowa, can comfortably be made the subject of a day trip from the city. The same applies to many destinations in Chapter 10, as well as to those in the Tarnów region (Chapter 8) and to Wadowice and Oświęcim in Silesia (Chapter 11).

Cracow

Cracow (Kraków in Polish) is nowadays Poland's third largest city, with a population of around 850,000 — a figure three times higher than the pre-war level. Inevitably, this means that the city has more than its fair share of urban sprawl, but the historic centre is of unusually large extent and a constant visual treat. In the whole of Central Europe, only that of Prague — which gets inundated with a far larger number of foreign tourists — is of comparable quality. There are important examples of every significant European architectural style and virtually every single street is of interest. An entire week's sightseeing can easily be filled without venturing beyond the municpal boundaries.

Cracow's centre falls into three distinct areas, each of which forms the subject of one of the itineraries below: the Old Town, which accounts for the bulk of the area; the Wawel, a hill crowned by the royal and ecclesiastical showpieces; and Kazimierz, for centuries a separate town, and one which preserves the most potent surviving reminders of the vanished culture of Eastern European Jewry. One point to note with regard to these is that the first is very largely pedestrianised, and the second entirely so. Although the attractions of the inner suburbs are far more thinly spread, they offer sufficient reward for those determined to get well and truly off the beaten tourist track. Within the outer environs are several exceptionally enticing destinations, some well-known, others generally overlooked.

The Old Town

Work on laying out Cracow's **Old Town** (Stare Miasto) began as soon as the city received its charter in 1257. A symmetrical pattern of streets and squares was adopted, though modifications to a strict chessboard plan had to be made in order to incorporate existing buildings. The Old Town was gradually enclosed by a powerful system of double defensive walls with

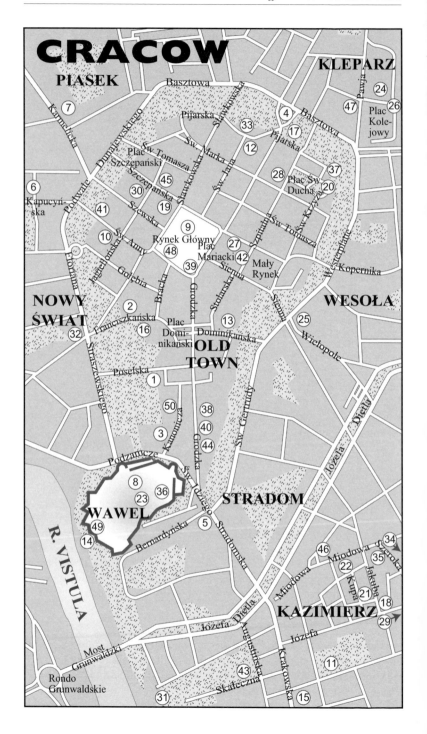

CRACOW

KLEPARZ

PIASEK

Basztowa

Karmelicka

⑦

Pijarska

Planty

㉔

Basztowa

㊼

Plac
Kole-
jowy

㉖

④

⑰

Su-Marka

㉝

Jana

Pijarska

⑫

Plac Św.
Ducha

Dunajewskiego

Św. Tomasza

Plac
Szczepański

Szczepańska

Planty

㉘

Plac Św.
Ducha

㊲

⑥

㊺

Szewska

⑳

Kapucyń-
ska

㉚

⑲

Sw. Krzyża

Westerplatte

㊶

④①

Św. Anny

Rynek Główny

⑨

㉗

Sw. Tomasza

Kopernika

⑩

Jagiellońska

④⑧

Plac
Mariacki

㊷

Mały
Rynek

WESOŁA

Floriańska

Gołębia

㊴

Sienna

NOWY

②

Bracka

Grodzka

㉕

ŚWIAT

Franciszkańska

Plac
Domi-
nikański

⑬

Dominikańska

Wielopole

㉜

⑯

Straszewskiego

Stolarska

Św. Gertrudy

OLD
TOWN

Poselska

①

Dietla

㊿

㊳

Kanonicza

㊵

Grodzka

③

㊹

Podzamcze

Sw. Idziego

WAWEL

⑧

㊱

㉓

STRADOM

R. VISTULA

㊾

Stradomska

⑭

Bernardyńska

⑤

㉞

㊻

Miodowa

Szeroka

㉟

㉒

Jakuba

Kupa

Miodowa

㉑

⑱

KAZIMIERZ

Dietla

㉙

Most
Grunwaldzki

Józefa

Augustiańska

Józefa

Rondo
Grunwaldskie

㊸

Skałeczna

Krakowska

⑪

㉛

⑮

KEY

1 Archaeological Museum	26 Main Railway Station
2 Archbishop's Palace	27 Mariacki Church
3 Archdiocesan Museum	28 Matejko Museum
4 Barbican	29 Old Synagogue
5 Bernardine Church	30 Old Theatre
6 Capuchin Church	31 Pauliłe Church
7 Carmelite Church	32 Philharmonic Hall
8 Cathedral	33 Piarist Church
9 Cloth Hall	34 Poper Synagogue
10 Collegium Maius	35 Remu'h Synagogue
11 Corpus Christi Church	and Cemetery
12 Czartoryski Museum	36 Royal Palace
13 Dominican Church	37 Słowacki Theatre
14 Dragon's Cave	38 SS Peter and Paul Church
15 Ethnographic Museum	39 St Adalbert's Church
16 Franciscan Church	40 St Andrew's Church
17 Florian Gate	41 St Anne's Church
18 High Synagogue	42 St Barbara's Church
19 Historical Museum	43 St Catherine's Church
20 Holy Cross Church	44 St Martin's Church
21 Izaak Synagogue	45 Szołayski House
22 Kupa Synagogue	46 Tempel Synagogue
23 Lost Wawel Exhibiton	47 Tourist Office
24 Main Bus Station	48 Town Hall Tower
25 Main Post Office	49 Wawel Castle
	50 Wyspiański Museum

towers and gates. In the nineteenth century, all but a small section of this was demolished and replaced with a shady park, the Planty, whose presence ensures that the Old Town retains its sense of separateness from the rest of the city. Virtually all its buildings are of some historic interest, and range over the full gamut of styles from Romanesque to Art Nouveau.

The main square, the **Rynek Główny**, forms the focal point of the Old Town, and of Cracow as a whole. Its dimensions are unparalleled by any other European square, with each side having an approximate length of 656ft (200m). However, it only gained its broad, spacious appearance around the middle of nineteenth century. Prior to then, most of the central space was occupied, in accordance with the normal Polish custom, by public buildings, shops and market stalls.

Only three of the structures in the open part of the square were saved from demolition, the largest being the **Cloth Hall** (Sukiennice), whose kernel dates back to the fourteenth century. In the 1550s, it was completely transformed by the Italian sculptor-architects who were employed at the royal court, who adapted the Renaissance architecture of their native land to the needs of Poland's harsher climate, creating a distinctive national style in the process. The overall conception of the project is generally attributed to Giovanni Maria Mosca, often known as 'Il Padovano' after his Paduan birthplace; the carved mascarons on the attic are probably by his Florentine colleague, Santi Gucci. Because the demolitions left the Cloth Hall in a very exposed position, it received a further major reconstruction in the 1870s, when the two long elevations were adorned with open arcades and projecting central sections.

The dank main hall on the ground floor, entered directly from the arcades, is still used for trading, albeit mostly souvenirs for sale to tourists. On either side is an old world café, each of which has turn-of-the-century decoration. Upstairs is a branch of the National Museum, the **Gallery of Nineteenth-Century Polish Painting**. This includes examples of all the leading artists of the period, including Piotr Michałowski, Józef Chełmoński, Artur Grottger and Jan Matejko, who is represented by several typical blockbusters, including *The Prussian Homage* and *Kościuszko at Racławice*. The former illustrates an event which took place on the Rynek Główny in 1525, when Albrecht von Hohenzollern, the last Grand Master of the Teutonic Knights and the first Duke of Prussia, formally accepted his uncle King Zygmunt the Old as his feudal overlord.

Alongside the Cloth Hall is a tall Gothic tower, the only surviving part of the **Town Hall**, the rest of which was pulled down in 1820 in an unfortunate act of civic vandalism by the government of the Republic of Cracow. A café and a satirical cabaret are housed in the tower's vaulted cellars, while the observation balcony at the top offers much the best view of the Old Town that is readily accesible to the general public.

The **church of St Adalbert**, the third building in the middle part of the Rynek Główny, is the oldest in the Old Town. It is named after Poland's first Christian martyr, who supposedly preached at the previous church on the spot immediately before leaving for his ill-fated mission to convert the heathen Balts. The foundations of this survive below the present church, which is twelfth-century Romanesque with an inevitable Baroque overlay.

Subsequent to the demolitions, the open part of the square was adorned with a **monument to Adam Mickiewicz**, the national bard. In December, this is the setting for one of the city's great annual traditions, the judging and display of new *szopki*. These are a unique local folk art, eschewing the normal format of the Christmas crib in favour of a chapel-like structure around which the Nativity scenes are depicted. *Szopki* can be made from almost any form of material; they are invariably brightly painted and are often mechanised. Examples can be seen in all the city churches during the Advent and Christmas seasons.

Many of the mansions lining the Rynek Główny are now shops or eateries and can thus be visited. Most have late Baroque or neo-Classical façades, although much older structures often lie behind and underneath. There is a particularly fine group on the east side — the Grey House (number 6) was Kościuszko's headquarters during the 1794 Insurrection; the Montelupi House (number 7) was Poland's first post office; the Salamander House (number 8) is named after the emblem on its portal; the Boner House (number 9) was built by the richest local banking dynasty of the Renaissance era; while the Gold Head House (number 13) has been a pharmacy since 1403. On the south side, St Anne's House (number 14) is the headquarters of the Polish diaspora; Wierzynek (number 16) is the most renowned restaurant in Poland; the Hetman House (number 17) retains splendid Gothic interiors; and the Zbaraski Palace (number 20) has a courtyard with loggias.

The Sign of the Rams (number 27) at the southern corner of the west side is now a cultural centre; its basement is home to the Piwnica Pod Baranami cabaret. Also on this side is the Krzysztofory Palace (number 35), which now contains the **Cracow Historical Museum**. This has a miscellaneous collection of objects relating to the city, including a display of *szopki* and the original costume for the Łajkonik pageant, a colourful annual folklore event which takes place 8 days before Corpus Christi. The latter was designed by Stanisław Wyspiański, the leading figure in the Young Poland (Młoda Polska) movement, the Polish equivalent of Art Nouveau.

Dominating the north-western end of the Rynek is the great civic **church of St Mary**, generally known as the **Mariacki**. Although it presents a homogenous appearance, with the main body of the building going up in the second half of the fourteenth century, construction work actually went on for nearly 200 years. The lower of the two towers serves as the belfry, while the higher, which is topped with a magnificent late fifteenth-century spire with eight turrets and a golden crown, was traditionally the main civic watch-tower. Every hour, a trumpeter sounds a fanfare, known as the *hejnał*, from the latter. The tune, which is broadcast at midday on Polish radio, and casts a haunting spell over the Old Town, was supposedly played by a watchman during one of the thirteenth-century Mongol raids. It ends abruptly in mid-phrase, in commemoration of the legend that it was at this point that he was shot through the throat by an enemy arrow.

The Mariacki is packed with outstanding art treasures, among which the gilded and polychromed late Gothic high altar has pride of place. Generally considered to be the greatest work of art ever created in Poland, it stands 42.14ft (12.85m) high and 36ft (11m) wide and was carved between 1477 and 1489 by the German sculptor Veit Stoss (known to Poles as Wit Stwosz). In the mornings, it is displayed in its closed position, with twelve reliefs of scenes from the lives of the Virgin Mary and Christ. At 12noon, it is opened to reveal the central shrine of the Dormition and Assumption of the Virgin, portrayed with over-life-sized figures carved in the round, and six more reliefs of the Nativity and the Passion. Stoss also carved the huge stone

Crucifix in the south transept, which stands alongside an equally grandiose Renaissance ciborium by Giovanni Maria Mosca. Other notable works of art are the fourteenth-century stained glass windows in the apse; the elaborate early Baroque choir stalls; five large altars by the eighteenth-century Venetian painter Giovanni Battista Pittoni; and the painted decoration of the vaults and walls by Jan Matejko. There are also numerous tombs and epitaphs to the leading burgher families.

To the rear of the Mariacki is the small late fourteenth-century **church of St Barbara**, which formerly served as its cemetery chapel. According to tradition, the Mariacki masons built it voluntarily in their spare time; the impetus for this may be have been to provide a church where services could be held in Polish, as masses in the Mariacki were then in German only. On the outside of the church is a Gethsemane chapel, with a depiction of Christ on the Mount of Olives by an unknown sculptor in the style of Stoss. Inside is a poignant early fifteenth-century Pietà by a local mason dubbed the Master of the Beautiful Madonnas. Behind the church is the Mały Rynek, a secondary market square originally used for selling meat.

From there, ul. Szpitalna leads north to plac św. Ducha, formerly the location of the Hospital of the Holy Ghost, most of which was pulled down at the end of last century and replaced by the **Słowacki Theatre**, a plush venue modelled on the Paris Opéra. Only the **church of the Holy Cross**, the hospital chapel, was saved from demolition. Its exterior is box-like in shape, with steeply pitched roofs, but the interior is one of the jewels of Polish architecture. The nave, built at the turn of the fifteenth century to a square groundplan, has a single central pillar from which springs an exquisite palm tree vault of sixteen separate ribs. A century later, it was adorned with delicate decorative paintings.

A little to the north-west are the only surviving parts of the medieval forifications. The **Barbican**, now stranded in splendid isolation in the Planty, was built at the very end of the fifteenth century as an outer defensive bulwark, and was linked to the walls by a causeway over a moat. A quasi-circular fort on the Arab model, specially designed in order to target the enemy flanks, it is the only one of its type in Central Europe. Seven small spire-crowned turrets give it a striking silhouette; the sentry walk below accommodated defenders armed with hand-held weapons, while the lower openings in the walls were for cannon. To the rear is a stretch of wall with three of the original forty-seven towers and the **Florian Gate**, the only survivior of the seven city gateways. In summer, the inner side of this wall serves as an informal open-air art gallery.

Adjoining the wall is the Arsenal, which is linked by covered bridge to a mansion on the opposite side of ul. Pijarska. Together these contain the **Czartoryski Museum**, which displays the collections amassed by the eponymous aristocratic family, firstly at Puławy and then in exile in Paris. There are antiquities from Egypt, Mesopotamia, Greece and Etruria; decorative art from all over Europe; and souvenirs of the Battle of Vienna of 1683, including the ornamental metal shield of King Jan Sobieski and a tent and weapons captured from the defeated Turks. Among the paintings are some fine Sienese Primitives and seventeenth-century Dutch works, including Rembrandt's *Landscape with the Good Samaritan*. However, the star attraction is *The Lady with an Ermine*, one of no more than ten easel paintings securely attributable to Leonardo da Vinci. It portrays Cecilia Galleani, the mistress of his patron Ludovico il Moro; the animal (*gale* in Greek) is included as a punning reference to the subject's name, and to Ludovico's nuckname of Ermelino.

Diagonally opposte the museum entrance is the **Piarist church**, a dignified example of eighteenth-century Baroque. The façade, by the Roman architect Francesco Placidi, is based on that of Il Gesù, the famous mother church of the Jesuits, but has an additional ornamental upper section. It is constructed so as to produce a clever illusionistic trick: when viewed from further down ul. św. Jana, the street is made to appear as a cul-de-sac.

The Florian Gate faces down ul. **Floriańska**, the city's most prestigious shopping street. It has a number of fine mansions, such as the Bells House (number 24) and the Negroes House (number 14), each of which is named after its portal carvings, as well as the Pod Różą (number 14), one of Poland's most venerable hotels. The Jama Michalikowa (number 45) is Cracow's most famous and beautiful café, once the meeting-place of the artists and writers of the Young Poland movement, and later of the celebrated Green Balloon cabaret. Inside, the two rooms still preserve their Art Nouveau stained glass, furniture and other decor, and also display theatrical souvenirs.

A couple of doors down is the **Matejko House** (number 41), where Cracow's most famous painter lived from 1873 to 1893, becoming a museum soon after his death. The rooms, including the studio with his easel and painting implements, have been left virtually untouched and are in themselves a vivid documentary record of the life of the period. Plenty of original paintings and sketches are on view, as well as some of the historic artefacts the artist kept as references for the vivid anecdotal detail at which he excelled.

Just off the north-western corner of the Rynek Główny is plac Szczepański, which has two more of the city's finest Art Nouveau buildings. The **Old (Stary) Theatre** actually dates back to the 1840s, but its stolid Historicist shape was transformed out of all recognition by the exuberant Young Poland decoration which was added. At the western end of the square, the Academy of Arts adopts the style of the Viennese Secession and is thereby the building which best encapsulates Cracow's era as an Austrian city. It is adorned with a relief frieze depicting the life of an artist designed by Jacek Malczewski, and is still frequently used for temporary exhibitions.

Standing in sober contrast to these is the **Szołayski House** on the eastern side of the square, which is now home to a branch of the National Museum. It is particularly strong in Gothic art, displaying a host of painted retables and statues brought from churches throughout the city and region; among these, the graceful *Madonna of Krużlowa* stands out. There is also a polychromed sandstone relief of *The Agony in the Garden of Gethsemane* by Veit Stoss, as well as a Crucifix by a member of his school.

From plac Szczepański, ul. Jagiellońska goes south to the academic quarter. Cracow has the second oldest university in Central Europe, founded by King Casimir the Great in 1364, and re-established in 1400 by King Władysław Jagiełło. The **Collegium Maius**, the original building of the latter foundation, is now preserved as a historic monument and tourist sight. It is centred around a peaceful two-storey patio with an overhanging coffered ceiling on the upper level and carvings of coats-of-arms on the balcony; there is also a pretty Baroque fountain, plus a number of architectural fragments saved from demolished buildings.

The interiors can only be visited on guided tours for which it is advisable to book in advance. On the ground floor are several classrooms, including an Alchemy Room. Upstairs are the main reception chambers, such as the Aula, a graduation hall lined with portraits of distinguished academics, and the Common Room, with an intricate spiral staircase brought from a house in Gdańsk. In the Treasury are several rectors' maces, including one donated by Queen Jadwiga which is the oldest of its type in Europe. Also on show are French tapestries, sixteenth- to eighteenth-century woodblocks from local printing houses, and a collection of historic scientific instruments. This includes the Jagiellonian globe, which was made around 1510 as part of a clock mechanism, and has the earliest known representation of the American continent.

Of the other University buildings, the most notable is the Baroque **church of St Anne** just around the corner. The third on the spot, it was built to commemorate the beatification in 1680 of the fifteenth-century Cracow theologian Jan Kanty, who was later canonized. Tylman van Gameren, the court architect in Warsaw, was entrusted with the commission, and he responded with a design which utilises a number of spatial tricks to produce a sense of grandeur which belies the limitations of the restricted site on which it had to be built. Most of the interior decoration is by the Italian sculptor Baldassare Fontana, who made all the altars and stuccowork, as well as the tomb of Jan Kanty. Other features include banners donated by King Jan Sobieski and a neo-Classical monument to the great astronomer Copernicus, who was, at least reputedly, a student at the University.

Immediately south of the Rynek Główny are two large monastic complexes of rival mendicant orders, both of whom established themselves in Cracow in the first half of the the thirteenth century. The **Domincan monastery** is marginally the older of the two, though the only traces of the original Romanesque structure are the lower walls of the cloister and the refectory on its northern side. Although badly ravaged by the great city fire of 1850, the church, which is dedicated to the Holy Trinity, was restored to an approximation of its previous Gothic appearance. The most important work of art is the bronze slab on the left wall of the chancel to the Renaissance scholar Filippo Buonaccorsi, which was designed by Veit Stoss and cast in Peter Vischer's famous bronze foundry in Nuremberg.

There are also several fine Mannerist chapels, including one to the first abbot, St Hyacinth (or Jacek), which is approached by a stairway from the northern aisle. The paintings illustrating his life are by Tommaso Dolabella, a seventeenth-century Venetian who was based at the monastery; the rest of the decoration is Baroque. At the end of the southern aisle is the ornate Rosary chapel, built as a thank-offering for Poland's victory in the Battle of Vienna.

The **Franciscan church** is best-known as the setting for the baptism in 1386 of the pagan Lithuanian ruler Jagiełło, an event which enabled the formation of a dynastic union between Poland and Lithuania, which lasted until 1795. It has a very curious shape, as the nave is adjoined by the Passion chapel, which is of almost identical dimensions. Like its Dominican counterpart, it was badly damaged in 1850 and restored in neo-Gothic. However, its appearance was radically changed at the turn of the century, when it was decorated by a team of Young Poland artists led by Stanisław Wyspiański, who was himself responsible for the great west window depicting God the Creator, the chancel windows of St Francis and the Blessed Salomea, and the murals at the east end with their varied floral, geometric and heraldic motifs. The cloister has a portrait gallery of Cracow bishops as well as fine but very faded Gothic frescos.

On the northern side of the Franciscan monastery is the **Archbishop's Palace**, which was the home of Karol Wojtyła for the decade prior to his election in 1978 as Pope John Paul II. The rambling complex on the southern side of the monastery was successively an aristocratic residence, a monastery of the Discalced Carmelites, and an Austrian-run prison. It now contains the **Archaeological Museum**, whose displays chart the early history of the Polish nation.

The southern part of the Old Town was originally a district known as Okół. It predates the area to the north, which is why it does not conform to the latter's chessboard layout; instead, it is centred on a north-south axis, ul. Grodzka. About halfway down this street is **St Peter and St Paul**, the first Jesuit church in Poland, built by a team of Italian architects at the turn of the seventeenth century in the pioneering early Baroque style of Il Gesù. Piotr Skarga, the celebrated preacher who was its first prior, is buried in the crypt. In the eighteenth century, a balustrade with statues of the Apostles was built on the street front, but the figures were ruined by pollution and have been replaced by modern copies.

Alongside is the eleventh-century **church of St Andrew**, whose twin-towered Romanesque exterior, built of regular limestone blocks, has been preserved largely intact. Its interior, however, was completely remodelled in an exuberant Baroque style by Baldassare Fontana, and was later adorned with a Rococo pulpit shaped like a boat, complete with mast and rigging. Since the fourteenth century, it has been part of a convent of Poor Clares, who moved from Grodzisko, described later in the chapter. Next on the street is the small Baroque **church of St Martin**, a sort of miniature version of St Peter and St Paul. It was built for Discalced Carmelite nuns, but for nearly two centuries has been the place of worship for the city's small Lutheran community.

A block to the west is ul. Kanonicza, arguably the most atmospheric street in the Old Town. Its houses are nearly all Gothic or Renaissance by origin; under Communist rule many were allowed to fall into a shocing state of dereliction, though a good deal of restoration work has since been undertaken. The **Wyspiański Museum** (number 9) displays sketches and memorabilia of the much-loved artist and playwright, including designs for stained glass windows and his visionary but abortive plans for the conversion of the Wawel into a full-blown Polish Acropolis.

Further down the street, the Chapter House (number 19) and Deanery (number 21) together contain the new **Archdiocesan Museum**. This displays works of art from churches throughout the episcopal province, with one room devoted to the hitherto inaccessible treasury of the Mariacki, which includes, in addition to valubale liturgical artefacts, a cycle of paintings of the life of St Catherine by Hans Suess von Kulmbach, a pupil of Dürer who spent part of his career in Poland. Another room contains memorabilia of Pope John Paul II, who lived there between 1951 until his appointment as an auxiliary bishop in 1958.

The Wawel

The **Wawel**, a 748ft (228m)-high Jurassic hill above the Vistula immediately south of the Old Town, is the most prominent feature of Cracow's skyline. It occupies a unique place in the hearts and minds of the Polish people and it is almost impossible to exaggerate its significance within the history of Poland, and its centrality to the oft-threatened sense of national identity. For five centuries the Wawel was the seat of the royal court and the setting for most of the greatest church and state occasions. Even after the loss of capital status, it continued to be the scene of coronations and the burial place of kings and national heroes, and during the Partition period was regarded as the most potent symbol of the subjugated nation.

Fittingly, the Wawel is of far more than symbolic importance, boasting Poland's greatest monumental ensemble and richest array of art treasures, and amply rewards an unhurried visit. The best way to begin a tour is to walk all the way round the it, to see its dramatic silhouette from as many angles as possible. On the west and south sides, the hill rises very steeply; from the Old Town, a cobbled pathway wends its way upwards, entering the precincts through the Renaissance Waza Gate.

To the left is the **cathedral**, the third on the site, which was begun in 1320, immediately after King Władysław the Short inugurted its role as the national coronation church. Considering its pre-eminenence, it is of surprisingly modest dimensions, with a very short nave, this being a direct consequence of the restricted space available on the hilltop. Although the main body of the building is uniformly Gothic, its overall appearance is very disparate as a result of the profusion of side chapels which were added down the centuries, their picturesque and colourful appearance more than com-

The surviving wing of the castle in Sandomierz (Chapter 8)

The Rynek in Sandomierz, with a view of the Town Hall (Chapter 8)

Caravans in the yard of the Gypsy Museum in Tarnów (Chapter 8)

A typical farmhouse of the Holy Cross Mountains region, now in the Ethnographic Park Tokarnia (Chapter 8)

pensating for the lack of stylistic unity. The lower part of the Silver Bells Tower on the right-hand side of the façade is a fragment of the previous Romanesque building, while the Clock Tower opposite is crowned with a large Baroque helmet. Behind the latter is the Zygmunt Tower, which can be ascended for a view over the Old Town. It houses the mighty Zygmunt bell, which is 6.39ft (1.95m) high, 8.52ft (2.60m) in diameter, and weights 11 tons. Cast in 1520, it requires upwards of eight people to ring it, and is heard only on major feast days.

Over the entrance door to the cathedral is a group of prehistoric bones which supposedly guarantee the building's continued existence. According to legend, they were taken from the dragon slain by Krak, but actually come from the shin of a mammoth, the skull of a rhinoceros and the rib of a whale. Focal point of the interior is the magnificent shrine of St Stanisław, a Cracow bishop who was murdered in 1079 by King Bolesław the Bold. He was not canonized until two centuries later, but was soon adopted as one of Poland's patron saints. The domed baldachin was designed in the 1620s by Giovanni Trevano, one of the architects of the Jesuit church of St Peter and St Paul, while the coffin with reliefs of the saint's life was made half a century later by the Gdańsk silversmith Peter van Rennen. In the presbytery beyond are the Baroque choir stalls and high altar.

The ring of chapels round the building, erected as mausoleums to kings, nobles and bishops, provide a second focus. Of these, pride of place belongs to the Zygmunt chapel on the southern aisle, whose gilded dome is among the most striking features of the cathedral exterior. One of the greatest and purest achievements of the Renaissance to be found outside Italy, it was built between 1524 and 1531 by the court architect, the Florentine Bartolomeo Berrecci. Although its rigorous geometry epitomises the ideals of the Renaissance, it differs from its Italian counterparts in the dazzling richness of its surface effects. The carved decoration, executed by a team of Italian sculptors, includes recumbent figures of King Zygmunt the Old, his son King Zygmunt August and the latter's wife Queen Anna, statues of saints and Biblical personages, and grotesques with mythological motifs. Germanic touches are provided by the grille and the silver altarpiece, which were both made in Nuremberg; the latter was designed by Albrecht Dürer's brother Hans and has paintings by his follower Georg Pencz on the reverse.

Alongside is the Waza chapel, built according to a similar format, alebit in the Baroque style, for the succeeding royal dynasty. Equally sumptuous, though in a very different way, is the Gothic Holy Cross chapel immediately to the right of the entrance doorway, which contains the red marble tomb of King Kazimierz Jagiełło by Veit Stoss and a cycle of Byzantine-style frescos by Ruthenian artists. The Lady chapel behind the high altar is likewise Gothic, though it was partially transformed into a Renaissance chantry for King Stefan Bathory by Santi Gucci. On its southern side, Berrecci made a simplified version of the Zygmunt chapel as a chantry to Bishop Piotr Tomicki; on the northern side is an equally imposing chantry to Bishop Piotr Gamrat by Giovanni Maria Mosca. In the ambulatory opposite are grandiose Baroque monuments by Francesco Placidi to King Jan Sobieski and his predecessor King Michał Korybut Wiśniowieski. The oldest royal tomb is that to King Władysław the Short at the eastern end of the northern aisle, diagonally opposite a Baroque altar which shelters a fourteenth-century Crucifix which belonged to the Blessed Queen Jadwiga. There are two other Gothic tombs: to King Kazimierz the Great in the southern aisle, and to King Władysław Jagiełło in the nave.

The Treasury is housed in a chamber off the northern aise. Its most notable items include the spear of St Maurice, which the Holy Roman Emperor Otto III donated to King Bolesław the Brave in 1000, the same year as the Cracow bishopric was founded; a Crucifix fashioned from two thirteenth-century coronets; and the sixteenth-century gold reliquaries of St Stanisław and St Florian. Among the priestly vestments is a mitre made for the canonisation ceremony of St Stanisław in 1253.

Further down the same aisle is a small crypt devoted to the two greatest Polish writers of the Romantic era, Adam Mickiewicz and Julius Słowacki. At the end of the aisle is the entrance to the Royal Crypts, which contain the actual sarcophagi of the monarchs, as well as other national heroes such as Tadeusz Kościuszko, Józef Poniatowski and Józef Piłsudski. The first two of these are buried alongside Poland's other great military hero, King Jan Sobieski, in St Leonard's crypt, one of the best-preserved Romanesque interiors in the country.

Directly adjoining the cathedral is the **Royal Castle**. Of the Gothic fortress, which was ravaged by fire in 1499, there remain the fortifications on the east side, notably the eccentrically shaped Hen-Foot Tower. Most of the remainder of the old building was replaced by a sumptuous new Renaissance palace for King Zygmunt the Old designed by a Florentine architect, Franciscus Italus, who was replaced on his death by Bartolomeo Berrecci. It is probably that the latter was responsible for the final appeance of the courtyard, a far more grandiose conception than any to be found in Italy. The most original feature is the third storey, which is at twice the normal height, with the columns, which are moulded into bulbous shapes at the usual position of the capital, rising straight to the huge overhanging wooden roof. Below the latter are frescos, now rather faded but recently well restored, illustrating antique themes.

Despite having been looted on many occasions, the royal apartments contain a priceless array of works of art. Prominent among these, and spread throughout the chambers, is what must still be regarded as one of the world's premier collections of tapestries, even although only 143 pieces survive out of the 356 fomerly housed there. Most were woven in sixteenth-century Flemish workshops to cartoons by Michiel Coxcie, and fall into three main series — illustrations of the Book of Genesis, landscapes with animals, and grotesque compositions based around the coats-of-arms of Poland and Lithuania.

As the Royal Castle is constantly the subject of restoration projects, it is something of a lottery as to which parts are open to the public at any one time.

The private apartments on the first floor are modest in scale. Of particular note is Zygmunt the Old's bedchamber, which contains the oldest tapestry in the collection, dating back to the fifteenth century and illustrating the medieval French poem, *The Story of the Swan Knight*. There are also some fine interiors within the towers, particularly the Alchemia in the former Łotietek Tower, which was used for experiments in alchemy. Its vault rests on a pentagonal pillar, and its walls are hung with Renaissance and Mannerist paintings, including *The Last Judgment* from the studio of Hieronymous Bosch.

The second floor contains the main reception chambers, beginning with the Audience Hall in the east wing. This has a remarkable coffered ceiling with 30 (out of an original total of 194) carved heads by the Silesian sculptor Sebastian Trauerbach, humorously portraying members of the various social strata of the period. The frieze, painted by Hans Dürer, illustrates the various ages of Man. Beyond the Tournament Hall, named after another Dürer frieze, are the Zodiac Room and the Planet Room, each of which has a 1920s reconstruction of its original astrological fresco. Tucked away in the north-eastern corner are three small rooms from the beginning of the seventeenth century — the bedroom and study of King Zygmunt Waza, and the chapel, which has a late Gothic triptych painted in a Cracow workshop. Among the large chambers in the north wing are the Eagle Room, the former royal court of justice, which contains a portrait of Prince Władysław Waza by Rubens, and the Senators' Hall, the largest in the castle, whose minstrel gallery testifies to its function as the setting for major ceremonial occasions.

The west wing of the Royal Castle houses a permanent exhibition entitled '**The Orient in the Wawel**'. Many of the items on display come from the booty captured in the late seventeenth-century wars against the Turks which culminated in the Battle of Vienna, and include several spectacular tents and banners made of silk and gold thread, as well as rugs, sabres, daggers, guns, harnesses, helmets, armour and rugs, notably the Persian-made Paradise carpet, which takes its name from the depiction of the Garden of Eden. The Polish court developed a much wider infatuation with orientalism, as is proved by the collections of Chinese and Hispano-Moorish porelain and Japanese lacquer.

A suite of Gothic chambers on the ground floor of the castle's east wing contain the **Crown Treasury and Armoury**. In the first room are the oldest items, found during archaeological excavations on the Wawel, as well as several minor royal possessions. The adjoining Jagiełło and Jadwiga Room contains the few surviving crown jewels — the Szczerbiec, the thirteenth-century coronation sword; a sixteenth-century sword used for dubbing ceremonies; and a banner made for the coronation of the third wife of King Zygmunt August. In the following room are objects which belonged to King Jan Sobieski, including a papal sword and hat and the mantle of the Order of the Holy Ghost. The remaining rooms contain a huge collection of weapons from all over Europe, as well as reproductions of the banners captured from the Teutonic Knights at the Battle of Grunwald, and the original banner of King Charles X of Sweden, won at the Battle of Rudnik.

Another permanent exhibition, '**The Lost Wawel**', occupies the former Royal Kitchens, which are entered from the gardens south of the cathedral. This is centred on the excavated foundations of the Rotunda of the Virgin Mary, which dates back to the tenth century and is thus one of the oldest churches in the country. In addition, there are medieval sculptures and everyday objects found during archaeological explorations of the Wawel, Renaissance lapidary fragments from the Royal Castle, and a large array of decorated tiles from the kitches' stoves. The traces of three other buildings — two Gothic churches and a Renaissance house — can be seen in the gardens themselves. They were demolished by the Austrians in the nineteenth century in order that a parade ground could be laid out.

At the western side of the hill, just beyond the Thieves' Tower, is the entrance to the **Dragon's Cave**. This was supposedly the haunt of a monster which terrified the local populace until it was slain by Krak, who fed it with animal skins stuffed with tar and sulphur which duly caused it to explode. On the terrace near the exit is a fire-breathing sculpture of the dragon, made in 1972 by a leading Polish sculptor, Bronisław Chromy.

Kazimierz

South of the Wawel hill is the district of **Kazimierz**, which is named after Kazimierz the Great, who founded it in 1335. It is likely that the king's intention was to create a distinctively Polish town to rival Cracow, which was then dominated by German merchants. The two towns were originally separated by a now vanished arm of the Vistula, though Kazimierz soon expanded over the river and right up to the foot of the Wawel by incorporating the erstwhile village of Stradom.

Kazimierz duly remained a completely separate municipality until 1791, and it ranked among Poland's most prosperous towns. As the German influence in Cracow waned, so did Kazimierz become increasingly Jewish in character. At the end of the fifteenth century, when the Jews had been expelled from Cracow's Old Town, a purely Jewish district was established in the eastern part of Kazimierz, separated by a wall from the larger Christian district to the west. As Jews from all over Europe fled to Poland to escape persecution, so was the Jewish district allowed to expand, taking over parts of its Christian neighbour. In 1818, the government of the Republic of Cracow pulled down the ghetto wall, thereby allowing members of the Jewish community to live wherever they chose. Jews exercised increasing dominance over Kazimierz right up until World War II, when the community was all but wiped out by the Nazis. These developments notwithstanding, the division of Kazimierz into eastern and western sectors remains very obvious to this day.

Starting with the Christian district, there are a couple of notable Baroque churches in Stradom, in the lee of the Wawel. The **Bernardine monastery** is the successor to one founded in the fifteenth century as a direct result of a proselitizing mission by the celebrated Italian preacher, St John Capistrano, which was destroyed by the Swedes in 1655. Its squat appearance, with the central dome concealed by the roofline, was necessitated by the requirement not to interfere with the firing lines from the Wawel. Inside, the principal works of art are a group of St Anne, the Virgin and Child by Veit Stoss and a seventeenth-century mural of the Dance of Death. Directly across the street is the **church of the Missionary Fathers**, a successful transplant of the grand late Baroque style of Rome.

In Kazimierz proper, the Augustinian **church of St Catherine** ranks as the purest Gothic building in the city, untrammeled by the usual later modifications. The grandiose south porch is the main entrance point: most unusually, there is no access to the church via the façade, which was never finished and is hidden behind the monastery wall. Another oddity is the covered bridge spanning ul. Skałeczna, which links the convent on the opposite side of the street with the so-called Hungarian chapel, where the nuns hold their services. Like the sacristy at the other end of the church, this is square in shape, with the vault resting on a single central pillar. The cloisters on the north side preserve medieval frescos depicting the history of the Augustinian order, while the chapter house now serves as the place of worship for Cracow's small Uniate community. Outside the church is a stumpy little fifteenth-century belfry, with a lower storey of brick and an upper of wood.

On a promontory above the Vistula at the end of ul. Skałeczna is the **Paulite monastery**, based around the Church of the Rock. This Baroque building, the third on the site, is one of Poland's leading places of pilgrimage, as it was supposedly the place where St Stanisław was murdered by King Bolesław the Bold, an event commemorated by a big procession held each year on the Sunday following the 8 May. Alongside the church, an archway frames a statue of the saint on a plinth which is placed in the pond where it is said that his body was dumped. The crypt serves as a national pantheon for Poles who have distinguished themselves in the arts: among those buried there are the Renaissance-era historian and cleric Jan Długosz, the painters Stanisław Wyspiański and Jacek Malczewksi, the composer Karol Szymanowski and the novelist Józef Kraszewski.

Kazimierz's market square, known as plac Wolnica, is dominated by the Renaissance Town Hall, now the home of an excellent **Ethnographic Museum**. On the ground floor are reconstructed interiors from rural farms. The first floor contains colourful traditional costumes from all over Poland, while the top floor is devoted to folk woodcarving and festivals. On the main ul. Krakowska just south of the square is the former **Trinitarian church**, which now belongs to a monastery of the Brothers of St John of God. It was built by Francesco Placidi, who resorted to his renowned repertoire of illusionistic tricks to maximize the façade's visibility on a street much too narrow to show it off to best effect.

To the north-east of plac Wolnica is the **church of Corpus Christi**, part of a monastery of Canons Regular. Like St Catherine's, it preserves most of its fourteenth-century architecture, though it was later enlivened by such late Gothic flourishes as the brick gable over the façade and the protruding bell tower. Moreover, it was profusely adorned with examples of local woodcarving throughout the seventeenth and eighteenth centuries, creating a sumptuous effect inside. The finest pieces are the choir stalls, whose backs have paintings illustrating the history of the Canons Regular, and the boat-shaped pulpit in the nave. One medieval stained glass window survives in the apse, while the south aisle has an epitaph to the great architect Bartolomeo Berrecci, who was murdered in mysterious circumstances in 1537.

North-east of the church is the old Jewish town. Following the demolition of the dividing wall, this was inhabited in the main by the most orthodox and conservative Jews, and was already in a somewhat rundown state by the time the Nazis transferred the population to the ghetto they had set up in Podgórze on the opposite side of the Vistula, prior to despatching them to the death camps. After the war, eastern Kazimierz was reduced to a state of semi-derliction, as Cracow's Jewish population, which once numbered 70,000, dwindled to around 200.

Since the fall of Communism, however, there has been a strenuous attempt to revive Jewish life in what is by far the best-preserved old Jewish quarter anywhere in Europe, one which boasts no fewer than seven historic synagogues. Among the new facilities, both on ul. Szeroka, are a Jewish café-restaurant cum hotel, and a Jewish bookshop. The latter, housed in a Renaissance mansion known as the **Jordan Palace**, arranges thematic tours which take in sights otherwise difficult of access. The regeneration of the district has received a huge fillip as a result of international box-office success of Stephen Spielberg's film *Schindler's List*, which won seven Oscars. It is based on Thomas Keneally's largely factual novel about a German industrialist who saved many of Cracow's Jews from extermination, and was shot on location in 1993.

At the southern end of ul. Szeroka, adjoining a rebuilt section of the municipal walls of Kazimierz, is the aptly named **Old Synagogue**, the oldest surviving Jewish temple in Poland. Founded at the turn of the sixteenth century, it was destroyed by fire in 1557 and rebuilt by an Italian architect, Matteo Gucci, in Renaissance style, albeit with an anarchronistic late Gothic vault. A prayer room for women, who were initially confined to the gallery, was later added to the northern side. The bimah, surrounded by a wrought-iron balustrade, has been restored to its original appearance; the late Renaissance holy ark on the southern wall has also been preserved. No longer used for worship, the Old Synagogue is now home to the Jewish Museum, which features collections of liturgical objects, paintings by Jewish artists, and photographs of life in pre-war Kazimierz and of sufferings at the hands of the Nazis.

On the eastern side of the street is the **Poper Synagogue**, an early Baroque temple which takes its name from the rich merchant who founded it in 1620. Its interior, a barrel vaulted hall, has been stripped of its decoration and is now used as an artistic studio for children. A little further north, on the same side of the street, is the Mikveh or **Ritual Bath House**, which dates back to the sixteeth century but was remodelled around the original pool 300 years later.

The **Remu'h Synagogue** on the western side of ul. Szeroka is the only one in Cracow which is still used for regular worship every Friday and Saturday. It dates back to 1558, replacing a wooden construction of 5 years earlier, and is named in honour of Moses Isserlis Remu'h, a scholar and miracle worker who was the son of the founder. Architecturally, it is very plain, but it preserves its furnishings, including the bimah, ark, cantor's pulpit and money box. The adjoining cemetery was desecrated by the Nazis, and a memorial wall was constructed after the war from smashed lapidary fragments. Excavations carried out during the same period uncovered hundreds of undamaged tombstones which had been buried as a precautionary measure during the seventeenth-century wars against the Swedes. By re-erecting these, the Remu'h has gained the only genuine Jewish necropolis of the Renaissance to be seen anywhere in Europe. The graves of the founder's family, including Moses Isserlis, can be seen immediately behind the synagogue.

Another Jewish cemetery, which supplanted the Remu'h after the latter became full, can be seen on ul. Miodowa to the east, just beyond the railway bridge. Although this is the only place in Cracow where members of the current Jewish community can be buried, it is left, in total contrast to its predecessor, in a largely unkempt state.

At the opposite end of ul. Miodowa is the **Tempel Synagogue**, where services are still occasionally held. It is much the largest and newest of the group, built in the 1860s for a reformist congregation whose liturgical use of both Polish and German was a bone of contention with local Jews of the orthodox tendency. The building resembles Historicist churches of the same period in its architecture and furnishings, which include stained glass, stuccowork and a white marble altar.

Also on ul. Miodowa, but entered from ul. Warszauera to the south, is the **Kupa Synagogue**. It dates back to 1643, but is in a very rough state, having lost virtually all its decoration, and is reduced to serving as a warehouse. A short distance to the south, between ul. Kupa and ul. Jakubia, is the **Izaak (or Ajzyk) Synagogue**, which was founded one year later. There are exterior stairways to the women's gallery, while inside is fine decoration made in the workshop of the great Italian-born stuccoist Giovanni Battista Falconi.

Round the corner on ul. Józefa is the **Wysoka (or High) Synagogue**, which was built in the second half of the sixteenth century. Its name is explained by its position on the first floor of the building, the ground floor having originally been occupied by shops. The synagogue was stripped of most of its decoration by the Nazis, though the money box, part of the ark and some polychromy survive. Offices of a conservation studio are now housed inside. At no.12 on the same street is a seventeenth-century house with the finest traditional courtyard in the district, stretching all the back to ul. Meiselsa to the rear and offering a fine view of the tower of Corpus Christi.

The Inner Suburbs

Beyond Cracow's core of the Old Town, the Wawel and Kazimierz is a ring of inner suburbs, all of which are historic, yet completely removed from the well-beaten tourist track. While it would be idle to pretend that any can match the attractions of the centre, they all have their distinctive character and at least a few monuments of note.

East of the Old Town is **Wesoła**, whose main axis is ul. Kopernika, a long curving street which connects with ul. Westerplatte on the inner ring road. There are several churches along its length, the first and oldest being that of St Nicholas, a twelfth-century collegiate foundation. The present building is largely Baroque, though traces of Romanesque architecture are visible on the outer walls. More interesting than the church itself is the lantern of the dead in its graveyard, a Gothic column set up, probably in the fourteenth century, for victims of leprosy, and brought to this site from a now vanished hospital. Just beyond the railway bridge is the Jesuit church, begun in 1909 but not finished until after World War I. It ranks among the finest twentieth-century Polish churches, particularly in respect of its decoration, which includes a number of huge sculptures by Xavery Dumikowski. At the end of ul. Kopernika are the Botanical Gardens, in whose grounds stands a late eighteenth-century astronomical observatory.

Kleparz to the north of the Old Town began as a suburb outside the protection of Cracow's walls, but Kazimierz the Great granted it a municipal charter and re-christened it Florencja. This name, which did not stick, was derived from the Roman martyr St Florian, whose remains were acquired by King Kazimierz the Just in 1184, who was anxious to provide Cracow with the holy relics it had hitherto lacked. The story goes that, just as the hearse was approaching the gates, the relics grew so heavy that the procession was unable to proceed any further, and so a church was duly founded on the site. Because of its vulnerable position, this has been seriously damaged or destroyed on six occasions, and the present building is a fairly modest Baroque design. On its southern side is the spacious plac Matejki, which commands a fine view of the Old Town skyline. The large monument to Poland's victory at the Battle of Grunwald in 1410 was erected to commemorate the 500th anniversary of the event, and endowed by the world-renowned pianist and statesman, Ignacy Jan Paderewski. Alongside is the Tomb of the Unknown Soldier, scene of the most solemn official celebrations. On ul. Krowoderska a few blocks further west is the convent of the Nuns of the Visitation, a well-preserved Baroque complex from the late seventeenth century centred on a fine Italianate church.

Piasek, the suburb west of Kleparz, is often still known by its old name of Garbary. It was developed by the Austrian authorities in the second half of the nineteenth century, and contains many grand buildings from this time, notably along its main street, ul. Karmelicka. This is named after the Carmelite monastery, whose Baroque church re-uses some of the masonry of its Gothic predecessor, which was destroyed in the Swedish wars. Inside are some fine examples of Baroque woodcarving, the stalls and the richly decorated high altar being outstanding. Adjoining the southern side of the church is a sizeable domed chapel by Giovanni Trevano, built to shelter a miraculous image of the Virgin and Child. At the southern end of Piasek, across the Planty from the University quarter, is the Capuchin monastery, which during Advent has some of the most elaborate *szopki* in Cracow on view in its church. Tadeusz Kościuszko and his officers had their swords blest at its Loretto chapel prior to launching the national insurrection of 1794.

Zwierzyniec, a much larger suburb stretching west from the Old Town, is known above all as the setting for celebrations and festivals. Many of the biggest open-air events — such as the masses held during Pope John Paul II's return visits to the city, which were each attended by an estimated two million people — are held on the Błonia, a park at the northern edge of the district. Just beyond its eastern end is the New Building, which contains the Gallery of Twentieth-Century Polish Painting. Outside stands a large monument to Stanisław Wyspiański, who is represented by many works, including his stained glass designs for Wawel Cathedral. There are also examples of many other leading Polish painters, notably Jacek Malczewski, Stanisław Ignacy Witkiewicz and Olga Boznańska.

The historic core of Zwierzyniec lies along the northern bank of the Vistula, where a Premonstratensian convent was founded in 1162. It has repeatedly been rebuilt, most notably at the turn of the seventeenth century in late Renaissance style. Girt with walls and towers, and pleasantly sited overlooking the river, it is notable mainly for its picturesque silhouette. Every Easter Monday, the Emaus fair is held outside, while the church is the starting-point for the Łajkonik pageant 8 days before Corpus Christi, which celebrates the repulsion of a Mongol raid in 1289. On the hill above, a site previously associated with pagan worship, are two more churches — St Margaret's, a late seventeenth-century wooden octagon, and the Holy Saviour, likewise Baroque but with the excavated remains of a pre-Romanesque church underneath. Outside the latter is a stone pulpit from which St Adalbert is said to have preached.

Further west is the Kościuszko Mound, raised on top of an existing hill in the 1820s as a tribute to the great patriotic leader. The idea was inspired by two pagan mounds in the outskirts of Cracow, and soil was brought from the United States, where he had fought in the Wars of Independence, as well as from the battlefields of Racławice, Maciejowice and Dubienka. Access is via a museum of Kościuszko memorabilia, and there is a fine view over Cracow from the top. At the foot of the mound is an Austrian fort, now converted into a hotel.

As a result of the First Partition of Poland in 1772, the area south of the Vistula was annexed by Austria. The village of **Podgórze** immediately opposite Kazimierz was given the status of a town; it was re-named Josephstadt in honour of the reigning Habsburg emperor, and developed as a rival to Cracow, though it never came near to achieving this. Not until 1915 did it become part of the city. In March 1941, the Nazis designated it as the site of the enclosed urban ghetto where all the surviving Jews of Cracow were forced to live, sealed off from the rest of the city. The ghetto was liquidated 2 years later, when the remaining inhabitants were despatched to the death camps.

On plac Zgody in the commercial heart of the quarter is the Pharmacy Under the Eagle (Apteka Pod Orłem), which was run by Tadeusz Pankiewicz, the only non-Jewish inhabitant of the ghetto. It is now a memorial museum of the period. Nearby, at no. 18 on ul. Józefińska, is the building which housed the Judenrat, the administration offices of the ghetto.

To the south rises a hill known as the Krzemonki, the setting for a big fair, the Rękawka, held on the Tuesday after Easter. On its northern side are the small Baroque church of St Benedict, which preserves traces of its Romanesque predecessor, and an Austrian fort which is due to be converted into an art gallery. The higher southern part of the hill is crowned by a 52ft (16m) high artificial mound which dates back to an indeterminate point in the Dark Ages. It has traditionally been assumed to be the grave of Krak, the founder of the city, but excavations have failed to uncover evidence that it was a burial site, so its function remains a mystery.

From the Krzemonki, the chimney of Oskar Schindler's enamel factory, located to the east on the opposite side of the railway tracks at ul. Lipowa 4, is clearly visible. It was one of many original locations used during the filming of *Schindler's List*. However, as the Płaszów concentration camp had been totally destroyed by the retreating Nazis, a mock-up was created in the recently disused quarry south of the Krzemonki. Most of this was removed after the film was completed, but the barbed wire fences and three barracks have been left as mementoes. The site of the Płaszów camp, which is marked by a Communist-era memorial, lies further south, a short distance west of the busy suburban station of the same name.

The Outskirts

There are several enticing desinations in the outskirts of Cracow, both within and outside the officical city boundaries. Each of the places described below makes for an easy half-day excursion from the city centre.

The westernmost suburb of **Bielany** lies about 6 miles (10km) away from the Old Town, or 3 miles (5km) from Zwierzyniec. At its eastern end is an extensive wood, the Las Wolski, at whose southern end is the so-called Silver Mountain (Srebrna Góra), on which stands a still-inhabited Camaldolese monastery. Founded in 1602 by Mikołaj Wolski, the Grand Marshal of the Crown, it was the first of several monasteries established in Poland by the order, which follows the Benedictine rule yet practises a very austere and largely eremetical existence, with few communal activities beyond the religious offices. Wolski obtained the design for the whole complex in Rome, which was executed by a German architect, Valentin von Säbisch. The façade collapsed and was replaced by a severe yet majestic twin-towered composition by an Italian, Andrea Spezza.

Entry is via a walled passageway which leads to a gatehouse above which the church towers can be seen, though it is only from the inner courtyard that the monumentality of the façade is evident. This forms the lynchpin of the complex's rigorously geometric layout, in which the monastic buildings lie on either side of the church, while the hermitages, which visitors can only see from a distance, are grouped in neat rows to its rear. The church contains a number of paintings by Tommaso Dolabella, but the main point of interest is the crypt, where the bodies of the monks are stored in niches until 80 years after their death. They are then exhumed and buried, though the skull is taken by one of the monks to his hermitage to serve as an aid to contemplation. It should be noted that while men can visit the monastery on any day of the year, women are admitted only for the Sunday morning masses, or on the the major religious feast days.

Still within the Las Wolski, about ¹/₂ mile (1km) north of the monastery, are the Zoological Gardens. A similar distance further north is the Piłsudski Mound, the highest of the four artificial hills in Cracow, built in emulation of its counterpart to Kościuszko. Beyond the eastern edge of the wood is **Wola Justowska**, a plush villa suburb which is named after the historian Justus Decius, private secretary to King Zygmunt the Old. His grandiose Renaissance palace, complete with a three-storey loggia, stands in its own small park. Sad to say, it currently lacks a function and is gradually falling into decay.

Tyniec, nowadays Cracow's south-westernmost suburb, lies on the Vistula, 7 miles (12km) from the city centre. Its name is inseparable from the Benedictine abbey, the order's first foundation in Poland, which was established in 1044. Some traces of the original Romanesque architecture survive, though the monastery has been subject to repeated modifications and rebuildings. Picturesquely set on a white limestone cliff directly above the river, it is enclosed within fortified walls dating back to the Gothic period. Entry to the complex is via a defensive gateway, beyond which is a courtyard with a stone well protected by an octagonal wooden pavilion. The church has a predominantly Baroque aspect, and is lavishly adorned with woodwork, including yet another boat-shaped pulpit. There is also a fine organ on which recitals are regularly held in summer, during which time the Gothic cloisters are opened to the public. During this season, the most attractive way of getting to Tyniec is by one of the excursion boats which run from the jetty below the Wawel.

Cracow's largest suburb is **Nowa Huta**, a planned satellite town with a population of nearly a quarter of a million people which stretches over much of the northern and eastern parts of the municipality. Its existence is due purely and simply to Communist infatuation with heavy industry and the concept of social engineering. Contemptuous of Cracow's royal, aristocratic and academic traditions, the post-war authorities aimed to attack them by building a huge new town right up against the city centred on a steelworks responsible for the majority of the country's production. By manning this with erstwhile peasants, it was believed that a class-conscious urban proletariat would emerge, and it was hoped that the traditionally strong religious beliefs of these people would be broken by the simple expedient of excluding churches from the town plan.

Beyond the purely physical aspect, this blueprint went badly awry. The workers imported from the countryside failed to develop as model Communist citizens, and the Roman Catholic church gained rather than declined in strength as a result of the inconveniences worshippers were forced to endure. Communism's demise has burdened the democratic authorities with the almost insoluble problem about what to do with this monumental disaster: the social and economic cost of closing it down would be much too great, yet the horrendous pollution for which it is responsible causes endless health problems throughout the conurbation and inflicts constant and continuing damage on the priceless architectural heritage of Cracow and the beautiful Jurassic landscape beyond.

Although built to a single plan, Nowa Huta's buildings are actually in a variety of styles, ranging from the debased neo-Classicism of the early Stalinist years of the plan, when arcaded frontages were favoured, to uncompromising examples of post-modernism. Ironically, the most prominent buildings are two huge space-age churches. By the 1970s, the Communists were finally forced to relent on the ban on building new places of worship, and the church of Our Lady Queen of Poland was raised in Bienczyce, a district to the north of Nowa Huta's centre. It is commonly known as the Ark because of its distinctive shape, and has a cavernous, multi-tiered interior whose focal point is an 26ft (8m)-high bronze of Christ Crucified by Bronisław Chromy. In the far northern district of Mistrzejowice is a newer church, consecrated by Pope John Paul II in 1983 and dedicated to a saint he had canonised a year before — Maximilian Kolbe, the Catholic priest who was incarcerated at Auschwitz for sheltering Jews, and who voluntarily accepted martyrdom in order to save a Jewish man from the gas chambers.

At the eastern edge of Nowa Huta is the erstwhile village of Mogiła, which escaped being engulfed by the modern development. Its two churches, which face each other across ul. Klasztorna, served the entire Nowa Huta population prior to the consecration of the Ark in 1978. St Barbara's, set in its own close, is an unexpected surprise, a rustic fifteenth-century wooden church of the type commonly encountered in Carpathian villages. It was remodelled in the eighteenth century, when the gateway-cum-belfry was added. The Cistercian monastery opposite was founded in the early thirteenth century but has been subject to many modifications and consequently exhibits sections in a variety of styles. In the presbytery and transepts of the church, and in the Gothic cloisters, are fine Renaissance murals painted by a resident monk, Stanisław Samostrzelnik. A short distance further east is the so-called Wanda's Mound, which dates back to an indeterminate period in the Dark Ages. It is named after the daughter of Krak, who offered herself up to the Vistula in preference to marrying a German lord, whereupon the locals are said to have raised this hillock in commemoration of her sacrifice.

An industrial site of a very different order can be visited in **Wieliczka**,

9 miles (15km) south-east of the centre of Cracow, just beyond the official city boundary. The Salt Mine, which has been a celebrated tourist attraction for over 200 years and is included on UNESCO's World Heritage List, is thought to be the oldest continuously functioning enterprise in the world, with an uninterrupted record which probably dates back to the eleventh century. Like all minerals, salt was the property of the crown, and in medieval times the production of this and other smaller mines accounted for up to a third of the revenue of the royal treasury. There are nine separate levels of mine workings, reaching to a depth of 1,072ft (327m) and linked by some 186 miles (300km) of passageways. The tourist circuit amounts to only 2 per cent of this and is confined to the top three levels, but even so the mandatory guided visit is quite strenuous, covering nearly 2 miles (4km) and lasting about $2^1/_2$ hours.

This begins with a descent down 394 wooden steps of a shaft sunk in the 1630s. A total of 20 chambers, all hewn by hand out of the solid salt, are visited in the first part of the trip, followed by a further 16 in the section of the mine designated as the museum; en route are several underground lakes. The first room, the Copernicus Chamber, has a statue of the celebrated astronomer, who is alleged to have been a visitor to the mine. Like all the other carvings to be seen, it is made from salt, the mine having spawned its own highly distinctive artistic tradition. Next is St Anthony's chapel, the oldest of the three places of worship on the circuit, dating back to the end of the seventeenth century.

The most magnificent chamber of all is the Blessed Kinga's chapel in the third level, which was begun in the 1870s, and continually embellished throughout the following half-century. Dedicated to the patron saint of Polish miners, the Hungarian-born wife of King Bolesław the Bashful, its dimensions are those of a substantial church, being 179ft (54.5m) long, 59ft (18m) wide and 39ft (12m) high. Its furnishings, including the high altar, pulpit, railings, chandeliers and bas-reliefs, are all made from salt. The last-named, notably a beautiful depiction of *The Flight of the Holy Family into Egypt* and a copy of Leonardo da Vinci's *Last Supper* rank as the finest achievements of the local salt sculptors.

On the same level are the Mikałowice Chamber, which has a spectacular wooden vault erected in the 1870s to prevent subsidence; the Vistula Chamber, which has what is claimed as the world's only subterranean post office; and the Warsaw Chamber, which serves as a sports hall and as a summertime sanatorium for sufferers of respiratory disorders. There then follow the chambers housing the museum, with displays on geological, historical and technical aspects of the mine. The most fascinating objects are the huge wooden treadmills and windlasses. A particularly fine example of the former is that in the Kraj Chamber; it dates back to the eighteenth century and was worked by four pairs of horses.

Most tourists return to Cracow as soon as they have seen the mine, but Wielicza has plenty of other historic buildings. On ul. Zamkowa, a short distance to the west, is the modest Gothic castle, which contains a museum of local archaeology and history, including a collection of around 200 old saltcellars. Of the town's churches, the most interesting is St Sebastian's to the north-west of the centre. It was built at the end of the sixteenth century, and has painted interior decoration by Włodzimierz Tetmajer, one of the leading artists of the Young Poland movement.

The Jura

The finest part of the Jurassic upland between Cracow and Częstochowa has been designated as the **Ojców National Park** (Ojcowski Park Narodowy). This consists of the 7 mile (12km)-long central valley of the River Prądnik, which joins the Vistula at Cracow, together with the final 3 mile (5km) stretch of one of its tributaries, the Sąspowka. With an area of just 6sq miles (16sq km), it is the smallest national park in Poland, and one of the smallest anywhere in the world. Nonetheless, it contains an amazing variety of attractions, including the 656ft (200m)-high cliffs framing the main gorge, spectacular isolated rocks fashioned by the weather into great natural sculptures, wild waterless ravines, some 210 caves, two very idiosyncratic churches, and the two most southerly of the chain of castles built in the Middle Ages to defend Poland's borders against Bohemian-ruled Silesia to the west.

The park is frequented by hundreds of types of butterflies, including many rare swallowtail types, while up to 15 of the 17 different species of bats known in Poland inhabit the caves. Among over a hundred different birds, the most numerous are dippers, wagtails and rock thrushes. Many rare plants, including some characteristic of both Alpine and Mediterranean regions, grow in the park, though the number has declined because of the effects of pollution from Nowa Huta and Upper Silesia. This has also affected the stock of fir trees, though these are being replaced by the managed plantation of more durable species endemic to the slopes, such as beeches, oaks, hornbeams and sycamores. Willows and poplars grow on the valley floor, while a unique feature of the area is the Ojców birch, which is smaller and shrubbier than the normal European silver birch. The park is probably the best place to observe the famous Polish 'golden autumn', being cloaked throughout September and October in truly spectacular reds and golds.

The main highlights can be seen in a day — or even less if travelling by car, as this is one of the few national parks in Poland where it is not necessary to walk very far to enjoy the best of the scenery. However, the park is so enchanting that few will want to economise on time there, particularly as it is so easy to escape into corners which are well off the beaten tourist track. A road, served by regular buses from Cracow, runs all the way through the park, hugging the banks of the Prądnik for most of the way. The red trail also passes along this road, with occasional detours on to neighbouring foot-paths; this is also the first section of the Eagles' Nests Trail. In the park itself there are four other colour-coded routes for walkers, which together penetrate its outer reaches, other than those to which access is forbidden for reasons of nature conservation.

The village of **Ojców**, 12 miles (20km) north of Cracow, is the main settlement within the park boundaries, spreading along the valley immediately below its second highest point, the Golden Mountain (Złota Góra). It was a spa resort in the nineteenth century, and although it has long lost that function, it still preserves a number of wooden buildings as a reminder of that era, and also continues to act as a small tourist base, with rooms available for rent in a number of private houses, and a campsite and lodge located off the main north-west road running out of the village.

Also accessible from this road is the clifftop castle, which was once the property of King Kazimierz the Great. It was inhabited until the 1820s, but thereafter was allowed to fall into disrepair, leaving only fragments of the walls, a restored octagonal tower commanding a fine view over the valley, and the entrance gateway guarded by mighty limestone boulders. In the centre of the village are two large buildings formerly used for spa purposes. One of these now contains the Ojców National Park Museum, which has separate sections on geography, archaeology, flora and fauna. The wooden house just to the south is home to the Regional Museum, with displays on local history and ethnology. Further on is a reserve of Ojców birches.

Beyond the southern end of the village, fronting the so-called Virgin Rocks, is a single isolated stump nicknamed Deotyma's Needle. Continuing onwards, the green trail leads eastwards away from the main road, leading in about 20 minutes to the fenced-off Dark Cave (Jaskinia Ciemna), which has proved a fruitful hunting ground for archaeologists, yielding evidence of human settlement that is at least 120,000 years old. Behind the cave is the Ogrojec, a natural courtyard enclosed on three sides by rocks, and a remarkable isolated rock known, because of its shape, as the Glove (Rękawica). The trail continues on to the Okopy hill, one of the finest panoramic viewpoints in the park.

On the opposite side of the valley, the black trail goes from the southern end of Ojców up the slopes of the Góra Chełmowa (1,568ft/478m), the highest point in the park, to Łotietek's Cave, which is reached after about an hour's walk. This is the largest of the park's caves, and the only one which is a regular tourist sight, with guides and electric lighting. In pre-glacial times, it lay at the foot of the valley floor, which is now 426ft (130m) below. It is named after the future King Władysław the Short (Łotietek), who hid there for several months from his arch-enemy, King Vaclav II of Bohemia. According to tradition, he slept in the last and largest chamber, now known as the Bedroom, and prepared his meals in the adjoining small room, now known as the kitchen. From there, it is worth doubling back to Ojców via the blue trail, which passes via the Cracow Gate (Brama Krakowska), a typical example of the natural rock gates so typical of the region.

The yellow trail leads from the northern end of Ojców westwards into the Sąspowka valley, the bottom of which is covered by lush meadows rich in wild flowers. Beavers were re-introduced to the stream in 1985, and quickly created a system of dams. The scenery is otherwise similar to that along the Prądnik, with numerous rock formations and caves. Particularly beautiful is the Koziarnia ravine, whose rocks are covered with shrubs and other vegetation. It takes no more than an hour to see the finest part of the valley, though the yellow trail continues onwards out of the park, re-entering it again near Pieskowa Skała.

By far the most popular walk from Ojców is the main red trail north, which initially follows the main road. Just beyond the northern fringe of the village is the Chapel on the Water, a charming example of folk architecture and decoration. Perched on stilts directly over the Prądnik, this was originally the spa bath house, but was modified into a place of worship in 1901, when the graceful little tower and steeple were added. Its location cunningly circumvented the Czarist edict which forbade the Roman Catholic church to construct new churches on solid ground. On the opposite side of the road a little further on is St John's spring, now enclosed by a gloriette. A little bridge leads from there over the river to a man-made cave cut into the rocks in which stands a statue of the Virgin Mary Immaculate.

The trail continues to the hamlet of **Grodzisko**, 1 mile (2km) on, passing several old mills en route. It leaves the main road at a bus stop, near which grow rare Italian asters, then ascends through a reservation of dwarf steppe cherries to the Hermitage of the Blessed Salomea. This curious little complex occupies the site of a medieval Poor Clares convent, one of whose superiors was Salomea, the sister of King Bolesław the Chaste. It was erected soon after her beatification in 1673, to plans by a Cracow priest and amateur architect, Jan Sebastian Piskowski, who offered a rustic interpretation of the grand Roman Baroque style of Gianlorenzo Bernini. In the main courtyard, a statue of St Clare atop a plinth is surrounded by five figures connected with the early history of the convent. Behind the chapel are three hermitages or prayer chambers and an obelisk resting on the back of an elephant, a composition directly influenced by Bernini's famous fountain in the Piazza Minerva in Rome. Lower down to the rear is Salomea's hermitage, equipped with a tiny altar and a stone bed.

At the far north-western end of the park, 2 miles (4km) from Grodzisko via the main road, is **Pieskowa Skała**. Immediately before the entrance to the village is one of Poland's most famous natural features, the 82ft (25m)-high rock known as Hercules' Club (Maczuga Herkulesa). Perched on the cliff above, protected on three sides by sheer drops and looking as though it belongs in a fairytale, is the castle, the only one along the Eagles' Nest Trail to survive as more than a shell. A Renaissance clock tower with loggia presides over the outer bailey, which is entered via a gateway adorned with the coats-of-arms of one of the former aristocratic owners. The round tower is a survivor from the original Gothic fortress, while the two Mannerist bastions — one of which is now a restaurant with a rooftop terrace — were added in the seventeenth century to make the defences more up-to-date. A Renaissance palace, which is five storeys high on the south side, and three on the others, is built round all four sides of the triple-tiered inner courtyard,

Świętez Krzyż, the monastery after which the Holy Cross Mountains are named (Chapter 8)

The open-air art gallery outside the Florian Gate, Cracow (Chapter 9)

The south front of the Wawel Cathedral in Cracow, with the Zygmunt and Waza chapels
(Chapter 9)

which is adorned with twenty-one vigorously carved mascarons and has a 148ft (45m)-deep well cut through the solid rock to the river below. The apartments are furnished in a variety of period styles ranging across the entire history of European interior design from Gothic to Biedermeier.

Adjoining the Ojców National Park to the west is the **Cracow Valleys Landscape Park** (Dolinki Krakowski Park Krajobrazowy) a much larger but far less strictly controlled area of protected landscape that is popular weekend walking country with Cracovians, though otherwise surprisingly little known. Its main tourist sight is the Wierzchowska Górna cave at the nothern end of the village of **Wierzchowie**, 3 miles (5km) south-west of Ojców by the yellow trail. With a length of 3,116ft (950m), it is by far the biggest cave in the whole Cracow-Częstochowa Upland, and is the only one, other than Łotietek, open for guided tourist visits. Two of the myriad number of small Jurassic valleys in the park lie just outside Wierzchowie: the black trail goes south-east through the Kluczwoda valley, while the yellow trail continues south-west through the Bolechowicka valley. The latter then travels west for a short distance before turning northwards into the Kobylana valley.

Even closer to Cracow yet even more off the beaten track is the **Tenczyń Landscape Park** (Tenczyński Park Krajobrazowy), which begins just beyond the western boundaries of the city and is likewise dotted with a host of tiny valleys. The most impressive rock formations are to be found in the Sanka valley, between the village of Mników, which lies within the suburban bus network, and Las Zwierzyniec, an extensive forest to the north.

For the remaining section of the Eagles' Nests Trail, the main jumping-off point is **Olkusz**, an old lead and silver mining town 11 miles (17km) north-west of Pieskowa Skała. The main building is the Gothic parish church of St Andrew, which was founded by King Kazimierz the Great, though altered on several subsequent occasions. It contains frescos of various dates, a Baroque organ, and a late fifteenth-century polyptych of scenes from the Life of the Virgin Mary and the Passion by the Cracow painters Jan Wielki and Stanisław Stary.

The village of Klucze, 4 miles (7km) north of Olkusz, is the entry-point for one of Poland's most extraordinary landscapes, the **Pustynia Błędowska**, the only desert in the whole of Europe. It stretches over an area of 12sq miles (32sq km), but was once considerably larger, and is receding all the time. Nonetheless, it has sandbanks and dunes which reach as high as 33ft (10m), while the vegetation around the River Biała Przemsza resembles that of an oasis. On very hot summer days, it is possible to see mirages.

The castle of **Ogrodzieniec**, 7 miles (12km) north of Klucze, stands 1 mile (2km) outside the town on the highest hill in the Cracow-Częstochowa Upland, the Góra Janowskiego. Kazimierz the Great's original fortress, perched atop the natural rock, was transformed in the sixteenth century into a splendid Renaissance palace by the Boners, a wealthy family of Cracow bankers. This was destroyed by the Swedes in 1655, but part of it continued to serve as a residence until 1610. Although now a roofless shell, it ranks among Poland's most evocative ruins, and has the benefit of commanding a sweeping view over the upland.

About 15$^1/_2$ miles (25km) north by various backroads are the twin fortresses of **Mirów** and **Bobolice**. More impressive than either of these, and a worthy rival to Ogrodzieniec, is the castle at **Olsztyn**, the penultimate stop on the Eagles' Nests Trail, just 7 miles (11km) south-west of Częstochowa, on whose urban bus network it lies. It is laid out on two parts, with a round watchtower crowning one outcrop of rock, and a keep on top of another, each of which offers a magnificent view.

Częstochowa

No place in Poland is more deeply imbued on the national consciousness than Częstochowa, which encapsulates so much that is paradoxical about the country. On the one hand, it is among Poland's largest industrial centres, with a skyline peppered with the smoking chimneys of textile factories and steelworks. On the other hand, the sole rival to their dominance, the Paulite monastery of Jasna Góra (literally, 'Bright Mountain'), ranks among the world's premier places of pilgrimage, one which, it is estimated, annually attracts larger numbers of the faithful than anywhere in Christendom other than Rome and Lourdes. The pilgrims come to venerate the miraculous icon of the Black Madonna, which since 1717 has held the official title of Queen of Poland, and is the most inescapable image in the country: at least one reproduction of it can be seen in virtually every Roman Catholic church in the land.

The special position that Jasna Góra and its icon hold in the hearts and minds of the vast majority of Poles is due to a rich tapestry of history and myth. Central to this is the tenuous position Poland has held on the map of Europe: at various times the Swedes, the Russians and the Germans have sought to annihilate it as a nation. Each of these traditional and non-Catholic enemies has laid siege to Jasna Góra, yet failed to destroy it, so adding to the icon's reputation as a miracle-worker — and the guarantor of Poland's very existence.

The icon, whose name derives from the heavy shading characteristic of the hieratical Byzantine style in which it is executed, came to Jasna Góra in 1384, 2 years after the monastery had been settled by monks of the eremitical Paulite order from Hungary. According to legend, it was painted from life by St Luke on a beam from the Holy Family's house in Nazareth, and this has been accepted without question by the faithful ever since. Scientific tests, however, have proved that it cannot be older than the sixth century, and it may even have been quite new at the time of its arrival at the monastery. Its first great miracle occurred in 1430, when it was stolen, allegedly by followers of the Czech reformer Jan Hus. The thieves had not gone very far before they found themselves unable to carry it because of its sudden increase in weight. They slashed the Virgin's face, which immediately began to shed blood, leaving a gash was retained after the icon was restored, and which can still be seen today.

In 1655, Jasna Góra withstood a six-week long siege by the Swedes, although it had only 250 defenders ranged against 4,000 attackers armed with superior weaponry. This ignited what turned out to be a hugely successful national fightback against the enemmy, who had occupied the rest of the country, with the exception of Zamość, against little resistance. Although it might seem reasonable to attribute the failure of the Swedish siege to the sophisticated modern defensive system built around the monastery earlier in the century, credit was bestowed on the Black Madonna. It has also been held responsible for subsequent triumphs, notably the failure of the Partitioning powers to capture Jasna Góra by force in the 1770s, and for the failure of the Nazis' attempt to blow up the monastery. However much these miracles can be disputed, there is little doubt that the cult of the icon, as orchestrated by by the Catholic hierarchy in the post-war years, played a key role in forging the popular front which eventually overthrew Soviet-imposed Communist rule.

The ideal time to visit Częstochowa is on one of the major Marian festivals, which fall on 3 May (Queen of Poland Day), 15 August (Feast of the Assumption), 26 August (Feast of Our Lady of Częstochowa), 8 September (Birth of the Virgin Mary) and 8 December (Feast of the Immaculate Conception). At these times, up to a million pilgrims converge on Jasna Góra, often in colourful traditional dress, many having made the journey on foot from their home town. Every year, for example, tens of thousands undertake the nine-day walk from Warsaw to celebrate the Feast of the Assumption.

Although they have been denuded of their military aspect, the walls and bastions enclosing the monastery mean that it still preserves a fortress-like feel. Entry to the complex, indeed, is still through four successive gateways, each one of which presented a formidable obstacle to an attacker. On the big feast days, the main masses have to be held in the open air, with the congregation standing on the brow of the hill, while the celebrants sit around a altar placed on the terrace above the eastern wall. The western and nothern stretches of wall are now laid out as a Way of the Cross, with large bronze sculptural groups depicting each of the stations set up on plinths outside.

The monastic church was originally a Gothic hall, but was completely transformed into a Baroque style following its destruction in one of the many fires which have ravaged Jasna Góra down the centuries. Sober from the outside, its interior decoration is mostly very restrained, though it has a few exuberant features, notably the colossal high altar in honour of the Virgin, and the two sumptuous family chapels off the southern aisle, both modelled on their their royal counterparts in the Wawel cathedral in Cracow.

Alongside is the Chapel of the Blessed Virgin, which to all intents and purposes is a separate church in its own right. Being the place where the Black Madonna is housed, it forms the centrepiece of the whole monastery. It is also the only part to retain much of the original Gothic architecture, though its walls are so encrusted with votive offerings that this is no longer obvious. Masses are said almost constantly from early morning until late evening and the constant flow of pilgrims means that it can often be difficult to catch more than a glimpse of the icon. Much of the time, it is invisible behind a silver screen, each raising and lowering of which is accompanied by a solemn fanfare intoned by a brass band hidden out of sight in the galleries. Even when on view (normally between 6am and 12noon, 3.30pm and 4.40pm, 7pm and 7.45 pm, and 9am to 9.10pm), only a small part of the actual picture can be seen, as the figures are almost invariably decked out in crowns and robes made of diamonds and rubies.

To the north of the chapel, a monumental stairway leads to the Knights' Hall, the monastery's principal reception room, hung with flags and paintings illustrating the history of the monastery. There are other opulent Baroque interiors, notably the refectory and the library, but although these are often featured in tourist brochures, they are not usually accessible to the public.

Jasna Góra's treasures are kept in three separate buildings. The most valuable liturgical items can be seen in the Treasury, which is housed in a chamber above the sacristy, and entered from the south-eastern corner of the ramparts. Among the objects on view are a sixteenth-century reliquary cross and silver monstrance donated by King Zygmunt the Old, a gold monastrance made to commemorate Poland's liberation from Swedish occupation, and various pieces of Meissen porcelain given by King August III.

At the south-western end of the monastery is the Arsenal, which is devoted to the military history of the fortress. It contains a magnificent collection of weapons, including Turkish war booty donated by King Jan Sobieski. Alongside is the 600th Anniversary Museum, documenting the monastery's story from a religious standpoint. Exhibits include the seventeenth-century backing of the Black Madonna, which illustrates the history of the miraculous image. There are also votive offerings from famous Poles, prominent among which is Lech Wałęsa's 1983 Nobel Peace Prize.

Another ancillary attraction is the stately 328ft (100m)-high tower, the tallest church belfry in Poland, which can be ascended for a view over the monastery and the city. Erected at the beginning of the century, it is a skilful pastiche of its fire-ravaged predecessor of exactly 200 years earlier. The newest part of the monastery is the south-eastern cloister, where open-air confessions are often heard: it was built in the 1920s in a bizarre blend of Rococo and Art Nouveau motifs.

Other than Jasna Góra, Częstochowa has very few sights. South of the monastery is the small Baroque church of St Barbara, which is, according to tradition, the place where the Black Madonna was slashed and shed blood. At the opposite end of the city, close to the railway station, is the massive neo-Gothic cathedral, which is remarkable mainly for its size. On plac Biegańskiego, midway along al. NMP, the arrow-straight 2 miles (3km)-long central boulevard, is the District Museum, which has a good archaeology section plus the usual local history material. There is also an Archaeology Reserve in the southern outskirts of the city, near the suburban station of Raków, displaying twenty-one excavated graves from the Lusatian culture of the sixth or seventh centuries BC.

Further Information
— Little Poland: The Cracow-Częstochowa Upland —

Places to Visit

Cracow

Archdiocesan Museum
ul. Kanonicza 19
Open: Tuesday to Saturday 10am to 3pm.

Archaeological Museum
ul. Poselska 3
Open: Tuesday to Sunday 10am to 2pm.

Cathedral Royal Crypts and Zygmunt Tower
Wawel Hill (Wyzgórze Wawelskie)
Open: Tuesday to Saturday 9am to 5pm, Sunday 12noon to 5pm.

Cloth Hall Gallery
Rynek Główny
Open: Tuesday, Wednesday and Friday to Sunday 10am to 3.30pm, Thursday 10am to 6pm.

Collegium Maius (Jagiellonian University Museum)
ul. Jagiellońska 15
Open: Monday to Friday 11am to 3pm, Saturday 11am to 2pm.

Czartoryski Museum
ul. św. Jana 19
Open: Wednesday, Thursday, Saturday and Sunday 10am to 3.30pm, Friday 10am to 6pm.

Dragon's Cave
Wawel Hill (Wyzgórze Wawelskie)
Open: June to September Tuesday to Sunday 10am to 3pm.

Ethnographical Museum
plac Wolnica 1
Open: Monday 10am to 6pm, Wednesday to Friday 10am to 3pm, Saturday and Sunday 10am to 2pm.

Historical Museum of Cracow
Rynek Główny 35
Open Wednesday, Friday, Saturday and Sunday 9am to 3.30pm, Thursday 11am to 6pm.

Kościuszko Mound and Museum
al. Waszyngtona
Open: Tuesday to Sunday 10am to 4pm.

Matejko House
ul. Floriańska 41
Open: Tuesday to Thursday, Saturday and Sunday 10am to 3.30pm, Friday 10am to 6pm.

New Building
al. 3 Maja 1
Open: Tuesday and Thursday to Sunday 10am to 3.30pm, Wednesday 10am to 6pm.

Old Synagogue (Jewish Museum)
ul. Szeroka 24
Open: Wednesday, Thursday, Saturday and Sunday 9am to 3pm, Friday 11am to 6pm.

Pharmacy 'Under the Eagle'
plac Zgody 18
Open: Monday to Friday 10am to 4pm, Saturday 10am to 2pm.

Royal Castle
Wawel Hill (Wzgórze Wawelskie)
Open: Tuesday to Sunday 10am to 4pm.

Szołyskich House
plac Szczepański 9
Open: Tuesday 10am to 6pm, Wednesday to Sunday 10am to 3.30pm.

Town Hall Tower
Rynek Główny
Open: Wednesday, Friday, Saturday and Sunday 9am to 3pm, Thursday 11am to 6pm.

Wyspiański Museum
ul. Kanonicza 9
Open: Tuesday, Wednesday and
Friday to Sunday 10am to 3.30pm,
Thursday 10am to 6pm.

Częstochowa
Archaeological Reserve
al. Pokoju 12
Open: Tuesday to Saturday 9am to 3pm.

Arsenal
Jasna Góra
Open: daily 9am to noon and 2pm to
5pm.

District Museum
plac Biegańskiego 45
Open: Tuesday and Thursday to
Saturday 9am to 3pm, Wednesday
12noon to 6pm, Sunday 10am to 3pm.

Jasna Góra Monastery Tower
Jasna Góra
Open: Monday to Saturday 8am to
4pm, Sunday 8am to 10.30am and
1pm to 5pm.

Jasna Góra Monastery Treasury
Jasna Góra
Open: April to September Monday to
Saturday 9am to 11.30am and 3.30 to
5.30pm, Sunday 8am to 1pm and 3pm
to 5.30pm, October to March Monday
to Saturday 9am to 10.30am and 3.30
to 4.30pm, Sunday 9am to 12.30pm
and 3.30 to 5pm.

600th Anniversary Museum
Jasna Góra
Open: daily 11am to 4.30pm.

Ojców
Castle
Open: 15 April to 31 October Tuesday
to Sunday 10am to 5pm.

Łokietek Cave
Open: May to October daily 9am to
4pm.

Ojców National Park Museum
Open: May to October Tuesday to
Sunday 9am to 4pm, November to
April Tuesday to Sunday 9am to 3pm.

Regional Museum
Open: Tuesday to Sunday 9am to 4pm.

Pieskowa Skała
Castle
Open May to September Tuesday to
Sunday 12noon to 5.30pm, October to
April Tuesday to Sunday 10am to
3.30pm.

Wieliczka
Castle
ul. Zamkowa
Open: Monday and Wednesday to
Saturday 8.30am to 2pm.

Salt Mine
Park Kingi
Open: 16 April to 15 October Tuesday
to Sunday 8am to 5pm, 16 October to 15
April Tuesday to Sunday 8am to 3pm.

Wierzchowie
Wierzchowska Górna Cave
Open: May to October daily 9am to
4pm.

Tourist Offices
Cracow
ul. Pawia 6-8
☎ 22-04-71 or 22-60-91

Częstochowa
al. NMP 65
☎ 413-60 or 434-12

10 • Little Poland: The Western Carpathians

Thee southern part of the old Krakowska province of **Little Poland** consists of the foothills and mountains of the **Western Carpathians** (Karpaty Zachodnie). Ever since tourism first became a popular activity around the middle of the nineteenth century, this has ranked among the most popular holiday destinations anywhere in Central Europe — and rightly so, as it contains a wealth of scenery which is considerably more varied than might be expected of such a compact geographical area.

Each of the separate mountain ranges has a distinctive character of its own. The crystalline High Tatras are the loftiest and most imposing part of the entire Carpathian chain and, together with the quite different but almost equally beautiful West Tatras, are still a virtually uninhabited wilderness area. A short distance to the east is the limestone range of the Pieniny, which is equally popular with visitors, largely because of the spectacular raft trip that can be taken through the Dunajec gorge.

The whole of the Tatras and the main part of the Pieniny have been accorded national park status. This honour has also been conferred on the central part of the Gorce and the Babia Góra massif in the Beskid Wysoki, and is due to be given to the Magura range in the western Beskid Niski. None of these is at all well-known outside Poland, and are thus ideal destinations for those who want to get really off the beaten tourist track. The other important range is the Beskid Sądecki, whose recuperative spa resorts offer an antidote to the more strenuous pursuits associated with its counterparts.

By far the most developed resort in the Western Carpathians, one which even during the Communist years was a regular fixture in English-language tourist brochures, is Zakopane. One of only a handful of places in the region large enough to be called a town, it lies directly below the Tatras, but also has the benefit of easy access to the other ranges, all of which are feasible targets of day trips. There are surprisingly few hotels in any of the other resorts, though plenty of accommodation is available in holiday homes which were formerly owned by trade unions, and in private houses, which display signs with the legend *pokoju* or *noclegi* if they have rooms to rent.

While it is possible to gain at least some acquaintance with the beauty spots of the region through travelling by car or by public transport, this is the one part of Poland where it is essential to walk to see the best of the scenery. Colour-coded trails comb all the ranges, and in the national park areas it is

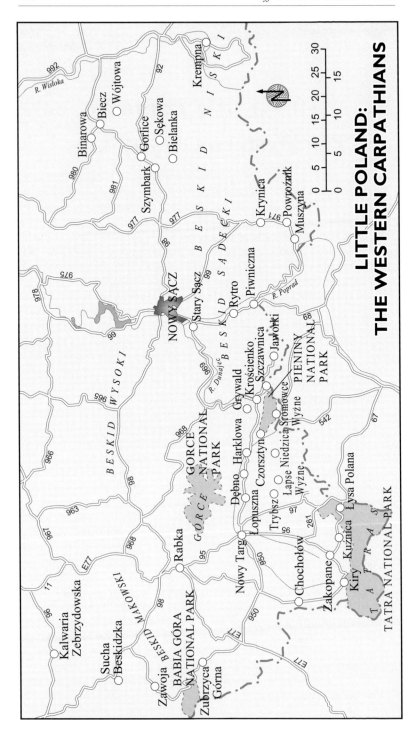

**LITTLE POLAND:
THE WESTERN CARPATHIANS**

mandatory to stick to these waymarked paths. Decent footwear is a pre-requisite when walking in the Carpathians, even although most paths present no technical difficulties. There are, it is true, some challenging routes, particularly in the Tatras, but even this range has plenty of easy low-level walks which are often equally rewarding. For those who wish to tackle some of the more ambitious routes, and do not want to have to return to a resort every night, there is a network of mountain refuges in each range, usually located in picturesque wooden chalets. Accommodation is basic and cheap, and is mostly in dormitories. Guests are never turned away, no matter how busy they might be.

Highly detailed maps of each range are available locally and elsewhere in Poland at a minimal cost: in addition to detailed local information, they show the course of all the trails very clearly. One important point to remember is that the international frontier with Slovakia cuts right through the Western Carpathians, often along mountain ridges, but that it is forbid-den to cross over to the other side at anywhere other than an official border post.

The Western Beskid Niski and Pogórze

As has already been mentioned in Chapter 7, the **Beskid Niski** and its foothills, the **Pogórze**, are divided into two sections, and mark the geo-graphical transition from the Eastern to the Western Carpathians, as well as the historic boundary between Red Ruthenia and Little Poland. Poles settled in the western Pogórze in the early Middle Ages, but the Beskid Niski remained virtualy uninhabited until much later, being settled mainly by the Ruthenian ethnic group known as the Lemks. (For more information on them, see the Bieszczady section in Chapter 7.) They retain a presence in the area, and indeed have staged something of a cultural revival since the fall of Communism. The most visible signs of their presence are their distinctive wooden churches, which can be found in the majority of villages throughout the Beskid Niski. Most were built for the Uniate rite, though many have since been taken over for Roman Catholic worship or for secular use. Wooden churches, this time built by ethnic Poles of Catholic faith, are a feature of the Pogórze, and indeed of the Carpathian foothills in general. These are far more obviously 'western' in appearance, though they have likewise changed very little in style down the centuries.

The oldest town in the Pogórze is **Biecz**. It was a place of some importance in the Middle Ages, thanks to its pivotal setting on the trade routes between Cracow and Hungary, and also had a morbid claim to fame as the seat of a school of public executioners. However, it was by-passed by the industrial development which affected many of the neighbouring towns, and now has a delightfully decayed appearance, its surviving historic buildings appearing incongruously grandiose for what is now little more than a village.

Of these, the finest is the parish church, which is set in a large enclosure with a detached belfry and a Renaissance entrance gate. Building began in the fourteenth century, but was not completed until the 1520s, resulting in a late Gothic hall design with elaborate net vaults. Inside are some outstanding late Renaissance and early Baroque furnishings, including the tomb of the magnate Mikołaj Ligęza, the high altar, the choir stalls, and the pulpit, which is adorned with relief carvings of musicians.

On the Rynek just to the west is the Town Hall, which is crowned by a tall slender Renaissance tower with a Baroque top. North of the church is the most substantial surviving section of the medieval wall. Another part of the fortifications encloses the burgher's mansion on ul. Węgierska to the south, which now contains part of the local museum. Its star attraction is an intact pharmacy with attached laboratory; ethnological exhibits and a collection of old musical instruments are also on display. A branch of the museum, focusing on local history, occupies another Renaissance mansion on nearby ul. Kromera.

Binarowa, 2 miles (4km) north-west of Biecz, has an attractive wooden church which is thought to date from around 1500. Its interior is completely covered with paintings: the ornamental polychromy on the vault dates from around the time of the church's construction, while the scenes on the walls were not added until the mid-seventeenth century. There are also some good furnishings, including a painted pulpit and folksy fifteenth-century carving of the Madonna and Child. **Wójtowa**, a similar distance south of Biecz, also has a wooden church, which is likewise sixteenth-century in date.

Gorlice, nowadays the largest town in the area, lies $8^{1}/_{2}$ miles (14km) south-west of Biecz. Its main claim to fame is as the place where Ignacy Łukasiewicz carried out his pioneering experiments in oil refining in the early 1850s, prior to sinking the world's first oil well in Bóbrka in the eastern Beskid Niski. The town's museum, located just off the Rynek on ul. Wąska, is primarily devoted to Łukasiewicz and the local oil industry. Although not in itself attractive, Gorlice is the main hiking base for the western Beskid Niski, which otherwise has very little in the way of accommodation, other than a few mountain refuges.

Sękowa, which lies just beyond the northern fringe of the Beskid Niski, 3 miles (5km) south of Gorlice, boasts the most southerly of the wooden churches originally built for Catholic use. The main body of the building, whose most prominent feature is its magnificent plunging roof, was constructed in the 1520s; the bell tower and the covered verandahs were not added until the seventeenth century. Known as *soboty* (literally, 'Saturdays'), the latter were built to shelter worshippers from isolated farms who arrived in the village late on Saturday night in order to participate in the early mass the following morning.

Part of the western Beskid Niski is due to be designated as the **Magura National Park** (Magurski Park Narodowy). The most valuable natural features of the intended park are the rock bastions, which are in various stages of decay, and the forests, which include many trees which are several centuries old. Over one hundred different birds nest in the area, including eagles, buzzards and woodpeckers, while indigenous animals include beavers, otters, wolves, lynxes and wildcats. From Gorlice, the blue trail goes southwards, skirting west of Sękowa prior to traversing Magura Małastowksa, the western of the two hill ranges in the park. The green trail goes south-east from Gorlice via the other range, the Magura Wątkowska, meeting up with the main red trail, which traverses the entire Beskid Niski, at the summit of Wątkowa (2,775ft/846m). A little further south is the junction with the blue trail.

At the southern end of the Magura Wątkowska is the village of **Krempna**, which lies 25 miles (40km) south-east of Gorlice on the bank of the still-young Wisłoka, a major tributary of the Vistula. Its wooden church, originally Uniate but now Catholic, dates back to the second half of the eighteenth century. The iconostasis from the same period is preserved inside, along with a fragment of another from the previous Orthodox church on the site.

Wooden churches can also be seen in three adjacent villages. That in **Kotań**, 1¹/₂ miles (3km) to the west of Krempna, stands in total isolation to the north of the village. It was also built in the eighteenth century, but no longer has its iconostasis, which is now in the Icon Museum in Łańcut. The church in **Świątkowa Mała**, a further 3km west, is a century older and has recently regained its partially-preserved iconostasis. Its counterpart in its twin community of **Świątkowa Wielka**, ¹/₂ mile (1km) to the north, is much larger and once again eighteenth-century in date.

Moving westwards from Gorlice, the first interesting village is the straggling community of **Szymbark**, some 5 miles (8km) away. In addition to a now-disused eighteenth-century wooden church, this has a small Ethnographic Park containing a number of reassembled rural buildings, including two windmills, two manor houses and several peasants' cottages. The 3 miles (5km) separating Szymbark and **Bielanka** to the south mark both a geographical and an ethnic transition, the latter being a leading centre of Lemk culture. Not only does it have a wooden church in the typical Lemk style, it is also home to a song and dance troupe which regularly tours abroad.

The Beskid Sądecki

The **Beskid Sądecki**, the next mountain range to the west, is somewhat higher than the Beskid Niski, with several peaks of over 3,280ft (1,000m). Nonetheless, it is best known as a place for recuperative holidays, being rich in mineral springs and having one of the two main concentrations of spa resorts in Poland. The Dunajec, one of the country's best-known rivers, separates it from the Podhale and Pieniny, while one of its tributaries, the Kamienica, forms the border with the Beskid Niski. Another Dunajec tributary, the Poprad, cuts right through the heart of the Beskid Sądecki, dividing it into eastern and western sections, the Pasmo Radziejowiej and the Pasmo Jaworzyny. A loop road, which closely hugs one or other river valley for almost its entire length, goes all the way round the latter, giving easy access to all places of interest in the range. The Beskid Sądecki is the westernmost territory inhabited by the Lemks, and thus also the most westerly outpost in Europe of Eastern Orthodoxy. Many of the villages, particularly in the south of the range, have wooden churches in the characteristic Lemk style, though most surviving examples date back only to last century and are seldom the equal of those to be found in the Beskid Niski and Bieszczady.

By far the largest town in the region is **Nowy Sącz**, which lies above the confluence of the Dunajec and Poprad, 25 miles (40km) west of Gorlice. Despite its name (nowy ≠ new), it has already celebrated its 700th anniversary, though it preserves only a handful of notable historic monuments and is primarily of interest for its museums and as a touring base. The Rynek, which has a bombastic Town Hall in the middle dating from the end of the nineteenth century, is the largest main square in the country after that of Cracow. A couple of blocks to the west is the Franciscan church, which still preserves much of its original Gothic shape. The parish church of St Margaret, just off the eastern side of the square, has not been so fortunate, having been subject to frequent alterations which have left it as a stylistic hotch-potch.

On the latter's southern side is the Gothic House, a former ecclesiastical residence which is now home to the Regional Museum. This contains several hundred works by the Lemk artist Nikifors, who gained an international reputation for the naive paintings he executed between the end of World War II and his death in 1968. Another highlight is an important collection of fifteenth- to eighteenth-century icons brought from the former Orthodox and Uniate churches of the region, many showing an obvious debt to Roman Catholic art. There are also a few examples of the work of the local fifteenth-century painters who formed, in conjunction with their counterparts in Cracow, the first recognizable Polish school of painting. Finally, the museum has an extensive array of folk art of the region, most of it with religious subject matter.

On ul. Joselewicza to the north of the Rynek is the former synagogue, which dates back to the seventeenth century and was later a leading centre of the revivalist Hassidic movement. It has lost its internal decoration and now serves as a commercial art gallery. Another gallery has been set up within the ruins of the castle beyond, which commands a fine view over the Dunajec. Built in the fourteenth century for King Kazimierz the Great, it was blown up by the retreating Nazis at the end of World War II.

The Ethnographic Park, one of the best *skansens* in Poland, lies 1¹/₂ miles (3km) east of the town centre in the district of Falkowa. It is due to expand considerably in the future, but around fifty redundant rural buildings have already been re-erected on the hilly site, and the interiors of a dozen or so of these, all of which are furnished in the appropriate style, can also be visited. They are grouped according to ethnographic regions, and include a special section devoted to Gypsy culture.

Nowy Sącz's older sister town of **Stary Sącz** lies 6 miles (10km) south, high above the Poprad, just before it joins the Dunajec. Its cobbled Rynek is among the quaintest squares in the country: the houses, which are only one or two storeys high, mostly date from the eighteenth century, and one of them contains a delightfully ramshackle local museum. To the south is the parish church, a Gothic building with Baroque decoration. More significant is the fortified convent of the Poor Clares to the east, which was founded in 1280 by the Blessed Kinga, widow of King Bolesław the Chaste. The Baroque frescos in the nave depict scenes from the life of the foundress, whose statue can be seen in the chapel devoted to her memory. Opposite the latter is the seventeenth-century pulpit, which incorporates a florid carving of the Tree of Jesse.

Rytro, 6 miles (10km) up the Poprad from Stary Sącz, is a small resort crowned by the ruins of a medieval castle. Its central location within the Beskid Sądecki makes it the best base for those wanting to make long hikes within the range. The western section of the red trail traverses the entire Pasmo Radziejowe, terminating at Krościenko at the foot of the Pieniny. It goes via several peaks, including Radziejowa (4,139ft/1,262m), the highest peak in the entire range. The green trail also goes all the way across the Pasmo Radziejowej, ending up at Szczawnica. There is a junction with the red trail at Przehyba (3,854ft/1,175m), enabling walkers to make a day-long circular trip from Rytro, with the alternative of stopping for the night at the refuge below the summit. The eastern part of the red trail crosses the Pasmo Jaworzyny via many of its main peaks, with two refuges en route; the first stage of this can likewise be used as the start of a circular walk. These trails, like all those in the Beskid Sądecki, are officially classified as easy, and present no special technical difficulties.

At **Piwniczna**, an alternative and slightly larger resort 3 miles (5km) beyond Rytro, the road down the left bank of the Poprad leads on to an official border crossing into Slovakia, 1¹/₂ miles (3km) further south. To continue round the Beskid Sądecki loop, it is necessary to cross over to the right bank of the river, which for the next 15 miles (25km) or so serves as the international frontier. **Żegiestów**, 9 miles (15km) upstream from Piwniczna, is divided into two distinct parts, with a spa quarter by the Poprad and an old village, complete with a wooden church, up the little valley to the north. Two of the following villages, **Andrzejówka** and **Milik**, likewise have Lemk churches; the former is on the main road, the latter lies up the valley of the same name.

A further 1¹/₂ miles (3km) on is **Muszyna**, a popular spa resort located on a short stretch of the Poprad which lies entirely within Polish territory, at the river's confluence with the Muszynka. The ruined castle dates back to the beginning of the fourteenth century, while a seventeenth-century inn in the town centre now houses the Regional Museum, with displays on local arts and crafts. Muszyna was for nearly half a millennium the property of the bishops of Cracow, and hence its parish church, which was built in the seventeenth century, has always been used for Roman Catholic worship.

Most of the nearby villages, on the other hand, have traditionally been inhabited by Lemks who adhered to the Uniate faith. In the three tiny valleys north of Muszyna are the villages of **Szczawnik**, **Złockie** and **Jastrzębik**, which each have a nineteenth-century wooden church complete with original iconostasis. However, the finest and oldest wooden church in the Beskid Sądecki is in **Powroźnik**, 5km from Muszyna along the loop road, which at this point starts to double back towards Nowy Sącz. Built in the 1640s, the Powroźnik church is a classic example of the Lemk style, with three onion domes of diminishing size. The central panel of the eighteenth-century iconostasis has been removed to make way for a Roman Catholic altar, but some older icons are preserved on the main walls, while the sacristy preserves murals from around the time of the church's construction.

Krynica, Poland's most famous spa, lies $3^1/_2$ miles (6km) north of Powroźnik at the terminus of the branch railway from Nowy Sącz, which closely follows the course of the loop road already described. Strung out along the wooded valley of the Kryniczanka, a tributary of the Muszynka, at an average altitude of around 1,968ft (600m), it first came to prominence in the middle of the nineteenth century, and soon developed into one of the most fashionable watering-holes of the Austro-Hungarian Empire. With the advent of Communism, it inevitably lost some of its lustre, but it is once again making a determined pitch at the foreign tourist market. Other than Zakopane, it is probably the Polish resort most commonly featured in package holiday brochures, profiting from the fact that it has a winter sports season in addition to its main summertime business of catering for walkers and recuperative holidaymakers.

The life of the town centres around its pump rooms, the principal one being on the main promenade, al. Nowotarskiego. Usually around ten different local mineral waters can be sampled there. Of these, the purple-brown *Zuber* has the reputation of being the most concentrated to be found anywhere in Europe, containing 24 grammes of solid matter per litre. Towards the northern end of the promenade is the valley station of the funicular railway which ascends to the summit of the Góra Parkowa (2,430ft/741m), which can also be reached from the town centre via the blue trail.

For a more ambitious walk, the obvious goal is Jaworzyna (3,654ft/1,114m), the highest point in the Pasmo Jaworzyny, with a mountain refuge below the summit. It can be reached either by the green trail from the north of Krynica, or by the red trail from the southern part of town, the latter being the first stage of the path all the way across the range to Rytro.

Also within easy access of Krynica are several small Lemk villages. **Mochnaczka-Niżna**, 3 miles (5km) to the north-east and reachable either by road or by the eastern section of the red trail, has two wooden churches, one from the mid-nineteenth century in the northern part of the village and a smaller one from the late eighteenth century towards the southern end. There are also two churches in **Tylicz**, 3 miles (5km) south along the valley of the Mochnaczka, which historically had a mixed Polish and Lemk population. The Catholic church dates back to the early seventeenth century, whereas its Uniate counterpart, nowadays the cemetery chapel, was built in the late eighteenth century. Tylicz is equally accessible from Powroźnik via a road along the serpentine course of the Muszynka, or from Krynica either by road or by following the red or green trails east, then switching to the black trail. A further 1¹/₂ miles (3km) south-east is **Muszynka**, which is located near the well-head of the eponymous river, and is centred on a fine late seventeenth-century wooden church.

The Pieniny

The **Pieniny** is a small and particularly beautiful chain which stands out from the other Carpathian mountains in being formed predominantly of limestone. Below its jagged white peaks are thickly wooded slopes, which look particularly glorious when cloaked in autumnal reds and golds. There are three distinct parts to the chain, each of which is divided by the frontier with Slovakia. The main central section, the Pieniny Właściwe, is separated from the Beskid Sądecki to the east by the River Dunajec, which also forms a spectacular gorge — a truly great natural wonder which has long been one of Poland's most popular tourist attractions — along the international border to the south. To the east is the Małe Pieniny (literally 'Small Pieniny') which lies across the Dunajec, divided from the Beskid Sądecki by the valley of the Grajcarek. Finally, the Pieniny Spiskie lies across the Dunajec from the south-western end of the Pieniny Właściwe, and forms the northern part of a small, time-warped rural region known as the Spisz, which historically belonged to Hungary and was populated mainly by Slovaks.

Although most tourists come on day trips from Zakopane, there are two little resort towns within the Pieniny catering for holidaymakers. **Krościenko**, which lies 21¹/₂ miles (35km) south-west of Stary Sącz on the main route between Nowy Sącz and Zakopane is, on balance, the better base for those wishing to walk in the range, as it has a bridge over the Dunajec and hence ready access to the trailheads. **Szczawnica**, 3 miles (5km) to the south at the confluence of the Grajcarek with the Dunajec, is a slightly more characterful place, with some nice old wooden houses and spa buildings in the eastern part of town. Its big disadvantage is that the only way of crossing the Dunajec is via the seasonal ferry, which stops operating in the late afternoon.

On the other hand, Szczawnica offers ready access to the Małe Pieniny, which actually has the highest peak in the range, Wysoki Skałki (3,444ft/ 1,050m). This lies right on the Slovak border, and is an easy ascent via the green trail from **Jaworki**, 4 miles (7km) up the Grajcarek from Szczawnica. This trail passes through a fine deep ravine, the Wąwóz Homole, which lies immediately south of the village. Jaworki is itself of interest for its late eighteenth-century wooden church, the most westerly surviving example of the characteristic architectural style of the Lemks. It passed from the Uniates to the Catholics after World War II, but still preserves its iconostasis.

Most of the Pieniny Właściwe has been designated as the **Pieniny National Park** (Pieniński Park Narodowy). It is compact and easily explored: the main ridge is just 7 miles (12km) long and has a maximum width of nearly 3 miles (4.5km). Despite this, the park has a rich flora, containing examples of well over half the vasular plants which grow in Poland. The main goal for walkers is the Three Crowns (Trzy Korony) massif which, as its name suggests, has three separate peaks, the highest being Okrąglica (3,220ft/982m). A stone stairway leads to a platform at its summit, which commands a memorable panorama over the Pieniny, the Dunajec below and the Tatras in the distance. From Krościenko, the simplest approach is to take the yellow trail from the western edge of town up to the Szopka Pass, then transfer to the blue trail, a walk that should take no more than 90 minutes in total.

The blue trail leads on via Zamkowa Góra (2,555ft/779m), which has a very ruinous medieval castle associated with the Blessed Kinga, to Sokolica (2,450ft/747m), the main peak in the western part of the range, with a wonderful view over the sharpest bend in the Dunajec. It then continues on to the Szczawnica ferry, while the green trail leads back to Krościenko. From the Szopka Pass, the western section of the blue trail continues right along the ridge to the park's north-west boundary, while the yellow trail descends via a gorge, the Wąwóz Sobczański, to the village of Sromowcze-Niżne, which lies near the head of the Dunajec gorge.

The only way of seeing the gorge to full effect is from the water itself, and raft trips along the river have been a major tourist attraction since the 1830s. These leave from **Kąty**, 3 miles (5km) upstream from Sromowcze-Niżne, and terminate at Szczawnica, a thrilling 9 miles (15km) long journey along the twists and turns of the river. Although it was a settlement in palaeolithic times, Kąty is now no more than a wharf with ancillary buildings. The usual way of getting there is via the circuitous road from Krościenko to Sromowcze-Niżne which travels all the way round the outside perimeter of the national park. This is plied by several buses daily, so car drivers need have no worries about being able to return to their vehicles at the end of the raft trip. An alternative means of getting to Kąty is on foot, by following the main blue trail until about halfway along the ridge, then descending via the red trail.

The rafting season runs from the beginning of May until the end of October, though these dates can change if water levels are exceptionally high. Passengers travel ten to a raft, which actually consists of five punts tied together with ropes. These are no longer the traditional dugouts carved from a single truck; nowadays, they are constructed from planks of spruce. A total of 500 raftsmen are based at the wharf. They work in pairs, each steering the raft with a long wooden oar. Rather incongruously, they are dressed in traditional highland costume worn directly over working clothes.

Just past Sromowce-Niżne, there is a wonderful view of the Three Crowns. At the Sharp Rock (Ostra Skała) beyond, the raft enters the gorge proper, as the river narrows to a width of only 164ft (50m). On the Polish side, the rocks rise steeply from the shore, whereas there is a footpath all along the Slovakian bank. The river itself constantly changes character, with fast shallow rapids alternating with slow deep stretches. Depending on the

The Chapel on the Water, Ojców (Chapter 9)

The rock formation known as Hercules' Club in the Ojców National Park (Chapter 9)

Pilgrims wearing traditional costume for the Queen of Poland Day celebrations in Częstochowa (Chapter 9)

View over the Pieniny mountains and the River Dunajec from the summit of the Three Crowns (Chapter 10)

water level, it takes between two and three hours to complete the trip, and prices are, by Western standards, remarkably reasonable.

Just beyond the western end of the national park is the village of **Czorsztyn**, whose existence is threatened by a huge unfinished hydroelectric dam project initiated during the Communist period which itself faces an uncertain future, having attracted widespread condemnation from both locals and environmentalists. High above the bank is a medieval castle, now very ruinous but impressive nevertheless, not least for the views it offers.

Facing it from across the Dunajec is its even more imposing counterpart in **Niedzica**, which lies at the far end of the Pieniny Spiskie. This castle was begun during the fourteenth century as a Hungarian frontier fortress; it was partially rebuilt in the early seventeenth century as a Renaissance palace and survives relatively intact. Part of it has been converted into a hotel, while another section houses the Regional Museum, with displays on the archaeology, art and ethnology of the Spisz.

Despite its proximity to the popular tourist centres and the Tatras, the rest of the Spisz region lies totally off the beaten track, practising a rural lifestyle that has changed little in centuries. **Łapsze Wyżne**, 6 miles (11km) to the west of Niedzica, has a wooden church of the 1760s with folksy Rococo furnishings, including a pulpit and several altars. A further 2 miles (4km) west is **Trybsz**, whose wooden church is 200 years older. Its painted interior decoration, which is dated to 1647, features Biblical scenes and portraits of saints on the walls and a mountain landscape view, undoubtedly inspired by the local scenery, on the ceiling.

The Central Podhale and the Gorce

Between the Pieniny and Tatra mountains lies a broad plateau known as the **Podhale**. It is populated by a proudly independent people known as the Górale (which literally means 'highlanders'), who maintain their own rich cultural tradition, particularly in the fields of costume, carpentry, music and dance. Immediately to the north is the **Gorce**, a mountain range which yields little to its more famous neighbours in terms of scenery and panoramic viewpoints, yet which remains, as a result of its relative inaccessibility, totally unspoilt and little visited.

From Krościenko, the main road towards Zakopane cuts right through the heart of the Podhale, by-passing a string of traditional farming communities en route. Some of these possess what rank among the oldest surviving wooden churches in Poland, the first being **Grywałd**, which lies 3 miles (5km) from Krościenko, and ¹/₂ mile (1km) north of the road. The church, which is at the southern end of the village, dates back to the late fifteenth century and adopts the archaic format of a square chancel. Most of the walls and ceilings are covered with charmingly naive folk paintings executed in 1618.

Its counterpart in **Dębno Podhalańskie**, 7 miles (12km) to the west, is among the most famous in the country and is known to have been built in the 1490s. The exterior is relatively conventional, and it is the quite amazingly well-preserved interior decoration which makes the church exceptional. The walls are covered with late Gothic paintings which include religious and hunting scenes as well as decorative motifs, all executed in bright colours which retain their freshness in spite of never having been restored. There are also some excellent furnishings, including the roodbeam, the high altar and the tabernacle, and there is even an intriguing musical instrument, a fifteenth-century dulcimer which takes the place of the bell during mass.

Harklowa, 1¹/₂ miles (3km) further on, has a similar though larger church. It lost its original murals in the nineteenth century, but was repainted in the 1930s. **Łopuszna**, another 1¹/₂ miles (3km) west, stretches up into the valley of the stream of the same name, right to the edge of the Gorce. The church, located in the lower part of the village, is very similar to Harklowa's, and was likewise repainted in the 1930s. To its west is a sort of miniature *skansen*, albeit one based on buildings already in situ. It is centred on an eighteenth-century manor house, and also includes several farm buildings.

Nowy Targ, 5 miles (8km) on, is the main commercial centre of the Podhale. The Dunajec is formed at its north-eastern edge from the confluence of its two headstreams: the Biały (ie White) Dunajec, which flows down the eastern side of the town, and the Czarny (ie Black) Dunajec, which arrives from the south-west then changes to an easterly course, dividing Nowy Targ horizontally. Unfortunately, the town has little in the way of sights, having been devastated by fire in the late eighteenth century: the only two monuments of note are the parish church of St Catherine to the north of the Rynek, which has a Gothic chancel and a Renaissance nave, and the wooden church of St Anne in the civic cemetery on the far side of the Czarny Dunajec.

However, it is well worth visiting Nowy Targ (whose name means 'New Market') on a Thursday morning for the sake of its market, the largest and most celebrated in Poland, which is held in the open area east of the Rynek. At the far end, farmers deal in the serious business of live animals and agricultural equipment. The best-known trade is in thick black and white wools; these can be bought in their undyed, freshly sheared state, or else as thick handknitted sweaters with fancy colour patterns. Other stallholders sell baskets, pottery, handmade toys and all kinds of religious and secular folk art. Recent years have seen an increase in the numbers of traders of the car boot sale disposition, many of them from Slovakia, Russia or the Ukraine.

Rabka, 13 miles (21km) north of Nowy Targ on the main transport routes to Cracow, lies at the north-western fringe of the Gorce. A quiet little spa town, its main historic monument is its seventeenth-century wooden church, which still preserves its original polychromy. Long deconsecrated, it houses the Regional Museum, with displays on the costumes, customs, arts and crafts of the Górale.

The whole of the central part of the Gorce has been designated the **Gorce National Park** (Gorzański Park Narodowy). It is a classic Carpathian landscape, with a definite character of its own. Much of it is forested, with oaks, limes and beeches on the lower slopes, and fir, beeches and spruces higher up, with the last of these now accounting, as a result of managed plantation, for over half the total number of trees. There are also many high mountain meadows and pastures comparable with those in the Bieszczady, and these often command magnificent views, notably over the ridge of the Tatras to the south. Over 900 different vascular plants, including many rare Alpine species, grow in the park, which is also the habitat of many birds, notably grouse, hazelhens, ravens and eagle owls. Although some of the initial ascents are quite steep, the marked trails are otherwise very easy going.

That the Gorce National Park lies off the beaten track even for Poles is due largely to the fact that it is well away from any main roads. Indeed, the only road of consequence which goes anywhere near is that from Krościenko to Mszana Dolna. It travels close to the park's north-eastern boundary at the Przysłop Pass, about 25 miles (40km) north-west of Krościenko. From the pass, the blue trail makes a horizontal traverse of the park, closely hugging the banks of its prettiest stream, the Kamienica, for the first half of the way.

Turbacz (4,296ft/1,310m) is the highest peak in the Gorce, though it actually lies just outside the official boundaries of the park. It can be reached on foot in about three hours from Nowy Targ by the green trail, or in a slightly longer period from Rabka by the red trail. The refuge just below the summit makes an ideal base for those wanting to spend several days in the range, though it is easy enough to return to the starting-point on the same day, whether directly or by means of a circular walk.

One recommended route is to follow the red trail east from Turbacz through the Długa Hala, a wold offering wonderful panoramic views of the Tatra ridge, then switch to the green trail for the ascent to Jaworzyna Krzemieniecka (4,044ft/1,233m), the highest point in the park. Returning to the red trail, there is the choice of following it all the way to Krościenko, with several possibilities of descending beforehand to the main Nowy Targ road, which is plied by regular buses, or of making a more direct descent to Łopuszna via the black trail. From the latter, there is a signposted detour to the Pucołomski Stawek, a tiny tarn with a tree-framed view to the Tatras.

The Tatras

The **Tatras** are the highest and most dramatic part of the Carpathians, and the only one to have alpine characteristics. Their total area amounts to some 288sq miles (750sq km), of which three-quarters lies within Slovakia. Despite its relatively small extent, the Polish sector contains a quite astonishing variety of landscapes: jagged peaks of well over 6,560ft (2,000m), sheer and inaccessible rockfaces, gentle wooded valleys cut by sparklingly clear streams, verdant meadows and wolds; sharply plunging waterfalls, and dramatically sited mountain tarns.

No matter what the season, the Tatras have something special to offer. In winter, the heavy snowfalls attract skiers and other winter sports enthusiasts; in spring, the lower ground is awash with colourful mountain flowers;

in summer, with the snow having melted from all but the highest levels, the whole range becomes accessible to walkers; while it is during the Polish 'golden autumn', which usually marks the final stages of the hiking season, that the landscape is arguably at its most beautiful. Moreover, the varied nature of the terrain means that there are marvellous walks of every conceivable level of difficulty, ranging from undemanding strolls to some of the most challenging hikes anywhere in Europe, often involving scrambling as well as ascents and descents via fixed ladders and chains.

Zakopane, the only resort in Poland to have gained an international reputation, is the gateway to the Tatras and the base for the overwhelming majority of its visitors. Located at the extreme southern end of the Podhale, $10^{1}/_{2}$ miles (17km) from Nowy Targ, it was an obscure highland village until the 1870s, when a physician, Tytus Chałubiński, set in motion the first moves towards its development as a recuperative health resort. Within a couple of decades, Zakopane had also become a leading centre of the Young Poland artistic movement. Inspired by the wooden farmsteads of the Górale, the painter Stanisław Witkiewicz, who himself had no formal training as an architect, developed the 'Zakopane style', a carefully defined theory which he put into practice in a series of highly original showpiece buildings. This was the first serious attempt to give the still-subjugated Polish nation a distinctive national architectural style and, although it failed to fulfil its creator's dreams of a successful transplant to other parts of the country, its influence on the town is still evident to this day. Thus Zakopane can claim to be an attractive place in its own right, despite the inevitable encroachment of the modern concrete blocks that are the hallmark of major resorts all over the world.

Witkiewicz's last building, designed immediately before World War I and constructed posthumously, is the Tatra Museum, which is located towards the lower end of the main pedestrian precinct, ul. Krupówki. It aimed to translate the local architectural idiom into the more durable materials of stone and bricks and was thus an important test case for the adaptation of the style to the types of buildings which would be required in cities. In the event, Witkiewicz's death and the onset of modernism meant that the experiment was taken no further. The museum itself makes a good introduction to the region, with displays on its flora, fauna, geology, history and ethnograhy.

Opposite stands the parish church, a neo-Romanesque building from the end of the nineteenth century, which replaced its smaller wooden counterpart on ul. Kościeliska, a short distance to the north-west. The latter only dates back to the 1840s, though it is little different in appearance from the Podhale village churches of the fifteenth century. Alongside is a stone chapel which is three decades older and thus the oldest surviving structure in Zakopane. Its cemetery contains the graves of many of the town's best-known citizens, including Chałubiński, Witkiewicz and the latter's son, the great experimental playwright, novelist and portrait painter Stanisław Ignacy Witkiewicz (otherwise known as Witkacy).

Further along ul. Kościeliska is the Villa Koliba, which was completed in 1892 as the first representative of the Zakopane style. Witkiewicz designed it as a sort of ideal home for a Ukrainian landowner, Zygmunt Gnatowski, and his plans were executed by a team of Górale carpenters. On the ground floor, the Highlander's Room houses the original owner's valuable ethnographic collection, while the Dining Room has furniture by Witkiewicz. Upstairs, the corridor and the master's and servant's rooms contain examples of applied art in the Zakopane style. On ul. Kasprusie, a few minutes' walk to the south-east, is the Villa Atma, the home of the composer Karol Szymanowski, and now a museum in his memory.

In the east of town, just off ul. Jagiellońska, is the Władysław Hasior Gallery, which is devoted to the work of the eponymous sculptor, Poland's leading practitioner of pop art. From there, it is a walk of about 20 minutes south to the Tatra National Park Museum, located beside a big roundabout, the Rondo Bystre. A short distance to the east is another Witkiewicz villa, albeit one not open to the public, the House 'Under the Firs' (Pod Jedlami). About 1 mile (1¹/₂km) further east is the Jaszczurówka chapel, which is likewise by Witkiewicz. It has a finely crafted high altar and colourful stained glass windows depicting the national emblems of Poland and Lithuania.

The formerly separate village and iron-smelting centre of **Kuźnice** (whose name means 'Smithy') lies 1 mile (1¹/₂km) south of the Rondo Bystre. A huge waterwheel remains as evidence of the industry that was once carried on there, but nowadays it is geared almost entirely to tourism. Not only is it the starting-point for trails into the mountains, it is also the ground station for the only cable car into the Tatras, one which provides ready access to the ridge for those unable or unwilling to walk, as well as a conveniently speedy means of ascent for serious hikers. It takes around 20 minutes to ascend to the summit of Kasprowy Wierch (6,510ft/1,985m), a journey made in two stages.

At the very opposite end of town, directly north of ul. Krupówki, is the valley terminus of the funicular railway to Gubałówka (3,673ft/1,120m), which can also be ascended via the steep but otherwise undemanding black trail to the west. Gubałówka is extremely touristy, but offers a majestic full-frontal view of the Tatras. Several trails lead off to the west, among them the black route to Mirów, which continues on to **Chochołów**, 7 miles (12km) north-west of Zakopane. This village consists entirely of old farmsteads, some dating back to the early nineteenth century, and has been placed under a protection order.

The whole of the Polish section of the Tatras, stretching from immediately beyond the southern municipal boundary of Zakopane, is designated as the **Tatra National Park** (Tatrzański Park Narodowy). Up to a level of 5,250ft (1,600m), it is covered with coniferous forest, with spruces predominating. There is also a wide range of flowers, including cowslips, crocuses, foxgloves, lilies and orchids. A sub-alpine zone then follows for the next 820ft (250m), with dwarf pines and hardy plants such as edelweiss and gentians. From 6,070ft (1,850m) to 7,545ft (2,300m) is an alpine zone of bare rocks interspersed only with mosses and the occasional solitary tree; the very highest levels are permanently under snow. Chamois and marmots live in the upper reaches of the mountains; lower down, the mammals include red and roe deer, badgers, foxes, otters, weasels, stoats, martens, wild boar, wild cats, lynxes, wolves and bears.

The Polish side of the Tatras falls into two distinct sections, with the dividing line falling at the Sucha Pass, 984ft (300m) south-east of the cable car terminal on Kasprowy Wierch. To the east lie the **High Tatras** (Tatry Wysocki), the only significant part of the Carpathians to have been glaciated during the last Ice Age. The rocks are crystalline, with granite predominating. Most of the summits are over 6,560ft (2,000m), and below them lie many picturesque mountain tarns. In general, the walks are more demanding than those further west and do not always make convenient day trips from Zakopane, though the four mountain refuges in the range cater for those who do not wish to descend every day.

The most famous beauty spot in the Tatras, Lake Morskie Oko (literally, 'Eye of the Sea'), lies in the easternmost part of the park. A paved road runs there all the way from Zakopane, but motorised transport is now banned from the last 7 miles (11km) of this, so cars and buses must stop at the large car park located 1 mile (1¹/₂km) south of Łysa Polana, the only official border crossing-point in the Tatras. The steep ascent can be speeded up by taking one of the horse-drawn vehicles which transport visitors in about an hour up to the old car park, just below the refuge on the north shore of the lake. Morskie Oko is generally described as the largest of the tarns in the High Tatras, though it may already have lost that distinction as a result of ersosion by scree. Nonetheless, the dark waters, the dripping waterfalls and the towering mountains above combine to memorable effect, and it is well worth following the path all the way round the shoreline to appreciate it from different angles.

The red trail leads up in about three-quarters of an hour to one of several Tatra lakes known as the Black Tarn (Czarny Staw). This offers a bird's-eye vista over Morskie Oko and an equally fine view up to Rysy (8,167ft/2,490m), which ranks as Poland's highest point, though its summit is shared with Slovakia. It can be reached in about three hours via the red trail; this is a strenuous route, albeit one amply rewarded by the gigantic panorama it offers over the whole range of the Tatras.

From the Morskie Oko refuge, the blue trail leads via a couple of summits to the Valley of the Five Polish Lakes (Dolina Pięciu Stawów Polskich), with many wonderful views en route. There are actually six tarns in all: two are minute, but the Great Tarn (Wielki Staw) is probably now larger than Morskie Oko. The same route leads onwards to the mighty saddle of Zawrat (7,081ft/2,159m), then past another Black Tarn and into the Dolina Gąsienicowa (which means 'Caterpillar Valley'), from where it descends towards Kuźnice. Alternatively, it is possible to double back to Morskie Oko from the Valley of the Five Polish Lakes via the yellow trail.

Zawrat is the second most westerly peak on the route of the most challenging walk in the Tatras, the Eagles' Perch (Orla Perć). This covers 17 summits, all over 6,888ft (2,100m) high, between Świnica 7,547ft (2,301m) and Krzyżne 6,930ft (2113m) and can be accomplished in a single day if the initial ascent is speeded up by taking the cable car. However, although frequently touted, this path is not only very exposed and vertiginous, it has also suffered badly from erosion and should really only be tackled in the company of a qualified mountain guide. Fine views of the Eagles' Perch ridge can be enjoyed from the blue trail and from various other routes easily accessible from the cable car.

The scenery of the **West Tatras** (Tatry Zachodnie) is quite different from that of the High Tatras. Its mountains are composed primarily of sedimentary rocks, mostly limestone and dolomite, with the crystalline sections mainly confined to the ridge along the border. There are only a few small tarns, but the concentration of caves is among the largest in Poland. For the most part, the walks, even to the summits over 6,560ft (2,000m), are far easier than in the High Tatras; they are also more comfortable day-trips from Zakopane, although there are three refuges within the range. The two main trailheads for the more ambitious routes are at Kuźnice and Kiry, the latter being a hamlet on the main road 4 miles (7km) west of Zakopane. In addition, the cable car's upper station at Kasprowy Wierch is a useful starting-point for walks, for example the straightforward westward section of the red route, which takes about three hours to travel along the ridge to Ciemniak (6,874ft/2,096m), from where it descends gradually towards Kiry.

The most easily recognizable mountain in the West Tatras is Giewont (6,212ft/1,894m) immediately behind Zakopane, a double peak whose outline is often likened to a sleeping knight — and which has thereby become the inspiration for a number of Arthurian-type legends. From Kuźnice, the blue trail leads up past the wooden Albertina convent through a broad wold, the Hala Kondratowa, before swinging round to ascend the higher of the Giewont's two peaks, which is crowned with a 49ft (15m) high iron cross. Towards the summit, there are fixed chains to help with the ascent. The journey back to Zakopane via the red trail travels below the broad west face of the mountain en route to the Grybowcu Pass, a fine viewpoint, before descending into the Dolina Strążyska.

The last-named is one of three gentle wooded valleys which lie in the northernmost part of the park, immediately beyond the municipal boundary of Zakopane, offering at least a taste of characteristic Tatra scenery for those who are not prepared to go for long or uphill walks. Immediately to the east is the tiny Dolina ku Dziurze, which terminates at a cave. A little further along is the Dolina Białego, which is cut by the prettiest of the streams, the Biały Potok, which courses along in a series of miniature cascades and waterfalls. By taking the yellow trail to the top end of this valley, it is possible to reach the equivalent place in the Dolina Strążyska by means of the black trail, so making for a pleasant circular walk.

Two of the most beautiful long valleys lie at the far western end of the Tatras. Immediately south of Kiry is the Dolina Kościeliska, where horse-drawn carriages can be hired by visitors, though these offer no real advantages, as the path (which is marked in green) is on level ground throughout. There are several caves, among them the Frosty Cave (Jaskinia Mroźna), the only one in the Tatras open as a regular tourist sight and equipped with electric lighting. There is also a pathway through the Mylna Jaskinia further south, though to see this it is essential to come equipped with a torch. At the top end of the valley, the black trail leads uphill from the refuge to a tarn, Smreczyński Staw, while the green trail continues up towards the border ridge.

Another green trail leads through the Dolina Chochołowska, the westernmost valley in the park: it has a car park at its entrance and is also served by buses during the summer. It likewise has a refuge at its far end, from where the trail leads up in another couple of hours to the border ridge, reaching the summit of Wołowiec (6,766ft/2,063m) via a short detour east along the blue trail. A good day-long walk is to continue along the ridge via Starobociański Wierch (7,137ft/2,176m), the highest peak in the West Tatras, to the Raczkowa Pass, descending via the green trail to the Siwa Pass, then along the black trail through the Dolina Starobociańska back to the middle of the Dolina Chochołowska.

The Beskid Wysoki and Beskid Makowski

The **Babia Góra massif**, which lies beyond the north-western end of the Podhale, is by far the most attractive part of the long chain known as the Beskid Wysoki (literally, 'High Beskids'). Forming part of the international frontier with Slovakia, it is a popular destination with both Poles and Slovaks, but is visited by few foreigners. Tourist facilities are accordingly very rudimentary, though the massif makes for a convenient day excursion from either Zakopane or Cracow.

From the former, the shortest approach is via **Zubrzyca Górna**, which lies directly below the southern end of the massif, some 25 miles (40km) north-west of Chochołów. The village preserves a number of wooden houses characteristic of the region, while some more imposing examples, including a large eighteenth-century manor house, have been collected together in the Ethnographic Park at its northern end.

Approaching from Cracow or Nowy Targ, the gateway to the massif is **Zawoja**, a straggling community situated on the banks of the River Skamica. It stretches for a full 7¹/₂ miles (12km) from end to end, making it the longest village in Poland, and perhaps even in Europe. As a tourist resort, it has yet to realize its potential, though it does have a few notable examples of vernacular wooden architecture, including an inn built in the 1830s and a church from half-a-century later.

The highest part of the massif, which has the distinctive conical shape associated with Eastern European 'witches' mountains', has been designated the **Babia Góra National Park** (Babiogórski Park Narodowy). It is the second smallest of Poland's national parks, though is among those most prized by naturalists, being of sufficient scientific interest to have gained admission to UNESCO's list of World Biosphere Reserves. One of its most characteristic features is the division of the vegetation into very distinct vertical bands. Up to a height of 3,770ft (1,150m), the slopes are thickly wooded, particularly with beech, fir and spruce trees; these then give way to spruce and rowans only. There follows a sector of dwarf mountain pines, while the highest areas have only grasses, mosses and lichen among the loose boulders.

Hundreds of different plant species grow in the park, which is particularly beautiful in late spring and early autumn; the rare laserwort is its symbol, while liverworts, pasque-flowers, rhododendrons and bilberries are all to be found in abundance. Around 115 different birds inhabit the park, including predatory types such as eagles, goshawks, sparrowhawks, buzzards, eagle-owls and ravens, as well as grouse, capercaillies and woodpeckers. There are also a number of wild animals, including deer, lynxes and wolves.

If driving, the easiest approach to the park is the Krowiarki Pass (3,234ft/986m), midway along the road between Zawoja and Zubrzyca Górna, which is equipped with a large visitors' car park. There is a choice of routes to Diablak (5,658ft/1,725m), the highest peak in the massif and itself part of the international frontier. Of these, the most straightforward is the red trail, which ascends via Sokolica (4,483ft/1,367m) and Kępa (4,988ft/1,521m), offering fine views of Diablak on the way. An enticing alternative is to follow the green trail, which ascends gently through the forest from the Krowiarki pass to the Markowe Szczawiny refuge in the very heart of the park. This is the junction of all the walking routes, and can be reached from various points in Zawoja by the yellow, black or green trails. From the refuge, it is a fairly steep ascent to Diablak via the yellow trail, which includes one short section with a fixed ladder ascent. The best option is to go up by one route and down by the other, a walk which should take around five hours in total. This is rewarded by the enormous panorama from the top of Diablak which on clear days (unfortunately quite rare) includes a sensational panorama of the entire ridge of the Tatras.

For those with more time to spare, the red and green trails continue northwestwards from Diablak along the frontier. At the Brona Pass (4,618ft/1,408m), the former descends to the refuge, whereas the latter continues along the Slovak border, traversing the peak of Mała Babia Góra (4,969ft/1,515m) before descending to the Jałowiecka Pass (3,335ft/1,017m) at the far end of the park. Outside the park's boundaries, but still within the Babia Góra massif, the most obvious goal is the summit of Polica (4,490ft/1,369m). This lies on the opposite side of the Krowiarki Pass, and can be reached from the car park by the eastern section of the red trail.

Sucha Beskidzka, which lies down the Skamica from Zawoja, about 12 miles (20km) away by road, marks the transition to the Beskid Makowski chain. The town's most diverting sight is the wooden eighteenth-century inn on the Rynek, arguably the finest of the regrettably few surviving historic examples of what was once a characteristic feature of Polish rural communities. Set in a landscaped park in the northern outskirts is the palace of the Komorowski family, a sixteenth-century Renaissance building with an arcaded courtyard which is now home to the Regional Museum.

In the northernmost foothills of the Beskid Makowski, 12 miles (20km) north-east of Sucha Beskidzka and 18¹/₂ miles (30km) south-west of Cracow, lies **Kalwaria Zebrzydowska**, which ranks second to Częstochowa as Poland's leading place of pilgrimage and is also one of the country's most distinctive and unusual historical sites in its own right. Dotted around the hillsides above the little town, a prestigious furniture-making centre, are over forty churches, chapels and ancillary structures built in imitation of the Holy Places of Jerusalem. The project, the brainchild of Mikołaj Zebrzydowski, the regional administrator of Cracow, got underway in 1600. Initially, the Jesuit architect Gianmaria Bernardoni was placed in charge of the work, but he was shortly afterwards replaced by Paul Baudarth, a goldsmith from Antwerp. Inspired by the splendid Mannerist buildings of his native city, he created a whole series of whimsical designs, often using highly elaborate groundplans. Although they can hardly be regarded as accurate reproductions of the Biblical-era buildings they purport to represent, they nonetheless show real flair and imagination in their diverse borrowings from the vocabularies of Classical, Byzantine and Oriental architecture.

The original circuit of buildings was dedicated to the Passion of Our Lord. In 1632, work began on building a second circuit devoted to the Virgin Mary, though it is intermingled with its predecessor, even sharing some of the same structures. Each of the circuits is the setting for a big annual pilgrimage. The more famous of these is at Easter and incorporates a costumed procession with mystery plays. It sets off in the early afternoon of Maunday Thursday and slowly proceeds along the first half of the Passion circuit. At dusk, it breaks for the night, to resume at daybreak on Good Friday, finishing at around 1.30pm with a re-enactment of the Crucifixion. A similar procession is held round the other circuit on 13 to 15 August to celebrate the Feast of the Assumption. For these events, pilgrims stream in from all over Poland, and the atmosphere is highly charged and emotional. At other times the hillsides are often completely deserted.

The focal point of the whole complex is the Bernardine monastery, much the largest of the buildings though also one of the most conventional, being a typical exmaple of Polish Baroque. Nonetheless, the church has some notable furnishings, such as the silver statue of the Virgin at the high altar, the carved choir stalls and the pulpit. Off the left-hand side of the chancel is the Zebrzydowski chapel, containing an image of the Virgin which has long had a reputation for its miraculous properties. Fronting the church is Paradise Square, which has a charming row of arcaded houses along its southern length. At the corner is St Raphael's chapel, the first stage on the two pilgrim circuits.

It takes at least a couple of hours to walk round the hillsides. First, it is necessary to follow the rough track which bears in a generally south-easterly direction down towards a brook bearing the Biblical name of Cedron, which is forded by the Angel Bridge. On the opposite side is the Church of the Sepulchre of Our Lady, one of Baudarth's most idiosyncratic designs. On the hill behind, known as the Mount of Olives, are the Gethsemane chapel and the Arrest chapel, while higher up, commanding a view back to the monastery, is the Ascension church.

Further south, the Cedron Bridge crosses back over the bridge to the pathway leading westwards up Mount Zion. At the top end of this are the two-storey Cenacle (the building where the Last Supper took place); the House of the Virgin Mary, which is constructed of unfaced red bricks; and the circular House of the High Priest Caiaphas. The path then leads northwards up another hill, on which stands the House of Pilate, a grand Roman villa in a hybrid Classical and Baroque style fronted by a porticioed balcony. Immediately in front is a covered walkway representing the Holy Steps, opposite which is the Chapel of the Heart of the Virgin Mary, easily recognizable from its curious beehive roof.

At the foot of the hill stands Herod's Palace, which is given an appropriately exotic appearance. The final hill, named Golgotha, is crowned with a series of buildings in a dignified Mannerist style, the most important being the Church of the Crucifixion, the Chapel of Unction and the Chapel of the Tomb of Our Lord Jesus. From there, it is just a short walk via the Chapel of the Virgin Mary Dolorous back down to the monastery.

Further information
— Little Poland: The Western Carpathians —

Places to Visit

Biecz
Biecz Museum
ul. Kromera 5 and ul. Węgierska 2
Open: Tuesday to Saturday 9am to
3pm, May to September also Sunday
9am to 2pm.

Gorlice
Regional Museum
ul. Wąska 7
Open: Tuesday to Sunday 10am to 4pm.

Kiry
Frosty Cave
Open: daily May to October 9am to
4pm.

Łopuszna
Manor House
Open: Wednesday to Sunday 8am to
4pm.

Muszyna
Regional Museum
ul. Kity 26
Open: Wednesday to Friday 9am to 4pm,
Saturday and Sunday 9am to 1.30pm.

Niedzica
Castle (Regional Museum)
Open: Tuesday to Sunday 9am to 5pm.

Nowy Sącz
Ethnographic Park
Open: May to September Tuesday to
Friday 9.30am to 4pm, Saturday and
Sunday 9.30am to 5pm, October to
April Tuesday to Sunday 10am to
2.30pm.

Regional Museum
ul. Lwowska 3
Open: Tuesday to Thursday 10am to
2.30pm, Friday 10am to 6pm,
Saturday and Sunday 9am to 2.30pm.

Rabka
Regional Museum
Open: Tuesday to Sunday 9am to 4pm.

Stary Sącz
District Museum
Rynek 6
Open: Tuesday to Sunday 10am to 1pm.

Sucha Beskidzka
Palace (Regional Museum)
Open: Tuesday to Sunday 10am to 3pm.

Szymbark
Ethnographic Park
Open: Tuesday to Sunday 9am to 3pm.

Zakopane
Tatra Museum
ul. Krupówki 10
Open: Tuesday to tSunday 9am to 4pm.

Tatra National Park Museum
ul. Chałubińskiego 42a
Open: Tuesday to Saturday 9am to 2pm.

Villa Atma
ul. Kasprusie 19
Open: Tuesday to Thursday, Saturday
and Sunday 10am to 4pm, Wednesday
2 to 8pm.

Villa Koliba
ul. Kościeliska 18
Open: Wednesday to Saturday 10am
to 2.30pm.

Władysław Hasior Gallery
ul. Jagiellońska 180
Open: Wednesday to Saturday 11am
to 6pm, Sunday 9am to 3pm.

Tourist Offices
Nowy Sącz
ul. Jagiellońska 46a
☎ 237-24

Zakopane
ul. Kościuszki 23
☎ 122-1

11 • Silesia

The old province of **Silesia** (known as **Śląsk** in Polish) has been one of Europe's most frequently disputed territories. At various times, it has been under predominantly Polish, Czech or German control, at others, all or parts of it have had at least a nominally independent status. Since 1945, all but a few of its westernmost tracts have been part of Poland, this being direct compensation for the loss of the country's Eastern Territories, which were incorporated into the USSR in 1939 as a result of a secret clause in the Nazi-Soviet Pact, and never given back.

Silesia was, together with Great Poland and Little Poland, a constituent part of the original Polish kingdom. Following the collapse of the monarchical system, the Silesian dukes, who were members of the royal Piast dynasty, were effectively the uncrowned kings of Poland. This system ended as a result of the Mongol invasions, and the duchy became detached from the rest of the country, and gradually fragmented. Firstly, it was divided by a line running diagonally north-east from the Golden Mountains into Lower and Upper Silesia. Each duke thereafter tended to divide his territory among his sons, so that eventually Silesia became splintered into eighteen separate principalities. Most of the rulers encouraged German settlers and recognised the King of Bohemia, the most powerful prince in the Holy Roman Empire of Germany, as their feudal overlord. As each line died out, its land was incorporated into Bohemia, which gained control of the entire province when the last of the Piasts died out in 1675. By this time, Bohemia itself had become part of the Austrian-dominated Habsburg Empire. In 1740, Frederick the Great of Prussia, launched an all-out war on Austria, his pretext being a dubious 150 year-old claim his ancestors had to one of the Silesian principalities. After changing hands several times, all but the southernmost part of Silesia was taken over by the Prussians in 1763, and became part of Bismarck's Germany in 1871. After World War I, those parts of Silesia still held by Austria were divided between Poland and Czechoslovakia. A plebiscite held under international supervision in 1921 resulted in Poland acquiring part of mineral-rich industrial conurbation just to the north, but the rest of Upper Silesia and all of Lower Silesia remained German until 1945.

Being a sizeable province, Silesia cannot be covered from a single base. Wrocław, the largest and most attractive city, makes a good centre for

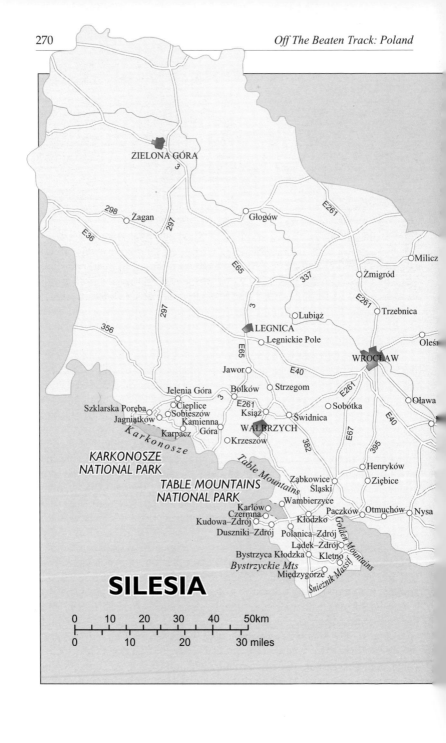

ZIELONA GÓRA

3

298 ○ Żagan

E36

297

E65

356

297

3

○ Głogów

E261

337

○ Milicz

○ Żmigród

E261 ○ Trzebnica

○ Lubiąż

▲LEGNICA
○ Legnickie Pole

E65

○ Oleśr

WROCŁAW

Jawor○

E40

Szklarska Poręba
Jagniątków

Jelenia Góra

○Cieplice
○Sobieszów
Kamienna
Karpacz ○ Góra

Karkonosze

KARKONOSZE
NATIONAL PARK

Bolków

E261

○ Strzegow

3

Książ○

WAŁBRZYCH
○Krzeszów

○Świdnica

382

○ Sobótka

E261

E67

○ Oława

E40

395

TABLE MOUNTAINS
NATIONAL PARK

Table Mountains

Karłów○
Czermna
Kudowa–Zdrój
Duszniki–Zdrój

Wambierzyce
○Kłodzko

Ząbkowice
Śląski

○Henryków
○Ziębice

Paczków○ Otmuchów
○ Nysa

Polanica–Zdrój
Lądek–Zdrój

Bystrzyca Kłodzka○ ○Kletno
Bystrzyckie Mts   Międzygórze

Golden Mountains

Śnieżnik Masyf

SILESIA

0	10	20	30	40	50km
0		10		20	30 miles

Oświęcim; The entrance to the concentration camp of Auschwitz, with the cynical Nazi slogan 'Arbeit Macht Frei' ('Work Makes You Free')

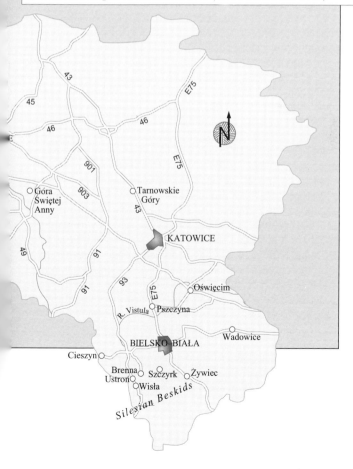

covering most of Lower Silesia, though the Sudeten Mountains along Poland's western border are too far away to make satisfactory day trips. However, there is abundant accommodation in the latter's two main holiday areas, the Karkonosze and the Kłodzko Region. Each of these has a choice of resorts and a variety of scenery, including an area designated as a national park. The Silesian Beskids, the mountain range in the far south of the province, make the most attractive base for exploring Upper Silesia, though many places there are also possible excursions from Cracow.

Wrocław

Silesia's chief city is **Wrocław**, the fourth largest in Poland. It is a place with a fascinating and complex history, most phases of which can be traced in its remarkable monumental legacy, which ranges from huge Germanic brick-built Gothic churches via elegant palaces and chapels in Viennese Baroque style to classic examples of utilitarian design from the early part of the twentieth century. Although Slav by origin, the city first began to be dominated by Germans in the early Middle Ages, and was generally known as Breslau. Having passed successively from the control of the Bohemian kings to the Austrian emperors and then to Frederick the Great's Prussia, it grew in the nineteenth century into one of Germany's leading industrial centres. So thoroughly Germanised had the city become, with Poles reduced to just over 3 per cent of the population, that it did not even feature on the shopping list of places Polish leaders were eager to acquire from the defeated Nazi Germany. In the event, it was allocated to Poland in more-or-less direct compensation for the Soviet annexation of the comparably-sized city of Lwów, and many of the latter's inhabitants were directly re-settled there, bringing several of their institutions with them.

The central area, laid out in an irregular chessboard pattern, spreads out from the spacious Rynek, which differs from other such squares in Poland in being dominated by leisure rather than commercial concerns. In the middle stands the Town Hall, the proud symbol of the city, whose appearance dates largely to the highpoint of local prosperity in the fifteenth century, when it was remodelled, using an unusual mixture of stone and brick, in a decorative late Gothic style. The east façade features an astronomical clock from 1580 and an elaborate gable, but is surpassed in magnificence by its southern counterpart, which juxtaposes huge Renaissance oriels, friezes of animals and foliage, and statues of saints and knights, along with an aged crone and a yokel. The latter are placed above the doorway leading to the vaulted cellars of the Piwnica Świdnicka, a tavern since the thirteenth century, which is named after the famous beer of the nearby town of Świdnica.

Nowadays the Town Hall functions as the city's Historical Museum, though the exhibits are overshadowed by their setting, one of the best preserved interiors of a medieval civic building to be found anywhere in Europe. On the ground floor are two surviving parts of the original thirteenth-century structure — the Burghers' Hall, which served as a covered market as well as the venue for important public meetings, and the Bailiff's Room, the office and courtroom of the local governor. Upstairs are the triple-aisled Knights' Hall, where the big civic receptions were held, the Strong Room, which served as the customs house and treasury, and the Princes' Room, which was built as a chapel but was later used as a meeting place by the rulers of Silesia's tiny principalities.

Among the cluster of modern buildings in the built-up centre of the square is Jerzy Grotowski's famous Laboratory Theatre, which for more than two decades was one of the world's foremost stages for experimental drama. The company was dissolved following its founder's emigration to Italy in 1982, and the tiny studio theatre is now used, generally once a week, for performances in his mode by visiting actors.

On the western side of the Rynek is a colourful group of mansions. The Griffin House at no.2 is one of several in the Flemish Renaissance style, while the Mannerist Waza Court at no.5, now a top hotel, is supposedly where King Zygmunt Waza stayed during secret negotiations for his dynastic marriage to Anna von Habsburg. Next door at no.6 is the House of the Golden Sun, with a Baroque façade and a suite of Renaissance interiors which now house the Museum of the Art of Medal Making.

At the south-west corner of the Rynek is a much smaller square, plac Solny, once the salt market, but now the haunt of flower sellers. Most of its buildings are nineteenth-century, with the former Stock Exchange on the south side being the most prominent. Off the north-west corner of the Rynek are two curious Baroque houses known as Jaś i Małgosia, linked by a gateway giving access to the close of St Elizabeth. The latter is the most beautiful of the brick Gothic churches that are so characteristic of the city, and its 295ft (90m) tower is the dominant feature of its skyline. Unfortunately, the main body of the church was burnt out under suspicious circumstances in 1976, and has as yet received only a partial restoration.

Facing the inner ring road just to the west is the only other surviving block of old burghers' houses. Across the road from them and down ul. Cieszyńskiego is the Arsenal, which dates back to the sixteenth century but was considerably altered by the Prussians a couple of hundred years later. Most of it is in a dilapidated state, but a section has been restored to house a branch of the Historical Museum. On the next street to the south, ul. Mikołaja, is the Gothic church of St Barbara, now the property of Russian Orthodox exiles from Lwów. It is accessible during the sung services on Saturday evenings and Sunday mornings; at other times, only the adjoining chapel is kept open.

A couple of blocks further south is the beginning of the maze-like former Jewish quarter, whose inhabitants fled or were driven from their tenements during the Third Reich and never returned. Discreetly tucked away on a tiny square halfway down an alley is the synagogue, a handsome neo-Classical building which has unfortunately been allowed to lapse into a terrible state of decay.

Immediately to the east is a quarter built in imitation of the grand neo-Classicism of the Prussian capital, Berlin. Indeed it was Carl Gotthard Langhans, one of Frederick the Great's court architects and the man responsible for the famous Brandenburg Gate, who built the palace on the northern side of ul. Kazimierza Wielkiego which now serves as the New University Library. He was also partly responsible for the Royal Palace on the opposite side of the street, which houses the Archaeology Museum, a survey of the prehistory of the region, and the entertaining Ethnographical Museum.

Further east, facing ul. Świdnicka, is the soaring Gothic church of St Dorothy. It is also known as the 'Church of Reconciliation' in honour of its foundation in 1351 by Charles IV, King of Bohemia and the future Holy Roman Emperor, as a thank-offering for the successful conclusion of negotiations with hisz Polish counterpart, Kazimierz the Great. Ironically, these confirmed Bohemia's dominion over Silesia, the trade-off being a renunciation of the former's claim to Poland. Unlike most of Wrocław's brick churches, this stayed in Catholic hands at the Reformation, serving as a Franciscan monastery. Its interior was whitewashed and littered with gigantic altars in the Baroque period, giving it a very different appearance from its counterparts, which still bear the hallmarks of having experienced four centuries of Protestant sobriety.

Behind St Dorothy's stands the Opera House, built in the late 1830s by Carl Ferdinand Langhans in a faithful continuation of his father's by then outmoded neo-Classical style. Facing it is another example of fourteenth-century Gothic, the church of Corpus Christi, which is distinguished by the delicate brickwork of its façade porch and gable, and by the elaborate interior vaulting.

A block east of the Rynek, at the junction of ul. Szewska and ul. Oławks, is a seminal example of German Expressionist architecture of the 1920s, the former Petersdorff store by Erich Mendelsohn. This concrete and glass building, the only one of several large department stores designed by the architect to have escaped modernisation, relies for its effect on the interplay between the projecting cylinder on the corner with the bold horizontals of the main street fronts.

The twin-towered St Mary Magdalene, a block to the north, is another illustration of the diversity of the brick churches built in the city during the fourteenth century: this one is unusual in having flying buttresses, giving it a slight Gallic accent. Funeral plaques and epitaphs are encrusted on its exterior, while the south side has a twelfth-century stone portal brought from the demolished abbey of Ołbin in the north of Wrocław. At the opposite side of the church is a separate entrance to a beautiful Gothic chapel, now a commercial art gallery.

Two blocks to the east is plac Dominikański, a vast open space on the site of a built-up area which was totally destroyed in World War II. At its northern end is the Dominican monastery, whose thirteenth-century church of St Adalbert is embellished with several lavish Gothic and Baroque chapels. Further east, the huge former Bernardine monastery stands in splendid isolation: there is a fine view of it from the nearby park. The last important example of Gothic brickwork in the city, the monastery was begun in the mid-fifteenth century and finished only a few years before the Reformation, whereupon it was dissolved and its barn-like church taken over for Protestant parish use. Severely damaged during the war, the church and cloisters have been reconstructed to house the Museum of Architecture. This offers a documentary record, using sculptural fragments and old photos, of the historic buildings in the city which perished in the war and have not been rebuilt. A little further along is the main Post Office building, which also houses the Museum of Posts and Telecommunications. It features two old mail coaches, historic equipment and a collection of stamps from the period of the Russian-controlled Kingdom of Poland.

Wrocław's most popular tourist attraction, the Panorama of the Battle of Racławice, is housed in a specially-designed rotunda in the park by the Bernardine monastery. This huge painting, 394ft (120m) long and 49ft (15m) high, was commissioned in 1894 to celebrate the stunning victory of Tadeusz Kościuszko's militia of scythe-bearing peasants over the Russian army at the village of Racławice between Cracow and Kielce. Although the third and final Partition of Poland, which wiped it off the map altogether, occurred the year after the battle, it was nonetheless viewed a century later by patriots of the still-subdued nation as a supreme example of patriotic will which warranted a fitting memorial. The painting was completed in just 9 months by Wojciech Kossak, one of Poland's finest artists, and Jan Styka, with help from seven other painters for the execution of specialist details. It was put on view in Lwów, then under the rule of Austria, the only one of the Partitioning powers which permitted nationalist propaganda of this kind, and remained there until it was damaged by a bomb in 1944. Wrocław, as the cultural heir to Lwów, then inherited it, but, because of its sensitive subject matter, was forced to keep it in storage until the advent of Solidarity in the 1980s enabled it to be put back on show. Visits, which are made in groups, must be booked in advance; headphones with English-language cassettes explaining all the details of the painting are available.

Across the park is the National Museum, whose entrance hallway contains some important examples of Silesian medieval sculpture, including the tympanum depicting the Dormition of the Virgin from the portal of the church of St Mary Magdalene, and the tombs of Dukes Henryk the Pious and Henryk the Righteous, the latter being one of the earliest funerary monuments to incorporate the subsequently popular motif of a group of weeping mourners. On the first floor are polychrome wood sculptures of the same era, including many examples of the *Beautiful Madonnas* characteristic of Central Europe, and foreign paintings from the fifteenth to nineteenth centuries. The top floor is devoted to Polish painting, though it also includes the prodigiously detailed *Entry of Chancellor Jerzy Ossoliński into Rome in 1633* by Bernardo Bellotto, the Venetian view painter who made such a valuable documentary record of eighteenth-century Warsaw. Other highlights are an unfinished historical blockbuster by Jan Matejko, *The Vows of King Jan Kazimierz Waza*, which is set in Lwów Cathedral; Piotr Michałowski's *Napoleon on Horseback*; and Jacek Malczewski's *Fatherland Triptych*.

From the National Museum, there is an enjoyable walk to be had to the west along the bank of the River Odra. This offers a series of views of the islands, churches and bridges of the ecclesiastical district across the water, and leads in a few minutes to the University quarter, a triangular-shaped area bounded by ul. Universytecka and ul. Grodzka.

Along the northern side of the former are three religious houses. First is St Vincent, which was founded as a Franciscan monastery by Henryk the Pious not long before his death at the Battle of Legnica. The Gothic church, one of the city's grandest, was severely damaged in the war and is not yet fully restored, but the Baroque monastic buildings overlooking the Odra are used by the university's Department of Philology. Henryk also founded the Ursuline Convent alongside, which served as the mausoleum of the Piasts who ruled the city during its period as an independent duchy. Last in the row is the fourteenth-century church of St Matthew, containing the tomb and memorial portrait of the seventeenth-century mystic poet and hymnodist Johann Scheffler, better known by his pseudonym of Angelus Silesius ('the Silesian Angel'). Facing the south side of the church is the Renaissance palace of the Opole Piasts, now the Faculty of Medicine, while across ul. Szewska is the Baroque residence of their cousins from Brzeg-Legnica, now the Institute of History.

Behind St Matthew's is the domed Ossoliński Library, which was originally built as a hospital by the Burgundian-born Jean Baptiste Mathey, one of the leading Baroque architects of Prague. The library collections are another legacy from Lwów, where they were assembled by the aristocratic family whose name they still bear; among the many treasures is the original manuscript of the Polish national epic, Adam Mickiewicz's *Pan Tadeusz*. Immediately to the west is the elongated plac Uniwersytecki. On its southern side is a dignified eighteenth-century palace, Dom Steffensa, currently home to the Institute of Anthropology. Opposite is the late seventeenth-century church of the Holy Name of Jesus, a typical example of the Counter-Reformation Baroque of the Habsburg lands. Inside, the ceiling is covered with a huge allegorical fresco of the cult to which the church is dedicated, the work of the leading Austrian decorative painter of the period, Johann Michael Rottmayr.

Adjoining the church is the 561ft (171m) long façade of the Collegium Maximum of the University, founded in 1702 by the Habsburg Emperor Leopold I, but not built until more than a quarter of a century later. The wide entrance portal bears a balcony adorned with statues symbolising various academic disciplines and attributes. A staircase adorned with frescos by Felix Anton Scheffler leads up to the main assembly hall or Aula, a spectacular Baroque interior fusing the arts of architecture, painting, sculpture and ornament. The huge illusionistic ceiling frescos by Christoph

Handke show the Apotheosis of Divine and Worldly Wisdom, and the University being entrusted to the care of Christ and the Virgin Mary. There are also portraits of the leading dignitaries involved in the founding of the University, trompe l'oeil likenesses of the great scholars of the past, and a statue of the founder, shown armed, bejewelled and crowned with a laurel.

From the eastern end of the University quarter, Most Piaskowy leads to the sandbank of Wyspa Piasek, which has a cluster of historic buildings crammed together in the centre. On the right-hand side is the University Library, occupying a former Augustinian monastery which also served as the Nazi military headquarters. Beyond is the fourteenth-century hall church of St Mary of the Sands, whose majestic interior features the most beautiful example of what is known as the Piast vault, an asymmetrical tripartite rib design peculiar to Lower Silesia. In the south aisle is the Romanesque tympanum from the previous church on the site, illustrating the dedication by its donor, Maria Włast. Across the road is the Baroque church of St Anne, now used by an Orthodox congregation.

Two elegant little painted bridges, Młyński and Most Tumski, connect Wyspa Piasek with the larger island of Ostrów Tumski, the site of the original Slav settlement. It is now the episcopal quarter, and has no fewer than five medieval churches. Just beyond Most Tumski is the fifteenth-century St Peter and St Paul, behind which is the hexagonal St Mark of a couple of centuries earlier. These are overshadowed by the much larger Holy Cross and St Bartholomew, which is really two churches, one on top of the other, the lower being too spacious and extensive to be regarded merely as a crypt. This double church was founded in 1288 by Duke Henryk the Righteous as his own mausoleum, but his tomb has now been removed to the National Museum. An elaborate Baroque monument to St Jan Nepomuk, with bas-reliefs illustrating his life, stands in the square outside.

Further east is the twin-towered cathedral, the main body of which was restored to its thirteenth-century form following war damage. It is entered via a richly carved portal, though only a few of the sculptures are originals, the others being nineteenth-century pastiches. Behind the high altar are three remarkable chapels. On the south side is St Elizabeth's chapel, with an integrated programme of architecture, frescos and sculptures created in the late seventeenth century by Italian followers of Bernini. In the middle is the Gothic Lady chapel, with the Renaissance funerary plaque of Bishop Jan Roth cast by the leading bronze founder of the day, Peter Vischer of Nuremberg. To the north is the Corpus Christi chapel, a perfectly proportioned and subtly decorated Baroque gem, built from 1716 to 1724 by the Viennese court architect, Johann Bernhard Fischer von Erlach.

Opposite the northern side of the cathedral is the tiny early thirteenth-century church of St Giles, the only one in the city to have escaped destruction by the Mongols, and still preserving some finely patterned brickwork. Down ul. Kanonia is the Archdiocesan Museum, a somewhat ramshackle collection of sacred artefacts. From the same street, there is access to the Botanical Gardens. Ul. Szczytnicka leads eastwards to plac

Grunwaldzki, which was converted into an airstrip in 1945 to allow the defeated Nazi leaders of to escape. At its southern end is the most famous of the city's bridges, Most Grundwaldzki, a masterly piece of engineering from 1910.

East of Ostrów Tumski is the city's most popular area of greenery, Park Szczytnicki. Its focal point is the Hala Ludowa, a huge hall built in 1913 by the municipal architect Max Berg to celebrate the centenary of the liberation of the city from Napoleon; this is still used for exhibitions, sporting events and other spectaculars. The unsupported dome has a diameter of 426ft (130m), and is an audacious piece of engineering even by present-day standards. Around the Hala Ludowa are a number of colonnaded pavilions by Berg's teacher Hans Poelzig, who made the city a driving force in the Deutscher Werkbund, the German equivalent of the Arts and Crafts Movement.

Also in the park is the Cubist-style Kindergarten, the only building by Le Corbusier in Eastern Europe. Together with the huge steel needle beside the hall, it is a legacy of the Exhibition of the Regained Territories, held in 1948. Other features of the park are a sixteenth-century wooden church brought from Kędzierzyn in Upper Silesia, an amphitheatre, a Japanese garden and pagoda, an artificial lake, and hundreds of different trees and shrubs, including oaks which are more than 600 years old. Across the road lie the Zoological Gardens, the largest in Poland.

Excursions from Wrocław

Wrocław is well placed for out-of-town trips, with enticing destinations lying within easy reach in all directions. Those described in this section are all easily manageable targets for excursions of a day or less, whether by car or public transport.

Oława, 17 miles (27km) south, was the birthplace of Maria Clementina Sobieska, granddaughter of King Jan Sobieski, wife of James, the 'Old Pretender' to the British throne, and mother of Bonnie Prince Charlie. Although badly damaged in the last war, there are still a few monuments of note. The neo-Classical Town Hall on the Rynek was designed by the great Berlin architect Karl Friedrich Schinkel, and retains the Baroque clock tower, complete with mechanical figures, of its predecessor. On the southwest corner of the square is the church of St Mary, which preserves its early Gothic chancel, though the rest of the building was remodelled in the sixteenth century in accordance with the changed needs of Protestant worship. North of the Rynek are the Baroque palace, a secondary residence of the Dukes of Brzeg-Legnica, and Schinkel's church of St Peter and St Paul.

A further 8 miles (13km) along the main road and rail lines south is **Brzeg**. Originally a fishing village on the bank (the derivation of its name) of the Odra, from 1311 it was the joint capital with Legnica of one of the Piast duchies. This status was retained until 1675 when the dynasty, which had played a prominent role throughout Poland's entire recorded history, finally died out.

The palace, located in tranquil isolation close to the river and west of the town centre, is among the finest in the country. From the medieval castle which preceded it there remain the chapel of St Hedwig's, which served as the mausoleum of the local Piasts, and the Lwów Tower. Most of the rest of the fabric dates back to the 1530s, and is the work of a team of Italian masons. It became something of a prototype design for an entire generation of Renaissance palaces in Poland, Bohemia, northern Germany and Sweden. Entry is via an extravagant gateway modelled on Albrecht Dürer's famous woodcut of a triumphal arch in honour of Emperor Maximilian. This features portraits of Duke George II and his wife, Barbara von Brandenburg, coats-of-arms, and two tiers of busts tracing the duke's genealogy.

The lofty three-storey courtyard differs from its Italian models in being designed to catch as much sunlight as possible. Although smaller than its royal counterpart in Cracow, it is more richly decorated, with the heraldic motif continued on the interior gate and antique-style medallions to the sides of the arcades. A suite of chambers on the second floor house the Museum of the Silesian Piasts. Exhibits include an impressive array of devotional sculptures, and a number of canvases by Silesia's greatest painter, Michael Willmann, including a powerful series of *The Four Doctors of the Church*.

Across from the palace is the Piast college, which was built some 30 years later. It has suffered far more from the ravages of time, but once more a school is functioning behind the great portal, in which Duke George's arms are joined by those of his wife's family. Directly opposite is the former Jesuit church of the Holy Cross, which dates back to the turn of the eighteenth century. Sober enough from the outside, its single interior space is encrusted with Rococo decorations.

Back towards the centre is the Town Hall, which belongs to the same architectural school as the palace, and again is an adaptation of an older structure, from which the tall belfry survives. It consists of two long parallel buildings, each terminating in a tower crowned by a bulbous Baroque steeple, joined together by the resplendent galleried façade. Further east is the Rynek, centred on the fourteenth-century hall church of St Nicholas. In the nineteenth century, the towers were heightened, a fact betrayed by the different colour of the bricks used in the upper sections. Inside is a varied array of memorial plaques of prominent local families.

West of Wrocław, the flatness of the Lower Silesian Plain is abruptly broken after about 19 miles (30km) by an isolated outcrop of rocks with two peaks, the higher of which is known as **Ślęża** (718m). One of the most enigmatic sites in Poland, it was used for pagan worship in Celtic times, and was later settled by the Slav tribe after whom the mountain and Silesia itself are named.

Ślęża is normally approached from the village of **Sobótka** to the north. The Regional Museum, housed in a Renaissance mansion south of the

Rynek, contains some notable archaeological finds. Outside the church of St Anne stands one of several curious ancient sculptures to be seen in the area; this consists of one stone placed across another, earning it the nickname of 'The Mushroom'. On the way up Ślęża is a large and voluptuous statue of a woman with a fish, while the summit has a carved lion. Exactly what these carvings symbolise remains a mystery: some certainly post-date the Christianisation of the area, but may nevertheless pertain to pagan rites. Five separate trails, some of them very stony, traverse the hillsides. A bit over an hour is the normal time needed for walking the most popular stretch, a direct ascent from Sobótka to the top of Ślęża by the route marked with yellow signs. The summit is spoiled by a number of ugly buildings including the inevitable television tower, while the neo-Gothic chapel is a poor substitute for the castle and Augustinian monastery which once stood on the spot. Ample compensation, however, comes with one of the most extensive panoramic views in Silesia.

Oleśnica, 19 miles (30km) east of Wrocław, was once the capital of a tiny Silesian duchy, and the palace still completely dominates the town. Originally a fourteenth-century fortress, it was transformed a couple of hundred years later into a magnificent residence in the German Renaissance style for a member of the Bohemian royal family. The elaborate gateway is carved with coats of arms, while the grandiose courtyard makes for a fascinating contrast with its Italianate counterpart in Brzeg. Most of the building is now used as offices, but there is also a small archaeological museum.

The Gothic parish church is linked to the castle by means of a covered archway, a legacy of its period as the ducal chapel; another reminder of this function comes in the grandiose tombs housed in the chancel. Oleśnica was a bastion of the Reformation and, although the church has now been returned to the Catholics, its arrangement of wooden galleries is a legacy of the Protestant emphasis on preaching. Extensive sections of the town walls survive, including an impressive gateway.

Trzebnica, 15 miles (24km) north of Wrocław, clusters round the Cistercian convent established in 1202 by Duke Henryk the Bearded and his wife, the German princess St Hedwig, who spent her widowhood in the convent, though she never took holy orders. Originally built in the Transitional style between Romanesque and Gothic, it was progressively remodelled and now has a predominantly Baroque appearance. The two portals are rare survivals of the medieval building; that on the façade, with a carving of King David playing the harp to Bathsheba and a maidservant, is of outstanding quality. Inside the church, the main feature is the Gothic St Hedwig's chapel to the right of the choir, added immediately after her canonisation in 1267. Her simple marble and alabaster sepulchral slab was incorporated in 1680 into a grandiose tomb lined with figures of mourners. At the same time, a considerably less ostentatious memorial to her husband was placed in the choir, its entrance guarded by statues of St Hedwig and her even more celebrated niece, St Elizabeth of Hungary.

North of Trzebnica lies a lake district with several nature reserves, centred on the two small towns of **Żmigród** and **Milicz**, which both lie in the valley of the Barycza, a tributary of the Odra. Until 1991, this entire region was traversed by Poland's best-known narrow-gauge railway; economic circumstances forced its closure, though there are hopes that it will be possible to revive it for excursion services. Milicz itself has a few sights of note. East of the centre is the half-timbered Church of Grace, one of several the Protestants were allowed to build in Silesia, following a concession forced on the Habsburg emperor in 1709. To the south-west of town is a neo-Classical palace, built at the very end of the eighteenth century for the local nobleman Joachim Karl von Maltzen, Prussia's London envoy. Its English-style park is the oldest of its type in Silesia.

One of Europe's most important bird reserves lies east of Milicz. Over 170 different water and moorland species breed there, while an even larger number use it as a stop-off point on their migratory path. Black and white storks, swans, herons, seagulls, cranes, cormorants and great crested grebes are among the species most likely to be seen, apart from the inevitable ducks and geese, while sea eagles are present for the entire winter. Autumn, as the birds prepare for migration, is by far the best season for a visit: they are less timid at this time and more likely to be found in groups and in the open countryside. There are marked trails throughout the area, and an observation tower at the Joanna Hill (Wzgórze Joanny) south of Milicz. Other parts of this lake district are forest reserves, in some of which wild boar and both red and fallow deer roam freely, though the marshy soil often means that stretches of this countryside are impassable.

Set just back from the Odra, about 34 miles (55km) downstream from Wrocław, the isolated village of **Lubiąż** stands in the shadow of one of the largest and most impressive monastic complexes in Central Europe. Founded by the Benedictines in the first half of the twelfth century, it was taken over by the Cistercians a generation later. Some medieval features are still evident, but are engulfed by the palatial Baroque buildings erected during a boom period following the disastrous Thirty Years War. The abbey's prosperity was short-lived, however: decline began as soon as Silesia came under Prussian rule in 1740, and continued apace until secularisation in 1810. Since then, the complex has served as a mental hospital, stud farm, munitions factory, labour camp and storehouse, in the process drifting into a state of semi-dereliction. After the fall of Communism, a foundation was established with the hope of attracting enough foreign capital to turn it into an international conference centre and hotel.

Pending a full restoration, the main attraction is the awesome exterior, and in particular the 223m long façade, whose uniformity is interrupted only by the twin towers of the church. Most of the latter's furnishings were removed during World War II, and a few small frescoes on the cupola of scenes from the lives of St Benedict and St Bernard are all that remain of the extensive decorative scheme by Michael Willmann, who lived in the monastery for the last four decades of his life. A few chambers in the north wing are open as a museum; these include the summer refectory, an elegant Baroque hall with pristine white stucco work and illusionist ceiling frescoes. Also worth a look is the village's parish church, St Valentine, likewise Baroque and with an altarpiece by Willmann, *St Valentine Healing the Sick*.

Northern Silesia

Northern Silesia is little visited by foreigners, and has few obvious sights. However, it does contain a number of historic towns which are, for very different reasons, well worth visiting.

The best-known of these is **Legnica**, some 43 miles (70km) west of Wrocław, whose name is primarily associated with the battle of 1241 which saw the invading Mongol hordes rout the combined Polish and Silesian army commanded by Duke Henryk the Pious. Oddly enough, the town was an immediate beneficiary of this disastrous defeat, becoming the capital of one of the three separate duchies into which Silesia was divided following Henryk's death in action. It remained a ducal seat until the last of the Piasts died in 1675, though latterly its role as their main residence was usurped by Brzeg, and it has ranked among the province's largest towns to this day.

At the northern end of the centre is the enormous castle, which is now occupied by administrative offices. Most of the structure is a Romantic era confection designed by the great Berlin architect Karl Friedrich Schinkel. However, it retains two towers from the medieval defensive fortress, plus the gateway in the form of a triumphal arch from the Renaissance palace which succeeded it. Outside is the early fifteenth-century Głogów Gate, one of only two surviving parts of the city wall.

To the south-west lies a well-preserved Baroque quarter. On the right are the Jesuit buildings, with the college and the church of St John united in a single, sweeping façade. Protruding from the eastern side of the latter is the brick Gothic presbytery of the Franciscan monastery which formerly occupied the spot. It owes its survival to its function as the Piast mausoleum, and has several sarcophagi on view inside, along with Baroque frescos illustrating the history of Poland and Silesia under the dynasty.

Across the road is the Regional Museum, housed in the former town mansion of the monastery of Lubiąż. Another fine palace of the same epoch, the Rycerska Academy, can be found in the street immediately behind, where the late fourteenth-century Chojnów Tower and a small section of the medieval wall can also be seen.

Beyond is the elongated Rynek, which has unfortunately lost much of its character as the result of the construction of hideous post-war blocks of flats. However, eight arcaded Renaissance houses, all brightly coloured and some decorated with graffiti, survive in the middle of the square. To their rear are the Baroque Town Hall and the nineteenth-century theatre, built in imitation of a Florentine Renaissance palace. There is also a fine but blackened eighteenth-century fountain dedicated to Neptune.

The far end of the square is closed by the twin-towered brick church of St Peter and St Paul, whose exterior was given a romanticised neo-Gothic remodelling. Fortunately, the fourteenth-century carved portals were retained, as was the architecture of the interior, whose furnishings include a late thirteenth-century font with bronze bas-reliefs, a Renaissance pulpit and a Baroque high altar. A couple of blocks to the north is another brick Gothic church, this time characterised by a gaunt, fortress-like exterior. Notwithstanding its dedication to Our Lady, it is still the place of worship of the rump of the town's once dominant Protestant community.

The actual site of the great battle with the Mongols lies 6 miles (9km) south-east of the city and is now occupied by the village of **Legnickie Pole**. According to tradition, Henryk the Pious was decapitated by the enemy and his mother, St Hedwig, was only able to identify his body because of his six-toed feet. A church was erected on the spot where the corpse was found, and in time became a Benedictine monastery, popularly but implausibly said to be the rather rustic Gothic building, which is more likely to be its successor, in the centre of the village. A Protestant parish for four centuries, the church has been secularised to house the Museum of the Battle of Legnica, which includes diagrams and mock-ups of the conflict and a copy of the tomb of Henryk the Pious, the original of which is in the National Museum in Wrocław.

The Benedictines, who had been evicted during the Reformation, returned to Legnickie Pole in the early eighteenth century and constructed a new abbey directly opposite. This was designed and built by Kilian Ignaz Dientzenhofer, architect of many of the greatest Baroque buildings of Prague, and illustrates his characteristic preference for varied geometric shapes and the interplay of concave and convex surfaces. The interior of the church, an oval nave plus an elongated apse, is exceptionally bright, an effect achieved partly by the white walls and partly by the provision of large windows designed to throw as much sunlight as possible on the altars and statues. Covering the vault are frescos by one of the leading decorative artists of the day, the Bavarian Cosmos Damian Asam. Above the organ gallery is a scene showing the Mongols, having hoisted Henryk's head on a stake, celebrating their victory, while the duke's mother and wife mourn over his severed body.

Głogów, 37 miles (60km) north of Legnica, is a former ducal capital nowadays mainly notable for its shock value. In 1945, the retreating Nazis turned it into fortress, which was completely destroyed by the Red Army. The historic centre has never been rebuilt and stands as an overgrown wasteland, encircled by the modern town that has sprung up to replace it. An abortive attempt was made to patch up the brick Gothic parish church, but clearly it was too badly damaged for full restoration. However, the Jesuit college, setting of E.T.A. Hoffmann's macabre short story, the cryptically titled *The Jesuit Chapel at G*, managed to survive, rising in defiance above the desolation. Inside, a photographic exhibition provides a poignant documentary record of the appearance of the town before its destruction.

In contrast, **Zielona Góra**, a further 37 miles (60km) north-west, suffered hardly any wartime damage. Its entire central area is also virtually free of any intrusive post-war development, and stands today as a remarkable patchwork of the varied architectural styles of turn-of-the-century Germany, with stolidly Historicist buildings standing alongside exuberant products of Jugendstil, the German version of Art Nouveau. The town has another, rather esoteric claim to fame, being the only place in Poland where wine is produced. This tradition is celebrated in a festival held each September.

A few older landmarks survive, including a couple of towers from the fifteenth-century ramparts, the Gothic church of St Hedwig and the much-remodelled Renaissance Town Hall in the centre of the Rynek. Most imposing of all is the parish church, an eighteenth-century example of the Silesian penchant for half-timbered ecclesiastical buildings. North-east of the centre, on al. Niepodległości, is the Regional Museum, which features a large collection of experimental sculptures by Marian Kruczek and examples of Jugendstil decorative art. Other departments of the museum are spread among various outlying villages. Of these, the most worthwhile is the *Ethnographic Park* at **Ochla**, 3 miles (7km) to the south, which reassembles a score of rural buildings from northern Silesia and western Great Poland.

Some 25 miles (40km) west of Głogów and 31 miles (50km) south-west of Zielona Góra is another old ducal capital, **Żagań**. Of its half-dozen historic churches, the finest is St Mary, which was formerly part of an Augustinian monastery. A high gabled Gothic hall church by origin, its interior, which has a Renaissance altar dedicated to the Holy Trinity, was completely remodelled in Baroque style. Further east is the first of two large market squares, the Stary Rynek, lined with a number of sixteenth- and seventeenth-century burghers' mansions, and the Gothic Town Hall, to which a Florentine-style loggia was appended in the nineteenth century. Beyond is the larger Nowy Rynek, with the Jesuit church on the north side.

Set in a park just to the south is the palace, which was commissioned in honour of the conferral of the duchy on Alfred von Wallenstein, the commander of the Imperial forces in the Thirty Tears' War. Most of it, however, was not built until later in the seventeenth century, and adopts a showy Italianate Baroque manner. It was badly desecrated during World War II, when its rich interiors were destroyed, and is now used as a cultural centre.

On ul. Ilwiańska in the suburb of Stary Żagań is the site of the notorious Nazi prisoner-of-war camp, Stalag VIIIC, now designated the Museum of Martyrology. Some 200,000 prisoners from all over the world, most of them officers, were incarcerated there; the film *The Great Escape* is based on a true episode in its history. A monument commemorates those who were murdered, while an exhibition room displays prisoners' beds along with samples of their hair, glasses, clothes and documents, plus photographs and a plastic model of how the camp once looked.

The Karkonosze

The 186 mile (300km) long Sudeten (or Sudety) mountains form a natural barrier between Silesia and Bohemia. Within the range are two of Poland's main holiday areas, the more northerly being the **Karkonosze**, the highest part of the chain. This is still better-known by its German name of Riesengebirge or 'Giants' Mountains': until passing to Poland in 1945 it ranked alongside the Black Forest and the Alps as Germany's most visited scenic region. Its popularity dates back to the turn of the nineteenth century, when it served as a potent inspiration to the German Romantics, who were attracted by the dramatic changes wrought by its volatile climate. Caspar David Friedrich, the movement's greatest painter, bequeathed many haunting images of the range set beneath luridly coloured skies with summits shrouded in mist.

The predominantly granite Karkonosze range rises abruptly in Silesia, but rather more gently in Bohemia. Its lower slopes are quite heavily forested, with fir, beech, birch and pine. At around 3,610ft (1,100m), these give way to dwarf mountain pines plus Alpine plants, some of them imported. Above 4,430ft (1,350m), there are no more trees, giving the summits an unusually stark appearance for this part of Europe. While primarily of interest for its hiking possibilities, there are also winter sports facilities, plus a smattering of historical monuments.

Jelenia Góra, which lies 37 miles (60km) south-west of Legnica, is the gateway to the area. Although its name means 'Deer Mountain', it has been a major industrial centre for the past five centuries, initially in the fields of glass and iron production, with high quality textiles, which were widely exported, taking over as the mainstay of the local economy in the seventeenth century.

The picturesque main square, plac Ratuszowy, is lined with an impressive series of late Renaissance, Baroque and neo-Classical houses. Despite their varied architectural styles, they form an unusually cohert group, all having whitewashed walls and an arcaded front at street level, providing welcome protection against the harsh winter climate in these parts. Unusually, retailing plays only a minor role in the life of the square: many of the premises are used as cafés and restaurants at ground floor level, while the upper storeys are subdivided into flats. Occupying the familiar central position on the square is the large mid-eighteenth century Town Hall, whose tower is one of the dominant features of the skyline.

To the north-east of the square rises the slender belfry of the Gothic parish church of St Erasmus and St Pancras. Epitaphs to leading local families adorn the outer walls of the church, while inside are abundant Renaissance and Baroque furnishings. Yet another prominent tower can be seen along ul. 1 Maja, the main shopping street to the east: originally part of the sixteenth-century fortifications, it was re-utilised a couple of hundred years later as the belfry of St Anne's chapel. The only other survivor of the town wall is yet another tower, located west of plac Ratuszowy.

Further down ul. 1 Maja is the Baroque chapel of Our Lady, now the property of an Orthodox congregation. At the end of the street, enclosed in a walled park-like cemetery, is another Baroque church, Holy Cross, built in the early eighteenth century by a Swedish architect, Martin Franze, on the model of St Catherine's in Stockholm. Though sober from the outside, the double galleried interior is richly decorated with trompe l'oeil frescos.

Set just below the wooded Kościuszko Hill to the south of the Old Town is the Regional Museum. Apart from changing temporary exhibitions, the display space is mostly given over to the history of glass from antiquity to the present. Due emphasis on local examples, with a particularly impressive twentieth-century section and a number of folk paintings on glass.

The best local viewpoint is the wooded hill to the west of town named after Bolesław the Wrymouth, the Polish king who is accredited as being the founder Jelenia Góra by dint of having established a fortress on this very spot. On the summit is an observation tower, freely accessible at all times, which commands a sweeping panorama of the town and the surrounding countryside.

Now officially part of the Jelenia Góra municipality, the old spa town of **Cieplice Śląskie-Zdrój** lies 5 miles (8km) to the south-west. The warm sulphur springs have attracted visitors in search of rest and recuperation for the past two centuries, and the heart of the resort is the Spa Park, whose delightful neo-Classical theatre regularly features concerts by its own resident orchestra and singers. On the southern side of the River Podgóra is another extensive area of greenery, the Norwegian Park. Within it is the Ornithological Museum, which has stuffed birds from around the world, with emphasis on local examples. Cieplice's broad main street is designated as a square, plac Piatowski. Its principal building is the large eighteenth-century Schaffgotsch Palace, named after the German family which formerly owned much of the town. There are also two Baroque parish churches, one for the Catholics, the other for the Protestants. Near the former is the pump room, where waters from four of the local springs can be sampled.

A further 3 miles (5km) south, still within the Jelenia Góra boundaries, is **Sobieszów**. Once again, there are two Baroque parish churches, both located off the main road: that built for the Protestants is appropriately plain in its architecture, while its Catholic counterpart is exuberantly decorated inside. In an isolated location on the south-eastern outskirts of the village is the Karkonosze National Park Museum, with displays on its geology, flora and fauna.

From there, the red and black trails offer a choice of ascents to Chojnik Castle, which sits atop the wooded hill of the same name. Founded in the mid-fourteenth century, the castle is celebrated in legend as the home of a beautiful man-hating princess who insisted that any suitor had to travel through a treacherous ravine in order to win her hand. Many perished in the attempt: when one finally succeeded, the princess chose to jump into the ravine herself in preference to marriage. The castle was badly damaged in 1675, not long after the addition of its drawbridge and the Renaissance ornamentation on top of the walls. Yet, despite its ruined state, enough remains to give a good illustration of the layout of the medieval feudal stronghold it once was. Part of it has been converted to serve as a basic hotel and restaurant, while the round Hunger Tower commands a wonderful view.

At the very edge of the Karkonosze, just south of Sobieszów but beyond the Jelenia Góra municipal area, is the village of **Jagniątków**, once home of the German novelist and playwright Gerhart Hauptmann, winner of the 1912 Nobel Prize for Literature. Having fallen foul of the Nazis he formerly supported, Hauptmann spent his last years in this isolated corner of his native province, staying on even after it came under Polish rule in 1945. The complicated psychological novels he wrote there have worn less well than his earlier naturalistic works, notably his drama of Silesian industrial life, *The Weavers*, which pioneered the use of a collective rather than an individual hero. Hauptmann's house, a spectacular Jugendstil mansion with a Great Hall lined with giant murals, is now a convalescent home for child victims of the industrial pollution of the Katowice conurbation. Because of this, plans to convert it into a museum have had to be forestalled, though visitors are free to go in to see the memorial room, which contains first editions of his most important works.

The upper reaches of the mountains have been designated as the **Karkonosze National Park** (Karkonoski Park Narodowy). Serious hikers can traverse the main ridge by following the entire length of the red trail, which closely hugs the frontier in covering all the main summits in the range. This is a strenuous day's walk, albeit one that can be facilitated by using the chair lifts at either end; it can be tackled more comfortably in 2 days by breaking for the night at one of the refuges along the way. Most visitors, however, make shorter trips into the mountains from a base in one or other of the Karkonosze's two main resorts, which are scattered communities located just outside the park boundaries at either end of the range.

Of these, **Szklarska Poręba** lies below Szrenica (4,467ft/1,362m) and just west of a major road crossing into the Czech Republic. The last section of the 11 miles (18km) journey from Jelenia Góra is among the most picturesque parts of the Karkonosze, with the road following the course of the Kamienna, one of the main streams rising in the mountains, which is joined along this short stretch by several tributaries. One of these, the Szklarka, forms a waterfall just before it joins the Kamienna. This favourite beauty spot is well signposted, and it can be reached in a few minutes from the car park and bus stop by the main road, at a point usually thronged with souvenir sellers.

The Kamienna splices Szklarska Poręba in two, with the main streets in the valley and the rest of the town rising high into the hills on either side. It is well worth following the stream all the way through the built-up part of the resort, as there follows another extremely picturesque stretch, featuring some spectacular rock formations, the Kruce Skalny, towering above the southern bank. Beyond, at the extreme western edge of town, is the Huty Julia, a celebrated glassworks, whose nineteenth-century core can be visited by guided tour on weekday mornings. From there, the black and red trails ascend into the mountains.

The latter enters the national park at the waterfall of the Kamienczyka, which is about a third of the way up the trail to Szrenica. Tumbling down the valley in a single slanting dive and beautifully framed by woodland, it is the most picturesque of the falls in the Karkonosze. A much quicker way into the mountains is by chairlift, which departs from the southern end of town, and goes up in two stages to the summit of Szrenica.

Karpacz lies 9 miles (15km) south of Jelenia Góra in the shadow of Śnieżka (5,255/1,602m), the highest peak in the Karkonosze. It is even more spread out than Szklarska Poręba: much of it is concentrated around one street, ul 1 Maja, which curves for some 2 miles (3km) uphill to the Hotel Biały Jar, the convergence point of three hiking trails and terminus of many of the buses.

The street follows a roughly parallel line to the course of the Łomnica, which rises high in the mountains and flows all the way through Karpacz, defining much of the northern boundary. There are two waterfalls within the town boundary, the lower having been altered to form a dam, whereas the upper preserves its rustic setting. The only other sightseeing attraction in Karpacz itself is the small Museum of Sport and Tourism, housed in an alpine chalet on ul. Kopernika. Below is the valley of the Dolna, which offers an excellent view up to Śnieżka.

Uphill from the Biały Jar, in the outlying village of **Bierutowice**, is the most famous building in the Karkonosze, the Wang chapel. For nearly 600 years, this twelfth-century Romanesque stave church — constructed without nails and featuring wonderfully refined carvings on its portals and capitals — stood in a village in southern Norway. By 1840, it had fallen into a state of disrepair, and was sold to King Friedrich Wilhelm IV of Prussia, who had it dismantled and shipped to this isolated spot, where it was punctiliously reassembled over a period of 2 years. The stone tower, added at the beginning of the twentieth century, is the only feature which is not original. In deference to Friedrich Wilhelm's wishes, it is still used on Sunday mornings for Protestant worship.

Immediately above the chapel is one of the entry points to the national park, and the blue hiking trail leads up into the mountains. Faster access is by the chairlift, whose station is halfway down towards the Biały Jar. This ascends directly to the summit of Kopa (4,510ft/1,375m), from where it is a walk of an hour or less to the top of Śnieżka. The path passes through the Kocioł Łomniczki, whose abundant upland vegetation includes Carpathian birch, gentian, cloves, Alpine roses and monk's hood. Only moss, lycopod, Alpine violets and lichen (of which 28 varieties have been identified) grow on the summit of Śnieżka itself, which is normally covered with snow for over half the year.

The final stage of the ascent can be made either by the steep and stony 'Zigzag Way' (the red trail) which takes the direct route, or the easier 'Jubilee Way' (the blue trail), which goes round the northern and eastern sides of the

*The Black Tarn
(Czarny Staw)
below the Rysy in
the High Tatras
(Chapter 10)*

*The Dolina
Kościelska, a
valley in the
West Tatras
(Chapter 10)*

The slopes of the cross-crowned Giewont, the mountain behind Zakopane (Chapter 10)

View northwards from the summit of Giewont (Chapter 10)

mountain. At the top is a large modern weather station-cum-refuge;. On a clear day, the view from Śnieżka stretches for 50 miles (80km), embracing not only other stretches of the Sudeten chain in Poland and the Czech Republic, but also Wrocław, Ślęża, Legnica and the Lausitz Mountains in Germany. However, good visibility is a rarity and the more usual misty effects at least offer a highly atmospheric consolation.

The red trail along the main ridge makes the most obvious basis for a walking route. One section particularly worth seeing is that immediately to the west of Śnieżka, which passes above two glaciary lakes, Mały Stam and Wielki Stam. A descent via the black trail, followed by a switch to the blue, leads back to the Wang chapel. However, it is advisable to go a bit further by the red trail, and descend by the yellow trail: this gives the opportunity of seeing the most picturesque rock formations in the Karkonosze, the Słonecznik and the Pielgrzymy.

The Sudeten Foothills

In the foothills of the Sudeten mountains lie several historic towns and villages well worth visiting if travelling between the Karkonosze and the Kłodzko Region; these are also feasible day-trips from either Wrocław or the mountain resorts themselves. Most of these places formerly belonged to the duchy of Jawor-Świdnica, which, although short-lived, was far more independently-minded than any of its counterparts, developing its own distinctive culture.

Since the fourteenth century, **Kamienna Góra** has been a major centre of weaving, the staple craft industry of the regional economy. The tradition is celebrated in the Lower Silesian Textile Museum on the main square, plac Wolności, which has a number of fine old houses, some of them arcaded. Nearby stands the Gothic parish church of St Peter and St Paul, while the Baroque Church of Grace, one of the group built in the early eighteenth century for Protestant worship, stands on a hillock at the southern side of town.

Kamienna Góra's main interest is as a jumping-off point for visiting the village of **Krzeszów**, 5 miles (8km) to the south, whose huge Abbey is among Silesia's most imposing sights. Initially founded by Benedictines from Bohemia, it was taken over by the Cistercians in the late thirteenth century and flourished during the Counter-Reformation, enabling the entire complex to be rebuilt in the Baroque style. The monastery then went into decline, and lay abandoned for over a century following the Napoleonic secularisation, but was re-settled by Benedictines in 1919.

Scattered throughout the village and its vicinity are a score of chapels forming a Way of the Cross, while within the walled close are the monastic quarters and two churches. Of these, the smaller, St Joseph's, was built in the 1690s for parish use. Its dedication was a reflection of the new Counter-Reformation cult of the Virgin Mary's husband, whose life is depicted in the fresco cycle along the walls by Michael Willmann. Executed with bold brushwork and warm colours, paying tribute to both Rubens and Rembrandt while seeming to anticipate the grace and lightness of French Rococo, this ranks as the painter's masterpiece. On the vault, Willmann continued the family theme by depicting various Biblical genealogies.

The monastic church, in the grand Baroque style, was begun in 1728 and finished in just 7 years — hence its unity of design. In the transept are three altarpieces by Willmann, but the most notable painting is a Byzantine icon which has been at Krzeszów since the fourteenth century. The nave ceiling frescos illustrate the life of the Virgin, and thus form a counterpart to the cycle in the parish church; that in the south transept depicts the martyrdom of the monks by the Hussites. Behind the high altar, entered from the south transept, is the mausoleum of the Jawor-Świdnica duchy, its vaults adorned with frescos narrating the history of the abbey. To the side are modest Gothic sarcophagi with the reclining figures of Dukes Bolko I and II, while the grandiose coloured marble tomb of Duke Bernard stands in the centre.

Bolko I, the founder of the duchy, gave his name to **Bolków**, which lies 12 miles (19km) north of Kamienna Góra. Although a ruin, Bolko's castle is still an impressive sight, both from afar, where it rises imperiously above the little town, and from close up, where the exposure of its massive walls gives a good insight into medieval construction techniques. Later converted into a Renaissance palace, it passed into the control of the monks of Krzeszów, and was finally abandoned as a result of Napoleon's suppression of the monasteries. A small museum on the history of the town has been set up inside, and the tower can be climbed for a huge panoramic view. In the lower town, the main features are the gaudily painted Gothic parish church and the sloping Rynek.

Some 12 miles (20km) north, about halfway towards Legnica, is the larger town of **Jawor**. On the Rynek are a number of Renaissance and Baroque patrician houses and the Town Hall, which preserves its four-teenth-century tower, but is otherwise a bulky neo-Renaissance structure from the end of the nineteenth century. The Gothic church of St Martin is a fine hall design, whose furnishings include Renaissance choir stalls and a Baroque high altar. However, the town's most intriguing sight is the half-timbered Church of Peace to the north-west of the centre. Its name derives from the Peace of Westphalia of 1648, which brought to an end the Thirty Years War, and was one of three (two of which survive) that Silesia's Protestant minority was granted permission to build. Both the material used — wood and clay only, no stone or brick — and the location outside the Old Town were among the restrictions imposed. Designed by an engineer, Albrecht von Säbisch, the church was cleverly laid out in order that a congregation of several thousand could be packed into a relatively modest space.

Strzegom, 12 miles (20km) east, is Silesia's oldest town and might even be the oldest in Poland, but the earliest reference to it, by Ptolemy in the second century, is beaten by Kalisz. An important centre for the extraction of granite and basalt, it is predominantly industrial, with few suggestions of its antiquity. The only notable monument is the lofty Gothic parish church, and in particular its elaborately carved entrances: The Last Judgment is illustrated on the façade, while the southern porch has a tympanum of The Dormition of the Virgin Mary.

About 11 miles (18km) south, in tranquil rural countryside only just outside the ugly sprawl of the mining town of Wałbrzych is the hamlet of **Książ**, which basically consists of a stud farm and a huge castle commanding a thickly wooded valley. The latter, seen at its best from afar, comprises sections in a range of architectural styles from the thirteenth-century Romanesque of Duke Bolko I's original fortress to nineteenth-century Romanticism. Part of it was transformed into a bomb-proof bunker for Hitler, but a few fine interiors remain. The most outstanding is the Baroque Maximilian Hall, with its carved chimneypieces, gilded chandeliers, a fresco of Parnassus, and coloured marble panelling.

Świdnica, some 9 miles (15km) east, was for long the largest Silesian town after Wrocław, and was one of Europe's leading brewing centres, its famed Schwarze Schöps being exported as far afield as Italy and Russia. Largely by-passed by industrialisation, and by modern warfare, it still preserves some of the grandeur befitting a former ducal capital. The Rynek forms the usual centrepiece and, as is so often the case, is predominantly Baroque, though the core of many of the houses is often much older. Two particularly notable façades are at number 7, known as The Golden Cross, and number 8, The Gilded Man. In the central area of the square are two fine but blackened fountains and the handsome early eighteenth-century Town Hall, which retains the tower and a star-vaulted chamber from its Gothic predecessor.

Off the south-western corner of the Rynek, the main street, ul. Staromiejska, curves gently downhill. The view ahead stretches past a number of Baroque mansions to the Gothic parish church of St Stanisław and St Wenceslas, whose belfry is the second highest in Poland. In front of the façade are a Baroque statue of the recently deceased St John Nepomuk and a late Gothic relief of St Anne, the Virgin and Child. On the main fifteenth-century portals, the two patrons join the group of Apostles framing the Madonna, while the Bridal Gateway on the north side of the nave has amusingly chauvinistic carvings of Samson and Delilah and Aristotle and Phyllis, so warning the bridegroom of woman's potential for corrupting man. After the Thirty Years War, the church was allocated to the Jesuits, who erected the large college building on the south side and filled the church's interior with Baroque furnishings, including the high altar, the organ and huge paintings, including some by Willmann.

Set in a quiet walled close north of the town centre, the Church of Peace was built in the 1650s for the Protestants, according to the conditions on construction applied at Jawor a few years before, and to plans by the same engineer. Although the smaller of the two, it is the more accomplished, and is generally considered to be the greatest half-timbered church ever built. Over 3,000 worshippers could be seated inside, thanks to the double two-tiered galleries, with a further 4,000 standing: all would be able to hear the preacher, and most could see him. The church's appearance was modified in the eighteenth century, as the Protestant community grew after Silesia came under the rule of Prussia. A vestibule was added to the west end, a baptistery to the east, while a picturesque group of chapels and porches was tagged on to the two long sides of the building. The latter served as the entrances to the private boxes of the most eminent citizens, whose funerary monuments are slowly weathering away on the exterior walls. At the same time, the interior was given a new set of furnishings — pulpit, font, reredos and the large and small organs.

Ząbkowice Śląski, 25 miles (40km) south-east of Świdnica, has gained the inevitable nickname of 'the Silesian Pisa' on account of its fourteenth-century leaning tower, situated just off the Rynek. Within a hundred years of its construction, the ground on which it was built had shifted so much that a storey was added perpendicular to the ground in the belief that this would help straighten it. In fact, the opposite occurred, and it now leans almost 5ft (1 1/2m) out of true. Although it looks like a defensive tower, it is actually the detached belfry of the church of St Anne, which stands in a peaceful garden behind. A few blocks south is the shell of the thirteenth-century castle, which was transformed into a palace for the Bohemian royal family by Benedict Rieth, the great architect of Renaissance Prague. It was burnt out in the Thirty Years War and, although the remains are substantial, there is little to suggest their former splendour.

The historic core of the former ducal capital of **Ziębice**, 10 miles (16km) east of Ząbkowice, is surrounded by significant sections of the medieval fortifications, the most impressive survival being the Paczków Gate. In the heart of the town is the thirteenth-century parish church of St Mary and St George, whose tower of roughly-hewn masonry contrasts with the brick-work of the rest of the façade. This is divided into paired sections, each with its own portal and gable, an arrangement mirrored inside, where the nave is divided down its axis by a row of columns, a feature characteristic of Bohemia but rarely encountered elsewhere. In the fifteenth century, the airy late Gothic aisled chancel was added, its arcades facing down each half of the divided nave, producing unusual spatial effects.

About 3 miles (5km) north of Ziębice is **Henryków**, site of the first Cistercian monastery in Silesia, founded in 1220 by Duke Henryk the Bearded, who named it after himself. Half a century later, the abbot Piotr compiled a chronicle in which appears, in the course of an otherwise Latin text, the earliest written sentence in the Polish language. The complex was greatly expanded in the late seventeenth and early eighteenth centuries in the monumental Baroque style then current. Furnishings of the same period, including several altarpiece by Willmann and some outstanding woodwork, fill the interior of the church, though its plain early Gothic architecture survives largely intact.

The Kłodzko Region

Jutting into Bohemia — to which it belonged for most of its history — and thus surrounded on three sides by different parts of the Sudeten chain, the **Kłodzko Region** is a rural area of rocky mountains, wooded hills and gentle valleys with some truly bizarre landscapes. Although ranking among the best walking territory in Poland, it caters equally well for the sedentary, thanks to the country's largest concentration of spa resorts with curative springs.

The region takes its name from its largest town, **Kłodzko**, which occupies a site of immense strategic importance, controlling access to several valleys, including what was long the main trade route between Bohemia and Poland. This role is given a very visual expression by the presence of two large fortresses rising on the heights above the River Nysa Kłodzka, which completely dominate the townscape.

The main survivor of the medieval fortifications is the Gothic bridge which provides a pedestrian approach to the Old Town. In the Baroque period, its defensive function being obsolete, it was embellished by a series of sacred statues and sculptural groups. On the opposite side from the centre is the Franciscan church, originally part of a Jesuit college. Facing it, a series of grand nineteenth-century mansions rise high above the river.

Higher up is the sloping Rynek, which has a number of fine old houses from various periods. Standing in the centre is the Town Hall, a swaggeringly self-confident building from the nineteenth century which retains the handsome Renaissance belfry of its predecessor. Just to the south is a smaller and quieter square dominated by the Gothic church of Our Lady, which contains, alongside abundant Baroque furnishings, the fourteenth-century tomb of the founder, Bishop Ernst of Pordolice, Rector of Prague University. West of the church is the Regional Museum, which features a collection of antique clocks in addition to the expected local displays. Immediately to the church's rear is the entrance to the Underground Tourist Route, which travels for some 1,968ft (600m) through the town's medieval storage cellars. These were re-discovered only a few decades ago, having lain abandoned for centuries.

From the end of the route, or from the Rynek, pathways ascend to the huge Prussian-built fortress, the more important of the two commanding the valley. Its former impregnability — which enabled it to withstand a siege in 1807 by Napoleon's all-conquering army — is still obvious, with the natural rock providing the first line of defence. It would take hours to travel along the whole length of its underground passages; some of these are so narrow that the only way along them is on hands and knees. As a complete contrast, there are superb views over the town and its surroundings.

The nearest resort to Kłodzko is **Polanica-Zdrój**, 9 miles (15km) to the west. It was only really developed in the twentieth century and is consequently less attractive than its neighbours, though it scores in its wide choice of accommodation. There is also an attractive Spa Park, which is ablaze with rhododendrons and azaleas in the late spring.

Lying just beyond the mountain ranges, Polanica is not ideally placed for quick access to the best scenery, but there are still some good walks in the immediate vicinity. South-west by the black trail are the Bystrzyckie Mountains; about $2^1/_2$ hours are required to ascend to the first main viewpoint, Wolarz (2,788ft/850m). A similar length of time is needed to reach the other summit within easy reach, Szczytnik (1,932ft/589m), via the yellow route going north-west; this has a neo-Gothic castle and a view over the glass-making village of Szczytna below.

A far more venerable spa, **Duszniki-Zdrój**, lies 6 miles (10km) west of Polanica. Despite the short distance between the two, their climates are quite different, Duszniki's being more fluctuating and extreme, with hotter summers and harsher winters. The town is a well-known cultural centre, with a handsome nineteenth-century theatre as a centrepiece of its spa quarter. In the first half of August each year, a Chopin Musical Festival, which usually features at least one world-famous pianist, is held, commemorating the concerts given during a convalescence there by the 16-year-old composer in 1826.

Duszniki divides into two halves, with the Old Town lying midway between the spa quarter and the railway station. On the Rynek, Renaissance and Baroque styles are mingled in the Town Hall and the burghers' houses, one of which bears a plaque stating that it was where Chopin lodged. Down ul. Mickiewicza is another fine square, plac Warszawy, where the former drapers' guild hall can be identified by the emblem of a lamb with the tools of the draper's trade.

The oldest street in town, ul. Kłodzka, is dominated by the Baroque church of St Peter and St Paul, which contains two fantastically ornate Rococo pulpits. That on the right is unique and rather morbid, being shaped like the whale which swallowed Jonah, with the creature's mouth fixed open to form a platform for the preacher; the Evangelists cluster under the whale's mouth, while the Church Doctors form the base of the sounding board which terminates in the Risen Christ.

At the bottom of the same street is the Museum of the Paper Industry, which occupies a large paper mill from the beginning of the seventeenth century. Not only is this one of Poland's most precious industrial buildings, its fine half-timbering, sweeping mansard roof and delicate rosette decoration make it a handsome piece of Baroque architecture. On a hillside to the south is a tiny chapel which now houses the Museum of the Chopin Festival, with documentary photographs and programmes of past events.

Further up is Nawojowa (2,214ft/675m), one of the two main viewpoints within easy reach of the town. The other, just to the south, is Ptasia Góra (2,414ft/736m), which is connected by the brown trail leading back to the spa quarter. Among longer hikes, the red trail leads south in about $3^1/_2$ hours to Zieleniec, the highest-lying village in the region and a noted winter sports centre. A short distance to its east is the Topieliska nature reserve, a high-altitude peat bog with tundra-like flora, including cotton grass and dwarf birch. A different section of the red trail goes west from Duszniki, arriving after a couple of hours at the ruined thirteenth-century Lewin Castle, another fine viewpoint.

Kudowa-Zdrój lies in a wide basin at the foot of the Table Mountains and the Lewińskie Hills, 10 miles (16km) west of Duszniki, and a couple of kilometres before a major road crossing into the Czech Republic. More than any of the other resorts in the Kłodzko Region, Kudowa preserves some of the feel of the era when it was patronised by international celebrities, Sir Winston Churchill among them.

A series of nineteenth-century villas set in their own spacious grounds give Kudowa a patrician appearance, but the town has no obvious centre other than the Spa Park. This has the largest sanatorium and pump room in the region, along with an extensive English-style park with over 300 different trees and shrubs. From there, it is an easy walk northwards to Kapliczne (1,377ft/420m), named after the Protestant chapel on its summit.

Just to the north of Kudowa is the village of **Czermna**, whose Baroque cemetery chapel is a curiously morbid attraction in an area otherwise associated with healthy living. Inside, the walls, ceiling and altar are covered with the skulls and bones of the dead of the Thirty Years' War, the Silesian Wars and the Seven Years War. In all, some 3,000 skulls are on view, with a further 21,000 kept in the crypt below.

The most attractive scenery in the Kłodzko Region — and arguably in the whole of Silesia — is found in the **Table Mountains National Park** (Park Narodowy Gór Stołowych), which stretches from Kudowa to Wambierzyce. Although relatively low, seldom rising above 2,950ft/900m, and almost as flat as the name implies, this range contains a quite stunning variety of different landscapes. It is particularly renowned for its fantastic rock formations — created by the erosion of the original soft sandstone — and luxuriant vegetation. The most convenient jumping-off point for a visit, particularly for those who do not want to do too much walking, is the hamlet of Karłów which lies 7 miles (11km) east of Kudowa via the serpentine 'road of a hundred bends'. However, Kudowa itself is a good base, particularly for those prepared to be more adventurous, and is also the only place in the area with much in the way of accommodation.

The best full day's walk in the mountains is the green trail from Kudowa. This passes through Czermna, then continues north-east to the first important group of rock formations, the Erratic Boulders or Błędne Skały, which are characterised by their quasi-geometric appearance. There the path has to twist and turn, squirming its way through what are often extremely narrow gaps between the gigantic rocks.

It is then about a further hour's walk along the same trail to an even more impressive outcrop, the Szczeliniec Wielki, which, at 3,014ft (919m), are the highest part of the Table Mountains. They lie directly above Karłów, and are approached by a flight of some 700 steps which were cut more than two centuries ago. The trail descends into and through a deep chasm known as 'hell', then passes through 'purgatory' before ascending to a belvedere called 'heaven', before winding its way back to its starting-point. On the way can be seen rocks which have been weathered into a wide variety of irregular shapes, attracting such nicknames as 'the camel', 'the elephant', 'the hen' and 'the sphynx'.

Further south, in the vicinity of the village of Łężno, the green trail passes the so-called Sawanna Afrykańska. This is a survivor of the otherwise vanished upper layer of the mountains, formed 50 million years ago when the region was similar to the African savannahs of today. Trees bent into umbrella shapes by the wind add to the uncanny impression of being in another continent.

The green trail continues southwards to Lewin; en route it intersects with the red trail, which doubles back to Kudowa. An alternative route is to take the red trail from Karłów eastwards to the largest and most scattered group of rocks in the area, the Rocky Mushrooms or Skalne Grzyby. Formed by an uneven decaying process, these take their name from what look like a crop of giant funghi, though many other shapes are in evidence. Further south, there is the option of switching to the yellow route to Duszniki or the blue route to Polanica, or else descending directly out of the range by means of the red route itself.

This leads in an hour or so to the pilgrimage centre of **Wambierzyce**, which is about 7 miles (12km) from Kłodzko by road. Somewhat extravagantly billed as 'the Silesian Jerusalem', it has been drawing the faithful ever since the twelfth century, when a blind man was cured there by praying at a statue of the Madonna and Child placed on a lime tree.

Perched above a broad flight of steps, the present basilica is the fourth on the site, though it retains the outer walls of its predecessor, which collapsed soon after it was built. Its monumental Baroque exterior gives no hint of the intricate layout inside, in which a modest-sized church is completely surrounded by a broad processional way, off which are a variety of chapels, grottoes and other nooks and crannies containing representations of scenes from the lives of Christ and the Virgin. The nave of the church is an octagon hung with six large altarpieces by Michael Willmann, while the oval presbytery has a cupola illustrating the fifteen mysteries of the rosary. A magnificent silver tabernacle from Venice bears the miraculous image, with a prodigious collection of votive offerings displayed to the side.

Scattered all round the village are nearly 100 shrines containing sculptures representing the minutiae of the Passion story. They are oddly grouped out of sequence, except towards the end, which culminates in the calvary on the hill facing the basilica. Halfway up is the Szopka, a large mechanical contraption controlling a series of Biblical and everyday scenes, laid out like miniature theatre sets. The work of a local nineteenth-century craftsman, Longinius Wittig, it took all of 28 years to make.

Some 9 miles (15km) down the valley south of Kłodzko is the peeling medieval town of **Bystrzyca Kłodzka**. It has a picturesque setting above the River Nysa Kłodzka, and the opposite bank offers a wonderful view of the distinctive tiered layout. Substantial sections of the walls survive, including the Kłodzko Gate, the Water Gate and the Knights' Tower. The last of these later became a belfry for the Protestant church, which dominates the smaller of the two central squares, the Mały Rynek. Now deconsecrated, it houses the eccentric Museum of Fire-Making, whose main attraction is a large collection of matchbox labels. In the middle of the main square, plac Wolności, is the Town Hall which has a nineteenth-century body tacked on to a Renaissance tower. Further uphill, the parish church of St Michael the Archangel features two well-crafted late Renaissance portals and a double-naved interior in the idiosyncratic Bohemian Gothic style.

At the extreme south-eastern corner of the Kłodzko Region, 8 miles (13km) from Bystrzyca, is the straggling community of **Międzygórze**. By the western end of the village is one of the region's most popular sights, the beautiful 89ft (27m) high waterfall of the Rover Wilczka. Not the least of its attractions is the number of angles from which it can be admired — the bridge directly above enables visitors to peer down at the roaring mass of water, while platforms placed at various levels on both sides of the river give a variety of downstream views.

Międzygórze is the starting-point for exploring the **Śnieżnik Massif** (Masyw Śnieżnika), the best of whose bracingly wild scenery can be seen in a day's walk. The red trail ascends steeply through lovely wooded countryside, taking about a couple of hours to reach the Na Śnieżniku refuge, set in total isolation at over 3,936ft (1,200m). It is then a much gentler ascent to the plateau-like summit of Śnieżnik (4,674ft/1,425m), the highest point in the Kłodzko Region, set right on the Czech border.

A variety of routes lead back to Międzygórze, but an alternative is to descend northwards by the yellow trail in the direction of the scattered village of **Kletno**. About an hour's walk on is the Bear's Cave (Jaskinia Niedźwiedzia); this can also be reached from the north by road, but note that buses are very scarce and that cars have to be left over $1/2$ mile (1km) away. Discovered in 1966 during work in the still-functioning quarry nearby, the cave takes its name from the predominance of bears among the twenty-four species of prehistoric animals whose bones have been discovered there. As yet, no trace of human habitation has been found, but this may appear in due course, as only a small part of the cave has been excavated. Meanwhile, a section can be visited by guided tour; its stalactites and stalagmites, the most impressive in Poland, have been given nicknames like 'the palace', 'the corridor', 'the Madonna and Child' and 'the bat'.

About 9 miles (15km) north of Kletno is **Lądek-Zdrój**, an eastern counterpart to the three resorts in the valley west of Kłodzko, of which it most resembles Duszniki, as it too has a historic centre as a counterbalance to the spa quarter. According to tradition, the waters were known for their healing properties as early as the thirteenth century, when the bathing installations were allegedly destroyed by the Mongol invaders. Whether that is true or not, they have certainly been applied scientifically since the beginning of the sixteenth century, and have attracted visitors as august as

Goethe and Turgenev. The spa buildings, in late neo-Classical style, are the most grandiose in the Kłodzko Region. At the heart of the ensemble is the main sanatorium, a handsome domed building with extravagantly sculpted porticos. In the Old Town, a sixteenth-century bridge over the River Biała Lądecka, a tributary of the Nysa Kłodzka, can still be seen. The Rynek is largely Baroque, with a number of fine gabled houses, above which soars the tall octagonal tower of the Town Hall.

Immediately east of town are the curiously named **Golden Mountains** (Góry Złote). An easy excursion is to follow the blue trail south-east, ascending within an hour to the ruined medieval castle on Karpień 2,545ft (776m) via a series of fantastically weathered rocks that are so typical of the region. Another group of these rocks can be seen by transferring to the green trail north to Lutynia, after which it is possible to circle back to Lądek.

Northern Upper Silesia

The name of Upper Silesia, an almost unrelievedly flat plateau stretching from the Kłodzko Region to the Beskids, is associated primarily with the huge industrial conurbation towards its southern end. However, the northern part of the region contains a number of fine historic towns.

Just east of the Kłodzko region is a string of fortified townships associated for most of their history with the independent principality ruled by the bishops of Wrocław/Breslau from 1195 until 1810. **Paczków**, 19 miles (30km) from Kłodzko, is so evocative of a walled town of the Middle Ages that it has earned it the nickname of 'the Polish Carcassonne'. In reality, it is very small-scale in comparison with its French counterpart, and differs significantly in being entirely untouched by the hands of romantically-inclined nineteenth-century restorers.

Nowadays, the mid-fourteenth-century ramparts form a shady prom-enade in the centre of the town: their visual impact has been diminished by the enveloping later buildings, though the wonder is that Paczków managed to grow so much without resorting to their demolition. Of the 24 towers, 19 still survive, as do 3,936ft (1,200m) out of the original 4,428ft (1,350m) of wall. The latter is pierced by three gateways — the square Wrocław Gate of 1462 and the cylindrical Ząbkowice and Kłodzko Gates from around 1550.

The area within the walls, set on a gentle slope, consists of just a handful of streets, but the Rynek has the proportions of a market square of a major city. In the familiar off-centre position is the Town Hall, so comprehen-sively rebuilt in the nineteenth century that only the belfry of its Renaissance predecessor is left. This commands the best view of the town, and can be ascended on request. Behind the square is the parish church of St John, itself a strongly fortified part of the town's protective system. Begun soon after the completion of the walls, it was under construction for a century, with the crenellated attic not added until the Renaissance period. A section was lopped off the tower in the early eighteenth century and replaced with an ornamental Baroque helmet. Inside, the box-like geometry of the design is particularly evident, with the chancel the same length as the main nave. The furnishings are almost all neo-Gothic, and give a fusty nineteenth-century feel to the interior.

Otmuchów, 9 miles (14km) east of Paczków, nestles between two artificial lakes formed by the damming of the River Nysa Kłodzka. The original capital of the prince-bishopric, it is nowadays sunk in rural obscurity, only springing to life with the summer influx of watersports enthusiasts.

Dominating the town is the castle, which guarded an extensive fortification system that has vanished but for one ruined gateway. The Romanesque fortress was transformed into a Renaissance palace in the sixteenth century, and in 1820 was sold to Wilhelm von Humboldt, founder of the University of Berlin and architect of Prussia's much admired educational system. He lived there in retirement, the liberal views he had championed having fallen from official favour. Nowadays, it is a sanatorium; there is unrestricted access to the courtyard, but permission is required to ascend the tower, which commands a fine view.

On the Rynek is the Renaissance Town Hall, adorned with a beautiful sundial. The square slopes upwards to a well-kept floral garden and the twin-towered Baroque parish church, whose interior is richly decorated with stucco work by Italian craftsmen, and large painted altarpieces, including several by Michael Willmann.

Otmuchów was supplanted as capital of the prince-bishopric by **Nysa**, 7 miles (12km) east. During the Counter-Reformation, this became a leading centre of Catholic education, earning the nickname of 'the Silesian Rome'. Industry was a latecomer to the town, but in recent times its name has become synonymous with the trucks made there for export all over Eastern Europe.

The skyline is dominated by the huge church of St James, which long served as the cathedral of the exiled bishops. Erected in just 6 years in the 1420s, it is a fine example of the hall church style, with nave and aisles of equal height, a design much favoured in Germany but rare in Poland. Another unusual feature is that, save for three reconstructed chapels, it has hardly been altered. Inside, many of the pillars have a pronounced sag, so crushing is the weight of the vault. Fenced off by elegant grilles, the chapels overflow with funerary plaques and monuments to the bishops and local notables. Beside the church is its squat detached belfry, which was under construction for 50 years but left unfinished.

Sadly, the vast adjacent Rynek was completely destroyed in the last war, and only the Dutch-style Weigh House has been rebuilt. However, the Baroque episcopal quarter to the south-east of St James' has survived in far better shape. The Bishop's Palace, reached down ul. Jarosława, is now fitted out as the local museum, with well-documented displays on the history of Nysa, including impressive stone fragments from demolished buildings. Opposite, on ul. Grodzka, is the Bishop's Residence, which was built right up against the ramparts.

Further up same the street is the complex of Jesuit buildings. The white-walled church is in the plain style favoured by the order, though its austerity is softened by some recently-discovered ceiling frescoes and a beautiful eighteenth-century silver tabernacle at the high altar. Adjoining it is the famous Carolinum college, whose students included the future Polish kings Michał Korybut Wiśniowiecki and Jan Sobieski.

South of the Rynek is the Monastery of the Hospitallers of the Holy Sepulchre. Now a seminary, this huge eighteenth-century complex originally belonged to an order which moved to Nysa from the Holy Land at the end of the twelfth century. The main features of the church are a reproduction of the Holy Sepulchre in Jerusalem, and a cycle of highly theatrical frescoes by the brothers Christoph Thomas and Felix Anton Scheffler.

Little remains of Nysa's long-renowned medieval fortification system other than the graceful fourteenth-century Wrocław Gate north of St James' and the much plainer Ziębice Gate west of the Rynek; the latter, which can be ascended during the summer months, is enlivened by a marble carving of a lion, brought to Nysa as war booty.

Opole, set on the banks of the River Odra about 30 miles (45km) upstream from Brzeg and 37 miles (60km) north-east of Nysa, was capital of the German province of Upper Silesia. Both the city and the surrounding rural area still contain a sizeable minority of German or part-German descent, this being one of the few parts of the confiscated territories where compulsory repatriation was not rigorously enforced.

The island in the Odra known as the Wyspa Pasieka is known to have been inhabited in the ninth century by a Slav tribe called the Opolanes. Here also stood the castle of the Piast rulers of the local duchy, which existed from 1202 to 1532, though little remains except for the round tower, which can be climbed for a panorama of the city. Its grounds have been converted into a park with a large artificial lake and an open-air amphitheatre, the setting for one of the country's big annual folklore events, the Festival of Polish Song held each June. Further north, there is a good view of the old town on the opposite bank, and in particular of the former wharf directly opposite, with a picturesque jumble of buildings rising directly from the river.

Four bridges link the Wyspa Pasieka with the city centre. The second of these, one of several structures in Opole built around 1910 in the Secessionist style, imitates the appearance of those in Japanese gardens, and was made so cheaply that it became known as the Groschen Bridge after the smallest coin then in circulation. It bears the curious coat of arms of the city, showing half an eagle and half a cross, the local Piasts having allowed one side of the family's traditional emblem to be replaced by a commemoration of the city's acquisition of a relic of the True Cross.

Just over the next bridge is the Franciscan church, a much-altered Gothic construction chiefly remarkable for the richly decorated chapel of St Anne off the southern side of the nave. Endowed by the local Piasts to serve as their mausoleum, it has a star vault studded with keystones of the family eagle and painted with floral and heraldic motifs. The two double tombs were carved around 1380 by a member of the celebrated Parler family of Prague. Although he was still alive, an effigy of Duke Bolko III was made to accompany that of his recently deceased wife, with a similar monument created in belated memory of his two ancestral namesakes. The retable, dating from the following century, shows Bolko I offering a model of this monastery to St Anne, while Ladislaus II presents her with a model of the great church of Jasna Góra in Częstochowa. By application at the monastery door, other parts of the complex can be seen, including the catacombs, which contain the unadorned coffins of other members of the dynasty and a number of fourteenth-century frescos.

Immediately to the north is the Rynek. It was badly damaged in World War II, but its colourful mansions have been well restored. The Town Hall in the middle, dating from the early Nazi years, is a pastiche of the Palazzo Vecchio in Florence. Housed in the former Jesuit college just off the Rynek is the District Museum, with a good archaeology section featuring exhibits from prehistoric to early medieval times. A steep stairway then ascends to the church of Our Lady, which occupies the spot where the martyred St Adalbert used to preach in his capacity of Bishop of Prague. Beyond are the tower of the fourteenth-century fortress and remains of the sixteenth-century town wall.

From the Rynek, ul. Książąt Opolskich leads past the Secessionist Bank Rolników, which was founded by the local Polish population in 1911, along with a newspaper, as a gesture of nationalist defiance. Further down the street is the cathedral, a conflation of fourteenth-century Gothic and nineteenth-century imitation of the same. To the right of the main altar is the allegedly miraculous, jewel-encrusted icon known as the Opole Madonna.

The Diocesan Museum, located in a block of modern ecclesiastical buildings to the north, was opened in 1987 as the first non-state museum in post-war Poland. On the ground floor are several outstanding Gothic sculptures, while upstairs are gifts to adorn the Opole Madonna donated by notables ranging from King Jan Sobieski to Pope John Paul II, and the fourteenth-century reliquary made to house the fragment of the True Cross. Exhibitions of contemporary religious art are often held.

By the side of the main road to Wrocław, 5 miles (8km) west of the city centre, is the Opole Village Museum (Muzeum Wsi Opolskiej). This *skansen* features some sixty examples of the rural architecture of the region, many of which are grouped in simulation of their original environment. Particularly notable is the early seventeenth-century wooden church from Gręboszów, a typical example of what is still the main place of worship in many Silesian villages. Another highlight is an eighteenth-century water mill in full working order; it is demonstrated on request.

One of the few interruptions to the unrelenting flatness of the Upper Silesian Plain is the hill 25 miles (40km) south-east of Opole on which stands the village of **Góra Świętej Anny**. Associated with the cult of St Anne, mother of the Virgin Mary, this is one of the principal places of pilgrimage in Poland, and is the scene for colourful processions on 26 July each year. Its mass popularity, which has always been associated with Polish nationalism, dates back to the mid-seventeenth century, when a Franciscan monastery was built on the site of the original votive chapel. High above the main altar of the church is the source of the pilgrimage, a tiny Gothic statue of St Anne with the Virgin and Child. Believed by the faithful to possess miraculous powers, it is usually decked out in gorgeous clothes. Below the monastery is the calvary, an elaborate processional way laid out in the mid-eighteenth century, with thirty-three chapels and shrines telling the story of the Passion. A large and rather less tasteful Lourdes grotto was added as the centrepiece in 1912.

Southern Upper Silesia

With one notable exception, the southern part of Upper Silesia sees hardly any foreign tourism at all. This is largely because of the presence of a huge industrial conurbation of about a dozen continuously built-up towns whose combined population of 2 million is even higher than that of Warsaw. As one of the last unmodernised black countries in Europe, the Upper Silesian Industrial District has gained international notoriety as an environmental disaster area. Yet this part of Poland is not without its attractions: just to the south are the westernmost parts of the Carpathian chain and several small historic towns, while the even the conurbation itself is not entirely devoid of interest.

Its largest city is **Katowice**, which had just 500 inhabitants at the beginning of the nineteenth century, and no more than 4,000 fifty years later, before ballooning into one of the industrial powerhouses of the Prussian state. Although not an easy place to get to grips with, lacking even a clearly defined centre, it nonetheless has a few sights, along with a surprising amount of greenery.

In the southern part of the centre, uphill from the main railway station, is the cathedral. Begun in 1927 and completed in 1955, it presents a modernistic re-think of the Classical idiom, with a centrally-planned interior based on a vast open space set under a huge dome. The stained glass windows, embroideries and sculptures all provide evidence show the continuing vitality of religious art in present-day Poland. A block to the west, ul. Kościuszki continues on to the Kościuszko Park, which has a commemorative monument to the victims of World War II and the Holocaust. At the southern end of the park is a walled close containing an early seventeenth-century wooden church and its detached belfry, brought from the village of Syrnia.

Most commercial activity is based in the northern part of the city centre, which is bisected by a long, broad street, ul. Wojciecha Korfantego, named in honour of the leader of the Upper Silesian Uprisings immediately after World War II which eventually resulted in Katowice and some of the other towns in the conurbation being transferred from German to Polish ownership. On this street is the Silesian Museum, which contains a collection of Polish art from 1800 onwards. Many of the country's leading painters, such as Piotr Michałowski, Jan Matejko, Stanisław Wyspiański and Stanisław Ignacy Witkiewicz, are represented. At the end of the street is an enormous roundabout (known simply as the Rondo) with a sports hall shaped like a flying saucer. In front of it is the Monument to the Silesian Uprisings, three tall shapes in the form of clipped wings, symbolizing each of the attempts to gain freedom from German rule.

Further west lies Katowice's largest recreation area, the Voivod Park, which is overlooked by its principal attraction, a big wheel of similar design and vintage to its celebrated counterpart in the Prater in Vienna. Those with the stomach to ride on it are rewarded with a grandstand view of the conurbation; trips of a considerably less hair-raising nature can be had on the chair lift which plies a triangular circuit round the park.

About another ¹/₂ mile (1km) westwards, just over the official boundary with the adjoining town of **Chorzów**, is the Upper Silesian Ethnographic Park, a *skansen* of around forty predominantly eighteenth- and nineteenth-century wooden buildings brought from rural communities in the Silesian Beskids and other parts of the province.

At the northern end of the conurbation is **Tarnowskie Góry**, a mining centre since the thirteenth century, and one preserving two of the most important historic industrial sites in Poland, both of which can be visited on guided tours. Just off the main road to Bytom is the Sylvester Mine, which dates back to medieval times and was formerly worked for silver, lead and copper. Some 5,576ft (1,700m) of underground passages are open, along with a couple of artificial caves. In the small museum alongside are examples of the old equipment, plus models of how the mine was worked and the water levels controlled. A wall map explains the connection between the levels of the mine and the Black Trout Shaft (Sztolnia Czarnego Pstrąg) some 2 miles (3km) away. At the latter, boat trips are run along one of the former drainage channels through rock-hewn gates. Each of these has a different name, with a legend attached: for instance, at one point any woman wanting to find a husband within the year is invited to rap on the wall. At the end of the trip, once the water has stilled, the reflection from the ceiling gives the uncanny illusion that it has disappeared altogether.

Just beyond the southern end of the Upper Silesian Industrial District, but a whole world away in spirit, is the small town and former ducal capital of **Pszczyna**, whose name features in a well-known Polish tongue-twister about a grasshopper climbing up a stalk. The Piasts established a hunting lodge there in the twelfth century, and this was repeatedly expanded and rebuilt, eventually becoming the predominantly Baroque palace which survives, with a number of nineteenth-century additions, to this day. Inside are many period furnishings, some brought from stately homes elsewhere in Poland. The most imposing chamber is the mirror-lined ballroom, which is the setting for concerts on the first and last Sundays of the month. To the rear of the palace is its English-style park, featuring exotic trees and shrubs, a lake with water lilies and an ornamental arched bridge. On the other side, the palace faces the late eighteenth-century Rynek, which is lined with mansions and a Protestant church in a characteristically restrained Baroque style. On ul. Parkowa, a few minutes' walk to the east, is the farmstead a small *skansen* with about a dozen old farm buildings from the surrounding region, including an eight-sided barn.

The one place in Upper Silesia which sees significant numbers of foreign tourists is **Oświęcim**, which lies 19 miles (30km) south of Katowice and 15¹/₂ miles (25km) east of Pszczyna. While its Polish name may not be very familiar, its German name of Auschwitz has gained international notoriety as a result of the wartime concentration camp where Nazi atrocities reached the very nadir of depravity. Ironically, Oświęcim was the capital of the only one of the Silesian duchies which was incorporated into Poland rather than Bohemia; thus its annexation by Germany in 1939 was based on a bogus historical precedent. Were it not for the presence of the concentration camp, it would be an unremarkable provincial town with no historic monuments of note.

As it is, Oświęcim has gained the reputation of being Poland's most ghoulish tourist attraction, and in recent years has gained an increasing flow of Western tourists, mostly on day trips from Cracow, though the overall number of visits is far lower than in the Communist period, when it was an obligatory place of pilgrimage with organized groups from throughout the Soviet bloc. Although many visitors to Poland feel unable to face up to coming to Auschwitz, those brave enough to come almost invariably find it a uniquely moving experience. The Polish authorities deserve much credit for the sensitive way they have cut through the conflicting propaganda that has been made about the history of the camp, producing a dignified memorial to those who died accompanied by explanatory material of scrupulous fairness.

Now designated the Museum of Martyrology, the original camp occupies the site of a pre-war Polish army barracks at the edge of town. It was set up in 1940, and was originally populated by Polish political prisoners who were used as slave labour for German industrial concerns. The following year, SS chief Heinrich Himmler designated Auschwitz as the main centre for the so-called 'Final Solution', the attempted mass genocide of European Jewry. In his own words, his choice was determined by 'its convenient location as regards communications, and because the whole area can easily be isolated and camouflaged'. A further consideration was the scope for expansion, and in due course two large subsidiary camps and over forty smaller ones were established nearby. From 1942, transports of Jews, many tricked into coming by promises of land re-settlement or jobs in non-existent factories, began arriving in sealed goods trains from all over Europe. Survivors of the journey were divided into those suitable and unsuitable for work. The latter, amounting to over 70 per cent of the total, were then herded into chambers arranged to look like shower rooms, which were then filled with Cyclon B gas. Death came within 15 to 20 minutes, whereupon the corpses were

The House of Pilate and the Holy Steps at Kalwaria Zebrzydowska (Chapter 10)

The Frogs' House in Bielsko-Biała (Chapter 11)

The façade of the Cistercian monastery of Lubiąż (Chapter 11)

The Rocky Mushrooms in the Table Mountains National Park (Chapter 11)

stripped of hair (which was taken for industrial use), jewellery and gold tooth fillings, then cremated. During the Communist period it was claimed that 4 million people were murdered at Auschwitz, but recent estimates suggest a more realistic figure of 1.5 million, of whom approximately 85 per cent were Jewish.

In the reception area, there are regular screenings of the film shot by the Soviet troops who liberated the camp in 1945; a couple of times daily, it is shown with an English soundtrack. Entry to the camp proper is via a gateway bearing the chilling inscription 'Arbeit macht frei' (Work makes you free). Many of the prison blocks now serve as specific memorials, complete with documentation, to the various nationalities who were murdered here — Poles, Russians, Czechs, Yugoslavs, Austrians, Hungarians, French, Belgians, Dutch and Italians — while another focuses on the broader Jewish perspective. Other blocks have displays on the general history of the camp, including such numbing exhibits as the vast piles of worn shoes, hair, brushes, broken spectacles, and the various personal effects confiscated from the prisoners. Between Blocks 10 and 11 is the execution wall where prisoners who broke camp rules were summarily executed. The latter block has a special significance for Poles, being the place where the now-canonized priest Maksymilian Kolbe, who voluntarily gave his life to save that of a Jewish man, was incarcerated. It was also the place where the first mass killings with Cyclon B gas were carried out in 1941 on 600 Russian prisoners-of-war and 250 sick inmates. The later gas chamber and mortuary stands at the opposite end of the complex, outside the camp fence.

Most Jewish victims, however, perished not in the original camp, but in its much larger subsidiary, known as Auschwitz II, which is surprisingly little visited by tourists. This lies 1 mile (2km) west in the village of **Brzezinka**, another place better known, for obvious reasons, by its German name, Birkenau. Facing certain defeat, the Nazis torched most of what was in essence a gigantic factory of death in a vain attempt to cover up their crimes, but 67 buildings out of a total of over 300 survive virtually intact. These include the complete set of brick barracks, built without foundations on marshy ground, which comprised the women's camp. They have been left in their original condition, complete with the three tiers of bunks spread only with straw, which accommodated an average of eight inmates on each level. The outlines of most of the other buildings, spread over an area of 425 acres, are still clearly visible, with the four gas chambers and crematoria surviving as substantial ruins at the far end, overlooked by the International Monument to the Victims of Auschwitz, which was unveiled in 1967.

Wadowice, which lies 19 miles (30km) south-east of Oświęcim and originally belonged to the same duchy, would, in the normal course of events, be a small and obscure provincial town. However, it has become a popular place of pilgrimage with pious Poles ever since 1978, the year one of its sons, Karol Wojtyła, the Cardinal-Archbishop of Cracow, gained election as the first-ever Polish pope, and the first non-Italian for 450 years. The event is widely regarded as a crucial turning-point in the struggles against Communist rule, and the pope has gained virtual deification in his homeland: within his own lifetime, streets and squares all over Poland have been named after him, and a host of statues raised in his honour. His birthplace on ul. Kościelna, just off the Rynek, is a museum devoted to his life, while the font at which he was baptised can be seen in the Baroque parish church on the square itself.

In the mountain foothills 15^1/$_2$ miles (25km) south of Pszczyna is the city of **Bielsko-Biała**, an important car manufacturing centre, best-known for the Fiat Cinquecento. As its name suggests, it was formerly two separate towns, which only united in 1951. Nowadays, it is hard to see the join, as the River Biała, the former dividing line, appears as no more than an unobtrusive stream in the heart of the city. However, Bielsko and Biała spent most of their history in different countries — the former belonged to the duchy of Cieszyn, which came under Bohemian control, while the latter, as part of the Oświęcim duchy, passed to Poland. Even although both came under Austrian rule during the Partitions, only Bielsko formed part of the small Silesian province, Biała being allocated to Galicia.

Bielsko's main street is ul. 3 Maja, a broad boulevard lined with turn-of-the-century tenements characteristic of the city. It terminates at plac Bolesława Chrobrego, above which stands the castle, which was originally Gothic but was substantially rebuilt in the nineteenth century. The interiors, which are of surprisingly modest dimensions, now house a collection of works of art from the Middle Ages onwards.

Rising above the twisting streets and alleys of the Old Town is the church of St Nicholas, which was recently raised to the status of a cathedral. One of a number of buildings in the city in the turn-of-the-century Viennese Secessionist style, it has a striking array of stained glass windows and a tall belfry which echoes the architecture of the Italian Renaissance. To the north are several reminders of the historical strength of Protestantism in Upper Silesia: the plac Luthra has the only statue of Martin Luther to be found in Poland, along with a neo-Gothic church which is one of three still-functioning Lutheran places of worship in Bielsko-Biała — a Polish record. This ensemble is completed by a cemetery situated a couple of blocks to the north.

Biała's centre is dominated by the neo-Renaissance Town Hall, whose tower provides a secular counterfoil to that of St Nicholas across the river. To the north is plac Wojska Polskiego, at the north-eastern corner of which is the city's prettiest Secessionist building, the Frogs' House, a former wine restaurant named after its amusing carvings. Just to the east is the neo-Classical Lutheran church, a late eighteenth-century preaching hall with several nineteenth-century embellishments, including a pulpit in the shape of a boat. An even more impressive pulpit of this type is the ornate Rococo creation, complete with a representation of Jonah emerging from the mouth of the whale, in the twin-towered Church of Providence at the south-eastern end of central Biała. The church itself is an excellent example of the opulent Baroque architecture favoured in the Habsburg Empire.

At the far south-eastern edge of Bielsko-Biała is the formerly separate village of Mikuszowice. Its seventeenth-century wooden church of St Barbara, set in a walled close by the River Biała, is an outstanding example of folk architecture, and one of the few, other than those in *skansens*, to be found within the boundaries of a major city. The skyline, with its bulbous bell turrets and steeply pitched shingle roofs, is very picturesque, while the strikingly geometric groundplan features a square tower and nave and a hexagonal chancel. A generation after its construction, the church's interior was adorned with a cycle of naive wall paintings illustrating the legend of its patron saint. There is also a fifteenth-century carving of the Madonna and Child in the left aisle.

The **Silesian Beskids** or **Beskid Śląski** are the westernmost section of the Carpathian mountain chain. They rank among the most popular holiday destinations among Poles, both for hiking in summer and skiing in winter, but are well off the beaten track for anyone else. This is in large measure due to the dearth of accommodation easily booked in advance, though there are plenty of rooms available in holiday homes and private houses. There is direct access into the mountains from the south-western extremity of Bielsko-Biała. It is a walk of about 3 hours along the red trail to the top of Szyndzielna 3,365ft (1,026m); the same trip can be made in less than 15 minutes by cable car.

Szczyrk, which lies in the valley of the River Żylica about 9 miles (15km) south-west of Bielsko-Biała, is the leading resort in the Silesian Beskids. It ranks second to Zakopane as the most popular ski centre in Poland; indeed, its international-class downhill route is generally considered to be superior to that of its rival. All year round, a cable car runs from Szczyrk to the summit of Skrzyczne 4,123ft (1,257m), the highest peak in the range; the energetic alternative is to walk up by either the blue or the green trail. The latter route continues southwards to Barania Góra on whose slopes is the spring which forms the source of the River Vistula (Wisła). This, Poland's greatest waterway, subsequently winds a serpentine 3,575 miles (1,090km) course through Oświęcim, Cracow, Warsaw and Toruń before disgorging itself into the Baltic just east of Gdańsk.

From Barania Góra, there is a choice of marked descents to the town of **Wisła**, which can also be reached from Szczyrk via the spectacular main road which makes a looping circuit through the valleys and passes of the range. There is also an even more circuitous rail link with Bielsko-Biała, the latter stages of which closely hug the banks of the Vistula, which has already taken on the dimensions of a significant river. The best hike from there is south-west via the blue and yellow trails to Stożek (3,208ft/978m), a fine vantage point which forms part of the border with the Czech Republic.

Ustroń, a few kilometres downstream from Wisła, stands just to the west of one of the most popular peaks in the Beskids, Równica (2,900ft/884m). This can be reached by the red trail, but it is also accessible by car or bus via a tortuous mountain road. South-west from Ustroń by the blue route is Czantoria (3,264ft/995m), another summit right on the Czech frontier.

On the eastern side of Równica, on the bank of the River Brennica, lies **Brenna**, the most isolated resort in the range. The course of the river has been terraced, allowing good opportunities for bathing. There is also an open-air theatre which is used for regional song and dance events on weekends throughout the summer.

Żywiec, 12 miles (20km) south-east of Bielsko-Biala, is located in a broad valley at the foot of three separate mountain ranges — the Silesian Beskids to the north and west, the Small Beskids or Beskid Mały to the north-east, and the Żywiec Beskids or Beskid Żywiecki to the south. The town is best known for its brewery, which annually produces 30 million litres of what is generally agreed to be the best beer in Poland. During the Communist era, almost all of this was exported in order to obtain desperately-needed hard currency; these days, happily, it is widely available throughout the country.

The castle was founded as a secondary residence by the Dukes of Oświęcim in the fifteenth century, and was adorned with an arcaded courtyard in the Renaissance period. In the nineteenth century, it was given a heavily Historicist remodelling by the Habsburgs, who also built the pristine white palace opposite. To the south of the complex lies a spacious landscaped park in which stands a whimsical eighteenth-century Chinese tea house.

Just to the east of the palace is the parish church of St Mary, a Gothic building with predominantly Baroque furnishings and a highly idiosyncratic galleried Renaissance tower which provides a landmark from all over the town. On the main ul. Kościuszki immediately north of the church is the District Museum, housed in a Baroque mansion; a little further on is one of the towers from the fortification system. Also worth seeing is the rustic wooden church of the Holy Cross on ul. Świętokryska, just off the western end of ul. Kościuszki.

Cieszyn, 19 miles (30km) west of Bielsko-Biała, is a true curiosity, a town which has been divided between two countries since 1920. Following the demise of the Habsburg Empire, what was then known as Teschen was claimed by both Czechoslovakia and Poland, each of whom had large numbers of nationals living there. The Conference of Ambassadors decided on using the River Olza as the frontier, allocating the right bank to Poland, while the opposite side (known as Český Těšín) became Czech.

At the highest point of the centre is the Rynek, dominated by the eighteenth-century Town Hall. Off the south-west corner of the square is the Gothic church of St Mary Magdalene, which contains the mausoleum of the Piast dukes who established an independent principality in 1290. The main street, ul. Głębocka, lined with an imposing series of Baroque, neo-Classical and Secessionist mansions, sweeps downhill from the Rynek towards the river. A block to the south is ul. Trzech Braci (Street of the Three Brothers), on which stands the well associated with the legend of the town's foundation. In the year AD810 the three sons of Leszko III of Poland met up at this spring after a long period of wandering around the country. They were so pleased to see each other again that they founded a town named 'I'm happy' (*cieszyć sie*) on the spot. From the foot of ul. Głębocka, it is only a few paces along ul. Zamkowa to one of the world's most improbable international frontiers, the Most Przyjazni. What was once a town centre bridge is now the crossing point into the Czech Republic; the return in the opposite direction is via the Most Wolności, about 2,296ft (700m) upstream. Both of these are heavily used, as both Cieszyn and Český Těšín retain substantial ethnic minorities to this day, many of whom commute to work across the border.

On the west side of ul. Zamkowa rises a hill crowned by a Gothic clock tower, the only surviving part of the Piast palace. From the top, there is a fine view over both sides of the town. Alongside stands one of the oldest surviving buildings in Poland, the chapel of St Nicholas, a Romanesque rotunda dating back to the eleventh century. Also on the hill are a neo-Classical hunting lodge and a Romantic folly erected to look like a ruin.

Further Information
— Silesia —

Places to Visit

Bielsko-Biała
Castle
ul. Wzgórze 16
Open: Tuesday, Wednesday and Friday 10am to 3pm, Thursday 10am to 6pm, Saturday 9am to 3pm, Sunday 9am to 2pm.

Bolków
Castle
Open: Tuesday to Sunday 9am to 3pm.

Brzeg
Palace (Museum of the Silesian Piasts)
plac Zamkowy
Open: Wednesday 10am to 6pm, Thursday to Sunday 10am to 4pm.

Bystrzyca Kłodzka
Museum of Fire-Making
Mały Rynek
Open: Tuesday to Sunday 10am to 5pm.

Chorzów
Ethnographic Park
Open: May to September, Tuesday to Friday 10am to 5pm, Saturday and Sunday 12noon to 7pm.

Cieplice Śląskie-Zdrój
Ornithological Museum
Park Norweski
Open: Tuesday to Sunday 9am to 4pm.

Duszniki-Zdrój
Museum of the Chopin Festival
ul. Wiejska
Open: Tuesday to Friday 10am to 3pm, Saturday and Sunday 1pm to 3pm.

Museum of the Paper Industry
ul. Kłodzka
Open: Tuesday to Sunday 10am to 5pm.

Jelenia Góra
Regional Museum
ul. Matejki 28
Open: Tuesday, Thursday and Friday 9am to 3pm, Wednesday, Saturday and Sunday 9am to 5pm.

Kamienna Góra
Lower Silesian Textile Museum
plac Wolności 11
Open: Tuesday to Sunday 10am to 3pm.

Karpacz
Museum of Sport and Tourism
ul. Kopernika 2
Open Tuesday, Wednesday, Friday
and Sunday 9am to 4pm, Thursday
11am to 6pm.

Katowice
Silesian Museum
ul. Wojciecha Korfantego 3
Open: Tuesday to Friday 10am to 5pm,
Saturday and Sunday 11am to 4pm.

Kletno
Bears Cave
Open: February to November
Tuesday, Wednesday and Friday to
Sunday 10am to 4pm.

Kłodzko
Fortress
Open: Tuesday to Sunday 9am to 5pm.

Regional Museum
ul. Łykasiewicza 4
Open: Tuesday 10am to 3pm,
Wednesday to Friday 10am to 5pm,
Saturday and Sunday 11am to 5pm.

Książ
Castle
Open: May to September Tuesday to
Friday 9am to 5pm, Saturday and
Sunday 9am to 6pm; April and
October Tuesday to Friday 9am to
4pm, Saturday and Sunday 9am to
5pm; November to March Tuesday to
Sunday 9am to 3pm.

Legnica
Regional Museum
ul. Partyzanków 1
Open: Wednesday to Sunday 11am to
5pm.

Legnickie Pole
Museum of the Battle of Legnica
Open: Wednesday to Sunday 11am to
5pm.

Lubiąż
Monastery
Open: June to September Tuesday to
Saturday 10am to 2pm, Sunday 11am
to 5pm.

Nysa
Regional Museum
ul. Jarosława 1
Open: Tuesday, Wednesday and
Friday to Sunday 10am to 3pm.

Ochla
Ethnographic Park
Open: Wednesday to Friday and
Sunday 10am to 3pm, Saturday 10am
to 2pm.

Oleśnica
Palace
plac Zamkowy
Open: Tuesday to Sunday 10am to 3pm.

Opole
Diocesan Museum
ul. Kominka 1a
Open: Tuesday and Thursday 10am to
12noon and 2pm to 5pm, 1st Sunday
in month 2pm to 5pm.

District Museum
ul. Zamkowa 2
Open: Tuesday, Thursday and Friday
10am to 4pm, Wednesday 10am to 6pm,
Saturday and Sunday 10am to 3pm.

Opole Village Museum
ul. Wrocławska 174
Open: 15 April to 15 October Tuesday
to Sunday 10am to 5pm.

Oświęcim
Museum of Martyrology
ul. Findera 11
Open: daily June to August 8am to 7pm;
May and September 8am to 6pm; March,
April and 1 October to 15 December
8am to 4pm; 16 December to 28 February 8am to 3pm.

Pszczyna
Palace
ul. Basztowa
Open: May to October Wednesday
9am to 5pm, Thursday and Friday
9am to 3pm, Saturday and Sunday
10am to 3pm; November to April
Wednesday 10am to 4pm, Thursday to
Sunday 10am to 2pm.

Farmstead
ul. Parkowa
Open: April to October Wednesday to
Sunday 10am to 3pm.

Sobieszów
Chojnik Castle
Open: Tuesday to Sunday 9am to 4pm.

Karkonosze National Park Museum
ul. Chałubinskiego 23
Open: Tuesday to Sunday 9am to 4pm.

Sobótka
Regional Museum
ul. św. Jakuba 18
Open: Wednesday to Friday 9am to 3pm,
Saturday and Sunday 9am to 4pm.

Tarnowskie Góry
Black Trout Shaft
Open Wed to Monday 9am to 2pm.

Sylvester Mine and Museum
Open: Wednesday to Mon 9am to 2pm.

Wadowice
Pope John Paul II House
ul. Kościelna 7
Open: Tuesday to Sunday 9am to
12noon and 2pm to 5pm.

Wrocław
Archaeology Museum
ul. Kazimierza Wielkiego 34
Open: Tuesday, Wednesday and Friday
10am to 4pm, Thursday 9am to 4pm,
Saturday and Sunday 10am to 5pm.

Archdiocesan Museum
ul. Kanonia 12
Open: Tuesday to Sunday 9am to 3pm.

Arsenal
ul. Cieszyńskiego 9
Open: Tuesday, Thursday and Friday
10am to 4pm, Saturday 11am to 5pm,
Sunday 10am to 6pm.

Ethnographical Museum
ul. Kazimierza Wielkiego 35
Open: Tuesday, Wednesday, Friday
and Saturday 10am to 4pm, Thursday
and Sunday 11am to 6pm.

Museum of Architecture
ul. Bernardyńska 5
Open: Tuesday, Thursday and Friday
10am to 4pm, Saturday 11am to 5pm,
Sunday 10am to 6pm.

Museum of the Art of Medal Making
Rynek 6
Open: Tuesday to Sunday 11am to 6pm.

*Museum of Posts and
    Telecommunications*
ul. Krasińskiego 1
Open: Monday to Saturday 10am to
3pm, Sunday 11am to 2.30pm.

National Museum
plac Powstańców Warszawy 5
Open: Tuesday, Wednesday, Friday
and Saturday 10am to 4pm, Thursday
and Sunday 11am to 6pm.

Panorama of the Battle of Racławice
ul. Purkyniego 11
Open: Tuesday to Sunday 8am to 7pm.

Town Hall (Historical Museum)
Rynek-Ratusz
Open: Wednesday to Friday 10am to
4pm, Saturday 11am to 5pm, Sunday
10am to 6pm.

University Aula
plac Universytecki 1
Open: daily 9am to 3.30pm.

Zielona Góra
Regional Museum
al Niepodległości 15.
Open: Wednesday to Friday 11am to
5pm, Saturday 10am to 3pm, Sunday
10am to 4pm.

Żagań
Museum of Martyrology
ul. Ilwianska
Open: daily 10am to 5pm.

Żywiec
District Museum
ul. Kościuszki 5
Open: Tuesday to Saturday 10am to
2.30pm, Sunday 12noon to 3.30pm.

Tourist Offices

Jelenia Góra
Ul I Maja 42
☎ 240-54

Kłodzko
ul. Wita Stwosza 12
☎ 37-40

Opole
ul. Książąt Opolskich 22
☎ 354-80

Wrocław
ul. Piłsudskiego 98
☎ 44-41-01

ACCOMMODATION AND EATING OUT

The following lists contain a selection of hotels and restaurants in Poland, grouped by chapter. Choice is not nearly so wide as in Western European countries, but is generally adequate. In the most popular holiday areas, hotels account for only a small percentage of the available number of rooms for rent, which are also available in tourist lodges, holiday homes, pensions and private houses. Similarly, in the cities the regular hotels are supplemented by a whole series of now-privatised lodgings which formerly served specific occupational groups such as teachers, army officers or policemen.

Most hotels have their own restaurant, and these usually rank among the safest recommendations for places to eat. In addition to hotel and other restaurants, there are also a wide variety of snack bars (designated simply as *bar* in Polish). Though of widely variable quality — particularly the sadly depleted ranks of the milk bar (*bar mleczny*), which specialize in dairy-based and vegetarian dishes — are surprisingly good, offering tasty traditional Polish dishes at almost unbelievably low prices.

Full lists of places to stay and eat can be found on the backs of the invaluable city and regional maps which have become something of a Polish speciality. Local maps can be purchased at almost any of the ubiquitous newspaper kiosks; wider national selections are available in bookshops. The city maps have A-Z street listings, details of public transport services and routes, and all kinds of useful addresses; the regional maps are similarly informative, and show the courses of the colour-coded walking trails as well as all the roads.

Hotels

All the major Polish cities and most of the main resorts are equipped with at least one luxury hotel. Orbis, the former state travel agency, runs 55 out of these, which still amounts to over half the national total, though the percentage is being eroded all the time as a result of the opening of new ventures by international chains. Western standards of comfort and service are offered — the corollary being that Western-type prices are charged. In Warsaw, rooms in such establishments can cost as much as £100 ($150) per person per night, but prices are not so steep in Cracow, Gdańsk and Poznań, the other cities which see large numbers of foreign visitors, and are markedly lower elsewhere.

However, the overwhelming majority of the hotels in the country, including virtually all of those in smaller towns and rural areas, charge £10 ($15) per head or less. At the upper end of the price category are a surprisingly large number of business-type hotels whose rooms have en suite facilities and colour televisions as standard. Levels of luxury decline progressively towards the bottom end of the scale, which is occupied by budget establishments titled *Dom Turysty* or *Dom Wycieczkowy*. These are spartan in every respect, but seldom unacceptably so.

Camping
There are some 400 campsites throughout Poland, all of which are listed on the *Campingi w Polsce* map, available from bookshops, some travel bureaux or the motoring organization PZMot. Predictably, most are concentrated in the main holiday areas, though they can also be found in the outskirts of most cities. One specifically Polish characteristic is that it is not necessary to bring a tent, as there are generally chalets for hire, which are particularly good value if travelling as a family.

Hostels
Poland is rivalled only by Germany for the largest number of official youth hostels (*schroniska młodzieżowe*). Over 900 are listed in the annual guide published by the national association (PTSM), whose central office is al ul. Chocimska 28, Warsaw (☎ 49-83-54 or 49-81-28). However, the majority of these are in school buildings, and operate for no more than a few weeks in summer. Only 130 youth hostels are open all year round; their addresses, plus a small selection of their seasonal counterparts, can be found in the official international handbook.

Cheap dormitory accommodation is also available in many of the *Dom Turysty* and *Dom Wycieczkowy* establishments, as well as in the refuges in all the main mountain areas, which exist primarily to enable walkers to accomplish long-distance hikes without having to make detours down to villages for the night.

Eating Out
Within Eastern Europe, the culinary prestige of the Polish kitchen is surpassed only by that of Hungary. It is a traditional, peasant-based form of cooking, the national dish being *bigos*, which consists of fresh and pickled cabbage with mixed meats boiled very slowly for a few hours, then re-heated on several occasions. Other popular specialities are the various forms of

pierogi, noodle-based dumplings stuffed with cottage cheese (*z serem*), cabbage and wild mushrooms (*z kapusta i grzybami*), a potato-based mix (*ruski*) or minced meat (*z mięsem*).

Soups (*zupy*) are also among the most distinctive parts of the national cuisine. The commonest are the rye-based *żurek*, which should taste different on every occasion, and which may include eggs, sausages or potatoes; and the beetroot-based *barszcz*, which can be either a sqicy consommé or a thick broth. Other favourites are *krupnik*, a barley soup with vegetables; *kapusniak*, which is made from pickled cabbage and potatoes; *flaczki*, which is based on stewed tripe; and *rosół*, a beef or chicken bouillon usually served with macaroni. In summer, various cold soups are generally on offer, including *chłodnik*, a creamy beetroot soup with vegetables; *botwinka*, which is made from baby beets; and various fruit soups, which go under the generic name of *zupa owocowa*.

Herring (*śledź*) is the most popluar alternative to soup as a starter. Except on the Baltic coast, river fish tend to crop up on menus far mor often than seafood, the most common being carp (*karp*) and trout (*pstrąg*). Note that these are almost invariably charged by weight, with the price quoted being for 100 grammes. Among poultry dishes, chicken (*kurczak*) is the most frequently encountered, though duck (*kaczka*) is also very popular. The ubiquitous breaded cutlet (*kotlet schabowy*) is the standard pork dish, the main alternative being knuckle (*golonka*), another dish generally charged by weight. Grilled steak (*bryzol*) and stewed rolled beef (*zraz*) are the commonest red meat dishes.

Favourite Polish sweets are pancakes (*naleśniki*), ice-cream (*lody*), jelly (*galaretka*), stewed fruit (*kompot*), milk pudding (*budyń*) and cake (*ciastko*). Beer (*piwo*), mineral water (*woda mineralna*) or juice (*sok*) are standard accompaniments to a meal, though the national beverage is vodka (*wódka*), which is always drunk neat, with each glass downed in a single gulp. There is a bewildering variety of different flavours, the most prestigious being *żubrówka*, which is make from bison grass. Tea (*herbata*), which is served in glasses with optional sugar and lemon but not milk, and coffee (*kawa*) are the two main hot drinks.

Currency and Money Exchange

Poland's currency is the złoty, which will, until the end of 1996, exist in old and new forms, with all prices quoted in both. The old złoty exits in note form only, with denominations of 50, 100, 200, 500, 1,000, 5,000, 10,000, 20,000, 50,000, 100,000, 500,000, 1,000,000 and 2,000,000 złotys, each of which bears a portrait of a famous figure from Poland's past. Because its value had become so badly eroded by the inflation which inevitably followed the introduction of the free market economy after the collapse of Communism, the new złoty was introduced in January 1995. It is worth exactly 10,000 old złotys and is itself divided into 100 grosz. There are coins of 1, 2, 5, 10, 20, and 50 grosz, as well as of 1, 2 and 5 new złotys. Additionally, there are notes of 10, 20 and 50 new złotys; later in 1995, these will be joined by 100 and 200 notes, and others with higher values will follow once the old złoty is finally withdrawn. The new złoty notes all have portraits of Polish kings, and are thus readily distinguishable from those they are replacing.

Exchanging cash is seldom a problem in Poland, as exchange shops (designated as *kantor*, or occasionally as *walut*) are found in all but the smallest towns, and are ubiquitous in the large cities, where many are open for very long hours, sometimes even round the clock. It is more difficult to change travellers' cheques than it used to be: by far the most reliable bank for doing this is PKO (or Pekao), which has branches in most towns of any size. Luxury hotels which also perform this service for their guests, but tend to charge a high commission.

Most major credit cards, on the other hand, are widely accepted by upmarket hotels, restaurants and shops, and by many travel bureaux. They can also be used to obtain cash advances at the banks with which they have reciprocal agreements, and again PKO is the most efficient in this respect.

Tipping
It is normal to round bills upwards, though it is not considered essential to do so, nor is anything higher than 10 per cent expected.

Telephones
The Polish telephone system has improved out of all recognition in the past few years, but is still likely to be in a state of transition for some time to come. It is possible to call abroad directly from most parts of the country, and the easiest way of doing this is to use the blue machines which operate on magnetic telephone cards. These can also be used for all other types of calls; otherwise, it is necessary to buy tokens (A if local, C if trunk), or else make a timed call from a post office. There are seldom problems in calling directly from one city to another, though it is best to check the appropriate dialling code first. However, other calls may be impossible without the intervention of the operator, and it is advisable to make these from main post offices.

Emergency numbers are: police 997, fire brigade 998, ambulance 999. The number for the long distance operator is 900, for the international operator 901. International codes are 001 for the USA and Canada, 0044 for the UK, 00353 for the Irish Republic, 0061 for Australia, 0064 for New Zealand.

Tourist Offices

The Polish National Tourist Office has the following branches in English-speaking countries:

UK	USA	275 Madison Avenue,
310-312 Regent	33N Michigan Avenue,	Suite 1711,
Street	Suite 224,	New York,
London W1R 5AJ	Chicago,	NY 10016
☎ 0171 580 8811	IL 60601	☎ 338 9412
	☎ 236 9013	

Accommodation and Eating Out

*** Expensive
** Moderate
* Inexpensive

The three hotel grades are approximately above £20 $30 £10-£20 $15-$30 less than £10 $15 respectively per person

Chapter 1
Mazovia

Accommodation

Ciechanów
Polonia*
ul. Warszawska 40
☎ 34-54

Łomża
Polonez*
ul. Rządowa 1a
☎ 54-61

Łódź
Polonia*
ul. Narutowicza 38
☎ 32-87-73

Savoy*
ul. Traugutta 6
☎ 32-93-60

Centralny**
ul. Kilińskiego 59-63
☎ 32-86-40

Grand**
ul. Piotrkowska 72
☎ 33-99-20

Łowicz
Zajazd Łowicki*
ul. Blich 35
☎ 41-64

Płock
Dom Wycieczkowy PTTK*
ul. Piekarska 1
☎ 240-61

Petropol**
al. Jachowicza 49
☎ 244-51

Pułtusk
Dom Polonii***
ul. Zamkowa
☎ 20-31

Warsaw
Garnizonowy**
ul. Mozowiecka 10
☎ 27-23-65

Polonia**
al. Jerozolimskie 45
☎ 628-72-41

Rempex**
Krakowskie Przedmieście 4-6
☎ 26-00-71

Saski**
plac Bankowy 1
☎ 20-11-15

Bristol***
Krakowskie Przedmieście 42-44
☎ 625-25-25

Europejski***
Krakowskie Przedmieście 13
☎ 26-31-04

Jan III Sobieski***
plac Zawiszy 1
☎ 658-44-44

Marriott***
al.Jerozolimskie 65-79
☎ 630-63-06

Victoria
Intercontinental***
ul. Królewska 11
☎ 27-92-71

Zajazd Napoleonski***
ul. Płowiecka 83
☎ 15-30-68

Eating out

Łódź
Halka
ul. Moniuszki 1

Złota Kuźnia
ul. Moniuszki 6

Warsaw
Arkadia
Rynek Starego
Miasta 18-20

Belvedere
Park Łazienki

Bong Seng
ul. Poznańska 12
(Vietnamese)

Delfin
ul. Twarda 42

Fukier
Rynek Starego
Miasta 27

Karczma Gessler
Rynek Starego
Miasta 21a

Kuchcik
Nowy Świat 64

Kuźnia Królewska
ul. Wiertnicza 24

Menora
plac Grzybowski 2
(Jewish)

Rycerska
plac Szeroki Dunaj 9-11

Staropolska
Krakowskie
Przedmieście 8

Szecherezada
ul. Zajązkowska 11
(Arabic)

Tsubame
ul. Foksal 16
(Japanese)

Wilanów
ul. Wiertnicza 27

Chapter 2
Great Poland and
Kujawy

Accommodation

Antonin
Pałac Myśliwski**
☎ 181-17

Bydogoszcz
Ratuszowy*
ul. Długa 37
☎ 22-88-61

Pod Orłem**
al. 1 Maja 14
☎ 22-18-61

Ciechocinek
Amazonka*
ul. Traugutta 5
☎ 42-71

Gniezno
Orle Gniazdo*
ul. Wrzesińska 25
☎ 38-16

Mieszko**
ul. Strumykowa
☎ 46-25

Inowrocław
Bast*
ul. Królowej Jadwigi 35
☎ 728-88

Kalisz
Europa*
al. Wolności 5
☎ 720-31

Prosna**
ul. Górnośląska 52-55
☎ 339-21

Leszno
Centralny*
ul. Słowiańska 30
☎ 20-22-10

Mosina
Morena*
ul. Konopnickiej 1
☎ 13-27-46

Poznań
Lech**
ul. św. Marcin 74
☎ 53-01-51

Rzymski**
al. Marcinkowskiego 22
☎ 52-81-21

Wielkopolska**
ul. św. Marcin 67
☎ 52-76-31

Meridian***
ul. Litewska (Park
Solacki)
☎ 41-12-01

Park***
ul. Majakowskiego 77
☎ 79-40-81

Poznań***
plac Dąbrowskiego 1
☎ 33-20-81

Strzelno
Dom Wycieczkowy*
☎ 237

Włocławek
Kujawy*
ul. Kościuszki 18-20
☎ 262-31

Zajazd Polski*
plac Wolności 5
☎ 250-51

Eating out

Bydgoszcz
Karczma Słupska
al. 1 Maja 28

Gniezno
Gwarna
ul. Bolesława
Chrobrego 35

Kalisz
Adria
ul. Piekarska 13

Leszno
Leszno
ul. Słowiańska 11

Poznań
Club Elite
Stary Rynek 2

Krakus
ul. św. Marcin 25

Smakosz
ul. 27 Grudnia 9

U Dylla
Stary Rynek 37

W-Z
al. Aleksandra Fredry 12

Chapter 3
Pomerania

Accommodation

Czaplinek
Czapla*
ul. Parkowa 1
☎ 552-55

Pomorska*
ul. Jagiellońska 11
☎ 554-44

Darłowo
Kubuś*
ul. Wojska Polskiego
63a
☎ 29-19

Kamień Pomorski
Nad Zalewem*
ul. Zaulek Rybacki 1
☎ 208-17

Kołobrzeg
Skanpol**
ul. Dworcowa 10
☎ 282-11

Solny***
ul. Fredry 4
☎ 224-00

Łeba
Dom Wycieczkowy
PTTK*
ul. 1 Maja 6
☎ 324

Morski*
ul. Morska 3
☎ 468

Międzyzdroje
Dom Wycieczkowy
PTTK*
ul. Dąbrówki 11
☎ 809-29

Amber Baltic***
ul. Bohaterów
Warszawy 26a
☎ 808-00

Słupsk
Zamkowy*
ul. Dominikańska 4
☎ 252-94

Rowokoł**
ul. Ogrodowa 5
☎ 272-11

Szczecin
Dom Rybacka*
ul. Małopolska 23
☎ 33-80-66

Dom Marynarza**
ul. Malczewskiego 10
☎ 22-24-61

Neptun***
ul. Matejki 18
☎ 24-01-11

Radisson***
plac Rodła 10
☎ 59-55-95

Szczecinek
Zamek*
ul. Mickiewicza 2
☎ 420-74

Świnoujście
Albatros*
ul. Kasprowicza 2
☎ 23-35

Dom Rybaka*
ul. Wybrzeże
Władysława IV 22
☎ 29-43

Eating out

Kamień Pomorski
Pod Muzami
Rynek

Słupsk
Karczma Słupska
al. Wojska Polskiego 11

Pod Kluką
ul. Kaszubska 22

Szczecin
Balaton
plac Lotników 3
(Hungarian)

Chief
ul. Świerczewskiego16

Pod Muzami
plac Żołnierza
Polskiego 2

Chapter 4
Royal Prussia

Accommodation

Chełmno
Centralny*
ul. Dworcowa 23
☎ 86-02-12

Elbląg
Dom Wycieczkowy
PTTK*
ul. Krótka 5
☎ 32-48-08

Dworcowy*
ul. Grunwaldzka 49
☎ 33-74-22

Elzam***
plac Słowiański 2
☎ 34-81-11

Gdańsk
Dom Nauczyciela*
ul. Uphagena 28
☎ 41-55-87

Żablanka*
ul. Dickmana 15-16
☎ 52-27-72

Jantar**
Długi Targ 19
☎ 31-35-29

Hevelius***
ul. Heweliusza 22
☎ 31-56-31

Novotel***
ul. Pszenna 1
☎ 31-56-11

Gydnia
Antracyt*
ul. Korzeniowskiego
19d
☎ 20-68-11

Bałtyk**
ul. Kielecka 2a
☎ 20-07-82

Gniew
Pałac Marysieńki**
ul. Zamkowa 2
☎ 26-37

Golub-Dobrzyń
Zamek*
ul. 1 Maja 28
☎ 24-55

Grudziądz
Nadwiślanin*
ul. 1 Maja 28
☎ 260-36

Pomorzanin*
ul. Kwiatowa 28
☎ 261-41

Kadyny
Kadyny Palace***
☎ 31-61-20

Kartuzy
Rugan*
ul. 3 Maja 9
☎ 81-16-35

Malbork
Zbyszko*
ul. Kościuszki 43
☎ 33-94

Zamek***
ul. Starościńska 14
☎ 33-67

Sopot
Miramar**
ul. Zamkowa Góra 25
☎ 51-80-11

Grand***
ul. Powstańców
Warszawy 12-14
☎ 51-00-41

Stegna
Unimor*
ul. Wczasowa
☎ 82-47

Toruń
Trzy Korony*
Rynek Staromiejski
21
☎ 260-31

Kosmos**
ul. Popiełuszki 2
☎ 270-85

Zajazd Staropolski**
ul. Żeglarska 10-14
☎ 260-60

Wdzydze Kiszewskie
Motel Pod Niedźwiadkiem*
☎ 86-12-85

Eating out

Gdańsk
Karczma Michał
ul. Jana z Kolna 8

Pod Łososiem
ul. Szeroka 54

Pod Wieżą
ul. Piwna 51

Retman
ul. Stągienna 1

Taverna
ul. Powrźnicza 19-20

U Szkota
ul. Chlebnicka 8-9

Gdynia
Róża Wiatrów
ul. Zjednoczenia 2

Sopot
Pod Strecha
ul. Bohaterów Monte Cassino 42

Toruń
Palomino
ul. Wielkie Garbary 14

Staromiejska
ul. Szczytna 2-4

Chapter 5
Warmia and Masuria

Accommodation

Frombork
Dom Wycieczkowy PTTK*
ul. Krasickiego 3
☎ 72-11

Słoneczny*
ul. Kościelna 2
☎ 72-85

Gierłoż
Dom Wycieczkowy*
☎ 44-29

Giżycko
Zamek*
ul. Lotnicza 1
☎ 24-19

Wodnik**
ul. 3 Maja 2
☎ 38-72

Kętrzyn
Agros*
ul. Kasztanowa 1
☎ 52-40

Kwidzyn
Miejski*
ul. Braterstwa Narodów 42
☎ 34-34

Saga*
ul. Chopina 42
☎ 37-31

Lidzbark Warmiński
Dom Wycieczkowy PTTK*
ul. Wysoka Brama 2
☎ 25-21

Zajazd Pod Kłobukiem*
ul. Olsztyńska
☎ 32-91

Mikołajki
Gołębiewski*
ul. Mrągowska 34
☎ 165-17

Król Sielaw*
ul. Kajki 5
☎ 163-23

Mrągowo
Mrongovia***
ul. Giżycka 6
☎ 32-21

Olsztyn
Dom Wycieczkowy PTTK*
Wysoka Brama
☎ 27-36-75

Warmiński*
ul. Głowackiego 6
☎ 33-67-63

Novotel**
ul. Sielska 3a
☎ 27-40-81

Olsztynek
Zajazd Mazurski*
ul. Gdańska 15
☎ 19-28-85

Ostróda
Drwęcki*
ul. Mickiewicza 7
☎ 30-35

Park**
ul. 3 Maja 21
☎ 22-27

Reszel
Dom Pracy Twórczej*
ul. Zamkowa
☎ 109

Ruciane-Nida
Dom Wycieczkowy PTTK*
ul. Mazurska 14
☎ 310-06

Eating out

Frombork
Pod Wzgórzem
Rynek

Giżycko
Mazurska
ul. Warszawska 2

Olsztyn
Francuska
ul. Mickiewicza 9a

Reszel
Zamkowa
Rynek

Chapter 6
Podlasie

Accommodation

Augustów
Dom Wycieczkowy
PTTK*
ul. Sportowa 1
☎ 34-55

Motel**
ul. Mazurska 4
☎ 28-67

Biała Podlaska
Zajazd Podlaska*
ul. Powstańców 4
☎ 353-40

Białowieża
Dom Wycieczkowy
PTTK*
Park Pałacowy
☎ 125-05

Iwa*
Park Pałacowy
☎ 122-60

Żubrówka*
ul. Olgi Gabiec 2
☎ 123-03

Białystok
Cristal*
ul. Lipowa 3
☎ 250-61

Turkus*
u. Zwycięstwa 54
☎ 51-12-11

Leśny**
ul. Zwycięstwa 77
☎ 51-16-41

Bielsk Podlaski
Unibud*
ul. Widowska 4
☎ 28-41

Siemiatycze
Zajazd Kmicic*
ul. Weska
☎ 55-24-31

Suwałki
Hańcza*
ul. Wojska Polskiego 2
☎ 32-81

Dom Nauczycielna**
al. Kościuszki 120
☎ 629-00

Wigry
Dom PracyTwórczej*
☎ 632-18

Eating out

Augustów
Albatros
ul. Mostowa 3

Białystok
Astoria
ul. Sienkiewicza 2

Grodno
ul. Sienkiewicza 28

Bielsk Podlaski
Podlasianka
ul. Mickiewicza 37

Chapter 7
Red Ruthenia

Accommodation

Chełm
Kamena*
ul. 1 Armii Wojska Polskiego 50
☎ 564-01

Jarosław
Turkus*
ul. 1 Maja 5a
☎ 26-40

Krasiczyn
Zamek*
Park Zamkowy
☎ 18-83

Krosno
Krosno-Nafta*
ul. Lwowska 21
☎ 220-11

Lesko
Motel*
ul. Bieszczadzka 4
☎ 80-81

Zamek*
Park Zamkowy
☎ 62-68

Leżajsk
Podmiejski*
ul. Studzienna 2

Łańcut
Dom Wycieczkowy
PTTK*
ul. Dominikańska 1
☎ 45-12

Zamkowy*
ul. Zamkowa 1
☎ 226-71

Pałaczyk**
ul. Paderewskiego 18
☎ 20-43

Przemyśl
Pod Białym Orłem*
ul. Galińskiego 13
☎ 61-07

Przemysław*
ul. Dworskiego 4
☎ 40-31

Rzeszów
Polonia*
ul. Grottgera 16
☎ 320-61

Rzeszów*
ul. Cieplińskiego 2
☎ 374-41

Sanok
Dom Turysty PTTK*
ul. Mickiewicza 29
☎ 314-39

Turysta**
ul. Jagiellońska 13
☎ 309-22

Ustrzyki Dolne
Strwiąż*
ul. Sikorskiego 1
☎ 303

Ustrzyki Górne
PTTK*
☎ 104

Zamość
Dom Wycieczkowy
PTTK*
ul. Zamenhofa 11
☎ 26-39

Jubilat*
al. Wyszyńskiego 1
☎ 64-01

Renesans*
ul. Grecka 6
☎ 20-01

Eating out

Łańcut
Zamkowa
ul. Zamkowa 1

Przemyśl
Karpacka
ul. Kościuszki 5

Rzeszów
Rzeszowska
ul. Kościuszki 9

Sanok
Max
ul. Kościuszki 24

Zamość
Centralka
ul. Żeromskiego 3

Royal Kadex
ul. Żeromskiego 22

Chapter 8
Little Poland:
Sandomierska

Accommodation

Baranów
Sandomierski
Zamek**
Park Zamkowy
☎ 55-48-76

Kazimierz Dolny
Łaźnia*
ul. Senatorska 21
☎ 102-98

Murka*
ul. Krakowska 59
☎ 100-36

Zajazd Piastowski**
ul. Słoneczna 3
☎ 103-51

Kielce
Centralny*
ul. Sienkiewicza 78
☎ 66-25-11

Lublin
Lublinianka*
Krakowskie
Przedmieście 56
☎ 242-61

Victoria*
ul. Narutowicza 58
☎ 270-11

Unia**
al. Racławickie 12
☎ 320-61

Nałęczów
Przepióreczka*
ul. 1 Maja 6
☎ 129

Orońsko
Zamek*
Park Zamkowy
☎ 219-16

Puławy
Dom Wycieczkowy
PTTK*
ul. Rybacka 7
☎ 30-48

Izabella*
ul. Lubelska 1
☎ 30-41

Sandomierz
Ciżemką*
Rynek 27
☎ 236-68

Dick*
ul. Sokolnickiego 3
☎ 231-30

Tarnów
Pod Murami*
ul. Żydowska 16
☎ 21-62-29

Polonia*
ul. Wałowa 21
☎ 21-33-36

Tarnovia**
ul. Kościuszki 10
☎ 21-26-71

Eating out

Kazimierz Dolny
Esterka
Rynek 13

Staropolska
ul. Nadrzeczna 14

Kielce
Winnica
ul. Winnicka 4

Lublin
Karczma Słupska
al. Racławickie 22

Wisła
Krakowskie
Przedmieście 59

Sandomierz
Winnica
Mały Rynek 2

Tarnów
Bristol
ul. Krakowska 9

Ke Moro
ul. Żydowska 13
Gypsy

Chapter 9
Little Poland:
The Cracow-
Częstochowa
Upland

Accommodation

Cracow
Pol Różą**
ul. Floriańska 14
☎ 22-93-99

Pollera**
ul. Szpitalna 30
☎ 22-10-44

Polski**
ul. Pijarska 17
☎ 22-11-44

Saski**
ul. Sławkowska 3
☎ 21-42-22

Cracovia***
ul. Focha 1
☎ 22-86-66

Francuski***
ul. Pijarska 13
☎ 22-51-22

Grand***
ul. Sławkowska
☎ 21-72-55

Pod Kopcem***
al. Waszyngtona
☎ 22-03-55

Częstochowa
Mały*
ul. Katedralna 18
☎ 433-91

Centralny**
ul. Piłsudskiego 9
☎ 440-67

Patria**
ul. Starucha 2
☎ 470-01

Eating out

Cracow
Ariel
ul. Szeroka 17
(Jewish)

Balaton
ul. Grodzka 37
(Hungarian)

Da Pietro
Rynek Główny 17
(Italian)

Eremitage
ul. Karmelicka 3

Hawełka
Rynek Główny 34

Kurza Stopa
plac Wszystkich
Świętych 9

Orbit
ul. Wrocławska 78a

Staropolska
ul. Sienna 4

Vil-Tera
ul. św. Krzyża 1
(Lithuanian)

Wierzynek
Rynek Główny 15

Częstochowa
Astoria
al. NMP 46

Polonia
ul. Piłsudskiego 9

Chapter 10
Little Poland:
The Western
Carpathians

Accommodation

Gorlice
Parkowy*
Park Miejski
☎ 214-60

Victoria*
ul. 1 Maja 10
☎ 206-44

**Kalwaria
Zebrzydowska**
Stadion MKS
Kalwarianka*
ul. Mickiewicza 16
☎ 492

Krynica
Belweder*
ul. Kraszewskiego 14
☎ 540

Rzymianka*
ul. Dąbrowskiego 15
☎ 22-27

Muszyna
Zamkowa*
ul. Zazamcze 1
☎ 161

Nowy Sącz
Panorama*
ul. Romanowskiego 4a
☎ 42-18-78

Beskid**
ul. Limanowskiego 1
☎ 42-07-70

Nowy Targ
Janosik*
ul. Sokoła 8
☎ 628-76

Rabka
Sława*
ul. Zakopiańska 2
☎ 761-20

Rytro
Pod Roztoką*
Rytro 186
☎ 151

Zakopane
Dom Turysty PTTK*
ul. Zapruskiego 5
☎ 632-81

Imperia*
ul. Balzera 1
☎ 681-21

Gazda**
ul. Zaruskiego 2
☎ 50-11

Giewont**
ul. Kościuszki 1
☎ 20-11

Kasprowy***
Polana Szymoszkowa
☎ 40-11

Zawoja
Hanka*
Zawoja-Składy 2
☎ 148

Eating out

Gorlice
Gorlicka
ul. Słoneczna 6

Krynica
Hawana
ul. Piłsudskiego 17

Czarny Kot
ul. Stara Droga 28

Nowy Sącz
Bona
Rynek 28

Roxana
ul. Jagiellonska 6

Nowy Targ
Scahller-Bräu
Rynek 38

Sucha Beskidzka
Kaczma-Zajazd
Rynek

Zakopane
Obrochtówka
ul. Kraszewskiego 10

Poraj
ul. Krupówki 50

Redykołka
ul. Kościeliska 1

U Wnuka
ul. Kościeliska 8

Zbyrcok
ul. Krupówki 29

Chapter 11
Silesia

Accommodation

Bielsko-Biała
Prezydent*
ul. 3 Maja 12
☎ 272-11

Magura**
ul. Żywiecka 93
☎ 465-45

Bolkow
Bolków*
ul. Sienkiewicza 17
☎ 341

Brzeg
Piast*
ul. Piastowska 14
☎ 20-27

Cieplice Śląskie-Zdrój
Cieplice**
ul. Cervi 11
☎ 510-41

Cieszyn
Motel**
ul. Motelowa 93
☎ 204-51

Duszniki-Zdrój
Miejski*
ul. Świerczewskiego 2
☎ 504

Jelenia Góra
Europa*
ul. 1 Maja 16
☎ 232-21

Jelenia Góra***
ul. Świerczewskiego 63
☎ 240-81

Karpacz
Biały Jar *
ul. 1 Maja 79
☎ 193-19

Skalny**
ul. Obrońców 5
☎ 197-21

Katowice
Polonia *
ul. Kochanowskiego 3
☎ 51-40-51

Silesia**
ul. Piotra Skargi 2
☎ 59-62-11

Kłodzko
Nad Młynówka*
ul. Daszyńskiego 16
☎ 25-63

Książ
Książ*
☎ 250-17

Kudowa-Zdrój
Kosmos*
ul. Buczka 8a
☎ 66-15-12

Legnica
Piast Tourist *
ul. 8 Lutego 7
☎ 200-10

Cuprum**
ul. Skarbowa 7
☎ 285-44

Międzygórze
Nad Wodospadam*
ul. Wojska Polskiego 12
☎ 20

Nysa
Piast**
ul. Krzywoustego 14
☎ 40-84

Opole
Zacisze*
ul. Grunwaldzka 28
☎ 395-53

Opole**
ul. Krakowska 59
☎ 386-51

Oświęcim
Muzeum*
ul. Findera 11
☎ 332-27

Paczków
Zacisze*
ul. Wojska Polskiego 31
☎ 62-77

Pszczyna
PTTK*
ul. Bogedaina 16
☎ 38-33

Szklarska Poręba
Motel Relax*
ul. Jeleniogórska 9a
☎ 17-26-95

Sudety**
ul. Krasickiego 10
☎ 17-27-36

Szczyrk
Dom Turysty PTTK*
ul. Górska 7
☎ 578

Świndnica
Piast*
ul. Marksa 11
☎ 52-30-76

Wrocław
Monopol**
ul. Modrzejewskiej 2
☎ 370-41

Polonia**
ul. Piłsudskiego 66
☎ 310-21

Saigon**
ul. Wita Stwosza 22-23
☎ 44-28-81

Dwór Wazów***
Rynek 5
☎ 44-16-33

Panorama***
plac Dominikański 8
☎ 44-36-81

Wrocław***
ul. Powstańców
Śląskich 7
☎ 61-46-51

Zielona Góra
Śródmiejski*
ul. Żeromskiego 23
☎ 44-71

Polan**
ul. Staszica 9a
☎ 700-91

Eating out

Bielsko-Biała
Teatralna
ul. 1 Maja 4

Brzeg
Ratuszowa
Rynek 1

Jelenia Góra
Pod Smokiem
plac Ratuszowy 15

Tokaj
ul. Pocztowa 6
(Hungarian)

Katowice
Karczma Słupska
ul. Mariacka 1

Kłodzko
Wilcza Jama
ul. Grottgera 5

Legnica
Adria
Rynek 27

Opole
Europa
plac Wolności 1

Pszczyna
Karczma Stary Młyn
ul. Parkowa

Wrocław
Dwór Wazów Mieszczańska
ul. Kiełbaśnicza 6-7

KDM
plac Kościuszki 5-6

Piwnica Świdnicka
Rynek-Ratusz 1

Pod Chmielem
ul. Odrzańska 17

Spisż
Rynek-Ratusz 2

Index

TRAVEL GUIDE LIST

Airline/Ferry details ....
....
....
....
....

Telephone No. ....

Tickets arrived ☐

Travel insurance ordered ☐

Car hire details ....
....
....

Visas arrived ☐

Passport ☐

Currency ☐

Travellers cheques ☐

Eurocheques ☐

Accommodation address ....
....
....
....

Telephone No. ....

Booking confirmed ☐

Maps required ....
....
....

DAILY ITINERARY

Date ....

Places visited

....
....
....
....
....
....

Accommodation ....

....

....

Telephone No. ....

Booking confirmed ☐

Notes:

Discover a New World with
Off The Beaten Track
Travel Guides

Austria

Explore the quiet valleys of Bregenzerwald in the west to Carinthia and Burgenland in the east. From picturesque villages in the Tannheimertal to the castles north of Klagenfurt, including Burg Hochosterwitz. This dramatic castle with its many gates stands on a 450ft high limestone cliff and was built to withstand the Turkish army by the man who brought the original Spanish horses to Austria.

Britain

Yes, there are places off the beaten track in even the more populated areas of Britain. Even in the heavily visited national parks there are beautiful places you could easily miss — areas well known to locals but not visitors. This book guides you to such regions to make your visit memorable.

Greece

Brimming with suggested excursions that range from climbing Mitikas, the highest peak of Mount Olympus, the abode of Zeus, to Monemvassia, a fortified medieval town with extensive ruins of a former castle. This book enables you to mix a restful holiday in the sun with the fascinating culture and countryside or rural Greece.

Ireland

Ireland not only has a dramatic coastline, quiet fishing harbours and unspoilt rural villages, but also the natural friendliness of its easy-going people. *Off The Beaten Track Ireland* will lead you to a memorable holiday in a country where the pace of life is more relaxing and definitely not hectic.

Italy

Beyond the artistic wealth of Rome or Florence and the hill towns of Tuscany lie many fascinating areas of this ancient country just waiting to be discovered. From medieval towns such as Ceriana in the Armea valley to quiet and spectacular areas of the Italian Lakes and the Dolomites further to the east. At the southern end of the country, the book explores Calabria, the 'toe' of Italy as well as Sicily, opening up a whole 'new' area.

Germany

Visit the little market town of Windorf on the north bank of the Danube (with its nature reserve) or the picturesque upper Danube Valley, which even most German's never visit! Or go further north to the Taubertal. Downstream of famous Rothenburg with its medieval castle walls are red sandstone-built villages to explore with such gems as the carved altar in Creglingen church, the finest work by Tilman Riemenschneider — the Master Carver of the Middle Ages. This book includes five areas in the former East Germany.

Czech and Slovak Republics

From the Alpine peaks of the High Tatras and the forests and lakes of the Sumava and the Krkonose Mountains, to remote hill-top castles and little-visited historic towns in Bohemia and Moravia, this book will take you to eleven different areas of the Czech and Slovak Republics and show you the lesser-known sights that reflect this country's identity.

Portugal

Most visitors to Portugal head to the Algarve and its famous beaches, but even the eastern Algarve is relatively quiet compared to the more popular western area. However, the book also covers the attractive areas of northern Portugal where only the more discerning independent travellers may be found enjoying the delights of this lovely country.

Scandinavia

Covers Norway, Denmark, Sweden and Finland. There is so much to see in these countries that it is all too easy to concentrate on the main tourist areas. That would mean missing so many memorable places that are well worth visiting. For instance, there are still about sixty Viking churches that survive in Norway. Alternatively many private castles and even palaces in Denmark open their gardens to visitors. Here is your guide to ensure that you enjoy the Scandinavian experience to the full.

Spain

From the unique landscape of the Ebrodelta in Catalonia to the majestic Picos d'Europa in the north, the reader is presented with numerous things to see and exciting things to do. With the mix of cultures and climates, there are many possibilities for an endearing holiday for the independent traveller.

Switzerland

Switzerland offers much more than the high mountains and deep valleys with which it is traditionally associated. This book covers lesser known areas of the high mountains — with suggested walks in some cases. It also covers Ticino, the Swiss Lakeland area near to the Italian Lakes and tours over the border into the latter. In the north, the book covers the lesser known areas between Zurich and the Rhine Falls, plus the Lake Constance area, with its lovely little towns like Rorschach, on the edge of the lake.

Northern France

From the sandy inlets of Brittany and the well-watered pastures of Normandy, the hugh flower festival of La Tranche, the eagle reserve at Kintzheim in Alsace et Lorraine, to France's loveliest wine route in Alsace. See the France that most visitor's miss, this book is your key to going Off The Beaten Track in Northern France

Southern France

From the windy beaches and huge sand dunes of Aquitaine, the grandeur of the Pyrénées, the medieval villages of early English Kings, the spectacular chasm of the Verdon Gorges to the quiet areas of the Camargue. This book will take you to fourteen different areas of Southern France and show you the lesser known sights that reflect this country's true identity.

Scotland

Heather-clad mountains, baronian castles and magnificent coastal scenery, all combined with a rich historical heritage, combine to make this an ideal 'Off The Beaten Track' destination.